A capital in conflict:
Dublin city and the 1913 Lockout

A capital in conflict:
Dublin city and the 1913 Lockout

....

Edited by Francis Devine
Series editors: Mary Clark & Máire Kennedy

Dublin
Dublin City Council
2013

First published 2013 by
Dublin City Council
c/o Dublin City Library and Archive
138-144 Pearse Street
Dublin 2

Comhairle Cathrach
Bhaile Átha Cliath
Dublin City Council

Decade of Commemorations

www.dublincommemorates.ie

Text © the contributors 2013
Concept © Dublin City Public Libraries and Archives

Designed by Yellowstone Communications Design
Indexed by Julitta Clancy
Printed by Hudson Killeen

PRINt
IRISH
CLÓBHUAILTE
IN ÉIRINN

ISBN – Hbk: 978 1907002113
ISBN – Pbk: 978 1907002106

Postcard showing the riots and baton charge which took place in Dublin on Sunday 31 August 1913.

Contents

'Simultaneous charge near Abbey Street', *Evening Telegraph*, 1 Sept. 1913.

Acknowledgements

A book of essays such as *A capital in conflict* is necessarily a collaborative venture. The editors have received kind assistance from a wide range of individuals and institutions, including: Dr Barbara Dawson, Director, and Elizabeth Forster, Administrator, Dublin City Gallery: the Hugh Lane; Gina Quinn, Director, and Sandra Farrell, Administrator, Dublin Chamber of Commerce; National Library of Ireland; Sisters of Charity, Seville Place; Noelle Dowling, Dublin Diocesan Archives; Cathy Hayes, Irish Manuscripts Commission; Irish Labour History Society Archives; Clare Hackett and Éibhlín Roche, Guinness Archives; Michael Corcoran, National Transport Museum; and Adam Shaw, National Co-operative Archive, Manchester.

Throughout this process, we have been encouraged by the support of the 1913 Committee and Pádraig Yeates, whose magisterial work *Lockout: Dublin 1913* is a touchstone for all subsequent works on the subject. Funding for the project has been provided by Dublin City Council's Commemorations Committee, while guidance and support have been provided by Margaret Hayes, Dublin City Librarian, and Brendan Teeling, Deputy City Librarian. Special thanks are due to the staff of Dublin City Library and Archive, who, as always, have been unfailingly helpful. Finally, the editors are grateful to each and every one of the contributors, for their timely and original essays, which have created this book.

Francis Devine
Mary Clark
Máire Kennedy

Foreword

....

Naoise Ó Muirí

Ardhmhéara Bhaile Átha Cliath
The Mansion House, April 2013

As Lord Mayor of Dublin, I am pleased to welcome you to this volume of essays, *A capital in conflict: Dublin city and the 1913 Lockout*. This is the first in a proposed series of publications by Dublin City Council to mark the Decade of Commemorations. Other projects will include seminars and symposiums, online databases and exhibitions.

At a distance of one hundred years from the historic events which shaped modern Ireland, we can now reflect on the legacy of those tumultuous years. This legacy was shaped by men and women who were prepared to make the ultimate sacrifice and to give their lives for Ireland. Today we are not called upon to die for Ireland – instead our task is to live and work for Ireland, to build up our society, to ensure equality for all, to welcome migrants to our shores and to sustain those who have left us for other countries. Most importantly, we should plan for a brighter future for those who come after us. This legacy is one which we should follow in dedicating ourselves to making our city and country a home for all who live here and a place of welcome for all others.

A capital in conflict brings together the views of a wide range of experts at the cutting edge of historical research. This volume offers a new and fresh perspective on the events of 1913 and is certain to stimulate interest and discussion throughout this centenary year of 2013.

Preface

....

Margaret Hayes

Dublin City Librarian
April 2013

Dublin City Public Library and Archive Services are proud to present new essays which contribute to a deeper understanding of Dublin in the turbulent period centred on 1913. This publication forms part of Dublin City Council's Decade of Commemorations (1912-1922) in which the Council marks the centenary of key historical events with a range of projects, programmes, publications and events.

The essays in this volume are researched and written by experts in different fields, covering labour history, social history, women's history, literary history, medical history, culture, biography and the Irish language. Events in Dublin are examined within the context of international labour movements. Dublin Corporation's role in the unfolding events is put under scrutiny, and a final chapter looks at how events and personalities were viewed by writers in the decades following 1913.

It is valuable to remember that by 1913 Dublin Corporation had established five free public libraries in the city: Capel Street, Thomas Street, Charleville Mall, Kevin Street and Great Brunswick (Pearse) Street. These libraries were supported by city councillors and provided in the working-class areas of the city, with the stated aim of encouraging the working man, woman, and their children, to seek a better life by giving them access to books and reading. This access would also enable Dubliners to participate in the cultural, literary and economic life of their city. Daily newspapers were provided, public talks and readings were organised, and many Dubliners of this period owed their education to the public libraries. In 1913, just as the Lockout was beginning, a new branch library was opened in the affluent township of Rathmines.

The aim of this publication is to commemorate and contextualise the events of 1913 by highlighting the social and cultural life of Dublin, to encourage new research, give a forum to emerging historians, and provide a new perspective on events surrounding the Lockout. Therefore the book is a social and cultural, rather than political, history of the city of Dublin during 1913.

Notes on contributors

Editors:

Contributing editor

Francis Devine, a retired trade union official, is author of *Organising history: a centenary of SIPTU, 1909-2009* (2009) and *A unique association: a history of the Medical Laboratory Scientists Associatioon, 1961-2011* (2011). An honorary president, Irish Labour History Society, former editor, *Saothar*, and trustee, Working Class Movement Library, Manchester. He is a member of the Decade of Centenaries Advisory Group and member Comhairle Bhéaloideas Éireann – The Folklore of Ireland Council.

Series editors

Mary Clark (B.A, Ph.D, Dip. Archival Studies) is the Dublin City Archivist. She was a member of the inaugural National Archives Advisory Council (1987-97) and was honorary secretary of the Irish Society for Archives (1981-5). Author of several articles and monographs, her book *Directory of history Dublin guilds* (co-authored with Raymond Refausse) won the Society for Archivists' Phillimore Prize in 1995.

Máire Kennedy (MLIS, Ph.D) is divisional librarian with Dublin City Libraries in charge of Special Collections, Early Printed Books and Manuscripts. She is author of *French books in eighteenth-century Ireland* (Oxford, 2001), two chapters in *The history of the Irish book*, volume III, (Oxford, 2005), and she has published widely in Irish and international journals. She is the editor, with Bernadette Cunningham, of *The experience of reading: Irish historical perspectives* (Dublin, 1999), and with Alastair Smeaton, of *Reading Gulliver* (Dublin, 2008).

Contributors:

Lydia Carroll holds a Ph.D from the School of Histories and Humanities at Trinity College Dublin. She recently published 'In the Fever King's Preserves, Sir Charles Cameron and the Dublin Slums', and is a contributor to *Leaders of the city, Dublin's first citizens 1500-1950*, edited by Ruth McManus and Lisa-Marie Griffith. She is a seventh-generation Dubliner, whose family have lived, worked and had business interests in the heart of Dublin for more than two centuries.

Patrick Coughlan retired from Guinness Brewery in 1993 after forty-one years' active service. He completed a Diploma in Industrial Relations in the Catholic Workers' College (College of Industrial Relations), 1961-1964.

Kate Cowan is currently working as a tutor in the history department in NUI Maynooth, where she is also in her second year of the MLitt research programme. Her thesis title is 'Youth of the nationalist community in the early twentieth century'. She is heavily involved in Scouting Ireland both nationally and internationally.

John Cunningham is a lecturer in history at NUI Galway, is currently co-editor of *Saothar: Journal of Irish Labour History*, and is a founding member (2013) of the Irish Centre for the Histories of Labour & Class. Among his published works are *Labour in the west of Ireland, 1890-1914* (Belfast, 1995), *'A town tormented by the sea': Galway, 1790-1914* (Dublin, 2004) and *Unlikely radicals, Irish post-primary teachers and the ASTI, 1909-2009* (Cork, 2009).

David Durnin is an Irish Research Council for the Humanities and Social Sciences Doctoral Scholar at the Centre for the History of Medicine in Ireland, School of History & Archives, University College Dublin. He holds an MA in the Social and Cultural History of Medicine (First Class Honours) from UCD. His current research project, entitled "'The War away from Home': Irish Medical Migration during the Great War Era, 1912-1922", explores the role and experiences of Irish medical personnel during the First World War.

Karen Hunt is Professor of Modern British History at Keele University, UK. She has published widely on many aspects of women's politics (transnational, national and local) and the gendering of politics from the 1880s to the 1930s, including *Equivocal feminists* (1996) and *Socialist women* (2002, with June Hannam). She continues to explore the life and politics of Dora Montefiore (1851-1933) as well as juggling a series of interconnected projects on aspects of everyday women's politics that include assessing the effect of women's enfranchisement on interwar local politics and the politics of food on the First World War home-front.

Leeann Lane received her research MA from University College Cork and her Ph.D from Boston College. She is Head of Irish Studies and Head of the School of Humanities at Mater Dei Institute of Education, a college of Dublin City University. She is the author of *Rosamond Jacob: third person singular* (Dublin: UCD Press, 2010). She has also published on the children's writer, Patricia Lynch, and on the co-operative writings of George Russell (Æ). She has recently been appointed by the government to the National Advisory Group on Centenary Commemorations.

Enda Leaney was educated at Dublin and Oxford. He is a former Government of Ireland Post-Doctoral Fellow and Lecturer in Modern History at the National University of Ireland, Galway and the University of Notre Dame, South Bend. He has published in a number of academic journals. In 2009 he was awarded the Public Library Research Medal by An Chomhairle Leabharlanna for his research on Digital Libraries. He works for Dublin City Public Libraries.

Ann Matthews received her Ph.D from NUI Maynooth. She published *Renegades: Irish republican women, 1900-1922* in 2010, and in 2012, *Dissidents: Irish republican women 1922-1941. In 2010, as* part of the NUI Maynooth Local History series, her work *The Kimmage Garrison: making billycan bombs at Larkfield,* was published. Other works include 'Vanguard of the revolution' in Ruan O'Donnell (ed.), *The Impact of the 1916 rising* (Dublin, 2008) and 'Cumann na mBan and the Red Cross, 1914-1916' in *Associational culture in Ireland and abroad* edited by Jennifer Kelly and R. V. Comerford (2010). She has written a drama called '*Lockout*', which will be staged this year, and is currently working on the history of the Irish Citizen Army 1913-1935.

Thomas J. Morrissey, S.J., studied pure history at UCD, took his MA and Ph.D from the National University of Ireland, was founder headmaster of Crescent College Comprehensive in Limerick, and director of the National College of Industrial Relations, Dublin. He is the author of some 13 books, which include - *William Martin Murphy* (Dublin, 2011); *William O'Brien, 1881-1968, socialist and trade union leader* (Dublin, 2007); *William J. Walsh, 1841-1921, archbishop of Dublin* (Dublin, 2000).

John Newsinger is Professor of Modern History at Bath Spa University. He has written widely on modern Irish history and published a number of books and articles in that area including *Rebel city: Larkin, Connolly and the Dublin labour movement*. His most recent books are *The blood never dried: a people's history of the British Empire* and *Fighting back: the American working class in the 1930s*.

Séamas Ó Maitiú has taught history in a Dublin city secondary school and in a number of third level institutions for many years. He holds an MA in Local History from NUI Maynooth, the dissertation for which was a study of Donnybrook Fair, subsequently published as *The humours of Donnybrook: Dublin's famous fair and its suppression* in the series Maynooth Studies in Local History. His Ph.D thesis in history from NUI on the history of the Dublin townships was published as *Dublin's suburban towns 1834-1930* by Four Courts Press. Further studies in the history Dublin and West Wicklow, where he has lived for many years, resulted in the publication of works on the the history of Jacobs the biscuit-makers, Wicklow stonecutters and the famine journal of Elizabeth Smith of Baltiboys.

Niamh Puirséil is a historian and writer. She has written widely on Irish politics and the trade union movement and including *The Irish Labour Party* 1922-73 (Dublin, 2007), the standard history of that party. She is a former editor of *Saothar,* the journal of the Irish Labour History Society and was joint editor, with Francis Devine and Fintan Lane, of *Essays in Irish labour history: a festschrift for John W. and Elizabeth Boyle* (Dublin, 2008). A former research fellow in the Centre for Contemporary Irish History, TCD, she has previously lectured in UCD and is currently writing a history of the Irish National Teachers' Organisation.

Ciarán Wallace is a Postdoctoral Teaching Fellow in Trinity College Dublin and is joint-convener of the Dublin City Research Group. His research interests include urban history, civil society and national identities in Ireland. He has published articles on these themes in the *Journal of Urban History* and *E–Rea Revue électronique d'études sur le monde Anglophone.* Ciarán's work has been supported by a fellowship from the Irish Research Council for Humanities and Social Sciences. He is currently working on a monograph *Divided city: Dublin and its unionist suburbs 1900-1916.*

Colin Whitston is Vice Dean Undergraduate Studies and Senior Lecturer in Industrial Relations with the National College of Ireland. Previously he was Senior Research Fellow at the Industrial Relations Research Unit at Warwick University, and then Senior Lecturer in Industrial Relations at Keele University. He received a scholarship from the National Union of General and Municipal Workers to study at Ruskin College Oxford, where he was awarded a Diploma in Labour Studies. As well as teaching in Ireland and the UK Colin has taught specialised courses in industrial relations in Germany and Slovakia, and has published widely on trade union organisation, policy, and membership. He has worked, and been a trade union representative in the rubber, engineering, construction and transport industries.

'Mounted police take possession of empty street', *Evening Telegraph*, 1 Sept. 1913.

Glossary

Askwith: Sir George Ranken Askwith was born on 17 February 1861. He was educated at Marlborough College and Brasenose College, called to the Bar, 1886, and appointed King's Counsel, 1908. In 1907, he entered the Board of Trade becoming Comptroller-General, Labour & Statistics Department, 1909. In 1911, he chaired the Industrial Council and in 1915 the Government Arbitration Committee under the Munitions of War Act. In 1913, Askwith was most celebrated for his role in conciliating and arbitrating industrial disputes. He died on 2 June 1942 as Baron Askwith of St Ives.

Bureau of Military History: The BMH 1913-1921 Collection is held at the Military Archives of Ireland. It is a collection of 1,773 witness statements, with a collection of contemporary documents, photographs and voice recordings, which were collected by the State between 1947 and 1957. The purpose was to gather primary source material for the revolutionary period in Ireland from 1913 to 1921. The collection was digitised, in a joint initiative of the National Archives and the Military Archives, and this collection is available for research free of charge at www.bureauofmilitaryhistory.ie.

Co-operative Wholesale Society: The CWS celebrated its 50th jubilee in 1913 and was the co-ordinating body for consumer co-operatives. The CWS assembled and packaged the food parcels that were sent to Dublin in 1913 and crew members of the first food-ship, *SS Hare*, were presented with the CWS Shilling Medal.

Dublin Castle: Dublin Castle was built on the orders of King John in 1204. It was the seat of British administration in Ireland, headed by the Chief Secretary for Ireland. In the 19th and early 20th centuries it housed the Local Government Board for Ireland, and the British intelligence unit in Ireland. It symbolised British rule and, as such, was hated and feared by sections of the population. Following the Anglo-Irish Treaty (1921) the castle was handed over to the Irish provisional government.

Dublin City Council: During the period 1841-2001, the term Dublin City Council was applied to the elected representatives who formed the local government of the city. There were 80 members of Dublin City Council in 1913. The persons who topped the poll in each electoral ward were known as aldermen and the remaining persons elected to Dublin City Council were known as councillors. Each year, Dublin City Council elected one of its members to serve as Lord Mayor of Dublin, with responsibility for chairing the City Council meetings.

Dublin Corporation: In 1548, the local government of Dublin City was incorporated, confirming its standing as a legal entity which was entitled to buy and sell property and to document its transactions by use of a city seal. The legal entity's full title was 'The [Lord] Mayor, Burgesses and Citizens of Dublin' and its short title was 'Dublin Corporation'. In practice, the term Dublin Corporation was usually applied to the elected members and unelected officials acting together. The use of the term Dublin Corporation was abolished under the Local Government Act 2001 and was replaced by Dublin City Council, which can now mean the elected representatives and/or the elected members and unelected officials acting together.

Free labour: The 'philosophy' of free labour was that trade unions sought to force workers into joining against their will, preventing those workers who wished to deal direct with their employer from doing so. Trade unions thus denied workers 'freedom' to sell their labour in their own manner. Popular among employers, including William Martin Murphy, 'free labour' saw trade unions as 'outside' agencies damaging the otherwise beneficial and benign relationship between employer and worker.

G.P.O.: The General Post Office was situated on Sackville (O'Connell) Street from 1818. The imposing building dominates the street and is particularly remembered for the part it played in the 1916 Rising as the headquarters of the rebels. In 1913 its situation near Nelson's Pillar, and across the street from the Imperial Hotel and Clery's department store, made it the centre of many events, including the 'Bloody Sunday' riots.

Home Rule: Home Rule is a term first used in the 1860s, it was variously interpreted by different political groups, from being a federal system within the United Kingdom, to denoting an autonomous Irish parliament. By 1912 the third Home Rule Bill was introduced by British Prime Minister Asquith. The bill was opposed by Ulster Unionists and Conservatives, and in 1913 it was defeated by the House of Lords. This delayed it for nearly two years, it was due to become law in September 1914, but was suspended at the outbreak of the First World War.

Industrial unionism: The organisation of all workers in the same industry into one union, giving workers greater bargaining power. Industrial unionism was designed to build greater unity and solidarity epitomised by slogans such as 'an injury to one is an injury to all' – classically seen as a 'Larkinite' slogan. Industrial unionism aimed to unite craft and general worker in one union and avoid sectionalism. It is an organisational concept associated with syndicalism.

Irish Trade Union Congress (ITUC): Formed in 1894, the ITUC was the 'trade union centre' for Ireland just as the Trades Union Congress had performed that role for Britain since 1868. By 1913, no Irish unions any longer affiliated to the TUC. The ITUC played little direct role during 1913, however, as industrial action was co-ordinated by Dublin Trades Council. From 1912, the ITUC was known as the Irish Trade Union Congress & Labour Party.

Labour Party: This could refer to the British Labour Party, formed in 1906; Irish Labour Party formed after a motion adopted by the Irish Trade Union Congress in 1912 but not fully operative in 1913; or the Dublin Labour Party, also formed in 1912 with no connection to the ITUC & Labour Party. In the Irish case, many of the same personalities were simultaneously involved in both political Labour organisations.

Larkinism: A term for James Larkin's tactics and vision of trade unionism. The Irish Transport and General Workers' Union sought to organise all workers, extensively used the sympathetic strike – 'one out, all out', and blacking of 'tainted goods', greatly alarming employers. 'Larkinism' was Larkin's personal blend of socialism, syndicalism and republicanism. Larkinism also sought the cultural as well as economic and social liberation of workers, O'Casey noting that Larkin wanted the rose along with the loaf of bread on a worker's table.

The National Society for the Prevention of Cruelty to Children (NSPCC) is a charity which grew out of a number of local societies founded in Liverpool, London, and other English cities, in the 1880s. Following an act of parliament passed to protect children from abuse and neglect in 1889, the NSPCC brought together all the existing branches of the society across Great Britain and Ireland.

National Transport Workers' Federation: The NTWF was founded in 1910 as an association of British trade unions catering for dockers, seamen and transport workers. In 1913, it assisted with the organisation and distribution of food aid to Dublin. The NTWF laid the foundations for the amalgamations that created the (British) Transport and General Workers' Union in 1922.

Parliamentary Committee: Both the ITUC and TUC executives had the title Parliamentary Committee and were elected annually at their respective Congress.

Parnellite: Supporters of the Irish Party politician Charles Stewart Parnell (1846-1891). Parnell's party supported Home Rule and the Land League. Such was his influence and popularity in Ireland that he was dubbed 'the uncrowned king of Ireland'. A love affair with Mrs Katherine O'Shea, wife of another member of the Irish Party, later alienated much of his support. The Parnell monument in Sackville (O'Connell) Street was paid for by public subscription and unveiled on 1 October 1911.

Recognition: The acceptance by an employer that the workforce may join the trade union of their choice and that this will be 'recognised' in direct negotiations on all matters between employer and the chosen trade union on behalf of staff.

Sackville (O'Connell) Street: In 1913 the street was officially called Sackville Street, Upper and Lower. However, in Nationalist and Irish language circles it was called O'Connell Street. *The Freeman's Journal* refers to it as O'Connell Street, and Thom's directory gives the Irish language form of Sackville Place as Plás Uí Chonaill. It was officially changed to O'Connell Street in 1924.

Suffragette: Those who campaigned for votes for women and were prepared to engage in civil disobedience and other public protests to highlight their cause. Suffragettes, generally, followed a radical programme and had connections with the labour and progressive movements. It was a term first applied in the United Kingdom to members of the Women's Social & Political Union.

Suffragist: A more general term for those campaigning for votes for women, whether female or male, radical or conservative.

Syndicalism: Syndicalism sought to replace capitalism at the point of production through a general strike of workers organised in 'One Big Union' (OBU). The industrial sections of the OBU would then manage their industries as part of a State Socialist society. The term originated in France in 1907.

Trades Council: A body consisting of branches of affiliated unions within a city or district. In 1913, Dublin Trades Council co-ordinated multi-union industrial action and thus administered the Strike Committee and distributed monies and food provided through the Trades Union Congress.

Trades Union Congress (TUC): Founded in 1868 as a 'union of trades', the TUC has been the British 'trade union centre' ever since, co-ordinating the actions and policy of affiliated trade unions. The first Special TUC to consider a single strike took place in Manchester in December 1913 to consider events in Dublin.

Yellow Union: The International Labour Organisation defines a company or 'yellow' union as one 'limited to a single company which dominates or strongly influences it, thereby limiting its influence'. Yellow unions were outlawed in the United States in 1935. Alternatively, as in 1913, a 'yellow union' van would be one set up - usually with financial backing from employers - to oppose a radical body - the ITGWU in 1913. John Saturnus Kelly's Irish Railway Workers' Trade Union was a 'yellow' union.

Sunday crowds outside the G.P.O. on 31st August 1913, show no sign of disorder prior to police baton charge, *Evening Telegraph*, 2 Sept. 1913.

Abbreviations:

BMH: Bureau of Military History

DCLA: Dublin City Library and Archive

DDA: Dublin Diocesan Archives

DEF: Dublin Employers' Federation

DTC: Dublin Trades Council or, its full title, Dublin United Trades Council and Labour League

DUTC&LL: Dublin United Trades Council and Labour League

GA: Guinness Archives

ITUC: Irish Trade Union Congress

ITGWU: Irish Transport and General Workers' Union

LRC: Labour Representation Committee

MAI: Military Archives of Ireland

NAI: National Archives of Ireland

NLI: National Library of Ireland

NTWF: National Transport Workers' Federation

TUC: (British) Trades Union Congress

1.

Who dared to wear the Red Hand badge? reflections on the 1913 Dublin Lockout

....

Francis Devine

The story of the 1913 Dublin Lockout is apparently familiar. However, apart from the contemporary account by employers' apologist Arnold Wright with its subtitle of denial,[1] it was not until Pádraig Yeates's 'substantial monograph' in 2000 that a full study appeared, although even this has been called 'essentially a reportage'.[2] Despite John Cunningham's interesting view of 'History Wars' over the Lockout (below), it was merely glanced at in general histories, reflecting a general neglect of labour history.[3] From the 1970s onwards, the Lockout received greater attention as labour history studies appeared but few delved far beyond the personalities of James Larkin and employers' leader William Martin Murphy, descriptions of the slums and, less commonly, some explanation of industrial relations contexts.[4] Larkin's feet of clay have been increasingly exposed in recent works and, in parallel, there have been attempts to rescue Murphy from the quagmire of 1913 and hail him as Ireland's first successful multinational capitalist and entrepreneurial industrialist, a committed Home Ruler whose fundamental goodness and care for his employees has been obscured.[5] For most, Seán O'Casey's plays, Donagh MacDonagh's ballad,[6] Liam MacGabhann's poem,[7] and – above all – James Plunkett Kelly's play *The risen people* and subsequent novel *Strumpet city* and its television adaptation by RTÉ arguably had greater impact on their imagination and perception of 1913 than scholarly or labour movement literature.[8] For school students, *Divided city* ignited new interest as did subsequent resources produced for the Leaving Certificate curriculum.[9] In Dublin, in particular, but throughout the labour movement generally, the 1913 'folk memory' should not be underestimated. Those who witnessed 1913 handed down their story. It is a discernable fleck in the cloth that is Dublin working class culture and explains why it is the Larkin monument and not Murphy's which commands O'Connell Street.[10]

Labour movement and 1913

This year, Irish labour will celebrate 1913. This was not always straightforward as history was distorted by the bitter split in the Irish Transport and General Workers' Union (ITGWU) in 1923-24.[11] In recounting the Lockout, the ITGWU made only the briefest references to Larkin in their 1959 Golden Jubilee publication, *Fifty years of Liberty Hall*.[12] Four years later, Donal Nevin's well-crafted, illustrated booklet for the Workers'

Union of Ireland (WUI) re-asserted the cult of Larkin as heroic chief leading Dublin's underclass.[13] In 1963, the WUI struck a commemorative Lockout badge, the first such until those simultaneously issued by ITGWU and FWUI in 1988, one depicting James Connolly and the other Larkin against the original Liberty Hall. These badges were confidence building measures towards the creation of SIPTU in 1990. In 2003, SIPTU produced a commemorative badge and James Larkin Jones (better known as Jack Jones), former General Secretary (British) Transport and General Workers' Union and International Brigade veteran, addressed their conference.[14] Splits had been healed and 1913 could again belong to all. In 2013, SIPTU is central to many events being co-ordinated by the 1913 committee, led by the flagship 1913 Tapestry Project launched by President Michael D. Higgins in Liberty Hall on 6 November 2012.[15]

What follows is not an attempt to 'tell the tale' of the Lockout but a brief examination of some of the major events. Some questions are raised for consideration during the centenary.

Turning points and phases

Within the essays that follow, Dublin city's economy, labour market, social and living conditions, culture – including Leeann Lane's discussion of contemporary literary debates, Séamas Ó Maitiú's assessment of the Gaelic League and Ciarán Wallace's analysis of the Municipal Gallery controversy – and politics are examined. The Lockout was the year's dominant event but much else was happening or was anticipated – not least Home Rule. The Lockout was the product of many pre-conditions but its first phase began on Thursday 21 August when newsboys refused to sell the *Irish Independent* in support of dismissed ITGWU men.[16] After meetings in Liberty Hall over the next weekend, ITGWU men abandoned their Dublin United Tramways cars on Tuesday 26 August. Events moved rapidly and the baton charges and violence of 'Bloody Sunday', 31 August, captured international press front pages and roused British Trades Union Congress (TUC) delegates meeting the next day in Manchester, Monday 1 September. On Wednesday 3 September, over 400 members of the Dublin Employers' Federation (DEF) locked out workers who would not forswear the ITGWU, whether members or not. The dispute changed from an innocuous, local one of issue to one of principle. It was now Lockout not strike.

During the second phase, employers and workers – as would occur in the imminent First World War – exchanged fire from entrenched positions. Employer weapons were the physical repression of workers by police, military and armed scabs, the law courts, an unremittingly hostile press and pulpit, and – in addition to Lockout – eviction and starvation. Food ships and strike pay from the international labour movement sustained the workers, steeled by Larkin and others' oratory and the uplifting weekly *Irish Worker*. Both sides made mistakes. Murphy's intransigence denied possible settlements. Sir George Askwith's public inquiry (29 September-6 October), TUC leaders and notable, concerned public figures – all brokered terms acceptable to the ITGWU. The price – implicit recognition of the union and, worse, its continued existence – was too high for Murphy who wanted only all out victory. The employers were increasingly seen as callous, malicious and uninterested in anything other than the ITGWU's destruction, irrespective of the human cost.

The ITGWU made errors. Kate Cowan, Karen Hunt and Ann Matthews examine attempts to take workers' children to 'Godless homes' in England (21-25 October). In contemporary parlance, this was a 'public relations disaster' and diversion of energy and resources, although the episode had 'no real bearing' on the dispute itself.[17] On 12 November, when James Connolly – acting as ITGWU General Secretary while Larkin was imprisoned – closed Dublin port 'as tight as a drum' in an attempt to land the knockout blow, shipping companies that had accepted ITGWU terms were driven into the intransigent Murphy camp. When the TUC's special congress on 9 December – the first such conference called to discuss a single strike since the TUC's formation in 1868 – again rejected industrial solidarity by 2,280,000 to 203,000 – a decision made easier by Larkin's personal abuse of notable TUC leaders – all prospects of either side winning outright evaporated. The stalemate that had endured since early September now awaited starvation and despair to break its cycle. The final phase occurred from early January 1914 when the drift back to work gathered pace. On 18 January, Connolly advised ITGWU members to return without, if possible, 'signing the document'. It was a bitter defeat for ITGWU and Dublin's workers. The imperative question became how to win the peace having lost the war. History shows that, eventually, they managed this quite well.

Economic and social conditions

In 1911, 304,802 people lived in Dublin, a city essentially bounded by Phoenix Park and the two canals.[18] Main employments were Guinness and Jacob's, administrative and civil service positions, and transportation – carters and dockers. Most jobs were 'unskilled' and casual: 17,223 general labourers, 3,081 carters and draymen, 4,604 messengers and porters. Competition for employment was intense, exacerbated by the continuous influx of those coming into the city off the land. Significant, persistent unemployment repressed wages. An average labourer's wage was about one pound a week, assuming he got a full week. For women, wages were as little as seven shillings. These rates were low by comparison with Belfast or large cities in Britain. There were 13,551 domestic servants, 4,294 dressmakers and milliners, 2,296 tailoresses, seamstresses and shirt-makers, and 1,246 charwomen. To raise such workers' wages required not just unionisation but their acceptance that 'an injury to one was the concern of all', a tenet central to Larkinism and one that challenged employer capacity to replace strikers with those from the reserve army of labour.

Low incomes were reflected in terrible living conditions and poor diet, examined by Lydia Carroll and Enda Leaney. A housing inquiry found that 87,305 people dwelt in appalling squalor in city-centre tenements, with 80% of families occupying only one room: 22,701 lived in 'third class' housing, officially termed 'unfit for human habitation'. Overcrowding and insanitary conditions meant disease was rife. The 1913 Public Health Report recorded that of 8,639 deaths, 1,444 were from tuberculosis (TB) and 4,642 from 'nervous, circulatory, respiratory and digestive diseases' like pneumonia, and diarrhoea, conditions synonymous with poverty and inadequate nutrition. There were 1,808 deaths of infants under one year of age. Alcohol and crime added to the desperation.

While most accept that such conditions were central to events in 1913, it has been argued that 'there are good grounds for arguing that the importance of social conditions has been grossly exaggerated and is even a red herring.'[19] This argument – part of a complex construct that seeks to explain the Lockout in the 'light of structural factors affecting Irish industrial relations' – has merit when read fully. However, for most workers, life was immediate, the daily search for basics impelling and – prior to Larkin's arrival – a lot that appeared given and unalterable. Those objectively reporting on conditions noted the passivity of those blighted. William Partridge –Amalgamated Society of Engineers (ASE) activist who became an ITGWU organiser – observed that 'the coming of Larkin had, for the first time, given the common people *hope*.'[20] It was thus not poverty itself – for such social tinder had lain dormant for years – but the new belief that it could be ended that transformed a tattered multitude into a ragged army. Shrewd employers like Murphy recognised and feared this new contagion known as 'Larkinism'.

Trade Unionism and the ITGWU

Craft unions were long-established in Dublin and most employers happily 'paid the rate'. The majority of workers, the unskilled, were, however, largely unorganised.[21] Industrial relations were autocratic and paternal. Trade unions thus represented a minority of the workforce before the ITGWU was registered on 4 January 1909 by dockers and quay workers, ordinary, poorly-educated men from Belfast, Cork, Dublin, Dundalk and Waterford, with Larkin as General Secretary.[22] It instantly transformed a supine labour movement, informed by four principles, if not new to the Irish movement, then applied, vigorously and consistently, for the first time: an Irish union for Irish workers; militant industrial unionism intended to create One Big Union; a socialist vision for the Workers' Republic – encouraged by the prospect of Home Rule; and an internationalism that would allow an independent Ireland to fight alongside other nations' workers for the global good. The trade union movement in the late 19th and early 20th centuries has been characterised as having been 'colonised' by British craft unions with minimal impact of the 'New Unionism' among the unskilled in the 1890s. It was about to change dramatically through 'Larkinism', 1907-14; and, later, Syndicalism, 1917-23.[23]

To gage the numerical impact of the ITGWU, Irish Trade Union Congress (ITUC) membership is revealing. It had 21,000 members in 1894 and 67,000 by 1901, representing almost entirely British-based and local craft unions. In 1909, after the ITGWU was admitted – having been initially opposed by conservative elements – ITUC strength was 89,000. This fell to 65,000 in 1910, and a mere 50,000 in 1911, indicative of trade conditions, before rising to 70,000 in 1912 and 100,000 in 1913. ITGWU membership grew from 1,200 in 1909, to 5,000 in 1910, 18,089 in 1911, 22,000 in 1912 and 30,000 in 1913, all year-end figures.[24] In addition, the movement was losing its caution and effects of 'mental colonisation' by 'amalgamated unions that stifled the emergence of a truly Irish expression of trade unionism.' Indeed, until the ITGWU arrived, it was not possible to talk of an *Irish* labour movement. In 1913, the ITGWU targeted tramway workers, recognising their strategic significance in controlling the capital's transport.[25]

Remarkably, as the Lockout commenced in August 1913, the ITGWU was less than five years old.

William Martin Murphy and the employers

There were several attempts to organise tramway workers before 1913. The Dublin and District Tramwaymen's Trade Union, formed in 1890, petered out by 1897. Revived in 1901 with Dublin Trades Council support, it enlisted city dignitaries to respectfully forward memorials to William Martin Murphy. Lacking self-confidence it was easily thwarted by Murphy, who, whilst tolerating representation, insisted upon docility. In 1908, even the leaders of a 'house union' were intimidated, bought off or, in one case, banished to Murphy's bus company in Paisley, Scotland.[26]

Murphy kept his men in check through autocratic management, providing little or no time off, and maintaining a reserve staff. 'Trouble-makers' always knew there were those ready to replace them. With a yellow union planned to preclude ITGWU incursion, tramwaymen were called to Liberty Hall on 28 June 1913. Larkin targeted powerhouse staff for if they came out, all trams stopped. By 12 July, 800 men had joined. Murphy tried to dissuade them but would not enter a public debate: 'we cannot disguise ourselves from the fact that an attempt is being made by an organiser outside the Company to seduce the men.' Directors had 'not the smallest objection to the men forming a legitimate Union (applause).' The matter became personal. *The Irish Worker* branded Murphy a 'damned liar' who had been 'driven from public life as a toady, renegade, an untruthful and dishonest politician, a false friend, a sweating employer, a weak-kneed tyrant', a view modified by Thomas Morrissey's broader portrait below. Larkin would meet him on any platform to prove he was a 'poltroon, liar and sweater' and 'that your only god is profit'.[27] Such language hardened Murphy's attitude. Used to his own way, Murphy feared the ITGWU threatened the social system that he utilised so well.

Dublin Employers' Federation

General employer resistance to the ITGWU was instant. In 1909, the union was effectively driven from Cork by an Employers' Federation and major battles took place in Wexford, 1911-12, and Sligo and north County Dublin earlier in 1913.[28] The Dublin Employers' Federation (DEF) was founded on 30 June 1911, to 'prevent strikes' and oppose 'intimidation and violence'. In classic 'Free Labour' parlance, men 'desirous of retaining or returning to their employment, are prevented from doing so.' The situation was 'very grave'. There was 'an urgent necessity for co-operation to protect the interests of employers.' DEF objects were 'mutual protection and indemnity of all employers of labour' and 'to promote freedom of contract between employers and employees.' Dublin employers learned well from their Cork counterparts. Two years previously, the situation there was bad but was now 'entirely satisfactory and they have experienced little or no labour trouble since the Federation was founded.' Murphy was conspicuous within the DEF provisional committee.[29]

On 3 September, 404 DEF employers issued the 'Odious Document', *the* document at the heart of the Lockout.

> I hereby undertake to carry out all instructions given to me by or on behalf of my employers and further I agree to immediately resign my membership of the Irish Transport and General Workers Union (if a member) and I further undertake that I will not join or in any way support this union.[30]

With blatant hypocrisy, employers themselves combined to deny the same right of combination to workers. Even those unconnected with the ITGWU were cast from work. By 22 September over 20,000 were locked out in city and county. From October, evictions began of those not paying rent – the Larkin family suffering this fate in December. The 'document' proved a tactical error. Trade unionists in Ireland and internationally would not tolerate denial of a basic human right – the right to organise. Solidarity was guaranteed.

Just as the ITGWU was less than five years in existence, the DEF was two years in being in July 1913.

Press

In our age of twitter and podcast, media coverage in 1913 is fascinating. In addition to constant misrepresentation by the establishment press – Murphy advantageously owning the *Irish Independent, Sunday Independent* and *Evening Herald* – the ITGWU was attacked by a 'yellow press' undoubtedly privately funded by Murphyites. From 28 August, Bernard Doyle's *Liberator* – Redmondite in character – reflected Nationalist fears for their usurpation by Labour. P. J. McIntyre's *Toiler* was a more threatening publication whose stock-in-trade was character assassination, the most infamous being that Larkin was, simultaneously, an Orangeman and son of Carey the informer – side by side pictures of father and son appearing as weekly proof. These papers' 'short and spiteful' lives were a peculiar compliment to the ITGWU. The 'sustained attack on the honesty of its leader', Larkin, failed as, by their own 'admission', workers 'remained loyal'.[31]

As John Newsinger details below, the ITGWU published *The Irish Worker* as a magnificent counterpoint. It was 'Larkinism congealed in print'.[32] Even for today's readers, *The Irish Worker* is exciting and fresh. Its impressive circulation – and beyond that its actual readership – attested to its appeal. It is the high point of working class journalism and one of Larkin's greatest achievements as, in addition to being editor, he contributed nearly 400 pieces. It attracted leading writers, poets and playwrights, and reproduced American, Australian and other international material. As Karen Hunt and Colin Whitston discuss below, the international establishment, labour and women's press carried analysis of Dublin's industrial chaos. An Irish struggle thus became uniquely internationalised.

Bloody Sunday and Lockout martyrs

On Friday, 15 August Murphy ordered *Irish Independent* despatch staff to leave the ITGWU or be sacked: 'As the Directors understand that you are a member of the Irish Transport Union whose methods are disorganising the trade and business of the city, they do not further require your services.'[33] Forty were immediately paid off. Newsboys, who had idolised Larkin since 1911, refused to sell the *Evening Herald* and Eason's van-men blacked papers. Scabs were brought in and scuffles broke out. On Sunday 17 August, 200 tramwaymen were sacked for not repudiating the ITGWU. Murphy personally visited Dublin Castle. The fruits of his call were evident in the reinforcement of Dublin Metropolitan Police (DMP) by Royal Irish Constabulary (RIC). The authorities abandoned any pretence at impartiality from the beginning.

1. Tram 282 with police escort, 1913.
National Transport Museum Collection

On Tuesday morning, 26 August, tramwaymen left their cars where they stood. Violence quickly erupted. After Larkin and Dublin Trades Council (DTC) officials – P. T. Daly, Partridge, Thomas Lawlor and William O'Brien – were arrested in their homes and deposited in Mountjoy Gaol on 28 August, the ITGWU summoned Connolly down from his union duties in Belfast. A major demonstration planned for Sackville (O'Connell) Street on Sunday 31 August was prescribed by order of magistrate, E. G. Swifte, coincidentally a Tramway Company shareholder. Freshly released from prison, Larkin, speaking from a Liberty Hall window, set fire to the proclamation saying he would attend on Sunday, 'dead or alive'.

Connolly and Partridge were arrested on Saturday 30 August but Larkin evaded arrest, hidden by Countess Markievicz. After overnight violence, the union agreed to transfer the proposed Sackville Street meeting to their social premises at Croydon Park, Clontarf.[34] Police were nevertheless stationed in large numbers in streets adjacent to

Sackville Street. It was later revealed that troops were confined to barracks in full uniform throughout Saturday and Sunday. Had the demonstration not been transferred, the consequences might have been significantly more horrendous than they were, as the colluding authorities were clearly prepared to wreak mayhem on any assembly.

2. Postcard, 'The arrest of Larkin in disguise'.
DCLA, Dixon slides

Rooms were booked in the Murphy-owned Imperial Hotel [now Clery's Department Store] in the names of Mr Donnelly and niece, Miss Gifford. They arrived at ten o'clock and were shown to rooms 13 and 24. At midday, Donnelly – Larkin disguised as a clergyman wearing Count Markievicz's frock coat – stepped onto the smoke-room balcony overlooking the street and shouted, 'I'm Larkin'. He was instantly arrested and police poured from their hiding places, setting about those around them. Most victims were neither ITGWU members nor trade unionists but citizens strolling along the capital's main thoroughfare. The *Daily Sketch* reported two dead, 460 injured and 210 arrested and the *Saturday Post* over 600 hospitalised, from infants to old folk. Partridge, addressing September's TUC, said many police were the worse for drink, a fact reported across Europe. Public outcry, at home and abroad, was intense. Such violence convinced TUC delegates – whatever about their leaders – to rally to Dublin's side. The *Daily Mirror's* graphic front page on Thursday 4 September, depicted wounded victims, homes vandalised by police, and Liberty Hall with its black drape, 'In Memory of Our Murdered Brothers.' It shocked British public opinion unused to wanton police violence. The TUC added its voice to those demanding a public inquiry, later dismissed by Larkin as a 'whitewash'.

'Bloody Sunday' remains Irish labour's most enduring image. It gifted the ITGWU the moral high ground. O'Connell Street's Larkin monument today surveys scenes which thousands have digitally stored from family lore, school texts, or *Strumpet city*. It roots trade unionism as an essential element of society, identified with the creation of the Irish state, integral to our culture. In addition to Bloody Sunday victims James Byrne and James Nolan, Liberty Hall's commemorative plaque also cites Kingstown Branch Secretary James Byrne, 16-year-old IWWU member Alice Brady who died after being shot by a scab, and Eugene Salmon, Jacob's striker and hero of the Church Street tenement collapse.[35]

BELFAST STRIKE.—Motor Vans delivering Goods in the Principal Streets of the City under Police Escorts.

3. Postcard of Belfast strike, 1907.

Private Collection

TUC funding

On 1 September, the TUC granted £5,000 for food aid. A nationwide collection followed, sustained until Christmas. The first food ship, *SS Hare*, emblem of the National Transport Workers' Federation (NTWF) fluttering aloft, docked on 27 September. For those who heard Larkin say that he would bring in food ships, to have stood on a cold quay and watch a ship actually arrive was an incredible experience. It explains workers' enduring faith in Larkin. It was an iconic moment, the 'Heroic Dublin' of today's Dublin Council of Trade Unions' emblem, through whose equivalent organisation food supplies were distributed.[3]

The TUC was – and is – criticised for sending food but denying industrial support. Larkin antagonised British trade union leaders but they were disinclined to sanction supportive strike action irrespective of Larkin. Dublin was not Devon or Dulwich,

Trades Union Congress Parliamentary Committee.

GENERAL BUILDINGS, ALDWYCH, LONDON, W.C.

Dublin Transport Workers' Dispute.

APPEAL FOR FUNDS.

To the Officers and Members of Affiliated Societies.

Gentlemen,—The Parliamentary Committee held a special meeting this morning for the purpose of receiving a report from the delegates appointed by the Manchester Congress to proceed to Dublin to help the Trade Unionists of that city to reassert the rights of free speech and of organisation and free meeting, and to inquire into the allegations of police brutality towards the citizens on Saturday and Sunday, the 30th and 31st of August.

After giving due consideration to the report (which is herewith appended), the Parliamentary Committee decided to at once arrange for a shipload of provisions being sent to Dublin, and for this purpose they have pledged the credit of the Trade Union movement to the extent of £5,000 (or practically one-halfpenny per member of the societies affiliated to Congress), and to issue an immediate appeal to the unions for funds in order that the supply of provisions for the men, their wives, and families may be continued as long as necessary.

The Parliamentary Committee make a strong and urgent appeal to all societies to respond generously, and invite the Executive officers to bring this pressing matter before their members without delay.

Cheques and post office orders should be crossed, and made payable and forwarded to Mr. C. W. Bowerman, General Buildings, Aldwych, London, W.C.

On behalf of the Parliamentary Committee,

J. A. SEDDON, *Chairman.*

C. W. BOWERMAN, *Secretary.*

September 23rd, 1913.

4. Trades Union Congress appeal for funds, 1913.

Report of the proceedings of the 46th annual Trades Union Congress, Milton Hall, Manchester, 1-6 September, 1913.

Private Collection

Derby or Dundee. Even if it had been, rule books would have been cited as to why sympathetic action was impossible. In addition, there was no precedent for a TUC-led general strike. Their parliamentary committee was instinctively hostile to the idea. Greaves suggested that had the TUC merely sanctioned the 'blacking of tainted goods', 'not only would Dublin employers have been defeated, but they themselves would have been immeasurably strengthened. They lacked the vision.' Dublin asked for action akin to that they unstintingly gave in 1911 to British mariners and railwaymen.[37] Instead, they got charity. Donations listed in the TUC Dublin Food Fund accounts testify to the spontaneous solidarity of miller and miner, docker and engineer, labourer and clerk, Temperance Leaguer and co-operator, women's activist and Christian Socialist. It became an historic debt that Irish workers attempted to repay in cash, foodstuffs and holidays for children during the 1984-85 British Miners' Strike.[38]

TUC funding was crucial. On 13 October, the ITGWU sought a 'temporary loan of £1,000 in cash to tide us over the present deadlock.' Food supplies had 'given us great strength but the long drag without money was very hard.' The United Builders' Labourers and General Workers of Dublin Trade Union (UBLTU), with 1,250 full benefit members out against an income of £8 per week, were chief among seven other unions sustained by TUC monies. In addition to providing meals to strikers' children and families, the ITGWU could pay strike pay. Between 8 December and 20 January 1914, the ITGWU claimed for 10,650 men at five shillings a week, 970 at four shillings a week, and 840 women at half-a-crown. Numbers fell to 9,800 men at the higher rate by 6 January. ITGWU cash-in-hand amounts fell as low as £144 by 6 January.[39]

The ITGWU Dublin No. 1 Branch strike committee distributed all strike pay and food aid. By 29 January, the TUC were not 'holding out any hopes that the food supply can be continued after this week.' Monies fell from over £2,800 a week in January to £800 in late March and £400 on 8 April. ITGWU accounts for TUC funds are shown in Appendix 1. TUC accounts show that £28,975 16s. was dispensed to Dublin, of which the ITGWU received £23,456 (88%). A further £62,889 6s. 6d. was paid to the Co-operative Wholesale Society for foodstuffs. DTC 1913 accounts, published on 25 November 1914, showed the TUC donated £38,976 with an additional £13,379 forwarded from the 'public in Ireland and the United Kingdom', a total of £43,314. Of this, the ITGWU received the lion's share, £35,794 14s. (82%). These figures demonstrate the unflinching solidarity of thousands of men and women most of whom had no connection with Dublin whatsoever, and the disciplined manner of distributing and accounting monies received.

After the formation of the Irish Trade Union Congress (ITUC) in 1894, the Irish movement increasingly stood apart from the British TUC. By 1900, when convening in Huddersfield, only one Irish union was in TUC affiliation. At the 1913 Manchester TUC, no Irish union was affiliated and only two Irish delegates were among the 560 present. In short, organic links between the Irish and British movements had diminished considerably, contributing to a recognition of two distinctly separate movements and trade union jurisdictions. This was reflected in TUC reluctance to tread where it might not have been wanted and DTC – the lead organisation more than the ITUC – and ITGWU keenness to take charge of an 'Irish' event.[40] How many people in Britain came to regard Ireland as different and entitled to that difference as the Lockout unfolded is unknown.

Thus, Yeates asserts that 'it is certainly a mistake to portray the TUC's action as some sort of betrayal of the Dublin men.' He praises the tireless efforts of James Seddon and Harry Gosling who accompanied the food ships and attempted to broker peace. He disagrees with Connolly's dismissal of TUC leaders as 'new recruits to the perfidious English ruling class that had always oppressed Ireland' but acknowledges that they 'rigged the debate' at the special TUC in December.[41] In this spirit, TUC-channelled solidarity – in cash, food and kind – can be heralded as a noble gesture. Contemporary British TUC and Labour Party should commemorate 1913 as a major event in British, as well as Irish, labour history. Ireland, in turn, might make formal recognition of its gratitude.

Liberty Hall

Liberty Hall's basement became a soup kitchen. Upstairs, in the evening, concerts and dramatic works entertained large audiences. Workers were drawn by what W. P. Ryan described as the Hall's 'spiritual electricity', whether ITGWU members or not. The ITGWU expressed workers' whole being, industrially, politically, socially and culturally. It was more than a 'mere trade union'.[42]

Liberty Hall – the old Northumberland Hotel – was first leased by the ITGWU in February 1912, rapidly acquiring its new title. As the Lockout developed, 'income was considerably higher than the demand for actual strike pay.' It is not uncommon for those administering strike pay to have amounts left after its distribution: some members return to work or disagree with the action, others are sick, have found alternative jobs or get waylaid by other business. Their benefits are held on their behalf rather than returned to union general funds. ITGWU Dublin No. 1 Branch secretary John O'Neill – very much an unsung hero – and General President Thomas Foran deposited surplus amounts in the safe until Christmas 'when there was something in the neighbourhood of £7,500.' Larkin was not told of this nest egg, not out of antipathy towards him but because of 'his talent for husbanding money'. Foran's objective – clearly accomplished

– was to be 'as economical as possible in the distribution of the funds of the Union.' A Christmas grant of around £2,000 was made to members and part of a large legal bill owed to the union solicitors, Smyth and Son, was paid off. In March 1914, the ITGWU were told that Liberty Hall was to be sold to a third party. There were suspicions that this was Murphy or a front organisation but Foran claimed it was the Ancient Order of Hibernians. Whoever the would-be purchaser was, had they succeeded in buying Liberty Hall from under the ITGWU it might well have been the union's death knell.[43]

Instead, on 23 April 1914, £3,426 14s. 3d. – 'practically all the balance of the funds' – was used, together with a £2,000 mortgage from Northern Bank, to purchase the premises.[44] Thus, Liberty Hall was – to a considerable extent – purchased from the unpaid TUC strike pay. Larkin subsequently made much of Foran and O'Neill's actions but they must be judged by the circumstances of 1913 not 1923. They were not motivated by anti-Larkin feeling other than recognition of his capacity to make grand gestures. Purchasing Liberty Hall was arguably the grandest gesture of 1914.

Irish Citizen Army

Following Larkin's release from Mountjoy Gaol on 13 November, a large torch-lit rally massed outside Liberty Hall in Beresford Place. Connolly demanded, 'The next time we go out for a march I want to be accompanied by four battalions of our own men. I want them to have their own corporals and sergeants and men who will be able to "form fours". Why should we not drill men in Dublin as well as in Ulster?' He wanted 'every man who is willing to enlist as a soldier to give his name and address' and had 'been promised the assistance of competent chief officers, who will lead us anywhere.' He knew 'nothing about arms at present. When we want them, we know where we will find them. (Laughter)' The laughter was a mixture of black humour and incredulity at the suggestion that beleaguered workers, severely punished by police and troops at picket lines, should organise their own defence force, the Irish Citizen Army (ICA). The following day, Captain J. R. 'Jack' White, who had been involved in the Citizen's Committee unsuccessfully attempting mediation, offered his military expertise.

Initially called the Transport Union Citizen Army, a notice appeared in *The Irish Worker*, for 'all men willing to join for progress of training' to attend Croydon Park where 'Captain White will take charge.' By 13 December, attitudes turned from dismissive amusement: 'At first looked upon as a mere piece of Liberty Hall heroics, it assumed a different aspect when it was discovered that regiments had actually been organised and drilling under the command of an experienced officer and competent NCOs was in progress nightly.' White was impressed by his charges: 'the material is as good as could be wished', a large proportion being 'old soldiers'. He explained his involvement, 'The

5. W. P. Ryan, *The labour revolt* and *Larkinism*, London, Daily Herald Office, 1913.
Private Collection

supreme object of Larkin at the present day I take to be emancipation from wage slavery and organisation into co-operative industries owned and managed by the workers.' Such a task required 'discipline and the simplest teacher of discipline is drill.' White pondered: 'whether the first fruit of our labours is the freeing of ourselves or the freeing of your country, time will show, but ultimately Ireland cannot be free without you nor you without Ireland. Strengthen your hand for the double task.' Seeds of the ICA can be detected along Cork quays in 1909 or during the Wexford Lockout. The ICA made an immediate difference at meetings and demonstrations. Actions beyond protective, industrial duties were not yet evident.[45]

Some argue that 'without 1913 there would have been no 1916.' While this is contestable, there is some logic to the case. Having created the ICA, secured Liberty Hall and appointed Connolly as Acting General Secretary in November 1914, the centrality of Liberty Hall to the 1916 Rising – if not, formally, the ITGWU itself – is undeniable. Rosie Hackett, IWWU member and long-term ITGWU employee, recorded in her witness statement: 'Historically, Liberty Hall is the most important building that we have in the city. Yet, it is not thought of at all by most people. More things happened there, in connection with the Rising, than in any other place. It really started from there.'[46] Larkin's departure for America in October 1914 is not fully understood – assuming Larkin himself fully understood. Perhaps the mental exhaustion that afflicted him just before the Lockout returned. It is difficult to fully appreciate the scale of the psychological, physical, political and social demands made upon him. He initially wanted P. T. Daly to succeed him but, after counsel from O'Brien and others, Connolly was appointed. Yeates argues that 'Connolly's growing preoccupation with the Citizen Army and insurrectionary plots suggests that he neglected the more mundane tasks involved in revitalising the union.' Some of this cannot be gainsaid but there is ample evidence that Connolly was an assiduous General Secretary, industrially and administratively. The scale of the reverse, onset of war and general union disorganisation – a product as much of Larkin's disinterest in basic administration as Lockout – were more limiting factors as Connolly summoned the first executive, chivvied branches for their subscriptions, and conducted strikes like that in the City of Dublin Steam Packet Company to the Rising's eve.[47]

The ITGWU's own view in their first published *Annual report* in 1918, stressed the significance of 1916, rather than 1913, for rising union fortunes:

> The wonderful renaissance of national sentiment which followed more than justified the prescience of the dead leaders. From the Union point of view, the immediate losses have been more than offset by the ultimate gain. Easter Week saved the Union. It cancelled out the reaction from 1913, and removed bitter prejudices which had blocked its progress. It linked up the Labour Movement with the age-long aspirations of the Irish people for emancipation from political and social thraldom, and formed a natural moratorium under cover of which it was able to make a fresh start on better terms with increased membership.[48]

Yeates indicates that 'reaction' from 1913 has been overplayed with the union recovering relatively quickly in most employments, in itself an indication of employer willingness – Murphy apart – to return to an industrial relations normality that included ITGWU. Even in 1918, although Easter Week was depicted as having 'saved the Union', the impending explosion in membership, spatially and industrially, could not have been foreseen. ITGWU membership collapsed from 22,935 in 1914, to 15,000 in 1915, and 5,000 by Easter 1916. It expanded to 14,920 in 1917, 67,827 in 1918, 101,917 in 1919 and over 120,000 in 1922. This period truly established the ITGWU as a national force and secured its long-term place in Irish life. And yet, it is now 1913 for which the union is best remembered in the public mind rather than 1916 or the syndicalist surge after 1917.

Politics

The antipathy of Nationalist and Unionist politicians to the ITGWU is indisputable. The political dividend for Irish Labour from the Lockout was surprisingly negligible, a fact partly explained by its organisational weakness. British government inaction, whether in Westminster or Dublin Castle, was extraordinary. Yeates rightly argues that 'no British city, least of all the capital, would have been left for five months with its industry paralysed, and a third of its population on the bread-line.' State indifference was a 'powerful argument in favour of Irish independence.' How many contemporary minds came to the same conclusion is unknown. Connolly was convinced – if he had not already been – and British Labour Party equivocation and prevarication, noted by Niamh Puirséil below, further fuelled his commitment to national self-determination. Lockout experience pushed Dublin workers towards a republican agenda more than a labourite one.

Women and children

Leeann Lane interestingly examines contemporary women's experiences through, in part, James Stephens's *The charwoman's daughter*. It helps answer the question as to who – in addition to well-intentioned peace brokers, those providing food and clothing as described by Kate Cowan and Ann Matthews, tolerant credit-granting shop-keepers and sympathetic intellectuals and artists – constituted 'Heroic Dublin'? The answer is found in images of Dubliners' grandparents or great grandparents staring anonymously from Enda Leaney's pictorial below. Among them are women who performed daily miracles to sustain and nourish their families. It is often overlooked that about 1,000 women were on strike and more locked out, sisters-in-arms of the men as ITGWU/IWWU members. Women were key activists – Delia Larkin, Countess Markievicz, Helena Molony. Was this the first occasion when women were so centrally and conspicuously involved in a major event – and involved, without question as equals and as of right? Children were among the strikers and those locked out. They became an increasing street presence begging for alms, and anxiety for their welfare was an important and increasing – if not long-lasting – social concern. It is incorrect to see 1913 merely as an adult, male event. The women of 1913 have not been studied as closely as for those involved in 1916. For many, like Markievicz and IWWU leader Louie Bennett, 1913 was unquestionably a formative political experience.[49]

Other factors

In the rather neglected 'epilogue' of Yeates' *tour de force*, he draws attention to a number of interesting phenomena. The ITGWU provided legal representation for over 400 members accused of various 'crimes' during the Lockout, in addition to standard workmen's compensation and accident cases. Greaves suggests that such 'large-scale defence of members involved in industrial disputes was an ITGWU innovation.' Yeates shows that 'only £3,842 6s. 4d.' was paid out by the union on 'unemployment benefit, travel and emigration' as it 'succeeded in extracting large amounts not only from the TUC's Dublin Fund but also from the new State Social Insurance Scheme in order to fund its industrial war', a further dimension to David Durnin's essay below. So, not alone did the ITGWU survive the conflagration but it acquired new skills and experiences and was, arguably, a much more sophisticated organisation after the event than it had been before. In modern parlance, unlike the DEF, the ITGWU proved to be a 'learning organisation'.[50]

Yeates observes that 'it was the strikers' misfortune that events coincided with the advent of motorised transport.' Its introduction proved more effective in avoiding pickets than slow moving drays but also more efficient and profitable. Dublin and transport historians suggest that street scenes can be dated pre- or post-Lockout, generally, by the absence or appearance of motor haulage. Motorisation meant fewer jobs and many 'victims' of the Lockout were simply replaced by motor power. Many were assisted with grants for the emigration train and boat by Liberty Hall. Some joined the Dublin Fusiliers en bloc in 1914 as the 'Dockers' Company'. On 24 April 1915 at Saint-Julien near Ypres, they 'advanced "in faultless order" to within a hundred yards of the village, then their line was swept away by machine gun fire.' Those that 'crawled back' gave 'three cheers for Jim Larkin'. Echoing Connolly's celebrated drape outside Liberty Hall at the war's outbreak, 'We Serve Neither King Nor Kaiser But Ireland', this group of Dubliners still served 'The Chief'. How many of those locked out suffered a similar fate is unknown but, by 1916, around 5,000 former ITGWU members had emigrated or enlisted.[51]

Won, lost or drawn?

The Lockout was initially regarded as a defeat for the workers. The ITGWU had no option but to ask members to seek to return individually and, if possible, not to sign the 'document'. Working people were starving, mentally and physically spent, and external assistance had dried up. The union was indebted and had lost many members. A 'depression' hung, like some fetid miasma, over Liberty Hall for months.[52] However, the ITGWU had gained new adherents and international prestige. Connolly concluded that it was a 'drawn battle' from which 'both sides are still bearing heavy scars.' Wright's *Disturbed Dublin* described the 'ignominious defeat of the attempt to establish a peculiarly pernicious form of syndicalism on Irish soil.' Reviewing Wright, Connolly wrote:

> The employers, despite their Napoleonic plan of campaign and their more than Napoleonic ruthlessness and unscrupulous use of foul means were unable to enforce their Document, unable to carry on their business without men and women who remained loyal to their Unions. The workers were unable to force the employers to a formal recognition of the Union, and to give preference to organised men.[53]

The working class had 'lost none of its aggressiveness, none of its confidence, none of its hope in the ultimate triumph. No traitor amongst the ranks of that class has permanently gained, even materially, by his or her treachery.' The ITGWU banner still flew 'proudly in the van of the Irish working class and that working class still marches proudly and defiantly at the head of the gathering hosts who stand for a regenerated nation, resting upon a people industrially free.'

1913 became a celebrated victory clutched from the jaws of a defeat employers were too exhausted to enforce. Workers gained a new sense of their own power and power was *the* issue that it was really all about. The labour movement became accepted stakeholders in a society which had to deal with the broad tenets of social democracy, if not socialism, the duty to care for the underprivileged.

Larkin and Murphy

Larkin's departure for America removed him from Ireland for over nine years. On his return, internecine animosities damaged the movement until both Labour Party and ITUC followed the ITGWU in splitting (1944-45). Increasing criticism of Larkin – whilst often valid and based on soundly researched evidence – often misses an essential point. 1913 would probably not have happened without him and certainly not in the manner in which it did. 'Larkinism' was Murphy's *bête noir*, the ghost he could not exorcise. Ironically, Larkin was increasingly more interested in recognition through conciliation and arbitration than through rampant confrontation, a fact lost on Murphy.[54] When tens of thousands lined Dublin's snowy streets in February 1947 to witness Larkin's cortège pass, the city paid respects to a man who, literally, raised them from their knees.[55] His achievements of creating the ITGWU and *Irish Worker*, inspiring and leading the Lockout, are unchallengeable testimony to greatness.

For those tempted to rehabilitate Murphy, the Lockout certainly could not have happened without him. It was his creation and he kept it alive when peace was possible. He was mainly responsible for making the whole episode a 'tragedy, and an unnecessary one.' Yeates is unequivocal:

> The twinkling, good-humoured face with its almost boyish expression and the sanctimonious piety in which he usually wrapped his sordid schemes, served only to underline the inner vindictiveness of his soul. Anyone who could leave thousands of workers on the bread-line, and tens of thousands of women and children under the threat of starvation to wring from the opponents a 'Carthaginian peace' deserves all the obloquy that posterity had bestowed upon him.[56]

Lessons

If Murphy is thus a pantomime villain, a Dublin audience today shorn of its economic sovereignty and assailed by public sector cuts, reduced salaries and pensions, increased taxes and a significantly diminished quality of life, might well shout 'look out behind you' should a Larkin miraculously reappear on the stage. Battle did not conclude in 1913. Progress since has been uneven. Would a social audit in 2013 compared to 1913 show workers to be in credit? Extreme, widespread poverty may have gone but things are relative. There are social housing shortages, permanent health crises, educational disadvantage, drug abuse and related violent crime, and mass unemployment. The spectre of mass emigration is returning. There is a constant media attack on trade unionism's collective values, to which society in fact owes many of its freedoms. The new 'documents' are the tenets of privatisation, deregulation, unregulated market capitalism, constant appeals to individualism and an ostrich-like approach to climate change, Third World hunger, indebtedness and exploitation. Trade union values are dismissed as 'old-fashioned' or 'belonging to the nineteenth century'. In its centenary year, 2009, SIPTU felt it was 'never more necessary if we are to win the struggle for control of our destinies and management of our own economic, social and political affairs' that 'lessons must be drawn from 1913's solidarity between trade unions, national and international.'

> The trade union movement fought for the whole of the working class not just the organised sectors. *The Irish Worker* through its mass readership countered the employers' message from the bosses' servant press. The trade unions provided social and cultural activities for its members as well as industrial and political leadership. The Lock-Out tried to outlaw a culture counter to capitalism. It failed

partly because it was so crude and ham-fisted. Today's attack is more subtle and all the more dangerous because of it. To honour the memory of 1913 we must begin, on an individual basis, to commit ourselves to trade union activity not just trade union membership. We must once again set out the task of regenerating a nation on 'the shoulders of a people industrially free.[57]

Larkin, in his 1914 ITUC presidential address, thought the 'workers emerged from the struggle purified and strengthened.' The outcome was the 'initiating of a new principle of solidarity inside the unions, and for the first time in the history of the world of labour … the principle had received universal recognition; viz 'An injury to one is the concern of all.'[58] Partridge cited *The Times* who 'declared, and the Employers realised' that 'you cannot smash the ITGWU'.[59]

That the ITGWU survived the Lockout was a great victory.

Many questions still remain regarding 1913. How did the rest of Ireland regard events in Dublin? How did Belfast Trades Council respond? Why has analysis of such a major event been under-played? Could it be that it was because the central issue in 1913 was a worker's right to join a union of her/his choice? After two decades of Social Partnership, union recognition remains a central – and for workers a growing – concern, despite an 'illusory' right to trade union membership enshrined in Bunreacht na hÉireann.[60] As the 'Decade of Centenaries' unfolds and government introduces stringent cuts and 'yellow pack' deals for public servants, powerful forces work to deny workers freedom of association.

As in 1913, society must ask itself, in whose best interests? Perhaps 1913 remains dangerously of the present rather than quietly in some antiquarian past?

The Red Hand Badge

An abiding legacy of the Lockout is SIPTU's Red Hand badge. In 1913, the ITGWU adopted an annual badge, starting with the Red Hand of Ulster struck as a disembodied red hand with gold lettering 'ITWU 1913'. For whatever reason, this badge fired the public imagination, became the emblem of a best-selling work shirt manufactured by the IWWU co-operative in Liberty Hall, and was worn as an ICA cap badge. ICA insignia still adorn the tunics of the Fintan Lalor Pipe Band, formed in 1912. Thousands were sacked or locked out for refusing to discard their Red Hand badge. On 11 October, *The Irish Worker* published 'Mac's' 'Who Fears to Wear the Blood Hand Badge?' to be sung to the air of 'Who Fears to Speak of '98'. After 1918, when the ITGWU reorganised, the Red Hand became the standard union emblem to honour those of 1913. Larkin repeated this for the WUI emblem in 1924. In 1990, when ITGWU and FWUI amalgamated to form SIPTU, the Red Hand remained the union emblem. 'Mac's' song is included here in hopes that it may be sung, for a song, like the sentiments it expresses, lies dead when left on a page.[61]

Who Fears To Wear the Blood Red Badge?

Who fears to wear the blood red badge
Upon his manly breast?
What scab obeys the vile command
Of Murphy and the rest,
He's all a knave and half a slave
Who slights his Union thus,
But true men, like you men,
Will show the badge with us.

They dared to fling a manly brick,
They wrecked a blackleg tram,
They dared give Harvey Duff a kick,
They didn't care a damn,
They lie in gaol and can't get bail
Who fought their corner thus,
But you men, with sticks men,
Must make the Peelers 'cuss'.

We rise in sad and weary days
To fight the workers' cause,
We found in Jim, a heart ablaze
To break down unjust laws,
But 'tis a sin to follow him,
Says Murphy and his crew,
Though true men, like you men,
Will stick to him like glue.

Good luck be with him. He is here
To win for us the fight,
To suffer for us without fear
To champion the right,
So stick to Jim, let nothing dim
Our ardour in the fray,
And true Jim, our own Jim
Will win our fight today.

Appendix 1:

ITGWU Strike Pay From Dublin Trades Council, TUC Fund, 1913-14

Week	Men 5/-	Amt	Men 4/-	Amt	Women 2/6	Amt	Total	Coh	Other	Nett demand
1 Nov	10,017	2,504	1,000	200	840	105	2,909	406	300	2,203
8 Nov	10,019	2,505	1,000	200	840	105	2,810	463	320	2,027
15 Nov	10,134	2,533	982	196	840	105	2,835	324	300	2,211
22 Nov	10,894	2,723	982	196	840	105	3,025	406	-	2,619
29 Nov	11,007	2,752	982	196	840	105	3,053	198	200	2,655
6 Dec	10,847	2,712	970	194	840	105	3,011	-	500	2,511
13 Dec	10,650	2,662	970	194	840	105	2,961	-	670	2,291
20 Dec	10,100	2,525	970	194	840	105	2,824	600	200	2,024
3 Jan	9,980	2,495	970	194	840	105	2,794	84	200	2,510
10 Jan	9,800	2,450	970	194	840	105	2,749	144	200	2,405

Source: ITGWU, Special List A8 (NLI, MS 13,913 (1))
Note that all amounts have been rounded up to nearest ten shillings
Coh – cash on hands
Amt – amount

Acknowledgement

I am grateful to Catriona Crowe, John Cunningham and Pádraig Yeates for their constructive observations on drafts of this paper.

Notes

1   Arnold Wright, *Disturbed Dublin: the story of the great strike of 1913-1914. With a description of the industries of the Irish capital* (London, 1914). W. P. Ryan, *The labour revolt and Larkinism* was published in pamphlet form by the *Daily Herald* in late 1913 to raise labour movement consciousness.

2   Pádraig Yeates, *Lockout: Dublin 1913* (Dublin, 2000); Emmet O'Connor, 'What caused the 1913 Lockout? Industrial relations in Ireland, 1907-1913', *Historical Studies in Industrial Relations*, no. 19 (Spring 2005), pp 101-21; p. 104.

3   Fergus D'Arcy, 'Larkin and the historians' in Donal Nevin, *James Larkin: lion of the fold* (Dublin, 1998), pp 371-9.

4   Fergus D'Arcy, 'Larkin and the Dublin Lock-out' in Nevin, *Larkin: lion of the fold*, pp 38-47; C. Desmond Greaves, *The ITGWU: the formative years, 1909-1923* (Dublin, 1984), pp 92-121; Dermot Keogh, *The rise of the Irish working class: the Dublin trade union movement and labour leadership, 1890-1914* (Belfast, 1982); John Newsinger, *Rebel city: Larkin, Connolly and the Dublin labour movement* (London, 2003); Francis Devine, *Organising history: a centenary of SIPTU, 1909-2009* (Dublin, 2009).

5   Emmet O'Connor, *James Larkin* (Cork, 2002); Thomas J. Morrissey, *William Martin Murphy* (Dublin,

2011); Andy Bielenberg, *Entrepreneurship, power and public opinion in Ireland: the case of William Martin Murphy* (www.ucc.ie/chronicon/bielen.htm).

6   For MacDonagh's 'Dublin City 1913', see Dublin Council of Trade Unions, *In Dublin city in 1913: songs and stories of the workers of Dublin* (Dublin, 1988) and John McDonnell, *Songs of struggle and protest* (Dublin, 2008).

7   Liam MacGabhann's 'The Citizen Army is out today, and if you wonder why' is reproduced in McDonnell, *Songs of struggle and protest*. It is best recited by Sam Nolan, stalwart DCTU corresponding secretary.

8   James Plunkett, *The risen people* (Dublin, 1978) and *Strumpet city* (Dublin, 2006). First broadcast in 1980, it is now available on DVD.

9   Curriculum Development Unit, *Dublin 1913: a divided city*, (Dublin, 1978, 1982); *Documents for the new Leaving Certificate history: case studies Dublin 1913: strike and Lockout* (www.edco.ie/_fileupload/1913%20Lockout.pdf) (2010).

10 For monument see 'Inscriptions on a monument' in Nevin, *Larkin: lion of the fold,* pp 365-6 and Devine, *Organising history,* pp 55, 606, 677.

11 For the split and creation of the WUI, see Devine, *Organising history,* pp 143-224.

12 Cathal O'Shannon (ed.), *Fifty years of Liberty Hall: the golden jubilee of the Irish Transport and General Workers' Union, 1909-1959* (Dublin, 1959), pp 30-53. Many claim there were 'no references' made to him. Whilst this is not strictly true, it was effectively so.

13 Donal Nevin, *1913: Jim Larkin and the Dublin Lockout* (Dublin, 1963).

14 Devine, *Organising history,* pp 605, 874.

15 SIPTU/NCAD, *'Let Us Arise': unravelling and understanding our past: the 1913 tapestry project* (Dublin, 2012) (http://1913committee.ie/blog/); and 'President launches 1913 Tapestry project' (http://1913committee.ie/blog/?p=653).

16 Yeates, *Lockout*, pp 8, 9, 12-13.

17 Ibid, p. 584.

18 The population of city and county was 477,196, Census of Ireland 1911.

19 O'Connor, 'What caused the 1913 Lockout?', p. 106.

20 Greaves, *ITGWU*, p. 84; Yeates, *Lockout*, pp xvii-xxx.

21 Seven out of ten workers in 1911 were found in 'largely unorganised, subsistence-wages employments', O'Connor, 'What caused the 1913 Lockout?', p. 108.

22 Greaves, *ITGWU*; Devine, *Organising* history; Francis Devine, *Organising the union: a centenary of SIPTU, 1909*-2009 (Dublin, 2009).

23 Francis Devine and Emmet O'Connor, 'The course of labour history', *Saothar 12* (1987), pp 2-4.

24 Devine, *Organising history,* pp 1004-5.

25 Emmet O'Connor, *A labour history of Ireland, 1824-2000* (Dublin, 2011), p. 291.

26 *Irish Worker*, 24 Dec. 1913; 'Meeting of Motormen, etc' (NLI, LO 83); *Irish Worker*, 26 July; 6 Dec. 1913. For a general description see Bill McCamley, *Dublin's tramworkers, 1872-1945* (Dublin, 2008).

27 Registered as 100T in 1890, the DDTTU actually affiliated to the ITUC, 1894-1896. It had collapsed by 1905. See Sarah Ward Perkins, *Select guide to trade union records in Dublin* (Dublin, 1996), p. 248.

28 Michael Enright, *Men of iron, Wexford iron foundry disputes, 1890 and 1911* (Wexford, 1987; 2012); K. S. Roche, *Richard Corish: a biography* (Dublin, 1912); Eugene Coyle, 'Larkinism and the 1913 County Dublin farm labourers' dispute', *Dublin Historical Record*, lviii, no. 2 (Autumn 2005), pp 176-90.

29 Provisional Committee, DEF, was Edward H. Andrews; R. W. Booth, JP; S. P. Boyd, JP; John Brown; William Crowe; H. M. Dockrell; F. J. Fisher; D. Frame; R. K. Gamble, chair; Sir W. J. Goulding; James Mahoney; Lawrence Malone; Frank V. Martin; William Martin Murphy, JP; T. R. McCullagh; John McIntyre; J. D. MacNamara; Thomas A. O'Farrell; J. A. Pearson; William Perrin; J. E. Robinson; J. Sibthorpe; William Wallace, JP; and J. Young. *Irish Worker*, 29 July 1911.

30 This document had to be signed by the worker and counter-signed by the foreman or supervisor.

31   John Newsinger, '"The Devil it was who sent Larkin to Ireland': the Liberator, Larkinism and the Dublin Lockout of 1913', *Saothar 18* (1993), pp 101-6; '"The curse of Larkinism": Patrick McIntyre, the Toiler and the Dublin Lock-out', *Éire-Ireland*, 30 (3) (1995), pp 90-102.

32   Greaves, *ITGWU*, p. 64; see also Devine, *Organising history,* pp 48-9; Nevin, *Larkin: lion of the fold;* 'The *Irish Worker*, 1911-1914', pp 152-8; Robert G. Lowery, 'Seán O'Casey and the *Irish Worker* (with an index, 1911-1914)' in *O'Casey Annual No. 3* (London, 1994), pp 33-114; John Newsinger, '"A lamp to guide your feet": the *Irish Worker* and the Dublin working class', *European History Quarterly*, 20 (January 1990), pp 63-99; and James Curry, *Ernest Kavanagh: artist of the revolution (1894-1916)* (Cork, 2012).

33   Cited in Breandan Mac Giolla Choille, 'Dublin labour troubles' in *Intelligence notes, 1913-16, preserved in the State Paper Office* (Dublin, 1966).

34   Members of the Irish Women Workers' Union set off in brakes for a picnic at the Scalp.

35   The Liberty Hall plaque is illustrated in Nevin, *Larkin: lion of the fold,* p. 399.

36   I was fortunate to have talked with some who were present that morning and, 50 or 60 years later, their amazement and gratitude were remarkable.

37   Francis Devine, 'The ITGWU and labour unrest in Ireland, 1911', *Historical Studies in Industrial Relations*, 33 (2012), pp 169-88; Conor McCabe, 'The context and course of the Irish railway disputes of 1911', *Saothar 30* (2005), pp 21-31; Conor McCabe, 'The 1911 railway strikes' (http://1913committee.ie/blog/?p=80) (2011).

38   The story of this solidarity is told in Jonathan Saunders, *Across frontiers: international support for the miners' strike, 1984-1985* (London, 1989); Emrys Bevan, 'Ireland and the South Wales miners', *Obair 2* (January 1985), pp 8-9.

39   Larkin to C. W. Bowerman, TUC, 13 October, 1913 (NLI, William O'Brien Papers, MS 13,921); ITGWU Special List A8 (NLI, MS 13,913 (1)); Devine, *Organising history,* pp 56-8.

40   TUC, *Forty-sixth annual report, 1913.* The delegates were J. Keogh, 5 Railway Cottages, Lansdowne Road, Dublin, for the National Union of Railwaymen, and J. Gillespie, 25 Chanchattan Street, Belfast, Shipconstructors' and Shipwrights' Association. Neither spoke.

41   Yeates, *Lockout*, pp 582-3.

42   James Curry and Francis Devine, *'Merry May Your Xmas Be and 1913 Free From Care': The Irish Worker Christmas Number, 1912* (Dublin, 2012), pp 13-14 and pp 5-6 of the facsimile; Manus O'Riordan*, Next to the revolution – the greatest event of 1916: Liberty Hall as a cultural centre: the early years* (Dublin, 2002).

43   ITGWU, *The attempt to smash the Irish Transport and General Workers' Union* (Dublin, 1924), pp 20, 77-81, 121, evidence of Foran and O'Neill under questioning by Larkin.

44   The sale was concluded on 1 September 1914.

45   *Irish Worker*, 22 Nov.; 13, 27 Dec. 1913. *Freeman's Journal* and *Irish Times*, 14 Nov. 1913. The reference to Ulster was to Carson's open drilling of the Ulster Volunteer Force. It has been suggested that the ICA had its origins in the dockside battles in Cork in 1909 and/or in the resistance to police repression in Wexford, 1911-12, but it finally came after the events of Bloody Sunday, 31 August 1913 with various vague suggestions being made in September and October. John Hanratty recalled that in mid October, 500 strikers went to the ITGWU social premises at Croydon Park, Clontarf, to register but nothing happened, nothing until after Connolly's November speech, see D. R. O'Connor Lysaght, 'The Irish Citizen Army, 1913-1916: White, Connolly and Larkin', *History Ireland*, vol. 14, no. 2 (March/April, 2006), pp 16-21. J. R. White, *Misfit* (London, 1930; reprinted Dublin, 2005).

46   Rosie Hackett, witness statement (MAI, BMH WS 546), reproduced and annotated in Francis Devine and Manus O'Riordan, *James Connolly, Liberty Hall and the 1916 rising* (Dublin, 2006), pp 48, 75-84.

47   Helga Woggon, '"Not merely a labour organisation': the Irish Transport and General Workers' Union and the Dublin dock strike, 1915-1916', *Saothar 27* (2002), pp 43-54; Devine, *Organising history,* pp 73-7. The dispute was not settled until after Connolly's execution.

48   ITGWU, *Annual report for 1918*, p. 6.

49   A view observed by Joseph E. A. Connell, 'Irish Women's Franchise League and Irish Women Workers' Union', *History Ireland*, 21, no. 1 (January/February 2013), p. 66.

50   Greaves, *ITGWU*, pp 120-1; Yeates, *Lockout*, pp 576-7.

51   Devine, *Organising history*, pp 66-8. Yeates furthers this discussion in *A city in wartime, Dublin, 1914-1918* (Dublin, 2011), pp 41-9, 54, 77, qualifying his earlier remarks in *Lockout*.

52   ITGWU, Dublin No. 1 Branch minutes, January-July 1914 (NLI, MS 7,298); Frank Robbins, *Under the starry plough: recollections of the Irish Citizen Army* (Dublin, 1977), pp 27ff.

53   *Irish Worker*, 28 Nov. 1914.

54   O'Connor, 'What caused the 1913 Lockout?'; Francis Devine, 'Larkin and the ITGWU, 1909-1912' in Nevin, *Larkin: lion of the fold,* pp 30-7.

55   'Death of a Titan', including Liam Mac Gabhann, 'Big Jim crosses the city' in Nevin, *Lion of the fold,* pp 353-66.

56   Yeates, *Lockout*, pp 581, 586.

57   Francis Devine, 'The 1913 Lock-out: a brief history' (http://www.siptu.ie/AboutSIPTU/History/The1913Lock-Out/).

58   ITUC, *Report of twenty-first congress, Dublin, 1-3 June 1914*, p. 37; *Irish Worker*, 17 Jan. 1914.

59   *Irish Worker*, 24 Jan. 1914.

60   *Report of the Constitution Review Group* (Dublin, 1997).

61   'The Union badge' in Francis Devine, *Organising the union*, p. 124 and for illustrations of badges see colour section in this work. See also (www.siptu.ie/aboutsiptu/ourlogo/ (from 1990)).

2.

The 1913 Dublin Lockout and the British and international labour movements

Colin Whitston

On 18 December 1913, 237 woollen textile workers (about two-thirds of the whole workforce) struck the Bliss Tweed Mill in the small town of Chipping Norton in the English Midlands in a dispute over trade union recognition. On Christmas Eve the *Oxfordshire Weekly News* described the dispute as 'Murphyism in Oxfordshire' as the company dismissed the strikers, and the strikers themselves clashed with police and strike-breakers on picket lines and demonstrations. In vivid parallels with the major struggle in Dublin, the town was split, violence flared, strikers were harassed by police, and strike leaders were jailed.[1]

The Lockout in Dublin was not a subordinate front in a wider battle between labour and capital, but it was – and supporters and detractors alike acknowledged this – set within a broad movement of working class mobilisation and employer counter mobilisation that spanned the end of the 19th and the start of the 20th centuries across states and continents. Furthermore, while the formation of the Irish Transport and General Workers' Union (ITGWU) was a decisive step towards an independent Irish labour movement, and while relations between the Irish unions and the British had atrophied over time, Ireland was still a part of the United Kingdom.[2] Thus, while the Lockout had many unique features, it cannot be fully described, nor its significance fully understood, as an exclusively Irish event.

This chapter sets out to show the common experience of militant labour organisation in this period through consideration of the international context, a principal feature of which was the discontinuous but explosive growth of trade union membership and associated struggles over recognition and the establishment of collective bargaining. From these struggles emerged, in the USA, Canada, the UK and much of Europe, both the outlines of state-supported industrial relations institutions, and the fault lines for continued social, political and economic clashes in the years following the First World War. Yet the wave of industrial action in the UK between 1910 and 1914 was not limited to newly organising workers trying to 'put manners' on the employers. It included a new wave of strike activity amongst those with well-established bargaining relationships.[3]

Another feature of the period, in the UK and beyond, was the influence of new and radical approaches to union organisation and purpose. Just as socialists played a prominent part in the organisation of the 'New Unionism' of the 1880s and 1890s in England, before the First World War syndicalism (or perhaps one should say syndicalists) played an important role, not only in the prosecution of strikes but in debates about the form that unions should take and their purpose. Syndicalism, at least in its British form, was a reaction to the failure of both parliamentary action and cautious trade unionism to transform – rather than reform – the conditions of the working class, seeing mass organisation as independent of party, a vehicle of social change, and a future form of worker-management of industry. Solidarity, ideas of industrial unionism, militancy and distrust of established leaderships were all prominent amongst those touched by these ideas. Militant action also exceeded previous norms as the British strike wave of 1910-14 was characterised by unusual levels of violence, against property and managers as well as in clashes with strike-breakers.[4]

Radicalism was not at all confined to the workers' movement. In the UK 'between the great dock strike [1889] and the First World War effective and permanent employers' organisations were formed on a national scale'.[5] In Germany also employers benefited from 'a strategy of conflict, a "class struggle imposed from above" ... by arbitrary police bullying and partisan court rulings'.[6] Some employers' organisations, the Shipping Federation for example, played a significant part in both periods (being founded in 1890 for the purpose of rolling back the gains of the 'New Unions' – in which it had considerable success). Others, including William Martin Murphy's Dublin Employers' Federation, established in 1911, were products of the newer wave of conflict. All of these, old or new, were a counter mobilisation against labour, politically and economically, and were characterised by aggression and, often, violence, whether exercised by troops, the police, or by armed 'free labour'.[7] Class struggle is portrayed often, and inaccurately, as something done by workers to employers – it is certainly also something done by employers to workers, and this is an especially important factor in this period. It was these features, among others, that earned this period in the UK the title of 'The Great Unrest'.[8]

The Lockout was also a significant determinant of the future of the Irish trade union movement, and of its relations with sister organisations in Britain. From its inception the ITGWU struggled with British unions and British union leaders to establish a fighting organisation free from interference and domination by 'mainland' interests. But it struggled *with* British unions and union leaders in the sense of struggle *alongside* too. The formation and growth of the ITGWU can be seen as part of the wider unrest, but of particular interest is the dual nature of relations with the British movement during the course of the Lockout. Solidarity with Dublin's workers, both rhetorical and practical, was both widespread and controversial. Larkin and Connolly were no strangers to the British movement, and participated in the amalgamation debates of 1914[9] that led, ultimately, to the formation of the Transport and General Workers, Union in Britain. In doing so they represented the radical wing in the debates, in alliance with those who had been most forward in supporting Dublin in 1913, and in opposition to those who proved most unwilling to extend the dispute. No account of the Lockout and its international significance would be complete, therefore, without consideration of the solidarity movement and the role of the TUC, and of the TUC Special Conference in December 1913 – the only occasion that such a conference had occurred since the founding of the TUC in 1868.

The Great Unrest – worker militancy in the UK and beyond

Across Europe, from the end of the 19th century, industrial unrest grew, such that 'What contemporaries would have noticed more than any other aspect of labour activity in the three decades before the First World War was the increase in the incidence of strikes and their scale.'[10] Boll identified major peaks in strike participation in France between 1905 and 1908, and 1910 to 1912, and in Germany between 1910 and 1914, as well as in Italy, Russia and the United States.[11] Between 1902 and 1904 general strikes occurred in Belgium, Italy, the Netherlands and Sweden – where a law was passed enabling the imprisonment of pickets – and strikes reached a peak in Spain in 1913.[12] In America a rising tide of industrial action led to the establishment of the Commission on Industrial Relations, whose history, aptly titled 'Age of Industrial Violence', speaks of '… near anarchy … and military rule' in the years 1910-15.[13] 1910 alone saw the Bethlehem Steel strike, a Cloak Makers' strike, the Chicago Clothing Workers' strike, the Los Angeles strike wave and the Philadelphia general strike.[14] In the USA, between 1900 and 1915, union membership more than trebled.[15] Somewhat later, in 1919, the Canadian government appointed a Royal Commission on Industrial Relations in Canada on foot of what has been called 'The Canadian Labour Revolt' whose progress echoed events in Europe and the USA.[16] Brown has argued that an over-emphasis on the national setting of the 1913 Lockout, and in particular the importance of the struggle for recognition in Ireland, has led to an underestimation of its significance in an international setting, and, in particular, of its place in the movement in the UK as a whole.[17]

The Dublin Lockout was not the last episode of industrial unrest in the UK before the outbreak of the First World War; that unhappy honour goes to the disastrous London Building Trades Lockout of 1914.[18] In England in 1909 there were 170,258 workers directly involved in strikes, in 1910 there were 385,085.[19] The 'Great Unrest' in the UK can be traced through the Tonypandy Lockout, strike and riots of 1910, to strikes of seamen, dockers and railwaymen in 1911, the London transport strike of 1912, the West Midlands engineering and metalworkers' strikes of 1913, and the Dublin and London Lockouts of 1913 and 1914.

Defining periods in history is, however, always fraught with difficulty.[20] If struggles between the Shipping Federation and English workers in 1911 are part of the 'Great Unrest', how are we to characterise the Belfast dock strike of 1907 that eventually led to the foundation of the ITGWU in 1909? Hobsbawm and Cronin, in separate works and using marginally different periodisation, argue that 1910-14 was one of 'three great leaps' in strike activity and unionisation in the UK – the period between the 'New Unionism' of the late 1880s and the immediate post-war struggles before the inter-war depression,[21] and this view gives us a better grasp of events domestically and internationally. Similarly, O'Connor posits three waves of labour militancy in Ireland between 1889 and 1923,[22] and these arguably cannot be viewed as separate from the structural conditions in Britain. These were 'the extension of British 'new unionism' to Ireland between 1889 and 1891 … pioneered by seafarers' and dockside unions' … A 'Larkinite' phase, and a third wave when, 'from 1917 to 1923, the ITGWU acquired a guiding influence and diffused a syndicalist character to unrest.'[23] Williams' account of the beginnings of the 'Great Unrest' makes the point clearly, itemising among the mining and transport strikes actions by the Glasgow thread workers, Bradford textile workers, boilermakers, ironfounders and Lancashire cotton operatives.[24] The breadth of this movement led White to argue that we can discern 'two unrests' in this period: the first comprised the battle for unionisation and recognition, the second an upsurge of action by 'members of established and recognised unions whether "old" or "new"'.[25] In general this breadth may be seen as a feature – in the UK at any rate – of the contradictory impact of economic conditions in the 'Indian Summer' of Edwardian capitalism. In contrast to the preceding period of rapid unionisation which occurred during the 'Great Depression', the period of 1910-14 was characterised by boom conditions and rising levels of employment, and, if only moderately, rising prices, but also of stagnating productivity.

The mixture of influences was to prove explosive. In textiles, and mining, for example, relatively backward production methods led to both 'driving' and rationalisation, while in the technologically more advanced areas of engineering, paradoxically, new methods could produce the same discontents. As a consequence, workplace relations between managers and workers came under new strains, and new patterns of relations between workers themselves emerged because 'skilled workers were antagonised and aggrieved but retained a good deal of collective strength, while unskilled workers achieved a new ability to transform long-standing grievances into organised militancy.'[26] The effects were seen particularly in the growth of union membership among metal workers: between 1910 and 1914 some 200,000 of the million workers added to the membership of the

TUC were from the Amalgamated Society of Engineers (ASE) and the Workers' Union (whose members were predominantly semi-skilled engineering workers).[27] Similar forces were at work in France and Germany: while the majority of strikes during 1910-14 were pay disputes, both the length of the working day and workplace discipline and effort levels were at issue, as where, for example, metalworkers in the Ruhr complained of 'nervous exhaustion' arising from technological change and speed-up.[28]

Nevertheless, a striking feature of the first two waves of industrial struggle was the role of transport workers and their unions, not only in the UK, but in Europe too.[29] In Ireland, as O'Connor argues, relative economic backwardness, coupled with the growth and strategic importance of the transport sector, meant that unskilled, general workers were better placed than most to extract gains from employers; that the General Unionism of the ITGWU was the best tool to hand; and that success in the transport sector acted as a 'bridge' to general workers more broadly.[30] In England many of the trade union recognition gains of the 1890s had been eroded in an employers' counter-offensive thereafter. In the English strikes of 1911, with more than 10 million working days lost, most involved were port and transport workers. There, as in Ireland, industrial action was closely coupled with union growth, with membership in the waterfront unions rising by some 250% between 1911 and 1912, and renewing as well as gaining new union recognition.[31] Although centred on docks and shipping, the movement of 1911 encompassed both independent and associated strikes among railway companies, and, on occasion, brought into action a range of other general workers, either in pursuit of their own demands, or in solidarity with others, or both. The most gripping case was Liverpool in 1911 where a strike movement among dockers drew in railwaymen and tramwaymen, power station workers and dustmen in what became a virtual general strike where 'the whole City of Liverpool was thrown into a state of siege',[32] a struggle that also drew in large numbers of women workers from the sugar and rubber industries amongst others.[33]

The explosion of action within the transport industries was also affected by general social conditions and the specific forms of exploitation that characterised them. While O'Connor argues that attempting to use social conditions as a factor in explaining the Dublin Lockout is a 'red herring',[34] historians of the English strikes, and of transport strikes elsewhere, emphasise the connections between poverty, powerlessness and militancy:

> Some historians have felt that the uprising of the ports in 1911 remains mysterious. The only mystery is why it took so long … After years of privation and oppression the seamen, dockers and carters left their work in droves and together took to the streets.[35]

SETTLEMENT OF THE RAILWAY STRIKE.

SUCCESSFUL ISSUE OF NEGOTIATIONS.

WORK TO BE IMMEDIATELY RESUMED.

WITHDRAWAL OF THE TROOPS.

SERIOUS RIOTS IN WALES.

TROOPS FIRE ON THE CROWD.

Late on Saturday night the great Railway strike was ended, as the outcome of conferences at the Board of Trade which had proceeded all day between the men's representatives, two representatives of the Railway Managers' Association, and Mr. Lloyd George and Mr. Sydney Buxton.

By the terms work is to be immediately resumed, and all men who present themselves within a reasonable time are to be reinstated. Conciliation Boards are to be convened for the purpose of settling forthwith questions in dispute, provided notice is given within fourteen days of the date of the agreement.

If the Sectional Boards fail to arrive at a settlement, the Central Board is to meet at once.

Questions in dispute not within the Conciliation Scheme of 1907 are to be settled by a conference between representatives of the Companies and their employes, and, failing agreement, by arbitration to be arranged mutually or by the Board of Trade. The above are to be temporary arrangements pending the report of a Commission of Five upon the working of the Conciliation Boards and what changes are desirable with a view to a prompt and satisfactory settlement of differences. The Commission will proceed to work expeditiously, and both parties give assurances they will accept its findings.

The Government have promised the Railway Companies they will propose legislation next Session providing that an increase in the cost of labour due to the improvement of the conditions for the staff would be a valid justification for reasonable general increase of charges.

The Home Office subsequently issued a statement that, in consequence of the settlement, orders had been given to immediately withdraw the troops. The fact of the settlement was telegraphed to the King.

Rioting broke out in Llannelly late on Saturday night. The mob attacked shops and looted them. Subsequently they attacked the residence of the magistrate who had read the Riot Act earlier, but they were prevented from doing serious damage. The rioters then looted some trucks on the railway line and set them on fire., One contained carbide, and when the flames reached this it exploded with terrific violence. One man was blown to pieces, and another so badly injured that he died immediately. Others are lying in hospital. At 3.30 yesterday morning an armoured train arrived, and matters quietened down.

A message from the Llanelly police received late last night states that four were killed outright in Saturday night's explosion. One man has died since, and eleven are detained in hospital.

Serious disturbances occurred at Lincoln late on Saturday night. A mob attacked the Great Northern and Midland Stations, the police being pelted with broken bottles, stones and other missiles. They made charge after charge with their batons. Hundreds of shop windows were broken, damage to the extent of thousands of pounds being done.

Serious rioting took place at Chesterfield on Saturday night, and as a result thirteen people were taken to hospital. A number of arrests were made.

1. End of the railway strike and riots in Llanelly, Wales.
Freeman's Journal, 21 Aug. 1911.
DCLA

For many workers the drive to organise and the insistence on solidarity were rooted in poverty wages and competition between workers. G. D. H. Cole wrote of the Bliss Tweed Mill strike that its significance lay in its attempt to break out of the circle of competitive pressure on wages in which country poverty reinforced urban poverty. 'Till the country worker is better off' wrote Cole 'he will always be tempted into towns to take the place of any town worker who endeavours to raise his wages.'[36] Equally, as Geary shows, appalling conditions in housing and the workplace were concrete factors in the spread of union membership and strike action in Germany, with urban overcrowding, accidents, and industrial diseases all contributing to labour militancy.[37]

Oppression and privation equally marked the conduct of disputes in England and Dublin. In Liverpool, on 'Bloody Sunday' (13 August 1911) 350 people were hospitalised after an attack on a mass strike meeting by the police and troops, while troops shot and killed two workers in another incident some days later.[38] In the same month, as a national rail strike commenced, workers blockading a struck line outside Llanelli in South Wales were fired on by troops of the Worcestershire Regiment: two died. The intervention of the troops had been ordered by Thomas Jones, a JP in Llanelli, and a shareholder in the Great Western Railway.[39] Ironically, this part of the Camarthen line was seen as politically sensitive, being 'the main route to and from the troubled provinces of Ireland.'[40] The dock strike in Hull also saw attacks on strikers by both the authorities and armed strike-breakers. But Hull differed from other strike centres in one important respect: not only were unions not recognised in the docks, but most of the strikers were not union members – and received no financial support from the unions. The latter fact, along with extremely inept handling of the dispute by union leaders who attempted to impose a settlement relating to their own members only, did much to inspire the riots so often cited as the common face of 'unrest'. In fact, the desperate circumstances of un-unionised strikers led to widespread deprivation and 'as *The Times* reported, "Hull is in far greater danger of famine than of mass violence."'[41]

This combination of recognition strikes involving mass action, organised employer attempts at union busting, and the use of force, were features of the international scene also. We may see the strike and lockout (again!) of miners in the South Wales coal field and the resultant 'Tonypandy Riots' as an opening action in the 'Great Unrest' in 1910, but it was common elsewhere. In France employers 'financed "yellow" unions, imported blacklegs and hired gunmen to intimidate pickets', while Radical politicians (notably Clemenceau) had, since the beginning of the century deployed the army in large numbers against strikers.[42]

STRIKE RIOT AT LIVERPOOL.

BATTLE IN LIME STREET

ONE HUNDRED PERSONS INJURED.

FIERCE FIGHT WITH POLICE

RIOT ACT READ.

RAILWAY STATION AS HOSPITAL.

Liverpool, Sunday.

A feature in connection with the Liverpool strike on Saturday was the conveying of a hundred lorries containing supplies from Edge Hill goods station. The 100 empty lorries, many driven by fruit and provision merchants, were taken to the station under an escort of 50 Scots Greys armed with sabres, carbines and ball cartridge, a hundred mounted constabulary, and over 200 foot police. Two magistrates, each with a copy of the Riot Act in his pocket, were in attendance. Three hundred tons of provisions and fruit which had been held up were removed to the centre of the city under an escort of military and police, the protective force this time including 100 men of the Warwickshire Regiment with the magistrates' clerk and four magistrates. There were considerable demonstrations of hostility but no violence.

The general outlook is exceedingly ominous. The Lord Mayor has wired the Board of Trade:

2. 'Bloody Sunday' in Liverpool, 13 August 1911. *Freeman's Journal*, 14 Aug. 1911. DCLA

Force was a familiar story in the coalfields of Australia and the USA too. One of the most impressive speakers invited by the South Wales Miners' Federation during their strike was 'Big Bill' Haywood, leader of the American Western Miners' Federation and founding member of the Industrial Workers of the World (IWW), whose activities featured regularly in *The Irish Worker* between 1911 and 1914.[43] The struggles of the American miners for union organisation were notoriously met by state and employer violence on a scale unimagined in the UK. In a series of vicious disputes, on the railways and in the mines in particular, US employers used troops, state, county and city police, and armed strike breakers in a murderous campaign of union suppression typified by the 'Ludlow Camp Horror' where state troops machine-gunned an encampment of striking miners and their families. The Pennsylvania state police ('Cossacks' as they were widely known) were particularly active in this way, and had been, ironically enough, 'fashioned … along the lines of Britain's Royal Irish Constabulary not as an antilabor measure but because … conditions in Pennsylvania resembled those of strife-torn Ireland.'[44]

The influence of the IWW spanned continents, inspiring transport, mining and lumber strikes in Australia and Canada. One such miners' strike, in Broken Hill, New South Wales Australia in 1909, had among its leaders Tom Mann, an English trade union veteran of the 1889 London dock strike who returned to England in 1910 and played a leading role in the 'Great Unrest'. Before his return from the USA James Connolly had been an organiser for the IWW. Also in 1910, he had taken Charles McKeevers' place as editor of the *Free Press*, and effectively as strike organiser in the McKees Rocks steel strike in Pittsburgh, after McKeevers' imprisonment. In that paper he had written on the 'Labor War in Ireland' covering the Cork dock strike, and a report of Mann's defence of black workers in South Africa and his attack on white racism there.[45] Mann and Connolly, both so prominent in the disputes in England and Ireland, are associated with syndicalist ideas and organisations – advocates of industrial unionism, aggressive class politics, direct action, solidarity and revolution. It is to the competing ideas and forms of action of the period that we now turn.

Industrial militancy and 'syndicalism' – new forms of organisation and struggle

Just as, in Dublin, the employers cursed the influence of 'Larkinism', in the rest of the UK as well as Europe, Australia and America, employers cursed class war unionism and syndicalism. In England *The Times* produced a whole series of articles on industrial unrest that centred on the syndicalist label.[46] So powerful was the perceived challenge of a revived labour militancy to the official order that many saw in it – whether hopefully or fearfully – the lineaments of a social revolution. Sir George Askwith, who chaired the Court of Inquiry into the 1913 Lockout, commented that 'nobody could understand the rapid and alarming spread of many of the strikes' in the movement of 1910-14,[47] and the British Foreign Secretary thought the 1912 coal strike could become revolutionary and that 'unless we meet the men there would be a civil war.'[48] Brown follows the ideas of Halévy and Dangerfield, French and American respectively, in explaining the widespread political as well as industrial unrest and violence of the time as a general breakdown of consensus and social ties, even to the point, in the case of Stone, of identifying a wave of irrationality.[49] Writing in the 1930s, Dangerfield's thesis was that the period prior to the First World War was one of a collapse of liberal certainties under the assault of nationalist, suffragist and militant labour movements.

But such interpretations are subject to periodic reassessment, and usually reflect very contemporary concerns – the descent into Fascism in Dangerfield's case. On the other hand, Yeates' monumental history of the Lockout has been criticised as too strongly formed by the perspectives of social partnership and the institutionalisation of industrial relations, a viewpoint wholly committed to the institutions and industrial relations practices of an Ireland riding the 'Celtic Tiger' after the disputatious years of the 1980s.[50] White pointed out that earlier British historians of the emerging welfare state after 1945 saw in the 1910-14 movement nothing of real significance to upset the narrative of the peaceful development of collective bargaining to its consensual heyday in the 1950s. By comparison, writers dealing with the development of workplace organisation and industrial action in the UK in the 1960s looked back at syndicalism with renewed interest, as a source of patterns of decentralised bargaining and rank and file 'insubordination' towards trade union officialdom.[51] One suspects an inevitable tension in the commemoration of the 1913 Lockout between those who would see it as a warning of the dangers of potential conflict unrestrained by political compromise, and those looking to a more militant approach to the current subordination of the trade union movement, a tension that should supress any inclination to the smug.

White is surely correct in his assessment that the 'interpretation of 1910-14 as a syndicalist uprising was never made out of whole cloth' but his further arguments about industrial tactics, structures of bargaining, intra-union relations and extensive solidarity do require serious consideration.[52] Strikes may be the result of a clash of class and economic interests, but they are organised, directed, won or lost, by men and women, and these bring the force of ideas to bear on their actions, and their actions animate and develop ideas. It is to those men and women, and to their ideas and activities that we turn next, and here again the Dublin Lockout reflects wider events. Four strands are important: the ideas that key trade unionists and socialists brought to the period, the forms of action adopted by workers, the character of relations between workers and union leaders, and the results of the period in terms of union structure and collective bargaining.

Tillett, Mann, Connolly, Larkin, De Leon, and Haywood: radical thinkers and activists of considerable diversity (and, occasionally, considerable antagonism) left their mark on this period in similar ways to the socialist organisers of the 1880s-90s. The exact relationship between these individuals (between any individuals) and the actions of masses of workers is difficult to specify, and the impact of their ideas, perhaps, impossible. Nor are things made any easier by the sheer variety of viewpoints that could, at times, group themselves under the banners of 'syndicalism' or 'industrial unionism'.[53] Historians of the movement as diverse as Hobsbawm and Williams have argued the facts, and failed to agree – although it must be said that Hobsbawm is too much the Marxist to be over-impressed by the influence of Marxists.

There is enough commonality, however, to provide a skeleton of ideas. First, there is the influence of socialist thinkers (largely Marxist in outlook, but divided to some degree on the principal agency of social change, but also, in France and America, anarchists) who were hostile to the existing structure and practice of the trade unions insofar as these were craft based, or in other ways exclusive, so as to add sectionalism to the already horrendous difficulties of worker organisation. There was also a widespread dissatisfaction with the partial and unstable results of 'political' organisation that was exclusively parliamentary in orientation. Thirdly, sectionalism and the limits of parliamentary politics had impelled unions, in the eyes of their critics, including in the pages of *The Irish Worker*, to adopt a self-defeating moderation that led not only to a failure to secure economic advances for workers, but which guaranteed their continuing subordination to the capitalist class and capitalist system. Workers' emancipation lay in the widest and most inclusive form of union organisation, solidarity and direct action, and, ultimately, in the control of industry by the workers themselves.

The radicals' criticisms of established unions however, were of great force. Even the Webbs noted in 1894 that the basis of trade unions was:

> primarily sectional in nature. They come together, and contribute their pence, for the defence of their interests as boilermakers, miners, cotton spinners, and not for the advancement of the whole working class.[54]

Even the survivors of the new general unions of the 1880s and 1890s had, by the turn of the century, come to depend on limited industrial and occupational groups. Connolly, among other Marxists, identified sectionalism and craft exclusiveness as the besetting weakness of the union movement, and of the class movement in general. Not only did it weaken industrial struggle, it formed an important element of the colonisation of the workers' movement by liberals and bourgeois nationalists.

Another important feature of developments at the turn of the 20th century was the degree to which the incorporation of unions into a regulated system of industrial relations complemented the lack of a class policy.

In Britain the ruling class accommodated labour aspirations by recruiting union organisers and members wholesale into local government, the factory inspectorate, school boards etc. Halévy notes that following the social reforms of the 1906 Liberal government:

> Ministers had considered themselves justified in utilizing the practical experience of labour possessed by trade union officials … The Trades Board Act had necessitated the appointment of 800 posts whose salaries reached in some cases to £1,000 a year. There was a deluge of applications … In 1911 the … National

Insurance Bill brought with it another batch of official posts to satisfy the hunger of trade union officials.[55]

Radicals did not oppose such appointments in principle. In 1913 Connolly stood as a Labour candidate in the Dock Ward of Belfast in order to strengthen the workers' voice in elections to the Insurance Commission. What he opposed was the degree to which labour representatives became both administrators and guardians of a barely modified system of exploitation. His election address followed what was always his plan, the unity of political and trade union advances, including proposals to enforce direct labour organisation, union recognition and compulsory union membership.

Nor were the radicals interested in engaging in conflict at every opportunity or at any cost. In the case of the New York Shirtwaisters' strike of 1910 Connolly showed how coordinated guerrilla action was more useful than adherence to the contract driven policies followed by the American Federation of Labour (AFL), the craft-based, main union organisation of the day. His advice – and it goes some way to dismissing the canard that industrial unionism was in its nature adventurist – was:

> ... fight only at the time you select, never when the boss wants a fight. Fight at the height of the busy season, and in the slack season ... absolutely refuse ... Even if the boss insults and vilifies your union and refuses to recognise it, take it lying down in the slack season, but mark it up in your little book ...[56]

Nor is it possible to maintain the idea that syndicalists (in Britain at any rate) were simply anti-political. Mann and Larkin were both members of socialist parties – both had been members of the Social Democratic Federation which was largely hostile to union activity, both later joined the Independent Labour Party, and both became Communists. When asked if he approved the repudiation of political action by the IWW Connolly, a founder of the Irish Labour Party, replied 'it will be impossible to prevent the workers taking it.'[57] In maintaining his industrialist principles, Connolly was eager to minimise the differences between syndicalists and parliamentary socialists broadly speaking. He noted that the emphasis in the labour movement in the early years of the 20th century had varied with the pace of industrial struggle, and the success or failure of elected socialists. He caricatured the divisions by saying that, during the eight hours agitation in the 19th century you could distinguish between old-style unionist and socialist by their wording of May Day resolutions – the unionist demanding the eight hour day, and the socialist demanding legislation for the eight hour day.[58]

That syndicalist policies never 'conquered' the labour and trade union movement is true, but, as Holton argued, they resonated with the activities and outlook of wide layers of workers who adhered in practice to:

the primary importance of direct action over parliamentary pressure as a means of settling grievances, the desirability of industrial solidarity between workers in different industries, and above all at this stage the need for rank-and-file control over industrial policy.[59]

Of course, it has to be said that in London in 1889, in Liverpool in 1911, and in Dublin in 1913, workers who followed Tillett, Mann and Larkin were not necessarily endorsing the socialist or syndicalist views of the leaders, although many were. Indeed, it is a feature of such periods of widespread unrest that a whole gamut of often contradictory ideas comes into play. An account of one of Tillett's meetings in the 1912 London dock strike tells how, after a pause to turn back a strike-breaking lorry, 'a foreign gentleman addressed the crowd on the need for revolution, and received loud cheers. Then Ben Tillett again resumes the platform'. By contrast, the agitation conducted by Edward Tupper of the National Sailors' & Firemen's Union (NSFU), while successful in spreading the strike on the Cardiff docks, relied in part on racist attacks, verbal and physical, on Chinese seafarers.[60] Women likewise were often seen as outside the ranks, or deliberately excluded from both unions and employment. The French syndicalists of the CGT (the Confédération Générale du Travail – or General Confederation of Labour, an anarcho-syndicalist dominated movement founded in 1895) commonly excluded women, and in 1913 the printers' union expelled a member, from both the union and his job, because he had secured work for his wife. 'The union still resented events at Nancy, a decade earlier, when women blacklegs, encouraged by bourgeois feminists, had broken a strike.'[61]

It might be said that the ITGWU was, on the eve of the Lockout, driven by four broad policies,[62] including independence from the British movement and the promotion of solidarity action as a directing idea for the working class as a whole. Larkin was a tireless advocate of both, but it is in the work of James Connolly – one time union activist and Socialist Labour Party organiser in Scotland, propagandist for the original party in the USA, organiser for the IWW and later a member of the American Socialist Party – that stands out as perhaps the clearest and most eloquent advocates of this new wave of union organising. In the English movement Connolly's political acuity was often less apparent, but the immediacy of the problem of solidarity in face of an aggressive employing class rings out in the propaganda of Mann and others. In the *Industrial Syndicalist* Mann analysed the labour process on the London docks and the rationalisation and the speed-up that accompanied it and the evils of casualisation. In arguing that workers could not delay in addressing these conditions he wrote '… who is to alter them? And to that there is only one reply; The men themselves must do it. Ah, but How? There is only one way: viz. by proper Industrial Organisation.'[63] Mann's observations on sweating and the accompanying dehumanisation of the workforce was echoed almost exactly by Connolly not a year later in an excoriating exposé of conditions on the Belfast docks where 'As a result of ... systematic slave-driving the average day's work was driven higher and higher, until 160, 180, and 200 tons as a day's work ceased to excite any comment or be considered anyway remarkable' until union organisation raised wages, while, Connolly argued 'the improvement of conditions and increased self-respect cannot be overestimated.'[64]

In the event men and women were to do it, not because Mann or Connolly told them to, but because they had to, and because they had to they also had to invent forms of organisation and action that overcame sectional divisions. These innovations led to important institutional results. The formation of the National Transport Workers' Federation in July 1910 (which refused, incidentally, to admit the ITGWU as a 'breakaway' union) brought together 16 unions and was not only a precursor to a wider amalgamation movement, but a key weapon in the transport strikes that followed, as well as a focus of support for the Dublin workers in 1913. They also found expression in non-institutional – even anti-institutional – practices such that Cronin argues that the '... fundamental strategic innovation of 1910-14 was the "sympathetic strike"'.[65] Not only were wildcat strikes common, so too was their use in order to extend the field of combat, so as to transform sectional demands into district or even national ones. The railwaymen were prominent in this respect, but so were the semi-skilled engineering workers of the English midlands who extended solidarity to women and the unskilled so that '... the weakest sections gained large advances with the support – and perhaps even, in the short run, at the expense of – their stronger comrades.'[66]

Such solidarity was, in part, a response to new initiatives and activities that harnessed workers' social norms and communities in service of direct action. In 1911 Connolly described the funding of the 1907 Belfast dockers' strike: 'We had not a penny in our funds when we struck. We paid 4s. strike pay on the tenth day of our strike, and 4s. 6d. on the second week. Of this sum more than half came from Dublin, the remainder came from street collections among the loyal-hearted workers of Belfast'[67] – the street collection in particular being a feature of IWW strike organisation in America, with which Connolly was familiar.

The IWW was famous for its use of song in union agitation, but its use was widespread in Ireland too.[68] In the 1910 Pennsylvania miners' strike, wives of striking miners were arrested for harassing strike breakers and the mine company's security personnel. Mother Jones ('The Miners' Angel' and IWW activist of Irish origin)[69]

> encouraged the women to bring their children to the sentencing. With no one to care for the children, the judge was forced to jail the women and their children. Mother Jones then instructed the women to sing all night long saying they were

singing to the babies. After residents living near the jail complained, the women and children were released.[70]

In the Belfast linen strike of 1911 Connolly used similar tactics to unify the workers and to humiliate the employers. The employers had introduced a speed up, and draconian rules of labour discipline, such that laughing, singing or even adjusting hair in working time would lead to dismissal. Once more, the dispute was organised with street and indoor meetings, street collections and the parade of the United Labour Band. This was done despite the protests of the Textile Operatives Society of Ireland, and, incidentally, of the clergy. Connolly would not let old forms of union structure stand in the way of new forms of worker organisation.

The strike was lost, and the women had to return without a wage increase. Yet Connolly urged the women to resist the disciplinary rules:

> If a girl is checked for singing, let the whole room start singing at once, if you are checked for laughing, let the whole room laugh at once, and if anyone is dismissed, all put on your shawls and come out in a body.[71]

Anderson notes that this had some success: '... one exasperated manager who sent a girl home for singing ... had to send for her again, work was only resumed once she returned and she was welcomed with a song.'[72]

Many accounts of the conduct of disputes in this period show workers adopting innovative tactics to generate solidarity. A letter from local business people to the *Oxfordshire Weekly News* complained, in the case of the Bliss Tweed Mill strike, of 'processions parading the streets singing battle songs of various descriptions ... largely comprised of the female element ... raising their voices to the highest possible pitch.'

Clashes between strikers, police and strike breakers occurred regularly, and several strike leaders were charged, including Thomas Winnet, known as 'Chippy Larkin' to his friends in comparison with James Larkin. Annie Cooper, a Bliss Tweed Mill worker for over 20 years, was jailed for 14 days after refusing to pay a fine for assault on a strike breaker. On her release she was met by a crowd of over 1,000, paraded with her family through the town accompanied by a brass band, and the Workers' Union presented her with a silver tea pot.[73]

These forms of solidarity were controversial for many union leaders, as was the fact that so many disputes were unofficial in origin. While a Larkin or a Mann could work with such explosions many union leaders could not. The new methods adopted by workers were seen as 'a calculated repudiation of the contemporary labour leadership' both political and within the unions.[74] The practice of solidarity tended always to overflow the bounds established by union leaders in respect of agreements and the use of conciliation, and everywhere presented a challenge to established procedures, a challenge exacerbated by the unofficial strikes in industries with existing conciliation methods. It was, perhaps, because of this that 'old unionists' were so prominent in the development of militancy tinged with conscious socialist and syndicalist ideas. On occasion the established leaders managed to put together a package that satisfied the immediate demands of strikers, but in three trade-wide cases settlements were engineered against the direct opposition of members, in weaving, mining and building trades. Such disputes between the authority of the central officials and the demands of militants in the localities meant that 'the *entire* period of 1910-14 saw the Amalgamated Society of Engineers in the throes of a bitter internal struggle.'[75] For many militants therefore, whether conscious syndicalists or not, these years were to entrench a distrust of trade union officials that was to colour the development of workplace unionism into the war years and beyond. According to Murphy 'To be "agin" the officials was as much a part of the nature of the syndicalist-minded workers of that time as to be "agin the Government" was a part of the nature of an Irishman.'[76] It was also to colour relations between the ITGWU and the British TUC and unions during the course of the Lockout itself.

British labour – Irish labour: solidarity and the TUC

'We asked', wrote Connolly, 'for the isolation of the capitalists of Dublin, and for answer the leaders of the British labour movement proceeded calmly to isolate the working class of Dublin ... And so we Irish workers must go down into Hell ... [and] eat the dust of defeat and betrayal'.[77]

Connolly's bitter and uncompromising analysis of the end game of the Lockout, and of the role of the British TUC, was probably as significant for the development of the union movement in Ireland as the Lockout itself, and the issue of solidarity – of solidarity of action rather than passive support – was one of the fault lines that divided the movement in the two countries. It was of course the practice of the boycott and sympathetic strike that so angered the Dublin employers. The young ITGWU used such tactics widely. Writing in the English *Daily Herald* in December 1913 Connolly not only defended the use of the sympathy strike, but recounted the victories of other unions, including skilled workers' unions, arising from sympathy action by the ITGWU.[78] Dublin workers' refusal to handle goods carried by non-unionists was a key weapon in bringing union organisation and bargaining to the agricultural labourers of the city's hinterland.[79] The union also used them internationally, and in support of British unions operating in Ireland. At the onset of the 1911 transport strike the ITGWU was mainly concerned with the prevention of strike breaking, although the strike itself spread rapidly to Dublin and Belfast. When, in the course of the Liverpool strike the Amalgamated Society of Railway Servants (ASRS) called a general strike in England and Ireland it appointed the ITGWU its agent in Ireland and the ITGWU paid the railwaymen's strike pay and refused to handle 'black' goods, leading to a retaliatory Lockout by the Dublin timber merchants. When, however, the timber merchants provoked another rail strike the English executive of the ASRS declined to call a general strike, leaving the Irish railwaymen to their fate.[80]

TRADES UNION CONGRESS DELEGATES.

Three of the delegates from the Trades Union Congress, at present in Dublin investigating the labour troubles. Left to right:—Mr. H. Gosling, Mr. John Hill, Mr. J. A. Sedoon.
(Photo by Lafayette.

3. TUC delegates in Dublin.
Freeman's Journal, 6 Sept. 1913.
DCLA

And yet, betrayal is not the whole story, as Connolly made clear in his assertion that '... in its attitude towards Dublin the working class movement of Great Britain reached its highest point of moral grandeur.'[81] The dramatic expression of support for Dublin can be seen in the 'Fiery Cross' campaign waged by Larkin on his release from prison in

November 1913. Prior to his release – and following on from Dublin's 'Bloody Sunday' – there were huge meetings around England, and the Dublin issue lost the government two by-elections.[82] Larkin's first appearance at the Free Trade Hall in Manchester not only filled the hall but upwards of 20,000 thronged the streets outside. Meetings followed in Birmingham, Cardiff, Edinburgh, Glasgow, Leicester, Hull, Liverpool and London. The London meeting was addressed by, Big Bill, Haywood – fresh from France with a cheque for 1,000 francs from French trade unionists.[83]

If public meetings had decided the course of events, the Lockout would have been a triumph for the ITGWU. Concrete support also came from the British TUC and affiliated trade unions in the form of money and food ships. Greaves has commented bitingly that 'the Dublin workers looked for solidarity, but they got charity.'[84] If so, it was 'charity' on a substantial scale, and the response of British workers was notable. Harry Gosling (original chair of the NTWF, member of the British TUC's parliamentary committee and TUC representative in Dublin) gave a dramatic account of the funding and loading of the first food ship, which brings to life the drama stirred by the Lockout within the British movement. Having pledged £5,000 credit on behalf of the TUC Gosling and his colleagues found that the ship they wanted was strike-bound in Salford docks. Unwilling, at first, to unload and re-load the ship, the strike committee relented and there was fierce competition among the dockers to do the work. Ironically, the cargo to be offloaded included casks of Guinness. In the course of the Lockout over £150,000 was raised by the TUC and affiliated unions, and at rallies in support of Dublin workers.[85] The support was in part a reflection of conditions within the English unions. The Sheet Metal Workers' Union had been busy expanding the role of its shop stewards and aggressively pursuing union growth and the closed shop. After 'Bloody Sunday' the Derby Branch proposed that the TUC send food ships 'every day', and the union made a grant and imposed a two shilling levy on members to support the ITGWU.[86]

But still, Greaves' words stand, as the leaders of the ITGWU themselves made plain. Larkin's tour of Britain brought in money, but his urgent message was for sympathetic industrial action. Given his reception, what stopped solidarity action? Williams' account, published in the 1950s, claimed that 'British railway and transport workers, hardly recovered from their own recent struggles, were in no position to undertake any such commitment.'[87] In hindsight it could be that the tide of militant action had turned, but Williams' argument has little force as it stands, not least because he fails to specify whether the 'war weariness' was that of the workers themselves, or of their leaders. Greaves' account is more credible, if overstated:

> The British wanted to settle, the Irish to win. What was required from England
> was action, not sympathy. But if there were to be industrial action in England

the TUC officials would have to give up their role of mediators and accept that of combatants. The arch opponent of such action was the railwaymen's leader, J. H. Thomas.[88]

Thomas' opposition would not have surprised Irish workers given the ASRS abandonment of its Irish membership in 1911. He was, however, not alone. Sexton, the general secretary of the National Union of Dock Labourers, and the man that sacked Larkin as an official of that union for his activities in Belfast and thus impelled Larkin to form the ITGWU, had been hostile to the Dublin strike from the start. The seamen's leader Havelock Wilson publicly attacked Larkin and 'Larkinism', much to Connolly's disgust, since, as Connolly argued, it had been the ITGWU intervention that rescued Wilson's union in the 1911 strike.[89]

Thomas' rejection of sympathy action was long-standing; he had argued with his own members that the doctrine would mean railwaymen being on permanent strike. Rhetorical flourishes aside, Thomas had larger issues on his mind, principal among them the necessity of gaining recognition from the railway companies, and this meant separating his union from any taint of 'syndicalism', understanding this to be a catch-all for the labour militancy of the 'Great Unrest', and

> ... in March 1914 Thomas got his first offer of formal institutional recognition. Larkin's revolutionary unionism thus provided the [company] directors with an incentive to treat with the more cautious reformists on their doorsteps.[90]

Not all of Thomas' members agreed with him. Three workers at Victoria Street Liverpool were sent home for following Larkin's appeal, and the whole workforce walked out. The strike spread to the docks, and to Birmingham, Derby and Gloucester.[91] In the London docks Harry Orbell, a leading official, reported that the union had immense difficulty in preventing sympathetic action, and said 'Should it come to a stoppage I think it will be of such magnitude as has never been equalled in any previous dispute.'[92]

For many if not most of the British leaders the Lockout stirred sympathy, but also caution, as the tumultuous events in Britain from 1910 onwards had also done. Tillett, still capable of the firebrand speech, had long advocated conciliation and compulsory arbitration instead of strikes as the route to permanent trade union recognition.[93] Governments – when they were not busy using 'a little persuasion with the bayonet'[94] – were coming to the view that intervention in disputes was a way of reducing disorder, and, crucially, of supporting and insulating union leaders in controlling the undisciplined outbreaks of their members. In many of the settlements of this period, including those largely rejected by the striking workers themselves, George Askwith of the Board of

Trade was foremost in arranging settlements. Such was his success that Tillett called him 'the most dangerous man in the country' insofar as his actions might persuade workers that they had a real stake in the capitalist system.[95]

How to explain the viewpoint of the leaders of the British TUC, beyond personal antipathy and rivalries? In Italy, in 1919, Gramsci sought an explanation for a similar problem as workplace committees struggled with a reluctant union leadership in a near-revolutionary situation. The unions, Gramsci argued, had, through many years of struggle, imposed a form of 'industrial legality' on employers, curbing the worst excesses of exploitation and arbitrary use of power. They had done this not only by struggle, but by making the unions dependable enforcers of collective agreements amongst workers as well as employers. Industrial legality stood, therefore, by discipline. Gramsci argued that 'industrial legality' was a tremendous gain for workers as a whole, but that trade union leaders came to regard it as more important than the sometimes transient actions of workers. They came, in other words, to defend 'industrial legality' from the perspective of the employers, against the very workers it had been created to protect.[96]

These contradictions frame the meeting of the extraordinary conference of the TUC on 9 December 1913. The TUC parliamentary committee had been attempting to broker a deal, and, probably at the prompting of Askwith, suggested to the Irish leaders a possible negotiation with a section of the Dublin employers. Larkin would not agree: before any meetings could be contemplated the ITGWU would have to know clearly the policy of the TUC, and he urged a conference of all the unions to consider the possibility of sympathetic action.[97] The Irish must have been encouraged in this approach by open support for co-ordinated sympathetic action even by those currently urging restraint, especially from Robert Williams of the National Transport Workers Federation.[98]

The TUC agreed, setting the date for the special conference – the first of its kind ever called – for 9 December. Delegates would only be accepted, however, from affiliated unions and Labour members of parliament. This decision excluded many Irish unions (and the British ASE which had not paid its dues), as well as representatives of the National Transport Workers Federation, which was not, of course, a trade union in its own right, allowing the TUC leadership a conference 'largely made up of the obedient official element of their own stamp.'[99] Not all historians agree. Yeates rejects the idea that the nature of the conference delegates enabled the TUC leadership to evade engagement with rank and file support for the Lockout, arguing that the composition of the conference was not irregular, and that it largely consisted of the same people who had been so supportive of Dublin at the TUC in September.[100]

In the event the special conference was calamitous for the Irish movement. Preceded by a final attempt by the TUC to broker a settlement, and an attempt which the ITGWU saw as an attempt to 'jockey' the union into a peace on the employers terms, the conference was dominated by recriminations and personal attacks. The morning session was taken up with debate on a motion moved by Tillett deploring 'attacks on British trade union officials'. In the afternoon debate returned to the immediate situation and the appeal from the Irish for an effective blockade of Dublin and an end to the free movement of strike breakers. In a confused and hurried session proposals for continued financial support vied with those for a further conciliation conference. A crucial amendment from Jack Jones of the Gas Workers' Union, setting a date for a complete boycott of Dublin traffic and a levy on all union members to support the Dublin strikers was lost by more than ten to one. 'The original motion, which implied that the men would be willing to ask for terms, was overwhelmingly carried.'[101] *En route* back to Dublin Connolly found a report in a morning newspaper that Thomas' union had already ordered strikers on Dublin's North Wall Quay back to work, on pain of losing their strike pay.[102]

Conclusions

The Dublin Lockout – a foundational episode in the history of the Irish labour movement – had an international context derived from a series of struggles between workers and employers across many countries as the development of capitalism on an international scale drew new social forces into organisation, and re-energised older trade union formations. The process was not contained within the first decade and a half of the 20th century, nor did it cease when world war threw the international order into a bloodbath – nothing in human history is so neatly accomplished. But it was a pivotal period for many working class organisations such that in the following decades only Fascism could threaten to dissolve wholly the gains of organisation, recognition by employers, collective bargaining and a political space for the working class within the capitalist polity. The significance for Irish labour of the Lockout was that, despite immediate defeat, the ITGWU and the Irish unions generally shared in this process. By 1915, despite the radical contraction of union membership, Connolly could announce some seven new agreements giving ITGWU members pay rises as the result of negotiations.[103]

Such an outcome was not inevitable, however, but depended on solidarity, militancy, and organisational capacity.

In 1871 the liberal economist J. S. Mill wrote:

> If it were possible for the working classes, by combining among themselves, to raise or keep up the general rate of wages, it needs hardly be said that this would be a thing not to be punished, but to be welcomed and rejoiced at. Unfortunately the effect is quite beyond attainment by such means. The multitudes who compose

the working class are too numerous and too widely scattered to combine at all, much more to combine effectually.[104]

In less than 20 years an international movement would be unleashed that would prove Mill wrong. In three great surges – whether by Hobsbawm's, Cronin's or O'Connor's measure – working men and women invented and used the tools that would, if not abolish, then radically curtail the divisions of skill, status, religion, nationality and sex that always have, and still do limit working class solidarity.

The Dublin Lockout was the attempt, by a combination of Irish employers, to confront that process, and to throw into reverse all relations between workers and employers. At huge human cost 'Murphyism' failed in Dublin, just as, in the end, it failed in Oxfordshire too. Increasingly, employers' organisations predicated on the destruction of the workers' capacity to organise adapted both their theory and practice to accommodation with the unions and the development of the institutions of conflict management that came to characterise the industrial relations systems of both countries. Similar paths were trodden by employers elsewhere. In Sweden, a Lockout of engineering workers in 1905 led to the 'December compromise' in which the Swedish employers' organisation (SAF) acknowledged the unions' right to organise and bargain.[105] In most of Europe these developments came rather later – after the First World War – with increasing institutionalisation of relations between unions and employers and state interventions to strengthen conciliation and arbitration mechanisms.

For the trade unions in particular the struggles of the 'Great Unrest' settled the ground for permanent union organisation among the most marginalised sections in the labour market. In Britain the First World War, and in Ireland the 1916 Rising and independence, eventually consolidated the development of general unionism. This consolidation did not, however, reflect the radical ambitions of many of the leading activists of the period. In Britain the syndicalist agitation made no lasting impact on either trade union structure or action, and in Ireland the aspirational slogan of 'One Big Union' never prevailed. But the drive to amalgamation and general unionism as a counter to sectional interests continued in the formation of the 'Triple Alliance' of the miners, railwaymen and dockers in Britain and the eventual creation of the Services, Industrial, Professional and Technical Union (SIPTU) as the successor union to the divided ITGWU and the Workers' Union of Ireland.

In both America and Britain these later developments were deeply influenced by militants who following from the 'Great Unrest' formed the cadres of militant workplace organisation and new political currents after the Soviet revolution. In France the syndicalist CGT, increasingly reformist and discredited by conformity to state policy in the First World War, became the centre of mass Communist influence in the Popular Front of the 1930s.

In the end, as Hobsbawm argued regarding the 'New Unionism' of the 1890s, 'Longer term, industrially varied economic and technological developments determined the structure [of trade unions]. The dockers and their flamboyant leaders provided the conjuncture for the big leap forward.'[106] The same may be said of the early years of the 20th century of the activists and militants of 'The Great Unrest'.

Union structure is not, however, the whole of the story. Connolly, for all his championship of industrial unions, saw in the federation and amalgamation movements of the day a subordination of 'fighting spirit' to centralised authority in unions that ran dead against his principles of solidarity, arguing that 'Into the new bottles of industrial organisation is being poured the old, cold wine of Craft Unionism.'[107] The period following the First World War saw both the decline of syndicalism as a distinctive theory of social transformation and what Hyman has called the 'consolidation of integrative trade unionism' which matched the evolution of industrial relations systems more generally.[108] From the 1920 Works Council *(Betriebsräte)* Act in Germany which 'domesticated' the radical Workers' Council movement of the war years, to the 1938 Swedish *Saltsjöbaden* agreement promoting industrial peace, the price of recognition seemed to be the abandonment of an independent class approach to work, politics and society.[109] The divisions between the radical and the reformist in labour politics and trade unionism developed more strongly in the wake of the Russian revolution and the slump of the inter-war years.

This history did not run smoothly, and individual lives, reputations and competing organisational forms and programmes litter its path. In America, the combination of employer hostility, political reaction and organisational instability destroyed the IWW. But the organising campaigns of the Conference of Industrial Organisations (CIO) in 1930s America, among whom were veteran organisers of the 'labor wars' of the period, cemented mass trade unionism in large manufacturing, and did it on an industrial basis. Despite periodic 'red scares', and an employing class seemingly always ready to resort to violence, America came to some settlement with union organisation in the National Labour Relations Act ('Wagner Act') of 1935.

That settlement was a long time coming, but its terms reflect the concerns and aspirations – in part at least – of the workers in the Lockout and elsewhere, and, despite all the national differences, is worth considering in some detail.

The US Commission on Industrial Relations set up in 1912 concluded that:

> We hold that efforts to stay the organization of labor or to restrict the right of employees to organize should not be tolerated, but that the opposite policy should prevail, and the organization of the trade unions and of the employers' organizations should be promoted ... This country is no longer a field for slavery, and where men and women are compelled, in order that they may live, to work under conditions in determining which they have no voice, they are not far removed from a condition existing under feudalism or slavery.[110]

In just such tones Connolly defended the ITGWU from its detractors on the eve of the Lockout. He wrote:

> ... out of this class of slaves the labourers of Dublin, the Irish Transport and General Workers' Union has created an army of intelligent self-reliant men, abhorring the old arts of the toady ... and trusting alone to the disciplined use of their own power ... to assert and maintain their rights as men.[111]

The 1935 Wagner Act established as state policy the encouragement of the:

> ... practice and procedure of collective bargaining ... by protecting the exercise by workers of full freedom of association, self-organization, and designation of representatives of their own choosing, for the purpose of negotiating the terms and conditions of their employment or other mutual aid or protection.[112]

These were the terms of settlement – beyond all other considerations – that the workers of Dublin – and of the Bliss Tweed Mills – sought in their battles in 1913.

What then, is the legacy of this period, and why should it be commemorated? The easy, optimistic answer, is to follow the logic of those historians cited above who see the establishment of peaceful, rule-governed systems of industrial relations as the necessary and welcome outcome of the battles of an 'immature' industrial society. We should celebrate, it seems, having 'got over' the fevers of those years, and congratulate ourselves on the eminently sensible arrangements that now ensure (mostly) industrial harmony: a sort of industrial relations version of the Whig theory of history. But it is much harder to make such a case in light of developments – nationally and internationally – since 2008.

The optimistic answer is less easy now, not just because of recession and unemployment, but because these phenomena increasingly disrupt the idea that there is a single 'we' to commemorate 1913. Here again, for all the national specifics, Ireland occupies its own space in an international development – not this time of workers' advance, but of a reassertion of the power, logic, and ethics of free market capitalism, and of the powers of its owners and ideologues.

This reassertion of capitalist domination is not new – it never really went out of fashion. In 1984 Hayek, a principal source of neo-liberal ideas in the UK, argued that The two alternatives to the market – collectivism and syndicalism – destroy not only 'wealth but freedom, whereas the market virtually eliminates coercion of men by other men.'[113]

In Ireland – throughout the European Union for that matter – trade union recognition is in decline, and the weakest in the labour market are losing not only the protections of collective bargaining, but the subsidiary protections of institutions such as Joint Labour Committees or their equivalents. Casualisation, privatisation, sub-contracting, and the commodification of social goods such as education and health, austerity and 'labour market reform' are undermining '… varieties of institutional structures which ensure that the employer-employee relationship is not primarily determined by market forces' but also by forms of social regulation including trade union activity.[114] What should be remembered from 1913 is that workers have their own interests, separate and opposed to those of the employers, that employers will seek to attack or subvert those interests, and that the capacity of workers to determine events otherwise rests on their own organisational capacity and consciousness.

Notes

1   Mike Richardson, 'Murphyism in Oxfordshire – The Bliss Tweed Mill strike 1913-1914: causes, conduct and consequences' in *Historical Studies in Industrial Relations*, 25/26 (Spring/Autumn, 2008), pp 79-102.

2   For a discussion of the role played by the ITGWU in the strikes of 1911, and of Irish internationalism and relations with the British movement, see Francis Devine, 'The Irish Transport and General Workers' Union and labour unrest in Ireland, 1911', in *Historical Studies in Industrial Relations,* 33 (2012), pp 169-88.

3   Joe White, '1910-1914 reconsidered' in James E. Cronin and Jonathan Schneer (eds), *Social conflict and the political order in modern Britain* (London, 1982), pp 96-112.

4   White, '1910-1914 reconsidered', p. 79.

5   Eric J. Hobsbawm, 'The "New Unionism" reconsidered', in Wolfgang J. Mommsen and Hans-Gerhard Husung (eds), *The development of trade unionism in Great Britain and Germany 1880-1914* (London, 1985), p. 16.

6   Klaus Schönhoven, 'Localism – craft union – industrial union: organizational patterns in German trade unionism' in Mommsen and Husung (eds), *The development of trade unionism in Great Britain and Germany,* p. 230.

7   In the case of the Dublin Lockout see Pádraig Yeates, *Lockout: Dublin 1913* (Dublin, 2001), pp 447-8 and elsewhere. For an example of military attacks on strikers in England see Ken Coates and Tony Topham, *The making of the labour movement: the formation of the Transport and General Workers'*

Union 1870-1922 (London, 1994), pp 351-2. Such violence was often a long term policy of employers elsewhere. Sergio Seguí, leader of the Barcelona Comité Obrero in the 1917 insurrection was shot dead in 1923 by gunmen from the employers' organisation Syndicato Libre. See Victor Serge, *Memoirs of a revolutionary* (New York, 2012), p. 68.

8   Coates and Topham, *The making of the labour movement*, p. 336.

9   Ibid., pp 536-40.

10   Dick Geary, *European labour protest 1848-1939* (Bristol, 1984), p. 104.

11   Friedhelm Boll, 'International strike waves: a critical assessment' in Mommsen and Husung (eds) *The development of trade unionism in Great Britain and Germany,* p. 80.

12   Kenneth Brown, 'The strikes of 1911-13: their international significance' in Donal Nevin (ed.), *James Larkin: the lion of the fold* (Dublin, 2006), p. 57.

13   Graham Adams, *Age of industrial violence 1910-15* (Columbia, 1966), p. 228.

14   The International Association of Machinists and Aerospace Workers, Local 24 (http://www.andrewsiam. org/labor_history.html) (18 July 2012).

15   Walter Galenson and Robert S. Smith, 'The United States' in John T. Dunlop and Walter Galenson (eds), *Labor in the 20th Century* (New York, 1978), p. 30.

16   George S. Kealey, '1919: The Canadian labour revolt', in *Labour/Le Travail*, 13 (Spring 1984), pp 11-44.

17   Brown, 'The strikes of 1911-13', p. 56.

18   Francis Williams, *Magnificent journey: the rise of the trade unions* (London, 1954), p. 270.

19   Coates and Topham, *The making of the labour movement*, p. 340.

20   That there was a 'Great Unrest' at all has been questioned. For a critical review of historians' treatment of the period see, for example, Deian Hopkin, 'The Great Unrest in Wales 1910-1913: questions of evidence' in Deian R. Hopkin and Gregory S. Kealey (eds), *Class, community and the labour movement: Wales and Canada, 1850-1930* (Canada, 1998).

21   Cronin, *Industrial conflict in modern Britain*, p. 93; Eric J. Hobsbawm, *Labouring men* (London, 1964), p. 187.

22   Emmet O'Connor, 'What caused the 1913 Lockout? Industrial relations in Ireland 1907-13', in *Historical Studies in Industrial Relations,* 19 (Spring 2005), p. 119.

23   E. O'Connor, '*Syndicalism, industrial Unionism, and nationalism in Ireland*', in Steven Hirsch and Lucien Van der Walt (eds), *Anarchism and Syndicalism in the colonial and postcolonial world, 1870-1940* (Leiden, 2011), p. 196.

24   Williams, *Magnificent journey*, p. 245.

25   White, '1910-1914 reconsidered', p. 80.

26   Cronin, *Industrial conflict in modern Britain*, p. 99.

27   Hobsbawm, 'The "New Unionism" reconsidered', p. 20.

28   Geary, *European labour protest*, pp 105-6.

29   Ibid.

30   O'Connor, 'What caused the 1913 Lockout?', pp 107-9.

31   Coates and Topham, *The making of the labour movement*, p. 375.

32   Williams, *Magnificent journey*, p. 250.

33   For a discussion of the Liverpool events and their longer term impact on union membership and industrial relations see Eric Taplin, 'The Liverpool general transport strike, 1911' in *Historical Studies in Industrial Relations*, 33 (2012), pp 25-38.

34   O'Connor, 'What caused the 1913 Lockout?', p. 106.

35   Coates and Topham, *The making of the labour movement*, p. 345. See also an account of pay, working conditions and labour control in attempts to unionise the New York Transit System in Emily A. Nelms, 'Moving forces: strikes and unionization within the transit systems of Dublin and New York City, 1895-1926', *HY674: Comparative Labor History* University of Alabama at Birmingham (1 May 2008).

36   Richardson, 'Murphyism in Oxfordshire', p. 80.

37   Dick Geary, 'Germany' in Dick Geary (ed.), *Labour and socialist movements in Europe before 1914* (Oxford 1989), pp 109-12.

38   Coates and Topham, *The making of the labour movement*, pp 351-2.

39   Neil Prior, 'Llanelli's 'forgotten' riot - 100 years ago' BBC News, Wales (http://www.bbc.co.uk/news/uk-wales-14529442) (31 Aug. 2012).

40   Ibid.

41   Coates and Topham, *The making of the labour movement*, p. 356.

42   Roger Magraw, 'Socialism, syndicalism and French labour before 1914', in Geary (ed.), *Labour and socialist movements in Europe*, p. 61.

43   David Howell, 'Taking syndicalism seriously', *University of the Witwatersrand History Workshop* (13-15 July, 1994).

44   Adams, *Age of industrial violence*, p. 194.

45   Donal Nevin, *James Connolly: a full life* (Dublin, 2005), p. 303.

46   Deian, 'The Great Unrest in Wales', p. 251.

47   Cronin, *Industrial conflict in modern Britain*, p. 100.

48   Brown, 'The strikes of 1911-13', p. 58.

49   Ibid., pp 61-3.

50   Paul Smith, 'Book Reviews: Pádraig Yeates, *Lockout: Dublin 1913*' in *Historical Studies in Industrial Relations,* 17 (Spring 2004), pp 147-50.

51   White, '1910-1914 reconsidered', pp 73-5.

52   Ibid., p. 80. See also White, '1910-1914 reconsidered', p. 80. See also Richard Hyman, 'Mass organization and militancy in Britain: contrasts and continuities', in Mommsen and Husung (eds), *The development of trade unionism in Great Britain and Germany*, pp 258-62.

53   Deian points out that, even among the militants authors of *'The Miners' next step'*, there were those who rejected the title of syndicalist. Deian, 'The Great Unrest in Wales', p. 251.

54   Alan Fox, *History and heritage: the social origins of the British industrial relations system* (London, 1985), p. 172.

55   Ibid.

56   James Connolly, 'Industrialism and the trade unions' in Desmond Ryan (ed.), *The workers' republic: a selection from the writings of James Connolly* (Dublin, 1951), p. 84.

57   Desmond Greaves, *The life and times of James Connolly* (London, 1961), p. 184.

58   James Connolly, 'Changes' in Ryan (ed.), *The workers' republic,* p. 57.

59   Bob Holton, *British syndicalism 1910-14: myths and realities* (London, 1976), pp 118-19.

60   Coates and Topham, *The making of the labour movement*, pp 363, 433.

61   Magraw, 'Socialism, syndicalism and French labour', p. 61.

62   Devine, 'The Irish Transport & General Workers' Union and labour unrest in Ireland, 1911'.

63   Coates and Topham, *The making of the labour movement*, p. 326.

64   James Connolly, 'Belfast dockers: their miseries and their triumphs' *The Irish Worker*, 26 Aug. 1911.

65   Cronin, *Industrial conflict in modern Britain*, p. 100.

66   Richard Hyman, *The Workers' Union* (Oxford, 1971), p. 60.

67   Connolly, 'Belfast dockers'.

68   See, for example, 'Who Fears to Wear the Red Hand Badge?' reproduced in Devine, 'The Irish Transport and General Workers' Union and labour unrest in Ireland, 1911'.

69   A plaque has been unveiled to Mary Harris – 'Mother Jones' in Cork, (http://motherjones175.wordpress.com/) (2012)

70   http://www.midwestlaborers.org/WLhistory.htm (23 July 2012)

71   W. Anderson, *James Connolly and the Irish left* (Dublin, 1994), p. 18.

72   Ibid.

73   Richardson, 'Murphyism in Oxfordshire', pp 94-7.

74   Cronin, *Industrial conflict in modern Britain*, p. 100.

75   White, '1910-1914 reconsidered', pp 84-5.

76   Ralph Darlington, 'British syndicalism and trade-union officialdom' in *Historical Studies in Industrial Relations*, 25/26 (Spring/Autumn, 2008), p. 103.

77   James Connolly, 'The isolation of Dublin' in *James Connolly: collected works, volume two* (Dublin, 1987), pp 322-4.

78   James Connolly, 'A titanic struggle' in Nevin, *Larkin: lion of the fold*, pp 236-7.

79   C. Desmond Greaves, *The Irish Transport and General Workers' Union: the formative years* (Dublin, 1982), p. 90. For a full account see also Eugene Coyle, 'Larkinism and the 1913 County Dublin farm labourers' dispute', *Dublin Historical Record*, lviii, no. 2 (Autumn 2005), pp 176-90.

80   Greaves, *ITGWU*, pp 60-5.

81   Connolly, 'The isolation of Dublin', p. 320.

82   Greaves, *ITGWU*, p. 109.

83   Bill Haywood, 'An American in Dublin' in *1913 Jim Larkin and the Dublin Lockout* (Dublin, 1964), p. 91.

84   Greaves, *ITGWU*, p. 104.

85   Coates and Topham, *The making of the labour movement*, pp 474-5.

86   Ted Brake, *Men of good character: a history of the National Union of Sheet Metal Workers, Coppersmiths and Domestic Heating Engineers* (London, 1985), p. 219.

87   Williams, *Magnificent journey*, p. 268.

88   Greaves, *ITGWU*, p. 103.

89   James Connolly, 'A titanic struggle' reproduced in Nevin, *Larkin: lion of the fold*, p. 235.

90   Coates and Topham, *The making of the labour movement*, p. 485.

91   Greaves, *ITGWU,* p. 103.

92   Holton, *British syndicalism,* p. 193.

93   Coates and Topham, *The making of the labour movement*, p. 293.

94   Williams, *Magnificent journey*, p. 249.

95   Emmet O'Connor, *James Larkin* (Cork, 2002), p. 47.

96   Antonio Gramsci, 'Unions and Councils' in *Selections from political writings, 1910-1920* (London, 1977), pp 261-8

97   Yeates, *Lockout*, p. 419.

98   Coates and Topham, *The making of the labour movement*, p. 487.

99   W. P. Ryan, 'The struggle of 1913: an overview' in Nevin, *Larkin: lion of the fold*, p. 176.

100   Yeates, *Lockout*, p. 487.

101   Coates and Topham, *The making of the labour movement*, p. 489.

102   Yeates, *Lockout*, p. 473.

103   James Connolly, 'The Dublin Lockout and its sequel', *Collected works*, V. 11, pp 355-6.

104   John Stuart Mill, *Principles of political economy* (London, 1871), pp 563-4

105   Olle Hammarström, Tony Huzzard abd Tommy Nilsson, 'Employment relations in Sweden' in Greg J. Bamber, Russell D. Lansbury and Nick Wailes (eds), *International and comparative employment relations: globalisation and the developed market economies* (4th ed., London, 2004), p. 255.

106   Hobsbawm, 'The "New Unionism" reconsidered', p. 49.

107   James Connolly, 'Old Wine in New Bottles' in P. Ellis (ed.), *James Connolly: Selected Writings*, (Harmondsworth, 1973), pp 175-8.

108   Hyman, *Understanding European trade unionism: between market, class and society* (London, 2001), p. 42.

109   Hyman, *Understanding European trade unionism*, p. 43. Also Hammarström (et. al.), 'Employment relations in Sweden', p. 256.

110   United States Commission on Industrial Relations, *Final report and testimony* (Washington D.C., U.S. Government Printing Office, 1916), p. 169.

111   James Connolly, 'The Dublin lockout: on the eve', *Collected works,* V. 11, p. 290.

112   The full text of the act is accessible from the National Labor Relations Board web site (https://www.nlrb.gov/national-labor-relations-act)

113   F. Hayek, *1980s unemployment and the unions* (London, 1984), pp 357-64.

114   Richard Hyman, 'The europeanisation – or the erosion – of industrial relations?' in *Industrial Relations Journal* 32:3 (Oxford 2001), p. 281.

4. Harry Gosling (on the right) and J. A. Seddon (with pipe), representing the
British Trades Union Congress, watching the discharge of a food ship in Dublin.
SIPTU Archive

3.

The 1913 housing inquiry: Sir Charles Cameron, public health and housing in Dublin

....

Lydia Carroll

Generations of vicissitudes[1]

When William Martin Murphy, owner of the Dublin United Tramway Company (DUTC), helpfully pointed out to his workers before the Lockout of 1913 began that his shareholders would continue to eat three meals a day, unlike workers who went on strike,[2] he was hitting them right where they were most vulnerable – with worries about where their next meal might come from. For the working classes of Dublin, this was no idle threat – most lived a hand-to-mouth existence, in overcrowded, disease-ridden tenements, where the little food that families could afford was cooked on the only means of heating and cooking, the open fire, in the one room that served all family needs. Walter Carpenter,[3] a leading figure in the Lockout, would later sum the situation up succinctly at the 1913 *Inquiry into the housing conditions of the working classes* when he said that 'every house should have a bathroom so that a man's shirt need not be taken out of the pot for his dinner to be put into it.'[4]

Throughout the 19th and early 20th centuries, Dublin was notorious for its unsanitary housing conditions. The situation had steadily worsened after the Act of Union in 1801, when there was a large exodus of the wealthier classes from the city, and the industries which had served their needs, such as poplin making and carriage making, were no longer required. Employment became largely casual labouring, and was seasonal and irregular, with very few sources of employment for women. The result was a large population on the very verges of pauperism, who were unable to afford anything but the most basic accommodation. For most of them, this accommodation consisted of one room, where whole families cooked, ate, slept, and died in ever increasing numbers in tenement rooms cannibalised into family spaces from former Georgian houses, originally designed to house one family in comfort. Water and sanitary facilities were primitive, usually one tap on the landing or in the yard, where one or two water closets or privies, shared by all families in the house, would also be situated. Many families, unable to afford even the smallest rent for a one-room dwelling, shared this room with lodgers.

The correlation between overcrowded, unsanitary dwellings and public health was increasingly brought to public attention in the course of the 19th century. Sir William Wilde, now better known as father of Oscar, was a renowned Dublin surgeon, with an interest in the use of statistics as a tool for social reform. The 1841 census, widely regarded as the first 'scientific' census, gave him an ideal opportunity; using the details contained in the 1841 and 1851 census, Wilde created a unique street classification, based on the 'wealth, character, more or less healthy position, and the occupations of their population'.[5] Wilde's correlation of street classification with the death rates of the inhabitants showed unequivocally that the mortality rates in poorer areas were significantly greater than those in wealthier areas. The situation at the time of the Lockout in 1913 was virtually unchanged since Wilde's research, and was corroborated by Thomas Willis, a Dublin apothecary, who made a survey of St Michan's parish in 1845 and proclaimed that:

> The stench and disgusting filth of these places are inconceivable ... in some rooms in these situations it is not an infrequent occurrence to see above a dozen human beings crowded into a space not fifteen feet square ... within this space they must eat and drink; men, women and children must strip, dress, sleep. In cases of illness the calls of nature must be relieved; and when death releases one of the inmates, the corpse must of necessity remain for days within the room ... I am speaking of an entire district, and state facts incontrovertible.[6]

Willis claimed that the inhabitants of the city had 'sunk into that state of abject misery for which there is no parallel in any country in Europe.'[7] A comparison of annual death rates in various cities in 1906 (Table 1) would show that this situation had been little changed,[8] although it should be borne in mind that Dublin's death rate had decreased from 37.5 in 1879, the year Charles Cameron became Superintendent Medical Officer of Health.[9]

Table 1. Table of death rates

Dublin	25.4	Stockholm	16.1
London	12.8	Berlin	16.5
Glasgow	19.0	Vienna	22.2
Brussels	14.9	Buda-Pest	23.4
Amsterdam	14.3	Prague	22.7
Copenhagen	16.0	Rome	20.1

This already appalling situation became even worse during and after the Great Famine, as desperate people made their way from the country to Dublin, exacerbating the problems of overcrowding. Native Dubliners now had to share the precarious employment opportunities with an incoming stream of immigrants, from a hinterland which was shedding labour throughout the 19th century, and also from the great European migrations. The minutes of the North Dublin Union reported that boats at the Dublin docks offloaded 'the sick and disabled sent from England and Scotland ... destitute persons broken down in constitution.'[10] After the May Laws were passed in Russia in 1882, there was an influx of Jewish immigrants.[11] By 1911, the census showed that almost a third of the residents of Dublin (29.67%) had not been born in the city,[12] and during the latter part of the 19th century, many native Dubliners, who had previously been classed as skilled tradesmen, found that they and their descendants had sunk to the lower socio-economic category of unskilled workers, with a consequent loss of income and status.

1. Sir Charles Cameron, Medical Officer of Health for Dublin, 1864-1921.
E. MacDowel Cosgrave, *Dublin and County Dublin in the twentieth century* (Dublin, 1907).
DCLA

Public health

The Medical Officer of Health for Dublin from 1864 to 1921, Sir Charles Cameron, was acutely aware of the effects of the slum problem on the health of the city, as is obvious from his regular reports to the Corporation, which revealed the same litany of diseases month after month, year after year, with the occasional upsurge caused by epidemics, such as influenza, measles or dysentery. It was increasingly obvious that the genesis of most of the diseases, and the majority of their victims, lay in the Dublin slums. Cameron's report in 1879 repeated exactly the same findings as Wilde and Willis a quarter of a century previously: 'a high death rate is the almost constant corollary of great density of population.'[13]

The crowded and unsanitary living conditions in the tenements, compounded by malnutrition and insufficient clothing, [which themselves] were aggravated by the high rate of unemployment. Diseases such as typhus, typhoid, smallpox, dysentery, tuberculosis, and the dreaded cholera, all had one thing in common – they found an easy and deadly foothold in the poverty-weakened bodies of the inhabitants of the Dublin slums.

Tuberculosis remained one of the deadliest killers, claiming twice as many victims as other contagious diseases; it was the most difficult disease to eradicate, retaining its hold long into the 20th century. Erroneously believed to be hereditary, it was one of the most easily spread by contagion and most quickly succumbed to by those who were malnourished and poorly clad and housed. In poorer areas, the infected person usually shared the same room, and often the same bed as others, which resulted in whole families being wiped out by the disease. Cameron campaigned for, and was successful in seeing established, an isolation hospital at the Pigeon House Road and a sanatorium outside the city at Crooksling.

Throughout most of the 19th century, Dublin had one of the highest death rates of any city in the British Isles and, while mortality in cities like London, Liverpool and Birmingham began to decline after the 1870s, all having a death rate under 20 per thousand in 1905, Dublin's mortality still stood at 22.3 per thousand.[14]

Employment and unemployment

Moreover, while the overcrowding in most British cities and in Belfast was caused by increased industrialisation, Dublin's industries, such as fine textiles and carriage making, declined during the course of the 19th century, and were not replaced by any labour-intensive industries. By the first quarter of the 20th century, most of the employment in Dublin was casual and seasonal, in brewing, biscuit making, in transport or on the docks – industries that employed workers during busy seasons, and let them go during slack seasons. What manufacturing industry did exist tended to be capital-intensive, rather than labour-intensive – for example, Guinness's brewery had a capital value of five million pounds, and employed 2,000 staff, compared with the York Street Spinning Company in Belfast, which had a capital value of £500,000, but employed 4,000 – 5,000.[15] Moreover, while large-scale industries, such as spinning and weaving, provided employment for women in other cities, the large industries in Dublin (apart from biscuit-making) provided mostly male employment – work for women in Dublin was mainly in dressmaking and domestic service. With a largely male workforce, and a high rate of male tuberculosis, many families could therefore drop very quickly from working class to pauper status by the death of a male breadwinner. As a result, a large proportion of Dublin citizens lived an insecure, hand-to-mouth existence, surviving 'by employing every mode which industry can prompt or human ingenuity devise in order to procure even the meanest supply of the common necessaries of life.'[16]

In 1904, Charles Cameron published at his own expense a small booklet entitled *How the poor live*.[17] We can only speculate as to why he published it at his own expense. Perhaps he wanted to publish it quickly – he was certainly the type of man who liked to take the initiative, and put a plan into action quickly as, for example, in June 1897, when he called a public meeting which resulted in the formation of the Association for the Housing of the Very Poor, and for which he circulated a detailed memorandum to those who were influential in Dublin.

His opening sentence in *How the poor live* announced unequivocally 'there are probably no cities in the United Kingdom in which so large a proportion of the population belong to the poorest classes as is the case in Dublin.'[18] He compared the housing statistics of Dublin with those of Belfast, Lancashire, Glasgow, Edinburgh and London, showing that Dublin had by far the highest proportion of dwellers in single rooms, and claiming: 'surely that is proof of the poverty of a large proportion of the population.'[19] Cameron described what he referred to as 'the banker of the poor' – the pawnbroker, showing an intimate knowledge of the reliance of the poor on this system:

> No inconsiderable number of the poor get out of their beds, or substitutes for them, without knowing when they are to get their breakfast, for the simple reason that they have neither money nor credit. They must starve if they have got nothing which would be taken in pawn … articles of very small value will be accepted by the pawnbroker, and some items of a slender wardrobe are exchanged for the price of one or more meals – so small a sum as sixpence may be obtained in this way.[20]

The booklet is a portrayal of a population of hardworking people on the verge of starvation, written by a man who witnessed the conditions first hand in his daily working life.

In his concluding section 'Betterment of the Poor' Cameron claimed that:

> it is not in the power of the Sanitary Authorities to remove all the evils from which the poor suffer … [but that] … They could, however, soften the hard conditions under which the poor, and still more the very poor, exist, [by providing] them with homes superior to those they now have, without increasing their rents … I have always maintained that it is only the poorest and most dependent classes of the community that municipalities should provide with cheap and healthy dwellings;[21]

In 1914 D. A. Chart stated that 24,000 men, more than a quarter of the adult male population, were engaged in unskilled labour, although Pádraig Yeates claims that more recent research, based on the 1911 census, 'suggests that there were 45,000 unskilled workers – a seventh of the entire population and a third of the labour force.'[22] Chart revealed that 'the average wage was about 18s. a week, and even so low a figure as 15s. or 16s. had been recorded - much of this irregular work.'

Workers earning this amount, it was pointed out, could not afford to pay more than 2s. 6d. a week for accommodation – an amount for which no landlord could provide decent accommodation (not that the landlords were concerned with much except their own profit). Chart described the situation whereby, if the breadwinner was unable to work, the wife, if she could, would go out to work as a charwoman. If she couldn't find work – and work for women was difficult to find in Dublin, then the family would be forced to try to get some assistance from a charity, or more likely, be forced to pawn their possessions – as Chart described it 'The clothes and furniture are pawned, the rent falls into arrears, and the financial equilibrium, always unstable, is completely disturbed. The housekeeper on 18/- a week is engaged in a never-ceasing hand-to-hand struggle … and this financial stress … turns the laughing girls of the poorer Dublin streets into the weary-eyed women of the tenement houses.'[23]

The Lockout

Chart was speaking on 6 March 1914, less than a month after the bitter and, from the workers' point of view, demoralising dispute known as the Dublin Lockout, one of the darkest periods in the many dark days of Dublin's history.

James Connolly, an ITGWU official, would express the situation somewhat more militantly at the beginning of the dispute. In *The Irish Worker* in August 1913, he wrote

> the Irish Transport and General Workers' Union found that before its advent the working class of Dublin had been taught by all the educational agencies of the country, by all the social influences of their masters, that this world was created for the special benefit of the various sections of the master class, that kings and lords and capitalists were of value; that even flunkeys, toadies, lickspittle and poodle dogs had an honoured place in the scheme of the universe, but that there was neither honour, credit, nor consideration to the man or woman who toils to maintain them all.

So, in 1913, Dublin city, with its high unemployment rate, where the poor and unskilled were desperate for any kind of work, might seem like an unlikely setting for industrial disputes. Employers held the upper hand – if a strike took place, they could take their pick of any number willing to take the strikers' place. And indeed, this was the case until the advent of the ITGWU, whose leader was James Larkin. Until this union arrived on the scene, most trade unions had been geared to the needs of skilled tradesmen, and were usually non-militant. The arrival of the ITGWU changed that – it unified and fought for the rights of unskilled workers, and it was willing to use militant methods, such as the sympathetic strike, in support of its demands. Already it had gained wage increases of around 25% for many unskilled workers in the early part of 1913, with a series of over 30 industrial disputes between January and August. It would seem that, in that year of 1913, a rebellious *zeitgeist* was beginning, a *zeitgeist* in which the worm of workers' dissatisfaction with their lot would at last began to turn.

By 1913 the ITGWU had about 30,000 members. Larkin's motto was 'an injury to one is an injury to all', and his main weapon became the sympathetic strike, whereby workers in firms not on strike would refuse to handle the goods of the firm where workers were on strike. These methods had begun to tip the balance of power in favour of the workers, and against employers. Larkin's main antagonist on the employers' side was William Martin Murphy. In 1911, he had founded the Dublin Employers' Federation, and in 1913, the year of the Lockout, he was president of the Dublin Chamber of Commerce. As one of the leading employers in the city – he owned the DUTC and the *Irish Independent* and *Evening Herald* newspapers - he was incensed by the increasing power of the ITGWU, and the strike methods that had become known as 'Larkinism'.

On Friday 15 August 1913 Murphy walked into the delivery department of the *Irish Independent* and told the workers to choose between their jobs and membership of the

ITGWU. He laid off 40 men and 20 boys on the spot, they placed pickets, and that evening the city newsboys refused to sell Murphy's other paper, the *Evening Herald*. The boycott quickly spread to other newspaper distributors, including Easons, and on 21 August, 100 tramway workers received the following notice from Murphy's company 'As the Directors understand that you are a member of the Irish Transport and General Workers Union whose methods are disorganising the trade and business of the city, they do not further require your service' – in other words, he was dismissing and locking out workers for being members of Larkin's union. A week later, on Tuesday 26 August, Larkin struck back at the beginning of one of the busiest weeks of the year, Horse Show Week, by calling out the tramway men. Two hundred drivers of the DUTC, all members of Larkin's union, left their posts, and the trams stopped running. Murphy called on other employers to support him, which they did by locking out workers, while workers for their part boycotted firms who supported Murphy's actions. Larkin stated that the situation was 'not a strike, but a Lockout of men by an unscrupulous scoundrel' – thus giving the dispute its iconic name of Lockout that still arouses strong feelings up to the present day.

Dublin citizens were soon given good reason to have strong feelings about the Lockout. As well as support from fellow employers, William Martin Murphy sought, and was given, the assistance of not only the Dublin Metropolitan Police, but also the Royal Irish Constabulary, to help quell the strikers. It soon became obvious that the agents of the law were on the side of the employers, rather than those who were locked out. On the first evening of the Lockout, as Larkin addressed a meeting outside Liberty Hall, a ring of policemen monitored the crowd.

Seán O'Casey witnessed the scene, and described them as 'massive constables [who] instinctively finger their belts, and silently caress the ever-ready club that swings jauntily over each man's broad, expansive hip.' When Larkin burned a proclamation banning a planned meeting in Sackville (O'Connell) Street, a warrant was issued for his arrest, and on Saturday 30 August there were riots throughout the city, during which the police baton-charged the crowds – one man, James Nolan, was caught in the riots and beaten to death by the police. An eye-witness account would state that Nolan was running from the riots along the quays when he was clubbed by three constables, but the inquest on his death did not attribute blame to the police, attributing Nolan's death to an accident caused by general rioting. Another man, James Byrne, would later die from injuries received that night. Nolan and Byrne were buried with large public funerals as martyrs of the Lockout.

Following these riots, most of the labour leaders decided to abandon the planned meeting, and instead marched peacefully to Croydon Park in Fairview on Sunday

31 August. However, Larkin was determined to make his address as promised, and appeared in disguise on a balcony of the Imperial Hotel – opposite the G.P.O. and owned by William Martin Murphy. The police arrested him and then turned their attention to what was mainly a peaceful Sunday crowd of people uninvolved with the Lockout. Contemporary photographs and eye-witness accounts would show that the police baton-charged Sunday walkers indiscriminately. Handel Booth, an English M.P., who was having lunch with his wife in the Imperial Hotel, described it as a 'mad scene'.[24] The police had drawn their batons, and were running in different directions. According to Booth, the crowd was 'an ordinary Sunday crowd. They were certainly bewildered, and did not know which way to turn.'[25] 'Up and down the road, backwards and forwards, the police rushed like men possessed … wildly striking with truncheons at every one within reach … many ran the gauntlet until the third or fourth blow knocked them senseless. Kicking the victims when prostrate was a settled part of the police programme. Three such cases occurred in a direct line with our window.'[26]

The baton charges lasted only about five minutes, but in that time up to 600 people were injured. Countess Markievicz's husband, Casimir, named it Bloody Sunday, comparing it to the shooting of Russian workers during a peaceful protest some years previously.[27] As news of the baton charges spread, riots broke out all over the city, and as the police brought some arrested men to Store Street Station, women in the Corporation Street flats shouted 'murderers'. That evening, the police returned to the flats, broke down doors and terrorised the residents, many of whom hid in fear. One man, John McDonagh, who was paralysed, was beaten as he lay in his bed, and when his wife intervened, she too was beaten. The police seemed to go out of their way to destroy the few possessions the people in the flats had, for example, a sewing machine that a woman was buying on hire purchase to try to earn money; in particular they destroyed any religious items that were in the homes. As the Dublin Corporation solicitor would say in evidence to the Disturbances Commission:

> damage to the household goods of these people is very much more grievous than damage to property belonging to persons in better positions … their little sticks of furniture they gathered together with infinite toil … and they can only be replaced after long and difficult struggle later on.[28]

Fall of houses in Church Street

As if the horrors of the baton charges and other attacks were not enough, the poor of Dublin faced a further blow two days later. At 8.45 on the night of 2 September, two tenement houses fell in Church Street. The houses, numbers 66 and 67, were just across the road from the Father Mathew Hall, and the rubble from the houses fell right across the road to the building. The houses were owned by a Mrs Ryan, who was collecting rents with her son and daughter when a rumbling was heard from number 66. An eye-witness recounted that there was 'a queer noise like an engine banging against a carriage', then he 'saw the street wall open up and bulge out ... and just as I got to the hall the side wall began rocking and bulging.'[29] The rumblings from number 66 gave sufficient warning to the residents of number 67, who managed to escape before it too collapsed. All of the victims lived in number 66.

TENEMENT DISASTER.

THE WORK OF RESCUE.

EIGHT DEATHS.

A PRIEST'S THRILLING STORY.

Rescue parties were still at work throughout yesterday, with a view to recovering bodies of persons, said to be still missing, from the ruins of the two tenement houses which collapsed in Church street on Tuesday night.

It is now clear that a large proportion of the occupants of the two four-storey buildings were fortunately absent when the collapse occurred, but there is grave reaso nto apprehend that the death-roll may still be augmented.

Throughout the day the scene of the calamity was visited by enormous numbers of citizens, and the Fathers of the Capuchin Church were active amongst the relatives of the victims, consoling them in their terrible bereavement.

The Freeman-Telegraph Relief Fund, opened in our columns, met with a most generous response throughout the day from all classes of citizens, and gives every promise of being supported in a manner which will, at all events, do something to relieve the sufferings of those who are not only stricken in grief, but rendered destitute by this awful calamity. Ample arrangements are being made to afford everyone an opportunity of subscribing to this most deserving object.

The Lord Lieutenant and Countess of Aberdeen have written a letter expressing their sympathy with the victims of the disaster.

2. Church Street disaster.
Freeman's Journal, 4 Sept. 1913.
DCLA

The tragedy could have been much worse; the caretaker of the Father Mathew Hall was also alerted by the rumbling before the fall of number 66, and dragged some children who were playing in the street into the Hall, no doubt saving their lives. The Hall itself was filled with children at a function, and there was a large group of adults in the Capuchin church next door, who luckily were not on the street when the houses collapsed.

The fall of two large tenement houses filled the immediate area with a great cloud of dust, hampering the rescue efforts for some time, as did the onset of darkness, the street lit only by poor quality street lighting. The lights in the Father Mathew Hall were turned full on, and volunteers stood on the rubble holding lanterns and candles to light the rescue scene. As the Dublin Fire Brigade began their rescue efforts, the full scale of the disaster became apparent, as the fallen houses gave up both victims and survivors. The final death toll would be seven – the victims named as Hugh Sammon (17), Elizabeth Sammon (four and a half), Nicholas Fitzpatrick (40), Elizabeth Fagan (50), John Shiels (three), Peter Crowley (six) and Margaret Rourke (55).[30]

The bare list of names hid a tale of great heroism in the person of young Hugh Sammon (usually named as Eugene Salmon, the name he is given on the 1911 census form for the family). In one of the most poignant stories to emerge from the incident, it was revealed that the 17-year-old Eugene had returned to number 66 several times to rescue his siblings, being crushed by the fall on his final journey to rescue his sister Elizabeth, who also died. Eugene had been locked out by Jacob's biscuit factory the week before, making him a victim of both the Lockout and the Church Street disaster.

Coming so soon after the baton charges, the raid on the Corporation Street flats, and the deaths of James Nolan and James Byrne, the Church Street tragedy unleashed a torrent of anger against the living conditions in tenement houses. The industrial unrest and the notorious slums, previously viewed as separate problems, now coalesced into one common problem – the housing conditions of the poor of Dublin.

The 1913 Housing Inquiry

Taken in conjunction with the heightened tension occasioned by the Lockout, the seven deaths in Church Street acted as a catalyst in persuading the government to hold a far-reaching inquiry, making the Church Street victims what has been described as 'the posthumous pioneers of reform'.[31] The Chief Secretary, Augustine Birrell, agreed, at the insistence of a deputation from the Irish Association of Municipal Authorities, to hold an inquiry into the housing conditions of the poor in Dublin. His first response was to announce that he would 'appoint a small departmental committee to inquire into the character and extent of the slum problem in Dublin',[32] but he acceded to the demand of the Lord Mayor of Dublin, Lorcan Sherlock, who insisted that the inquiry must take place in public, as 'the citizens … do not believe that a private inquiry will throw the necessary amount of light on the ownership of the slums.'[33] The Lord Mayor went on to say that it was known that some members of Dublin Corporation were tenement owners, that it was the Corporation who must be 'the chief administrative authority in connexion with any large scheme of housing reform' and that 'nothing short of a public inquiry … can elicit the facts and enlist the support of private munificence.'[34] A further dimension to this was a short piece in *The Times*,[35] written by 'Our own correspondent', in which it was inferred that Lord Aberdeen also disagreed with Mr Birrell on the nature of the inquiry, although Lord Aberdeen denied that there was any disagreement.

APPALLING DISASTER IN THE CITY.

TENEMENTS COLLAPSE.

FAMILIES BURIED IN DEBRIS.

SEVERAL KILLED AND INJURED

RUINS IN FLAMES.

An appalling disaster, involving the death of several people, occurred in Dublin last night.

Two large tenement houses in Church street, near the Four Courts, collapsed about half-past eight, burying a number of families in the debris.

The tenements were occupied by some sixteen families, and in all between forty and fifty people were involved.

Men, women and children were buried in the ruins, and tons of debris had to be cleared away before they could be reached.

The work of rescue was continued through the night. By half-past one o'clock the bodies of thirteen people had been recovered. Five were dead.

There were instances of great heroism in the work of rescue. A lad of seventeen, name d Eugene Salmon, after carrying a number of children out of the house was killed while endeavouring to carry his little sister to safety.

a fracture of the skull, his condition leaving practically no hope of surviving.

At one o'clock there were ten persons altogether brought to hospital, three being dead and two in a very critical state.

It is stated that there were altogether fifteen families living in the two tenements, the number of occupants, so far as could be ascertained, being 42.

The premises 66 were, according to the landlord, Mrs. Brigid Ryan, who lives in 86 Church street, occupied by the following:—

Mr. and Mrs. Salmon and four children, parlour and shop.

Mr. and Mrs. Shields and four children, drawingroom.

Mr. and Mrs. Benson (no family), two-pair back.

Mr. and Mrs. Fitzpatrick and four children.

Mrs. Fagan and two daughters, top back.

In the adjoining house, 67, the families are given as follows:—

Mrs. Quinn and her daughter, shop and parlour.

Mr. and Mrs. Dignam and daughter, drawingroom.

Mr. and Mrs. Dempsey and two children, first back room.

Mrs. Carty and two daughters, two-pair front.

Mrs. Oxbury, two-pair back.

Mr. and Mrs. Devlin and two children, top front.

Mrs. Fagan and child, top back room. Both are stated to be safe, but at 1 o'clock the only others accounted for were the two Fitzpatrick boys, and Mr. and Mrs. Carty, who are seriously injured, and a young woman named Doyle, suffering from slight injury and shock.

Soon after the catastrophe, Dr. Kelly, of the Richmond Hospital, was on the scene and remained up to an early hour this morning. Dr. McCurry, of the Coombe Hospital, also rendered valuable assistance. Rev. Father Paul, O.S.F.C.; Rev. Father Laurence, O.S.F.C.; Father E. O'Callaghan, C.C., St. Paul's, and Father Kennedy, C.C., North Anne street, were early arrivals and adminis

3. Report on Church Street disaster.
Freeman's Journal, 3 Sept. 1913.
DCLA

The eventual decision was that a local inquiry would be conducted by a commission consisting of members of the Local Government Board for Ireland (LGBI), so the Corporation got its public inquiry as demanded, but not from a body of inquiry that they would favour.

The LGBI had been formed in 1872 to replace the old Poor Law Commission. As well as taking on the responsibilities held by the commission, the new board now also had responsibilities in areas such as disease eradication, sanitary services and housing, and was the official arbiter on such matters throughout the country. It had a fraught relationship with most councils, seeing it as its principal remit to keep them in order and investigate any suspicion of wrongdoing. It had the authority to curb their rating powers, and could refuse requests for borrowing powers. It was often accused of putting British government interests above the needs of Irish citizens, and over the years gathered a wide range of information on local authorities. From 1918 on, Sinn Féin gradually eroded the power of the board, encouraging many local councils to resist its authority.[36] Councils with a Sinn Féin majority were encouraged to pledge allegiance to the Dáil rather than the Local Government Board – for example, they refused to supply the records of meetings.[37] The Irish headquarters of the board was in the Custom House, and it is widely accepted that one of the main reasons for the burning of the Custom House in 1921 during the War of Independence, was to destroy the records they held on the various councils throughout the country.[38]

Since its inception, the LGBI had had a particularly antagonistic relationship with Dublin Corporation, and had moved against them on several occasions; for example in 1897 the Board had forced the resignation of three sanitary officers, and as recently as 1906 Surgeon David Edgar Flinn, on behalf of the board, had published a highly critical *Report on the sanitary circumstances and administration of the city of Dublin, with special reference to the causes of the high death-rate.*' Much of the antagonism between the two bodies arose from the (probably justified) belief of the Corporation that the LGBI, while criticising its efforts to improve housing, frequently stymied those efforts by its own actions and decisions. For example, the Corporation was criticised for allowing an influx of rural labourers into the city, which exacerbated the unemployment crisis; in fact, in 1906, the Corporation had tried to make two years' residency in the city a condition of employment, only to have this condition disallowed by the LGBI. Even further back, in the 1870s and 1880s, the Corporation's scheme to clear and redevelop the Coombe and Plunkett Street areas of the city with housing for the poor was abandoned due to the high costs involved, largely caused by the exorbitant compensation awarded to the owners of dilapidated property in the area – this compensation was set by the LGBI. Instead of developing the area for the housing needs of the poor, the Corporation was obliged to simply clear the area, and rent the sites at a loss to the Dublin Artisans' Dwellings Company, who built houses at rents the poor were unable to afford. This resulted in the poor being displaced and being forced to move to another slum area, exacerbating rather than alleviating the problems. On previous evidence, therefore, it seemed inevitable that, in any inquiry conducted into housing by the LGBI, the emphasis would be on the perceived ineptitude of Dublin Corporation, with little sympathy for the underlying difficulties faced by them in trying to solve the tenement problem.

The final decision was to hold an inquiry that fell squarely, and many believed, inadequately, between a private inquiry and a vice-regal inquiry. The first public sitting took place on 18 November 1913, at the Council Chamber, City Hall. There were four members on the committee: C. H. O'Conor (presiding); J. F. MacCabe; and A. P. Delany, all LGBI inspectors, and S. Watt, a member of the LGBI's internal staff. The Housing Committee of the Corporation would later express concern on the composition of this committee, on the grounds that the situation in Dublin was complex, and that the committee should include experts who were used to 'dealing with social problems or eminent sanitarians',[39] claiming that:

> officials devoid of any experience of the general administrative work of the Corporation could not take that wide and sympathetic view of the origin and advancing stages of this great social problem, and the numerous difficulties which lie in the path of the Local Authority in endeavouring to solve it.[40]

The inquiry called 76 witnesses, including, among others, aldermen, councillors, and officials of Dublin Corporation, clergymen, trade union officials, and private individuals with an interest in housing matters. One of the most closely questioned witnesses was Sir Charles Cameron, whose title was given as Executive Sanitary Officer and Medical Superintendent Officer of Health for Dublin.

The eclectic mix of witnesses clearly shows the difference between this inquiry and many others that had been held into Dublin's health and housing problems. Middle-class reformers found themselves giving similar evidence to trade union officials, sharing a common belief that the root of the industrial unrest that had resulted in the Lockout had its roots in the living conditions of the Dublin poor.

The newspapers published statements from outraged middle-class reformers, such as E. A. Aston,[41] who claimed that 'The heather of revolt against intolerable conditions of life has been dried in the one hundred thousand inhabitants of the twenty thousand single tenement rooms of Dublin.'[42] While *The Irish Times*, perhaps more concerned about social unrest than the living conditions of the poor stated 'The members of the

ITGWU live for the most part in slums like Church Street. Their domestic conditions make them an easy prey to plausible agitators.' William Martin Murphy not surprisingly thought that the slums had nothing to do with the industrial unrest, and that the tenement problem was being exploited by the ITGWU for their own ends.[43]

4. Church Street, after the collapse of houses, 1913.
DCLA, Dublin in Decay: images from 1913

Most of the witnesses called gave a roughly similar account of the horrendous conditions in the Dublin tenements, albeit with the evidence slanted towards their own particular concern – for example the dangers of immorality were stressed by clergy and the fault of the employers emphasised by the trade unions. However, by far the most searching questions were directed at the Public Health Office of Dublin Corporation, and in particular at the man in charge of that office, Sir Charles Cameron.

When the inquiry committee issued its report the following February, the following two charges would be made against him, based on questions put to Cameron by the inquiry committee.

1. 'That Sir Charles Cameron has taken on himself a dispensing power in relation to the closet accommodation stated to be necessary under the Bye-laws relating to tenement houses ...' [44]

2. 'Sir Charles Cameron [has] taken on his own shoulders the responsibility of dispensing in certain cases with the Bye-laws governing tenement houses and with the conditions laid down by the Corporation in regard to rebates ...' [45]

The report also claimed that there had only been 'a slight reduction in the death-rate in Dublin from all causes in recent years ...' [46]

It is worthwhile examining the questions and answers in some detail:

The criticism about water closets resulted from questions that began with the president of the committee, Mr O'Conor, asking Cameron 'how many water closets do you consider necessary for so many people?'[47] to which Cameron replied: 'I have a very strong opinion that every family should have one water closet ... if a water closet is common to two or more families – it is never in a sanitary state.'[48] While the Corporation bye-laws required one water closet for every 12 families, Cameron readily admitted that such requirements were not enforced when, 'in the exercise of my own judgement, I do not think it wise to'.[49] He qualified this statement following further questioning, by giving his reasons for dispensing with the requirements of the bye-laws: 'in many cases we find it more desirable to have only one closet – if we have two they both get into a bad state no matter how many notices are served.' He went on to say that his officials served about 20,000 notices on unsanitary water closets each year. In a later question session Cameron further explained his reasons for using discretion in implementing the bye-laws, when he claimed that one half of the tenement population could in practical terms be discounted when calculating the number of water closets, as:

> I can positively state, on the authority of the leading sanitary officers and my own observation, that the women never use these water closets put up in the yards ... secondly the children don't use them; they use the floors or the yards.[50]

The latter statement was corroborated by members of the inquiry committee, who admitted in the 1914 report:

> having visited a large number of these [tenement] houses in all parts of the city ... we are quite prepared to accept Sir Charles Cameron's evidence, that the female inhabitants of the tenement houses seldom use the closets.[51]

This point was made in the early pages of the report, but was not used to qualify their criticism later in the report of Cameron's 'dispensing powers' regarding water closets. It is also worth noting, that *The Irish Times*, which gave a summary of the report 'From our London Correspondent', also saw fit to omit this point, but did include a large headline 'SIR CHARLES CAMERON'S DISPENSING POWERS', and repeated the criticism without any reference to Cameron's reasons for exercising discretion.[52]

However, a far more damaging accusation was made against Cameron in the report, when it stated that he had given tax rebates to landlords without abiding by the regulations. The report focussed particularly on rebates given to three landlords who were members of Dublin Corporation: Alderman G. O'Reilly, Alderman Patrick Corrigan and Councillor James Crozier. According to the inquiry's report, there were 5,322 tenement houses in Dublin, of which a maximum of 102 were owned by members of Dublin Corporation.[53] Tax rebates for landlords of houses with a rateable valuation of under £8 had been introduced by the Dublin Corporation Act 1890 in an effort to encourage landlords to improve sub-standard tenements. In his 1914 publication *A brief history of municipal public health in Dublin* (written in response to the report of the inquiry) Cameron stated:

> A great many applications for rebates were made, and a large proportion of them refused. In a *very small* proportion of the houses granted rebates all the conditions for them were not present. In the case of the Building Bye-laws they are not always strictly complied with if there is a sufficient reason for not insisting on all of them being observed.[54]

With regard to rebates, Cameron admitted:

> I will always take a liberal view, even though I may not be strictly in accordance with the bye-laws. I want to give the reason. Well, I say I had two objects in view:

first, the improvement of places that never would have been improved so much except for the rebate of rates, and secondly, also that these places would be let at lower rates to these people who find it very difficult to pay this 2/- or 2/6 a week. Now, I may have been wrong, but that was the view that I took, and I would like to say this: on no single occasion, with regard to rebate of rates, has any member of the Corporation ever called on me personally, or sent a message to me, with one solitary exception; that is the case of Councillor Crozier.[55]

Cameron explained further that he re-examined Crozier's house, which had been refused a rebate, made a suggestion for an improvement that would allow a rebate to be made, and when this improvement had been made, he certified the house as fit for rebate.[56] Cameron would later contend that, while 'there may be a trifling laxity in not strictly enforcing the conditions justifying rebates',

the laxity is not due to favouritism but to the desire to see the dwellings of the poor being kept in a better state than they otherwise would be ... if the Corporation discontinue rebates many dwellings now in good condition would become more or less insanitary.[57]

In the section of the report dealing with tax rebates on tenements, the inquiry committee is somewhat disingenuous in its reporting of evidence, stating:

We think it desirable in connection with this subject to refer to some matters which came under our notice relative to tenements and other property owned by members of the Corporation ... the total amount of rate remitted last year was £3,819, a matter of some importance to the Ratepayers.

In its report, the committee stated that 'at an interview subsequent to the inquiry' they had learned that most of the tenement property was owned by a large number of small owners, and immediately named the members of Dublin Corporation who owned property. In a response to the report, the housing committee of the Corporation revealed that of the total amount of £3,819 given in rebates, an amount of £6 0s. 6d. was given to landlords where discretion in the strict appliance of the regulations was exercised. The housing committee stated that:

the introduction of the larger sum of £3,819 immediately preceding the mention of the names of the three members of the Corporation and the omission of all mention of the actual amount alleged to have been improperly received leaves much to be desired in the way of impartial reporting, or safeguarding against the false impression on the public mind as to the actual facts, which the peculiar construction of the paragraph in the report was undoubtedly bound to create.[58]

The housing committee of the Corporation took further issue with the report of the inquiry committee regarding comments on Charles Cameron's 'discretion' in strictly implementing the regulations regarding tax rebates, claiming that 'there was an attempt in its conduct to put the Corporation on its trial, and to enlarge on any of its actions which could be criticized.'[59] They (accurately) stated that the report took over a page to give their comments on the rebate which amounted to £6 0s. 6d., and 'about five lines … to say as little as they possibly could on the subject of the Dublin death rate and its decline during Sir Charles Cameron's period of service.'[60] It is worth examining this latter point in more detail.

During the inquiry, J. F. MacCabe asked Cameron if, 'during that time, since that time, 1879 [the year Cameron became Superintendent Medical Officer of Health] the death rate in Dublin has diminished very considerably?'[61] However, in the report, the inquiry committee contradicted this, claiming that '… there has been a slight reduction in the death-rate in Dublin from all causes in recent years … '.[62] While they did not define 'slight' or 'recent years', the facts would seem to contradict their statement on both counts: the death rate in Dublin in 1880 was 37.7 per thousand, in 1900 it was 30.3, and this had been reduced to 21.6 in 1913, the year of the inquiry, a substantial reduction by any standards. The number of tenements had been almost halved in the same period, from 9,760 in 1880,[63] to 5,322 in 1913,[64] but the report did not stress this reduction, which would have perhaps vindicated Cameron's work, but emphasised the fact that more people were now living in tenements, and that the density per house was greater than in 1880. That this was a demographic rather than a sanitary problem was not considered.

However, this masks the great inroads made by Charles Cameron and his staff into Dublin's death rate, helping to reduce it from 37.5 in 1879, the year Cameron took over responsibility for public health, to 17.6 in 1920, the year before he died. Comparison with other cities should not mask the improvements in the mortality figures for Dublin, improvements that were hard-won, in conditions that were worse than in other cities; improvements that could be wiped out almost overnight with an unexpected and uncontrollable epidemic.

This improvement in the death rate was illustrated graphically in the report of the housing committee replying to the LGBI report on the housing inquiry

> In 1880, the first year that Sir Charles Cameron was Medical Superintendent Officer of Health, the death rate in the city was 37.7 per 1,000 persons living, and the death rate from the principal infective diseases 7.9. In the previous year the two rates were 37.5 and 6.2.

In the 10 years ended in 1886 the mean death rate from all causes was 31.5, and from infectious diseases 4.4.

In the 10 years ended in 1896 the two rates were 29 and 2.9.

In the 10 years period 1897-1906 the two rates were 27.5 and 2.9.

In the following five years the mean death rate from all causes was 22.8, and from infectious diseases 2.2.

The mean death rate in the years 1912 and 1913 was 21.6, and from infectious diseases 2.4.[65]

A measure of the work done under Cameron's tenure as Medical Officer of Health can be gauged from the following statistics: from 1851 until 1877, a period of 26 years, about 200 houses in Dublin had been closed. In 1879, the year he took over as Superintendent Medical Officer of Health, Cameron immediately prepared a handbook of instructions for sanitary inspectors, and himself 'resolved to personally inspect every tenement house in the city, and also some hundreds of small cottages occupied by very poor people.'[66] By the end of 1880, that is, in one year under Cameron's stewardship, 602 houses and 204 cellars had been closed.[67] In 1881, Cameron and his staff obtained orders to close '447 houses, 161 rooms in other houses, and 99 cellars ... '.[68] Cameron enforced the construction of several hundred water-closets in tenements, and by October 1879, 743 water closets had replaced back-yard privies, with the hope expressed by Cameron that, within a year, water closets would be in nearly every tenement dwelling in the city.[69] In 1882, Cameron had a survey done which showed that 'in all Dublin there were 15,531 WCs and 11,269 privies.'[70] By 1892, he could report that 'very few privies now exist in Dublin – the water carriage system has been nearly completed.'[71] In 1892, he also produced a list of vacant sites (see below), and urged the Corporation to use 'the ample powers' conferred on local authorities by the Housing of the Working Classes Act, 1890 (53 and 54 Vict., chap. 70).

Appendix:

List of cleared spaces in Dublin

(Source: R.P.D.C.D., 1892, vol. 1, pp 200-08, 'Report by Sir Charles Cameron,
Medical Officer of Health, In re Powers possessed by the Corporation with respect
to ruinous buildings and the sites upon which houses formerly stood'.)

SOUTH SIDE		
Back Lane	frontage 57 feet by 54 feet in depth	(4 houses down)
Bow Lane, off Aungier-street	frontage 90 feet by 90 feet in depth	(8 houses down)
Bride's-alley, Mill-yard and Draper's-court	frontage 117 feet by 45 feet in depth.	(4 houses in ruins and 10 houses down)
Bull-alley	frontage 240 feet by 96 feet in depth.	(7 houses down)
Cannon-street	frontage 63 feet by 21 feet in depth.	(3 houses down)
Cook-street (3 spaces)	No. 1 Space, 54 feet by 51 feet	}
	No. 2 Space, 15 feet by 60 feet in depth	} (5 houses down)
	No. 3 Space, 24 feet by 42 feet in depth	}
Kennedy's-lane and O'Keeffe's-cottages	frontage 30 feet by 39 feet in depth	(22 houses down)
Meath Market	frontage 270 feet by 144 feet	(30 houses down)
Moss-street, corner of Bracken's-lane	frontage 30 feet by 24 feet in depth.	(3 houses down)
Myler's-alley, east side	frontage 54 feet by 24 feet in depth .	(3 houses down)
Patrick's-close, from Myler's-alley to Patrick-street	frontage 246	(8 houses down)
Power's-court: there are five spaces in this court:-	No. 1 Space: frontage 102 feet by 111 feet in depth.	(13 houses down)
	No. 2 Space: frontage 27 feet by 33 feet in depth.	(1 house down)
	No. 3 Space: frontage 33 feet by 30 feet in depth.	(3 houses down)
	No. 4 Space: frontage 24 feet by 45 feet in length.	(1 house down)
	No. 5 Space: frontage 111 feet by 42 feet in depth.	(7 houses down)
Ross-lane and Derby-square	frontage: 298 feet by 129 feet in depth.	(21 houses down)
Temple-bar:	frontage: 45 feet by 24 feet in depth.	(2 houses down)
Do. Corner of Crown-alley	frontage: 126 feet by 63 feet in depth.	(4 houses down)
Thomas-court	frontage: 239 feet; depth 40 feet	(13 houses down)

SOUTH SIDE		
Walker's-alley	frontage: 246 feet by 156 feet in depth.	(5 houses down, also long yard)
Wood-street, Oliver's-alley, Arthur's-lane and portion of Golden-lane	frontage: 1,081 feet, area about 11/4 acres.	(40 houses down)

Total houses taken down: 198

NORTH SIDE		
Arbour-place	frontage: 93 feet by 51 feet in depth.	(4 houses down)
Benburb-street (corner of Blackhall-place)	frontage: 63 feet by 63 feet in depth.	(3 houses down)
Beresford-street	frontage: 138 feet by 147 feet in depth.	(5 houses down)
Beresford-street	frontage: 63 feet by 117 feet in depth.	(3 houses down)
Butler's-court	frontage: frontage 234 feet by 42 feet in depth.	(11 small cottages down)
Bull-lane	frontage: 330 feet by 120 feet in depth.	(30 houses down)
Greek-street	frontage: 153 feet by 75 feet in depth.	(6 houses down)
North King-street	frontage: 57 feet by 120 feet in depth.	(3 houses down)
Old Abbey-street	frontage: 40 feet; depth 25 feet.	(2 houses down)
Potter's-alley, Marlborough-street	frontage: 160 feet; depth 25 feet	(7 houses down, or nearly down). Potter's-alley and the site of the old Glass Works, constitute an area of considerable size, on which about 40 houses could be erected.
Phoenix-street	frontage: 138 feet by 84 feet in depth.	(8 houses down)
West Arran-street	frontage: 66 feet by 72 feet in depth.	(4 houses down)

86 houses taken down

Conclusion

This list shows beyond doubt that Charles Cameron had his finger on the pulse of slum housing in Dublin and that, after 18 years of frustrating and repetitive slum clearance, he remained unbowed in his efforts to point out their duties to the Corporation. By 1913, under Cameron's tenure as Medical Officer of Health for Dublin, 4,263 houses and 1,190 cellars had been closed, and Dublin, no longer a midden city, had mains drainage.

However, these facts could not overcome the more dramatic revelations reported in the inquiry and its report, despite concerted efforts by Cameron and Dublin Corporation to point out the difficulties they faced, and the work they had done in spite of these, they did not come out of the inquiry without significant damage to their reputations. Most of the 'revelations' of the 1913 inquiry had been known to the authorities for decades, outlined in detail in previous enquiries. However, unlike previous enquiries, the 1913 inquiry and report became a catalyst for housing reform. Unfortunately, the First World War and later political unrest in Ireland meant that housing problems as a subject assumed less importance, and it would be several more decades before the tenement system finally came to an end in Dublin. However, the Lockout and the emotions it engendered, the victims of the Church Street disaster, the unfairly damaged reputation of Sir Charles Cameron, the criticism of the work of Dublin Corporation, were an important part of a momentum that would eventually see an improvement in public health and housing in Dublin.

Notes

1   *Reports and printed documents of Dublin Corporation,* henceforth cited as R.P.D.C.D., 'Report of the housing committee upon the report of the departmental committee appointed by the Local Government Board to inquire into the housing conditions of the working classes of the city of Dublin', vol. 2, no. 120 (1914), p. 158.

2   Pádraig Yeates, *Lockout: Dublin 1913* (Dublin, 2000), p. 7.

3   Walter Carpenter was born in England in 1871. He was a chimney sweep by trade – the 1901 census states he was 'a master chimney cleaner', while the 1911 census gives his occupation as secretary, Socialist Party of Ireland. He was also secretary of the Communist Party and was General Secretary of The International Tailors, Machinists and Pressers' Trade Union (colloquially known as 'the Jewish Union'). He was an outspoken campaigner for women's suffrage and equal pay for women, and gave graphic evidence of conditions in the slums to the 1913 housing inquiry. He died in 1926. Two of his sons, Peter and Walter Patrick, joined the Irish Citizen Army, and were active in the 1916 Rising. Walter Patrick later fought in the War of Independence and became president of the ITUC in 1959. Joe Mooney, 'Walter Carpenter - from sweep to revolutionary - a forgotten figure from the 1913 Lockout' (www.1913committee.ie).

4   Joseph V. O'Brien, *Dear dirty Dublin: a city in distress, 1899-1916* (Berkeley, CA, 1982), p. 138.

5   William Wilde, *Special sanitary report on the city of Dublin*, appended to the Census of Ireland 1841, p. lxviii.

6   Thomas Willis, *Facts connected with the social and sanitary condition of the working classes in the city of Dublin* (Dublin, 1845), p. 45.

7   Ibid., p. 21.

8   *Thoms Directory* (1907), p. 342.

9   Charles Cameron became Public Analyst for Dublin in 1862, and Medical Officer of Health for Dublin in 1874, Superintendent Medical Officer of Health in 1879, taking overall control of Dublin Corporation's Public Health Office in 1881. He was made a freeman of Dublin in 1911. Throughout his career, he was an outspoken campaigner on behalf of the poor of Dublin, waging war on the tenement system. At the end of his tenure, the death rate in Dublin had been halved, as had the number of tenements. His expertise was recognised internationally, but his reputation nationally was compromised by unfair comments on his performance in the *Report of the 1913 housing inquiry*. He continued to serve the people of Dublin until his death at the age of ninety in 1921.

10   *Minutes* of the North Dublin Union, 14 April, 1947.

11   The 'temporary' May Laws of 1882 were the major cause of Jewish emigration from Tsarist Russia. After the assassination of Tsar Alexander II in March 1881, the authorities clamped down on known revolutionaries and found a scapegoat in the Jews, organising pograms that were repeated in 1882, 1883 and 1884.

12   Charles A. Cameron, *A brief history of municipal public health administration in Dublin* (Dublin, 1914), p. 7.

13   Charles Cameron and Edward Mapother, R.P.D.C.D., 'Report on the means for the prevention of disease in Dublin', vol. 1, no. 63 (1879), p. 344.

14   Cameron, *A brief history*, p. 13.

15   Mary E. Daly, 'Late nineteenth- and early twentieth-century Dublin', in D. Harkness and M. O'Dowd (eds), *The town in Ireland* (Belfast, 1979), p. 223.

16   *Report of the Sick and Indigent Roomkeepers' Society*, 1857, p. 14.

17   Charles A. Cameron, *How the poor live* (Dublin, 1904). A note on the first page, in what appears to be Cameron's writing, states 'Presented to National Library of Ireland May 8, 1905.'

18   Ibid., p. 1.

19   Ibid.

20   Ibid., p. 3.

21   Ibid., pp 22-23.

22   Yeates, *Lockout*, p. 31.

23   D. A. Chart, 'Unskilled labour in Dublin, its housing and living conditions', Dublin: *Journal of the Statistical and Social Inquiry Society of Ireland*, vol. XIII, part XCIV (1913/14), pp 160-75.

24   Donal Nevin, *1913: Jim Larkin and the Dublin Lockout* (Dublin, 1964). Booth was Liberal M.P. for Pontefract, 1910-18.

25   Ibid.

26   Ibid.

27   Yeates, *Lockout*, p. 69.

28   Ibid., p. 72.

29   *Irish Independent*, 4 Sept. 1913.

30   *Irish Times*, 5 Sept. 1913.

31   O'Brien, *Dear dirty Dublin,* p. 150.

32   *The Times,* 22 Oct. 1913.

33   Ibid.

34   Ibid.

35   *The Times,* 8 Nov. 1913.

36   Joseph Robins, *Custom House people* (Dublin, 1993), p. 93.

37   Jason K. Knirck, *Imagining Ireland's independence: the debates over the Anglo-Irish Treaty of* 1921 (Plymouth, 2006), p. 52.

38   Michael Corcoran, *Our good health: a history of Dublin's water and drainage* (Dublin, 2005), p. 78.

39   R.P.D.C.D., vol. 2, no. 120 (1914), p. 156.

40   Ibid.

41   Ernest Albert Aston was born in Dublin in 1873. He trained as an engineer, and worked as a local government inspector before becoming a journalist and sub-editor of *The Irish Times*. He was a founder member (1911) of the Housing and Town Planning Association of Ireland. At the 1913 inquiry he presented proposals for a comprehensive plan for the city. He was a founder member of, and the driving force behind, the Greater Dublin Reconstruction Movement (1922), which formulated a comprehensive plan to solve the problems facing Dublin after the civil unrest that occurred between 1916 and 1922. He died in 1949.

42   E. A. Aston, *Freeman's Journal*, 4 Sept. 1913.

43   Murray Fraser, *John Bull's other homes: state housing and British policy in Ireland, 1883-1922* (Liverpool, 1996), p. 108.

44   *Report of the Departmental Committee appointed by the Local Government Board for Ireland to inquire into the housing conditions of the working classes in Dublin* (Dublin, 1914) (cd. 7317) (henceforth cited as Report 1914), Par. 28.

45   Ibid., Par. 30.

46   Ibid., Par. 13.

47   *Report of the Departmental Committee appointed by the Local Government Board for Ireland to inquire into the housing conditions of the working classes in Dublin* (Dublin 1914) (cd. 7273) (henceforth cited as Evidence 1913), qs. 1082.

48   Ibid.

49   Ibid., qs. 1086, 1087.

50   Ibid., qs. 6032.

51   Report 1914, Par. 11.

52   *Irish Times,* 18 Feb. 1914.

53   Report 1914, Par. 9 and Par. 29.

54   Cameron, *A brief history*, p. 79.

55   James Crozier. A vet by profession and a Unionist, he was a councillor in Dublin Corporation. He was part of a committee set up to solicit funds to help workers with strike pay during the Lockout.

56   Evidence 1913., qs. 7317.

57   Cameron, *A brief history*, p. 80.

58   R.P.D.C.D., 1914, vol. II, p. 165.

59   Ibid., p. 166.

60   Ibid.

61   Evidence 1913, qs. 1405.

62   Report 1914, Par. 13.

63   Report 1914, Par. 14.

64   Report 1914, Par. 9.

65   R.P.D.C.D., vol. 2, no. 120 (1914), pp 163-4.

66   Cameron, *A brief history*, pp 66-7.

67   Ibid., p. 67.

68   Ibid., p. 68.

69   Ibid., p. 12.

70   R.P.D.C.D., 'Statement of the duties carried out by the Public Health Department of the Corporation of Dublin', vol. 1, no. 26 (1892), p. 235.

71   Ibid., p. 236.

— "Irish Times."

τιζτε loυτα ι mbaιle άτα cliατ.

5. Decayed houses in Dublin, (1). Middle Abbey Street, (2). Charles Street, (3). Church Street, (4). Arran Street. *An Claidheamh Soluis*, 31 Jan. 1914.

DCLA

4.

'Medicine in the city': the impact of the National Insurance Act on health care and the medical profession in Dublin

....

David Durnin

Introduction

By 1913, Dublin was firmly established as Ireland's medical capital.[1] The development of this identity owed much to the strength of the city's medical infrastructure. Dublin was home to a collection of dispensary and Poor Law services, voluntary hospitals, general practices and lunatic asylums. Aside from these services and institutions stood some of Ireland's most prestigious medical schools and licensing bodies. Two of the country's leading educational establishments, University of Dublin (Trinity College) and University College Dublin offered medical courses which were among the most popular in the country. The Royal Colleges of Physicians and Surgeons, along with the Apothecaries Hall, an examining body for apothecaries, licensed Ireland's medical professionals. Together, this collection of medical services and educational institutions brought many medical professionals to the city. General practitioners, physicians, surgeons and newly qualified medical graduates flocked towards Dublin throughout the 19th and 20th centuries in search of education and employment. By 1913, approximately 16% of Ireland's entire medical profession resided in the county.[2] In the early 20th century, Dublin's population, in contrast to the national trend, increased.[3] The region's medical institutions and services were forced to expand to cater for the growing number seeking health care. The purpose of this chapter is to map the medical infrastructure available to Dublin's population in 1913 and examine the issues faced by the medical professionals within this system. It is not possible in the space of a short chapter to examine each of the region's medical services in significant detail.[4] Instead, this chapter, due to the strength of source material available, will focus primarily on Dublin's voluntary hospitals.[5] As Mary E. Daly points out, voluntary hospitals played a much more important role in providing health care in Dublin than in most other locations in Ireland and thus provide an appropriate point of study.[6] Laurence Geary and Daly have completed extensive studies on Dublin's voluntary hospital system. Geary has outlined its 18th- and 19th-century beginnings and Daly has explored its subsequent development in the 1930s.[7] This chapter seeks to explore the difficulties faced by these institutions in 1913 and analyse how these problems affected their ability to provide health care for Dublin's population in the early 20th century.

One of the most significant threats to Dublin's voluntary hospitals in 1913 was the National Insurance Act. Introduced in 1911, this act aimed to alleviate the working class of the burdening cost of health care. The act offered sickness, disability, maternity and sanatorium benefits to insured persons in Ireland. Its introduction was a complicated process that divided opinion among workers, employers and the medical profession.[8] Debates among these groups regarding the act continued well into 1913 and beyond. Dublin's hospital governors were especially concerned about the impact of the act on their institutions. In their 1913 *Annual report*, the Board of Superintendence of the Dublin Hospitals, which inspected many of the city's hospitals, including Dr Steevens', the Meath and Cork Street Fever Hospital, criticised the act for 'affecting general hospitals unfavourably'.[9] By examining the benefits of the National Insurance Act and the debates surrounding their effect on Dublin's medical infrastructure, this chapter seeks to examine the impact of the act on Dublin's voluntary hospital system in 1913.

Dublin's medical infrastructure

In the early 20th century, Dublin was an unhealthy city when compared to many other British regions.[10] In 1900, the Local Government Board for Ireland (LGBI) appointed a special committee, including John Moore and R. L. Swan, presidents of the Royal College of Physicians and Surgeons respectively, to inquire into the public health of Dublin city. The committee explored the high rates of disease and mortality in the city and made various recommendations, including improvements to housing in the city and to the processes of notification of contagious diseases.[11] However, by 1913, disease and ill health remained a significant problem in Dublin. There was a notable increase in incidences of typhus, enteric fever, diphtheria, scarlet fever and measles when compared to previous years. As Greta Jones has shown, tuberculosis was particularly prevalent and posed a significant threat to the health of the city.[12] The LGBI claimed the spread of these infectious diseases was largely a result of living conditions within the city.[13] In a special report attached to Ireland's 1913 LGBI report, Dr Thomas Browne, medical inspector for Dublin County Borough, stated that many of the original outbreaks were traced back to tenement housing that was 'filthy and overcrowded'.[14] For those that sought treatment for their illnesses in medical institutions, there was no shortage of Dublin hospitals to provide medical care.

By 1 January 1913, Dublin was home to 32 hospitals that provided 3,200 beds for the sick and wounded.[15] Table 1 in the appendix provides the names and the details of these hospitals. Many of the hospitals were voluntary institutions established during the 18th and 19th centuries to cater for various religious and charitable groups.[16] These hospitals treated patients free of charge and relied on philanthropic support to remain open. The majority of the hospitals, including the Adelaide (1858), Royal City of Dublin

(1832) and Mater Misericordiae (1861), were general hospitals that admitted patients suffering from a variety of illnesses including diphtheria, rheumatism and bronchitis.[17] Other hospitals were specialised, the Rotunda (1745), Coombe (1826) and Holles Street (1894) were maternity hospitals. The Hardwicke Hospital (1803) and Cork Street Hospital (1804) provided care for those suffering from fever. Each voluntary hospital was controlled by a board of governors and a medical staff. The number of governors and the wider structure of the board varied according to each hospital's charter. For example, the Royal City of Dublin Hospital had 21 governors, many of which were prominent medical professionals, including Gibbon Fitzgibbon, Fellow of the Royal College of Physicians in Ireland (RCPI). A small panel was chosen from the 21 to micro manage the institution and this panel was rotated on a monthly basis with other governors taking the mantle.

One of the primary functions of the small panel was to keep track of hospital admissions. Dublin's voluntary hospitals were established for the relief of the sick poor. During the 19th century, many of the institutions retained a strict religious ethos that governed admissions policy. The Adelaide, Meath and City of Dublin hospitals were all established as Protestant institutions for the treatment of the Protestant poor. Catholics had little opportunity to benefit from their care and instead looked to other voluntary hospitals, including the Mater Misericordiae, for treatment.[18] However, as the century progressed, regulations governing admission into voluntary hospitals eased and many people were admitted who would have been previously considered unsuitable. In 1913, the Royal City of Dublin Hospital governors proclaimed that the institution was 'entirely unsectarian with illness, accident or suffering being the sole claim for relief.'[19] By the early 20th century, there was also a change in the class of patient treated. Instead of caring solely for the destitute poor, Dublin's voluntary hospitals often treated those from outside the destitute class. As was the case in Britain, the destitute instead found themselves seeking admission to local Poor Law Hospitals, like the Richmond, Whitworth and Hardwicke Hospitals which were associated with Dublin's North and South Dublin Union workhouses.[20]

The admission of those from outside the destitute class brought in much needed funds for some hospitals as governors sought fees for treatment from those who could afford to pay. In 1913 Dr Steevens' Hospital received £1,224 from paying patients, the Royal Victoria Eye and Ear received £1,536 and Cork Street Fever Hospital received £2,471, over a quarter of their total annual income.[21] Financial management was one of the great responsibilities for hospital governors as institutions struggled to maintain a firm financial footing based on the principles of charity and philanthropy. Throughout the 19th century, Dublin's voluntary hospitals, like their British and American counterparts suffered financial hardships.[22] Therefore, while the fiscal uncertainty that plagued

Dublin's hospitals was far from a 20th-century phenomenon, the financial wellbeing of these institutions was at one of its worst ever stages by 1913. There were a number of reasons for this; firstly, Dublin's population had expanded far beyond the levels of the immediate post-famine era. While the national population was declining, the number living in Dublin increased significantly. The county population increased by 17% when compared to 1851 statistics, while the city population increased by 18%. In total, an extra 72,000 were living in Dublin when compared to 1851 levels.[23] Population growth forced the expansion of Dublin's hospital system as more people sought medical care. New wards were built and whole buildings constructed. The Meath Hospital, established in 1753, provided accommodation for 100 cases in 1851 but by 1913 had expanded its wards to cater for 160. St Vincent's Hospital also increased its accommodation by 60%.[24] Despite these additions, overcrowding was common. According to the Royal City of Dublin Hospital governors, 'if the hospital had 100 more beds available, they would all be filled to overflowing.'[25] Many of those seeking treatment in Dublin's hospitals were not residents in the county. In 1913, the Royal City Hospital admitted 1,536 patients from various parts of Ireland and Britain, including Roscommon and Liverpool.[26] Mrs Noel Guinness, member of the Linen Guild of the Royal City of Dublin Hospital, at the annual meeting of the Guild, criticised the pressure placed on Dublin hospitals by those resident in other counties as 'most major operations and serious cases of illness had to be sent to the city for medical treatment from all parts of Ireland, owing to the lack of nursing appliances and medical aid in country infirmaries.'[27] She claimed that by 1913, Dublin had become the 'dumping ground of all Ireland, and Ireland might be the dumping ground for the whole world.'[28]

While hospital governors and medical staff were in many cases, willing to care for additional patients, the risks posed to the institution by overcrowding were simply too great. As a consequence of increase in patient numbers, hospital expenditure rose to unprecedented levels threatening the very existence of the institutions. In 1913, governors of the Rotunda Lying-in Hospital authorised the construction of new buildings. This cost the institution in the region of £2,000, almost a quarter of its annual income.[29] As well as increasing the size of wards, governors had to ensure that their institution was well equipped with the latest advancements in medical science. This brought further expense to the hospitals as x-ray machines were installed or updated and operating theatres completely overhauled. On 13 January 1913, medical staff at the Meath Hospital requested governors to invest heavily in the construction and fitting out of two new theatres. According to the staff, the numbers requiring operations had increased rapidly over the past few years and costly improvements needed to be carried out.[30] Governors often sought alternative solutions to save on equipment expenditure, including a reliance on the medical staff to provide their own instruments. The governors of the Meath Hospital, when appointing a dental surgeon, were swayed in their decision after a letter was received by one of the candidates, Mr William Ogilvy stating 'if I am elected as Dentist, I shall supply all the instruments, sterilizer, dental chair, and other small things that may be necessary. The hospital will not be put to any expense.' Ogilvy was subsequently appointed to the post on the strength of his promise. Later in the year, when he lodged a request to the board for a new dentist chair, Ogilvy was instructed to refer back to his application letter.[31]

Financial worries for Dublin's hospitals also increased in 1913 as a consequence of the labour troubles prevalent throughout the city. During the outbreaks of violence, hospitals were forced to admit and treat a significant number of patients. On 6 September 1913, *The Irish Times* reported that some 300 people were treated in the space of 24 hours in Jervis Street Hospital following riots throughout Dublin city. The influx of patients was so sudden that the hospital abandoned normal admissions procedures – names of admissions were not taken and all medical staff, including resident students and nurses, was called to give assistance.[32] The range of injuries was wide. One policeman was treated after being struck in the face with a hammer while standing in a doorway. An ambulance car carrying injured people to the hospital was also set upon by a mob armed with stones and broken pipe.[33] Smaller disturbances continued throughout the month of September. On 26 September 1913, Sir Patrick Dun's Hospital admitted 20 men suffering from injuries after a riot among railway men on Lombard Street. Several others were treated in Jervis Street and Mercer's Hospital.[34] This influx of admissions increased hospital expenditure as additional fuel, food and medical supplies were required.

Indeed, the acquisition of supplies was also a concern for hospital governors during this period. In September 1913, as coal companies became involved in the labour disputes, many of the Dublin hospitals' coal supplies were depleted. The timing of this issue was particularly troublesome for hospital authorities. Usually, many of the Dublin hospitals re-opened beds in September that had been closed for the summer months. Due to fuel shortages these beds remained closed and furthermore, many hospitals were forced to close additional beds.[35] This limited their ability to provide medical care to Dublin's population. The stock of cotton wool and surgical dressings was also dangerously depleted by October 1913. While companies in England were prepared to provide dressings to Dublin's hospitals, they simply could not get the supply shipped and delivered owing to labour disputes in Ireland's capital. Under normal circumstances, the dressings available to Dublin hospitals would have lasted some two to three weeks, giving time to resolve the issue. However, the riots and the large number of injuries that required treatment meant that dressings were in heavy demand. Therefore, medical staff were forced to save on dressings whenever they could and wait for the delivery of new supplies later in the year.

BLOODSHED NIGHT AND DAY

APPALLING SCENES IN CITY

FIERCE BATON CHARGES.

HUNDREDS INJURED.

TWO MEN DEAD.

THE HOSPITAL RECORD

JERVIS STREET, 320; MERCER'S, 50; DUN'S, 65

MR. LARKIN ARRESTED

IN THE IMPERIAL HOTEL.

Fierce conflicts with the police, which gave rise to numerous baton charges, took place in the city on Saturday and yesterday.

As a result of these conflicts, a man named James Nolan, of 8 Spring Gardens, off Ballybough road, who was admitted to Jervis street Hospital on Saturday night, died from his wounds yesterday morning. He sustained a fracture of the base of the skull, caused, as it is alleged, by the stroke of a policeman's baton.

Wild scenes of excitement were witnessed in several parts of the city. There were repeated charges by the police, as the result of which over 200 people were treated in the various hospitals for scalp wounds.

A second death is reported to have occurred yesterday—that of a man who was treated at Jervis street Hospital and was subsequently conveyed to his home.

Yesterday Mr. Jim Larkin fulfilled his promise to address a meeting in O'Connell street. At half-past one o'clock he appeared on the balcony of the Imperial Hotel, disguised as an elderly gentleman, and proclaimed his identity to a crowd in the street.

Superintendent Murphy and a body of police immediately rushed into the hotel and effected his arrest.

When he appeared in custody a crowd gathered in the street and cheered him vigorously. The police repressed the demonstration and a series of fierce baton charges took place.

At the intersection of Princes street and O'Connell street a gathering of about 30 people was hemmed in between two lines of police. Everybody in the crowd was batoned vigorously and numbers were seriously injured.

During the afternoon rioting occurred in different parts of the city and many tramcars were attacked. On the Inchicore line the military were called out to reinforce the police.

On Saturday fresh warrants were issued for the arrest of Messrs. Larkin, Partridge and Connolly. The two latter were arrested on charges of provoking a breach of the peace. Mr. Partridge was allowed out on bail and Mr. Connolly, who refused to give bail, went to prison for three months.

Early on Sunday morning the Strike Committee decided to abandon the proclaimed meeting in O'Connell street and announced that a demonstration would be held in Croydon Park.

It was stated at Jervis street Hospital last night that the number of cases treated at that hospital yesterday and on Saturday was 320.

The Lord Mayor of Dublin purposes demanding a public inquiry into the conduct of the police and will instruct the Law Agent of the Corporation to appear at the inquests on the victims of baton charges.

charged forward, and with drawn batons laid round them with considerable effect.

PRUSUIT IN MARLBOROUGH STREET.

The crowd were pursued by about a score of constables up Marlborough street, past the Pro-Cathedral, and many had their flight accelerated by the application of policemen's truncheons. In the crash of stones and bottles a number of business establishments suffered, big breaches being in some of their windows. There was a cessation for a time, and the groups of police were opportunely augmented. Shortly before 11 o'clock, notwithstanding the precautions taken to prevent the formation of crowds in the streets, the police had another trying experience. A number of them were drawn up on the footway in Earl street between Messrs. Beckers' and Messrs. Boyers' establishments, and also on the opposite side. Suddenly a hail of stones, many being rough fragments of granite, and broken bottles came flying from along Talbot street and the corners of Marlborough street. Again the police followed up the rioters with promptness, and, with drawn batons attacked them. Down Lower Marlborough street about fifty of the roughs fled, and were afforded protection in a number of the houses. While the officers were following up the fugitives a volley of broken bottles and a few tumblers were hailed from windows in that section of the street. An exciting episode in this charge was that, while one young fellow was fleeing from the advancing police, he fell in front of an approaching motor car. Before the speed of the car was actually arrested a fine athletic young constable seized him by the middle and pulled him out of danger.

SATURDAY NIGHT SCENES.

BATON CHARGES IN O'CONNELL STREET.

When the excitement was at its height in Talbot street and North Earl street on Saturday evening there were repeated scenes also in O'Connell street, near Nelson's Pillar. Numbers of people, who were attracted apparently through curiosity to witness what was proceeding, found themselves frequently within dangerous distance of the police in their charges up to the O'Connell street end of North Earl street. A large body of police was on duty in the vicinity along O'Connell street, more along Henry street, and a third body in Prince's street. Whenever the stampedes appeared to be general one body or other of the police, rushed in and used their batons on the foremost of the crowd, and more than once individuals came in for rather severe treatment. In one case a young man, who was well ahead in one of these rushes from the danger zone, actually ran into a line of police who were charging up the centre of O'Connell street. He received a rather severe mauling.

After a number of experiences of this kind the crowd became anxious of any sign of excitement, and the least appearance of a police movement caused the people to disperse quickly.

AT O'CONNELL BRIDGE.

SEVERAL PERSONS INJURED.

There were a series of baton charges at O'Connell Bridge, where a large crowd had gathered. The police charges were continued along Eden quay, and at O'Connell Bridge and there was some hooting. The police, who were drawn up near O'Connell's Monument, were ordered to charge, and there was a vigorous attack on the crowd. A number of people who had pressed around out of curiosity were sufferers. Several persons were knocked down, and bleeding heads were common. Plain clothes officers assisted the uniformed constables, and this led to a number of unfortunate incidents. People in the crowd, not aware of the identity of the plain clothes men, resented their interference, with the result that there were unfortunate instances of innocent spectators suffering in common with more

men. Some angry expressions were directed to the officers as they passed along, but no attempt was made to rescue the prisoner. By twelve o'clock the streets had quieted down, and except for the presence of groups of policemen the Pillar and the streets running off it presented much their usual Saturday night appearance. In the attacks made on the policemen stationed in and about Talbot street some of the men were struck but not seriously injured. In the course of the evening Inspector Campbell was knocked down by a hackney car in Earl street but escaped without any worse consequence than a slight scratch.

SUNDAY SCENES.

MR. LARKIN'S ARREST.

There was not a policeman to be seen in or about Beresford place yesterday, when from 11 o'clock onward groups of people began to collect in front of Liberty Hall. Apparently however, large bodies of police were held in readiness within a short distance of the place, for during the morning from 10 o'clock onwards a number of large detachments of constables filed down Abbey street and on to Store street.

The first evidence of any unusual animation in Beresford place was the assembling of a large number of two horse brakes. These were quickly filled by members of the Irish Women Workers' Union, who had arranged for an excursion to the Glen of the Downs.

There were thirty-six brakes in all, and these were formed up in processional order. Led by a four-in-hand, they proceeded along Eden quay, the occupants of the brakes waving flags and singing "A Nation Once Again." They turned into O'Connell street and proceeded as far Parnell Monument, round which they wheeled, and retraced their line of route along the other side of the street across O'Connell Bridge, and on their journey.

Cheering and Booing.

Occasionally there were outbursts of cheering as the procession passed through O'Connell street, to which the crowds who had assembled on the footpaths responded.

Passing tramcars were vigorously hooted and booed by the women and children on the brakes. At this time not more than half a dozen constables were to be seen on duty in O'Connell street and they made no attempt to interfere with the demonstration.

The first appearance of activity on the part of the authorities with regard to the proclaimed meeting in O'Connell street was presented by the march of a strong body of sixty D.M.P. and R.I.C. men who took up a position at the corner of O'Connell street and Eden quay.

Within ten minutes other strong bodies of constabulary were in possession of the entire of O'Connell street, being disposed at points from Parnell Monument across the bridge to Carlisle Buildings and Westmoreland st.

All the intersecting streets were also guarded by strong forces.

At the corner of O'Connell street and Eden quay a large crowd apparently attracted by curiosity gathered around the police detachment. When their numbers had grown to some proportions, orders were given to disperse the crowd, and this was done without any display of force.

1. Hospitals overcrowded after 'Bloody Sunday'.
Evening Telegraph, 1 Sept. 1913.
DCLA

88

To overcome the difficulties caused by the events of 1913 and offset the growing financial commitment it was essential for governors to raise hospital income levels. Dublin voluntary hospitals collected income from various sources. Student fees were one notable source of income. In 1877, representatives from ten Dublin hospitals, including the Adelaide, Mater Misericordiae and Sir Patrick Dun's, met to agree a standard fee for students and apprentices in hospitals.[36] Many of these hospitals had close relationships with the city's medical schools that continued into and beyond 1913. The University of Dublin (Trinity College – TCD), University College Dublin (UCD) and the Royal College of Surgeons in Ireland (RCSI) all offered medical courses in Dublin. TCD was well-established as a centre of excellence in medical education.[37] By 1913, TCD offered 12 qualifications in medical related fields, including the Bachelor in Medicine (MB), Bachelor in Obstetrics (BAO) and Diploma in Public Health (DPH). UCD, which became a constituent college of the National University of Ireland in 1908, had a strong tradition of educating Catholic students at its former medical school on Cecilia Street which had been in operation since 1858. UCD offered six qualifications in medical related studies, including Doctor of Medicine (MD) and Master of Surgery (M.CH).[38] As part of the medical curriculum, each Dublin medical school required its students to acquire residency in local hospitals. This involved observing patients on the wards or receiving instruction in the operating theatres, depending on the course of study followed. Some of the universities had well-established relationships with particular hospitals. TCD, for example, had a strong connection with Sir Patrick Dun's Hospital. Dun's Hospital was visited daily by the medical and surgical staff, and clinical lectures were delivered to students twice each week for eight months of the year.[39] Aiming to provide students with an insight into the most prevalent diseases, clinical hospitals offered specialised classes and courses. In Dun's, clinical teaching on the diseases of women was given twice a week. In the special fever wing, regular clinical instruction was given throughout the year. Pathological and bacteriological demonstrations were given in the laboratories on a weekly basis. Special demonstrations were also given on diseases of the skin. A department for the treatment of throat, nose, and ear diseases was in operation in the hospital and this offered the opportunity to provide instruction in these subjects. There was also a department for dentistry, which allowed TCD to offer a Bachelor and Master in Dental Science.[40]

Various courses were also added to Dublin's medical education system in reaction to the diseases that were particularly widespread. In 1913, the medical profession and the LGBI sought to create a specialised course on the treatment of tuberculosis (TB). The Allan A. Ryan Home, a small Dublin hospital that offered 25 beds for the treatment of those suffering from consumption, established a two week programme of instruction for the treatment of TB. This was soon superseded by a full six month certificate course.

Dublin's clinical hospitals including the Adelaide, Royal City of Dublin, Doctor Steevens' and Jervis Street, also came together to offer a postgraduate course of clinical instruction in tuberculosis. The LGBI recognised this as part of the qualification 'required by them for appointment as medical superintendent in hospitals or dispensaries established by County Councils.'[41] The course commenced on 6 January 1913, was three months in duration and offered clinical instruction on the 'pathology, diagnosis, treatment and general management of TB.'[42] By providing additional courses like these, Dublin hospitals were able to boost their income, while at the same time provide the necessary instruction towards assisting medical professionals in their treatment of some of Dublin's most prevalent diseases.

GOVERNMENT DEPARTMENTS, IRELAND.   885*d*

List of Institutions approved by the Local Government Board for Ireland in pursuance of Section 16 (1) (a) of the National Insurance Act, 1911, for the treatment of cases of Tuberculosis.

Forster Green Sanatorium, Fortbreda, Belfast ; Royal Sanatorium for Consumptives, Newcastle, Co. Wicklow ; Crooksling Sanatorium, Brittas, Co. Dublin ; Heatherside Sanatorium, Doneraile, Co. Cork ; Rossclare Sanatorium, Killadeas, Co. Fermanagh (26 patients) ; Peamount Sanatorium, Lucan, Co. Dublin (52 patients) ; Allan A. Ryan Home Hospital, Pigeon House Road, Dublin (cases requiring isolation or Tuberculin treatment) ; Rostrevor Sanatorium, near Warrenpoint, Co. Down ; County Clare Sanatorium, Ennis ; Our Lady's Hospice for the Dying, Harold's Cross, Dublin (advanced cases) ; House of Rest, Camden Row, Dublin (advanced cases) ; St. Patrick's Hospital, Wellington Road, Cork (advanced cases) ; Jervis Street Hospital, Dublin (surgical cases) ; Dublin Skin, Cancer, &c., Hospital, Hume Street (surgical cases) ; St. Vincent's Hospital, Dublin (surgical cases).

2. *Thom's official directory*, 1913.

DCLA

Student fees, while offering significant financial benefits to some Dublin voluntary hospitals, were not the only income stream. The institutions also relied on income from other sources, including the Dublin Hospital Sunday Fund (DHSF). The fund, founded in 1874, was controlled by a steering committee, elected each year, which organised various fundraising events throughout the year for the benefit of Dublin's voluntary hospitals. A collection, organised by the fund committee, took place in churches throughout various parishes one Sunday a year. Dublin's hospitals applied to the Committee of Distribution for funds and the committee, led by Viscount Monck, a Justice of the Peace for Dublin, decided which hospitals received the available funds. Not all of Dublin's voluntary hospitals benefitted from the scheme. On its foundation in 1874, the Catholic Archbishop of Dublin refused to give the fund his backing. Archbishop Cullen argued that the centralised system of fundraising was not beneficial for Dublin's voluntary hospitals. As a result, the fund was financed primarily through collections at Protestant churches and locations throughout the diocese. Due to the absence of Catholic participation in the raising of the funds, it had long been decided that both the Mater Misericordiae and St Vincent's Hospital, two Catholic institutions, would be excluded from receiving any monies raised.[43] This stipulation remained in place throughout 1913 and it was not until the following year that the fund committee made a public appeal for Catholics to come on board and join in for 'the relief of Dublin hospitals'.[44] In total, 16 hospitals benefitted from the fund, including Sir Patrick Dun's Hospital, Dr Steevens', the Rotunda and the Adelaide. The sum of £3,120 was distributed among them with each hospital receiving different amounts depending on the committee's decision.[45]

Aside from the DHSF, the majority of Dublin's voluntary hospitals relied on income derived from their own subscription schemes. Through this system, prominent members of society and the general public contributed various sums of money to the hospital on an annual basis. A hospital's governor was essential in raising subscriptions as they utilised their standing in local society to encourage friends and colleagues to subscribe. Subscriptions varied in value depending on the financial resources of the contributor, with the most common subscription rate standing at £1-1-0. More prominent members of society regularly contributed a significantly larger sum through their subscriptions and bequests. Catherine Clarke, who lived in Rathmines at the time of her death, left an estate of over £38,000. The majority of this was given to Dublin's charitable institutions, including £2,000 to both St Vincent's Hospital and the Mater Misericordiae.[46] Geary has shown that many of the contributions to Dublin's hospitals throughout the 18th and 19th centuries were motivated by both social obligation and a large degree of self-interest.[47] The same can be said for those contributing to Dublin's hospitals in 1913. Many who donated sought some recognition in return. On 10 February 1913, Maxwell Arnott, one of Ireland's leading horse trainers and a member of the prominent Arnott family, promised a contribution of £25 per year to the Meath Hospital on the condition a bed be named in his honour.[48] William Carson, board member of the Great Northern Railway, contributed £25 to the Royal City of Dublin Hospital, with the stipulation that a plaque dedicated to his wife be erected above the bed. Many of Dublin's voluntary hospital beds, as a consequence, were named after prominent members of Dublin's population.

Dublin hospitals undoubtedly benefited from the generosity of the region's population. However, their over-reliance on charitable donations was a flawed financial model which played victim to downturns in public financial support. By 1913, income derived from subscriptions had decreased significantly in comparison with previous years. According to some, 'only for people dying occasionally and leaving legacies the hospitals could not be kept up at all.'[49] When combined with an increasing demand for their services, the difficulty caused by the labour movements and the rising cost of care, Dublin's voluntary hospital system was in serious difficulty. To survive, hospitals took out substantial bank overdrafts. In December 1913, Mercer's Hospital had an overdraft of over £4,000, the Royal City of Dublin, c. £7,000 and the Meath Hospital owed a balance of £8,000.[50]

In December 1913, Ulster Bank requested that the Royal City Hospital make some attempt to lower its financial commitment to the bank as this was 'spiralling out of control'.[51] Hospital governors were compelled to examine ways of increasing subscriptions. However, before attempting this, it was essential to recognise and overcome one of the primary obstacles affecting income levels – the National Insurance Act.

NATIONAL HEALTH INSURANCE COMMISSION (IRELAND).

PEMBROKE HOUSE. UPPER MOUNT STREET, DUBLIN.

Commissioners.—Joseph A. Glynn, Chairman ; Walter S. Kinnear, Deputy-Chairman : William J. Maguire. Medical Commissioner : Mrs. M. L. Dickie.
Secretary.—John Houlihan.
Assistant Secretary.—Pierce Kent.
Accountant.—D. P. Gallagher.
Private Secretary to Chairman.—J. B. Shortt.
First Class Clerks and Assistant Accountants (arranged alphabetically).—J. A. Duffy, V. J. Fielding, J. E. Finn, W. R. Maconkey, J. A. M'Carron, A. F. J. Moran, C. J. Murphy.
Second Class Clerks and Examiners (arranged alphabetically).—C. F. J. Bell, P. Bradley (acting), R. W. Bresland, J. Calveley, D. J. Coveney, P. Dempsey. W. Dunne, G. T. Fidler, D. Finn, J. Fitzgerald, J. W. Gentleman, E. J. Gillgan (acting), J. S. Godden, T. J. Healy, A. Hollinshead|(acting), W.J. Kavanagh. H. A. M'Cartan (acting), J. O'Brien, C. J. O'Connell, E. O'Neill, J. Rogerson, R. J. Sheridan, J. B. Shortt, H. A. Sloan, T. Turner.
Assistant Clerks.—P. J. Byrne, J. W Bourke, C. A. Brennan, T. V. Brennan, J. Bonfield, A. J. Carrigg, E. P. Connell, T. P. Corby, T. J. Dunne, P.J. Finlay, T. J. Harding. W. Harley, M. Keegan, T E. Linton, T. M'Kenna, V. M. P. MacMahon, V. E. M. Mac-Swiney, B. E. Mulvin, H Paisley, V. Parslow, F. W. Powell, J. P Reardon, J. S. Robinson (Supervising), F. J.Shouldice, J. R. Spencer, T. Sugrue, T. J. Wilson (Supervising).
Typists.—Nineteen.

OUTDOOR STAFF.

Chief Inspector.—Cecil H. Darley.
Inspectors.—J. Cassedy, S. Clandillon, F. Guy, T. Roche, W. Walker, Mrs. N. H. Walker.
Assistant Inspectors.—G. A. Armstrong, J. C. Austin, S. J. Bolton, Miss J. M. Campbell, Mrs. M. Cosgrave, T. Concannon, Miss E. Donnelly, J. M. English. J. L. Graves, E. Hutchinson, Miss S. Johnstone, J. P. Kennedy, J. H. Killough, R. F. Mack, H. P. Moloney, P. M'Closkey, R. J. Thompson, R. V. Walker, J. B. Wells.
Health Insurance Officers.—Twenty-five.
Medical Officers.—John O'Donoghue, Charles Dickson.
Assistant Medical Officer.—Seamus O'Beirn.
Legal Adviser.—J. F. Culhane.
Actuary.—J. G. Kyd.

COUNTY BOROUGH COMMITTEES.
Names and Addresses of Temporary Clerks.

Belfast.—W. Adair, 64 Royal-avenue, Belfast.
Cork.—Alderman P. H. Meade, Barrack-street, Cork.
Dublin.—The Town Clerk, City Hall, Dublin.
Limerick.—Laurence O'Donnell, 6 Lower Mallow-street, Limerick.
Londonderry.—Sir F. Henry Miller, Guildhall, Londonderry.
Waterford.—T. J. Morrissey, 16 St. Ursula-terrace, Waterford.

COUNTY COMMITTEES.
Names and Addresses of Temporary Clerks.

Antrim.—Alexander Millar, County Court House, Belfast.
Armagh.—T. E. Reid, Court House, Armagh.
Carlow.—R. F. Keogh, Court House, Carlow.
Cavan.—Peter Levins, Court House, Cavan.
Clare.—Daniel O'Brien, Court House, Ennis.
Cork.—T. M'Carthy, Court House, Cork.
Donegal.—Bernard M'Fadden, Court House, Lifford.
Down.—John Fleming, Court House, Downpatrick.
Dublin.—A. Keogh-Nolan, 11 Rutland-square, Dublin.
Fermanagh.—Thomas Maguire, The Orchard, Enniskillen.
Galway.—W. G. Fogarty, Court House, Galway.
Kerry.—Edmund Harty, County Hall, Tralee.
Kildare.—Thomas Langan, Court House, Naas.
Kilkenny.—F. W. Doheny, John's Bridge, Kilkenny.
King's.—C. P. Kingston, Court House, Tullamore.
Leitrim.—John F. Keany, Cloonaghmore, Glenfarne, Enniskillen.
Limerick.—John J. Quaid, 82 O'Connell-street, Limerick.
Londonderry.—T. B. Adams, County Court House, Londonderry.
Longford.—Michael M'Cann, Court House, Longford.
Louth.—Valentine Warren, Bachelor's Walk, Dundalk.
Mayo.—J. T. Kelly, Court House, Castlebar.
Meath.—B. A. Grogan, Court House, Navan.
Monaghan.—D. C. Rushe, Court House, Monaghan.
Queen's.—Henry G. Scully, 2 Church-street, Maryboro'.
Roscommon.—William Kilmartin, Abbey-street, Roscommon.
Sligo.—John R. Keating, 13 Castle-street, Sligo.
Tipperary (N.R.).—William O'Brien, Court House, Nenagh.
Tipperary (S.R.).—Jeremiah Ryan, Court House, Clonmel.
Tyrone.—Claude C. Hamilton, Court House, Omagh.
Waterford.—Thomas B. Boyle, County Offices, Dungarvan.
Westmeath.—J. T. Roche, County Chambers, Mullingar.
Wexford.—N. J. Frizelle, Court House, Wexford.
Wicklow.—T. J. O'Reilly, Court House, Wicklow.

3. *Thom's official directory*, 1913.

DCLA

National Insurance Act

On 16 December 1911, the National Insurance Act received royal assent. The act was designed to give protection to workers, primarily those involved in industrial work, who lost income as a consequence of illness. Workers, employers and the state financially contributed to the arrangement, with friendly societies administering the benefits to their members. The scheme was also open to voluntary contributors including those from the self-employed, who if they wanted to join were required to pay both the worker's and employer's portion.[52] The act offered five benefits to the insured – medical, maternity, sickness, sanatorium and disability. There were distinct differences in the application of the act in Britain and Ireland. Ireland, in contrast to Britain, was home to few friendly societies. In Britain, membership of these societies reached almost six million, while in Ireland the number of members stood at 40,000.[53] Even allowing for differences in population, this was still a significant variance. As a consequence, the number of insured persons in Ireland was minimal as opposed to the percentage in Britain. By 1913, only 16 % of Ireland's population was insured under the provisions of the act.[54] In addition, after much debate among Irish medical professionals, their national associations (British Medical Association and Irish Medical Association) and political parties, it was decided to implement the act in Ireland without medical benefit attached.[55] Therefore, medical attendance by a general practitioner and medicines was not offered to the insured worker. With few insured and less benefits offered, it would appear that the impact of the act in Ireland may have been minimal. However this was not the case as far as medical care in Dublin was concerned. A significant number of those insured resided in Dublin. For example, 22.9% of people in Dublin County Borough were insured as opposed to 3.63% in Mayo.[56] Also, even without medical benefit, employers, workers and the state still contributed a significant financial sum to satisfy the terms of the act. This financial commitment, along with the provisions of the act itself had a detrimental impact on medical care and the medical profession in Dublin throughout 1913.

Impact on health care and the medical profession in Dublin

In principle, the benefits of the National Insurance Act were designed to ease the negative impact of illness on the insured. However these provisions caused some serious problems that threatened to undermine the processes of medical care in Dublin. Firstly, the National Insurance Act was primarily responsible for a significant decrease in Dublin voluntary hospital income streams. As was the case in Britain, subscriptions to Dublin's hospitals deteriorated following the introduction of the act.[57] Income from subscriptions for the Royal Hospital for Incurables decreased from £2,007 in 1910 to £1,533 in 1913. There were also decreases in subscription income for many of the other hospitals

The Insurance Act Explained.

This Act will come into force on July 15th, 1912, if nothing occurs in the meantime to prevent the working of it.

As it will affect all manual workers over 16 years of age, and all others over this age whose incomes do not exceed £160 a year, we give a concise summary of the principal clauses.

INSURANCE IS COMPULSORY.

For workers of either sex who earn less than £160 a year.

For all engaged in manual labour, no matter how much they are paid.

The age limits for both classes are 16 to 70.

VOLUNTARY INSURANCE.

Anybody and everybody who is not included in either of the classes that come under the heading of compulsory, and who is dependent for a living on some regular employment, such as small shopkeepers and tradesmen, etc., working on their own account and earning less than £160 a year, may become voluntary contributors.

RATES OF PAYMENT.

IN ENGLAND.

Men pay	... ...	4d a week.
Women	... ...	3d. a week.
Employers	... ...	3d. a week.
The State nominally pays		2d. a week.

IN IRELAND.

Men pay	... ...	3d. a week.
Women	... ..	2d. a week.
Employer	... ...	2½d. a week.

The reason for the lower rates in Ireland is that the Medical Benefits—about the only good thing in the whole Act—do not apply to this country.

4. *Irish Worker*, 13 Jan. 1912.

DCLA

including Steevens', Royal Victoria Eye and Ear and the Meath. The Board of Superintendence of Dublin Hospitals surmised that 'in a boom year, when charitable subscriptions might be expected to be heavy, there can be only one explanation for their extraordinary smallness, and the explanation is the Insurance Act'.[58] Indeed, many contributors to the insurance scheme felt that the levies applied by the act alleviated them of any further financial responsibility towards health care in Dublin and thus discontinued their philanthropic support of Dublin's hospitals. A similar reaction to new legislation had threatened the voluntary hospitals in the late 1830s, following the introduction of the Irish Poor Law.[59] Hospitals went on a public relations offensive in an attempt to improve the situation. The governors of the Royal City of Dublin Hospital, in their annual report, proclaimed that:

> It is to be feared that many of the usual supporters of the hospital have refrained from subscribing in the belief that the National Insurance Act affords some set off as against the expense of dealing with sickness in hospitals. This is by no means the case.[60]

While investigations and pleas were carried out, the possibility of implementing cost-cutting measures was examined and in some cases, new measures implemented. Expenditure on non-essential medical equipment was curtailed. The Royal City of Dublin and the Meath hospitals considered closing beds.[61] The City of Dublin Hospital examined the possibility of treating more of those seeking admission in their own homes rather than in the hospital wards. However, the housing conditions of the poorer classes rendered this idea 'useless and dangerous'.[62] Mercer's Hospital in an attempt to control finance introduced a new admissions clause - 'any patients sent in from this date until further order in excess of the number authorised by the Board shall have to be paid for by the medical gentlemen authorising the admission.'[63] Governors of Mercer's also prohibited the admissions of country patients, those from outside the county boundary, who were not paying for treatment. Therefore, ironically, the National Insurance Act, designed to ease the impact of illness on the worker, instead contributed largely to the curtailing of hospital services in Dublin in 1913.

Maternity benefit, which covered the cost of medical attendance by a registered medical practitioner or certified midwife at childbirth, posed a further threat to Dublin's hospitals. Maternity benefit was part of a wider movement to protect infant and maternal health, a constant societal concern in the early 20th century.[64] Infantile mortality was particularly high in Dublin. In January 1913, the Dean of St Patrick's Cathedral dedicated his sermon to the issue arguing that much had been done to reduce the rate, particularly by female voluntary helpers. However, there was much more to do and he encouraged the wider support in the movement to protect children's health.[65] Assisting women with the costs of childbirth through the provision of maternity benefit appeared to be a positive step. However, in reality it seriously threatened the very existence of maternity hospitals in Dublin. It was decided, on the introduction of the act, that maternity benefit would only be offered to women who gave birth away from the maternity hospital. Those who gave birth in maternity hospitals would not receive the 30 shillings offered under the provision, as hospital care was free of charge.[66] This caused 'considerable apprehension' for the maternity hospitals in Dublin, as they feared women would opt for the shilling over hospital care and thus completely undermine their *raison d'être*.[67] If there were no patients, the likelihood of encouraging philanthropic donations was greatly diminished.

Equally important, as noted, Dublin's hospitals were great teaching centres. The maternity hospitals were no different, and unlike some of the other hospitals, they received a significant amount of income from pupil fees.[68] A decrease in patient admissions would have seriously diminished the hospitals' capacity to provide education to medical students and thus hospital income would have been greatly affected. By 1913, governors of Dublin's maternity hospitals had seen enough to know that the impact of the Insurance Act was highly detrimental. In response, they came together to enter into negotiation with friendly societies to recommend their insured women to go into the hospital, where they would receive nine days treatment at the cost of 5s. This 5s. came from the 30s. provided under the provisions of the act. For those women who preferred to be treated at home, the hospitals would send their staff to the woman's house for the same fee.[69] This agreement satisfied Dublin's maternity hospitals. The fees offered under the insurance act offered some assistance towards the hospitals' constant financial struggle. More importantly, it encouraged women to avail themselves of the services offered by Dublin's maternity hospitals and cemented their prominent place in providing care to mother and infant.

Sickness benefit, designed to reduce the negative financial impact of illness on workers who were forced to take time off work due to sickness, also threatened Dublin's medical infrastructure. According to the act, sick workers would receive their entitlements on the production of a medical certificate. Dublin's medical personnel were prepared to issue these certificates but only at a rate of remuneration which they considered to be adequate. On 18 March 1913, a conference between the County Insurance Committees and the Irish Commissioners of National Insurance took place. This meeting was organised to discuss the allocation of a £50,000 grant given by the British Exchequer towards dealing with the issue of medical certification. It was agreed that the grant would be 'distributed on a capitation basis by the different Insurance committees among medical practitioners on a panel who agree to provide all medical certificates required by approved societies and Insurance committees.'[70] It was decided to offer Dublin doctors a rate of remuneration of 9d. for medical certificates. Doctors were outraged by the offer. On 12 April 1913, at a specially convened meeting, the 'whole medical profession of Dublin' opted to reject the terms offered as 'totally inadequate'.[71] All Dublin doctors were urged to show solidarity on this and 11 medical practitioners who had already signed an agreement with the Insurance Commissioners were encouraged to withdraw their names from the panel in a 'doctor's strike'. Yet, solidarity among all levels of Dublin's medical profession was rare. Dr Maurice Hayes, member of the Conjoint Committee of the British and Irish Medical Associations, gave a brief synopsis of this, 'in Dublin, as in all large cities and capitals, there is a certain attraction to young men just qualified to remain in the capital, and these men, starting in Dublin without any resources to keep them going until they get practice, are quite ready to accept societies [work] … at a very small rate.'[72] This division between the established Dublin medical professional and their newly qualified counterparts continued throughout 1913. Insurance commissioners also looked outside the county boundary and appointed medical officers to travel into Dublin to certify sick workers.[73] This arrangement, while wholly impractical, continued to operate until the following year as Dublin medical personnel maintained their opposition to what they believed to be wholly inadequate fees.

Sanatorium benefit was introduced to provide workers with 'free maintenance in a sanatorium or hospital while undergoing treatment for tuberculosis.'[74] It too had an impact on medical care in Dublin. As noted, the tuberculosis epidemic in Ireland was a major problem for Dublin health authorities. The city's slum housing conditions, widespread in 1913, encouraged the spread of the disease. Voluntary organisations like the Women's National Health Association played a significant role in trying to lessen the impact of the disease in Dublin.[75] With the introduction of sanatorium benefit through the National Insurance Act, it was hoped to encourage the working man to enter sanatoria quickly. According to Jones, the worker often resisted entering a hospital or sanatorium fearing that their income would suffer.[76] By providing some financial security, the act attempted to combat this reaction. However, in reality, by 1913 the National Insurance Act had little effect on admissions to sanatoria. This was partly because the number of beds available in specialised institutions for the treatment of tuberculosis was nominal. To combat this, under the provisions of the National Insurance Act, funds were earmarked for the construction of new TB hospitals in Ireland. A sum of £145,623 was provided under the act for this purpose.[77] Using some of this money, construction of the new Peamount Sanatorium was completed. In addition to the Crooksling Sanatorium, Peamount offered care and accommodation for Dublin's TB sufferers. The Meath Hospital also using funds garnered from the provisions of the act, established wards for the reception and treatment of surgical and advanced cases of tuberculosis.[78] From 1 May, three beds were put in each ward and two beds were rented to Dublin County Council at a cost of £100 per year. Further plans to develop the site to provide a fully equipped TB dispensary on the grounds of the hospital, which would be controlled by Dublin County Council were also discussed.[79] This new dispensary was fully operational two years later. Therefore, sanatorium benefit, unlike the other provisions of the National Insurance Act, posed no real threat to Dublin's medical infrastructure. Instead, it offered the finance necessary for the expansion and improvement of services. However, the uptake and use of this funding by Dublin authorities was slow and as a consequence, the impact of sanatorium benefit on healthcare in Dublin during 1913 was minimal.

In contrast, one provision that many Dublin workers felt would be instantly beneficial was medical benefit. Medical benefit was offered in Britain under the provisions of the National Insurance Act. It covered attendance by a medical practitioner and also provided for any medicines required. Its omission from the National Insurance Act (Ireland) caused much controversy.[80] On 4 February 1913, a parliamentary committee was established to consider and report on the advisability of expanding the benefits available to the insured.[81] The committee held interviews with various prominent members of Dublin's trade unions, employers and members of the medical profession with the hope of finding some consensus on the issue.[82] Opinions varied among individuals but those interviewed held positions that enabled them to provide some insight into the views held by the majority in each sector. Chaired by Lord Ashby St Ledger, former Paymaster General of the British Government, and including various personnel from the National Health Insurance Commission, the Treasury and the LGBI, the committee adopted an interrogative style of questioning hoping to find a solution to the medical benefit question. Richard O'Carroll, representative of the Dublin United Trades Council and Labour League, was interviewed by the committee.[83] The Council and Labour League represented some 40,000 workers in the city and county. According to O'Carroll, Dublin's workers were unanimous in their demand for the extension of medical benefits.[84]

William Martin Murphy, in his capacity as president of Dublin's Chamber of Commerce was also examined. Murphy and his fellow chamber members, the principal employers of labour in Dublin, passed a resolution against the extension of medical benefit to Ireland.[85] Murphy believed that the adoption of medical benefit was not an urgent issue. Instead, he hoped Ireland would adopt a 'wait and see' approach and examine the long-term effects of medical benefit in England before committing itself to the legislation.[86] Of course many of Dublin's employers were also concerned with the cost involved in providing medical benefit. F. G. Coldwell, representative of the Mercantile Association of Dublin, a body of 1,400 traders and manufacturers who employed a great number of workers in the Dublin area, complained that the legislation would 'mean a considerable increase in cost, and would mean a considerable tax, both upon the workers and upon the employers, without any real increased benefits.'[87]

Conflicting attitudes between employees and employers aside, the attitudes of the Irish medical profession, particularly those based in Dublin, played a key role in the eventual decision not to extend medical benefit to Ireland. Members of the medical profession interviewed by the committee, while not against the principle of medical benefit, were wary of participating in a system that would hurt the earning power of the profession. As a consequence, those interviewed made it apparent that any medical personnel involved in the provisions of medical benefit would have to be properly remunerated for their services. Maurice Hayes, when asked to provide the committee with an acceptable figure of payment, quoted 21s. as a base capitation fee for doctors to attend to an insured worker and dependents.[88] This rate was treble the fee agreed in Britain and completely unworkable.[89] The reluctance of high-standing general practitioners to undertake contract work was another major obstacle. As Barrington has argued, many well-established medical personnel saw contract work, in contrast to work in voluntary hospitals and general practices, as demeaning and detrimental to their status.[90] Some of the few friendly societies that existed in Ireland were urged to continue to offer their own medical benefit clause, but by 1913 it was still not legislatively obliged to do so. The subsequent release of the committee's report in August was met with little reaction by employers and employees.[91] Instead, the issue of medical benefit fell into the background as confrontations between both parties developed into the Dublin Lockout later in the month. However, for Dublin's medical institutions and profession, the battle against the threat of the National Insurance Act continued into the following year.

Conclusion

By 1913, Dublin's medical infrastructure was well established and provided medical care to a population suffering from various ailments and diseases. However, the events of 1913 threatened to expose the many cracks that were underlying the foundations of this system. In particular, the labour disputes and the National Insurance Act combined to seriously threaten the already fragile system of voluntary hospitals in Dublin. The rising cost of care, perpetuated by labour difficulties in the city, coupled with an increasing demand for hospital beds, placed Dublin's voluntary hospitals under severe pressure. The National Insurance Act, rather than assist these institutions in their desire to provide a good standard of care, only perpetuated the financial difficulties experienced by Dublin's hospitals. The act reduced an already weak source of income with its effect on voluntary hospital subscription rates and caused much division among the city's medical profession.

The impact of many of the issues that arose in 1913 continued beyond the end of the year. The issue of finance for Dublin's voluntary hospitals in particular proved to be a long-lasting problem for hospital governors and continued well into the 20th century.[92] The National Insurance Act and the rigorous debates concerning it also continued until the latter half of 1914. Dublin's medical profession continued its opposition and looked towards achieving favourable terms for the region's medical personnel. However, the outbreak of the First World War distracted the medical profession from these problems as doctors and voluntary hospital governors within the city focussed on providing care to returning sick and wounded soldiers. As a consequence, the issues that threatened the system of medical care in Dublin and the city's medical profession's preoccupation with the National Insurance Act receded for a brief period.

Appendix

Table 1. Dublin Hospitals, 1913

Hospital	Year of Establishment	Received Grants from Parliament	Number of Beds	Received Paying Patients
Drumcondra Hospital	1818		35	(+)
Adelaide Hospital	1858		137	
Allan A. Ryan Home Hospital for consumption	1910		25	
Children's Hospital Temple Street	1872		90	(+)
Dublin City Hospital for Diseases of Skin and Cancer – Holles Street	1899		15	
Coombe lying in hospital and Guinness Dispensary	1826	✔	68	(+)
Dr Steevens' Hospital	1720	✔	200	(+)
Fever Hospital and House of Recovery, Cork Street	1804	✔	270	
Hardwicke Hospital (House of Industry)	1803	✔	77	
Incorporated Orthopaedic Hospital of Ireland, Merrion Street	1876		80	(+)
Jervis Street Hospital	1718 (Rebuilt 1886)		130	
Mater Misericordiae Hospital	1861		345	
Meath Hospital and County of Dublin Infirmary	1753	✔	160	(+)
Mercer's Hospital	1734		81	(+)
Monkstown Hospital	1835		25	(+)
National Children's Hospital	1821		45	
National Lying-in Hospital, Holles Street	1894		60	(+)
Our Lady's Hospice for the Dying, Harold's Cross	1879		110	(+)
P. F. Collier Memorial Dispensary for Prevention of Tuberculosis	1911		N/A	
Provident Infirmary and General Dispensary	1873		N/A	(+)
Richmond Hospital (House of Industry)	1810	✔	87	
Rotunda Lying-In Hospital	1745	✔	130	
Royal City of Dublin Hospital – Baggot Street	1832 (Rebuilt in 1893)		124	(+)

Hospital	Year of Establishment	Received Grants from Parliament	Number of Beds	Received Paying Patients
Royal Hospital for Incurables, Donnybrook	1743	✔	213	
Royal Victoria Eye and Ear Hospital	1844	✔	82	(+)
St Vincent's Hospital and Dispensary	1834		160	
Simpson's Hospital for blind and gouty patients	1779		70	
Sir Patrick Dun's Hospital	1808		104	(+)
Skin, Cancer and Urinary Hospital	1911		24	(+)
St Michael's Hospital	1874		50	
Westmoreland Lock (Government) Hospital	1792	✔	100	
Whitworth Hospital (House of Industry)	1817	✔	60	

(+) – Denotes that paying patients are received

Source: *Medical directory of Ireland* (London, 1913), pp 1541-3.

Table 2. List of witnesses interviewed by the committee appointed to inquire into the extension of Medical Benefit under the National Insurance Act to Ireland

Name	Association
The Countess of Aberdeen	Women's National Health Association
Dr E. Whitley Allsom	Conjoint Committee, IMA, BMA.
Dr Marion Andrews	Slainte Approved Society
A. B. Barrand	Prudential Approved Society
P. Bourke	Vice-Chairman, Limerick Board of Guardians
P. Bradley	President, Cork County Land and Labour Association
Dr S. B. Coates	Conjoint Committee, IMA, BMA.
F. G. Coldwell	Dublin Mercantile Association
John Cotter	Clerk, Cork Board of Guardians
W. Crimmins	South Dublin Board of Guardians
D. J. Daly	St Finbar's Diocesan Health Insurance Society
G. J. Daly	St Finbar's Diocesan Health Insurance Society
Dr T. A. Davidson	Conjoint Committee, IMA, BMA.
D. Denehy	Cork District Trades Council
W. J. Dollar	Chairman and Managing Director, Duke Line Shipping Company

Name	Association
D. P. Gallagher	Accountant, Irish Insurance Commission
Mary Galway	Secretary, Women's Textile Operatives Society of Ireland
Dr J. P. Garland	Poor Law Dispensary Medical Officer, Dublin
Samuel Gibson	Ex-President, Chemists and Druggists' Association
C. W. Gordon	Londonderry Chamber of Commerce
Dr Maurice Hayes	Conjoint Committee, IMA, BMA.
J. Hutchinson	General Secretary, Irish National Foresters
Dr R. J. Johnstone	Vice-Chairman, Conjoint Committee, IMA, BMA.
Revd. P. Kerlin	Derry Diocesan Friendly Society
J. G. Kyd	Actuary to Irish Insurance Commission
T. Lawler	Limerick Federation of Friendly Societies
Dr P. G. Lee	Conjoint Committee, IMA, BMA.
E. J. Long	Limerick Chamber of Commerce
D. Lynch	Chairman, North Dublin Board of Guardians
P. Lynch	Cork United Trades and Labour Council
Revd. T McCotter	Down and Connor Diocesan Health Society
Dr D. A. McCurdy	Conjoint Committee, IMA, BMA.
W. J. McNulty	Londonderry Trades Council
J. Murphy	Belfast Trades Council
W. M. Murphy	Dublin Chamber of Commerce (president)
R. S. H. Noble	Orange and Protestant Friendly Society
P. Nolan	Waterford Trades and Labour Council
J. D. Nugent	Ancient Order of Hibernians Approved Society
R. O'Carroll	Dublin United Trades Council and Labour League
R. P. O'Connor	Limerick Trades and Labour Council
M. J. O'Lehane	Parliamentary Committee, Irish Trades Union Congress and Irish Drapers' Assistants' Association
Dr W. J. O'Sullivan	Conjoint Committee IMA, BMA. (Limerick)
A. P. Phelan	Waterford Chamber of Commerce
D. D. Sheehan	Member of Parliament for Mid-Cork and President of Irish Land Labour Association
S. Suffern	Chemists and Druggists' Society of Ireland
N. Thompson	Union Friendly Society
Sir W. J. Thompson	Registrar-General for Ireland
A. W. Watson	Chief Actuary, National Health Insurance Joint Committee
D. M. Watson	Vice-President, Pharmaceutical Society of Ireland

Name	Association
K. B. Williams	Cork Incorporated Chamber of Commerce and Shipping
H. Kingsley Wood	National Amalgamated Approved Society

Source: *Appendices to the report of the committee appointed to inquire into the extension of Medical Benefit under the National Insurance Act to Ireland* **[Cd.7039] H.C. 1913, xxxvii, pp iii-iv.**

Notes

1   See Mary E. Daly, *Dublin the deposed capital: a social and economic history, 1860-1914* (Cork, 1984); Mary E. Daly, 'A tale of two cities: 1860-1920', in Art Cosgrove (ed.), *Dublin through the ages* (Dublin, 1988), pp 113-32.

2   This is an approximate number based on figures from *Medical directory for Ireland* (London, 1913), p. 2. The returns of the *Medical directory* are not complete. Figures were based on individual medical practitioners submitting information. This did not always occur and thus, some information was outdated.

3   W. E. Vaughan and A. J. Fitzpatrick, *Irish historical statistics: population, 1821-1971* (Dublin, 1878), p. 3.

4   For studies on Ireland's dispensary system, asylums and Poor Law institutions see Catherine Cox, 'Access and engagement: the Medical Dispensary Service in post-Famine Ireland', in Catherine Cox and Maria Luddy (eds), *Cultures of care in Irish medical history, 1750-1970* (Basingstoke, 2010), pp 57-78; Mark Finnane, *Insanity and the insane in post Famine Ireland* (London, 1981); Virginia Crossman, *The Poor Law in Ireland, 1838-1948* (Dundalk, 2006).

5   A significant repository of material relating to Dublin's voluntary hospitals is held in the National Archives of Ireland (2007/128; BR2006/86; 2D/36/36; 2D/38/52), Trinity College Dublin (Adelaide Hospital Collection) and the Royal College of Physicians of Ireland (DCHC/1).

6   Mary E. Daly, '"An atmosphere of sturdy independence": the state and the Dublin hospitals in the 1930s', in Elizabeth Malcolm and Greta Jones (eds), *Medicine, disease and the state in Ireland, 1650-1940* (Cork, 1999), p. 235.

7   See Laurence M. Geary, *Medicine and charity in Ireland, 1718-1851* (Dublin, 2004); Daly, 'Atmosphere of sturdy independence', pp 234-52.

8   For a discussion on debates leading up to the introduction of the National Insurance Act in Ireland see Ruth Barrington, *Health, medicine and politics in Ireland, 1900-1970* (Dublin, 1987).

9   *Fifty-sixth annual report of the Board of Superintendence of the Dublin hospitals, 1913-1914,* [Cd.7576], H.C. 1914, xix, 44, p. 5.

10   Daly, *Dublin;* Greta Jones, *'Captain of all these men of death': the history of tuberculosis in nineteenth and twentieth century Ireland* (Amsterdam, 2001), p. 11.

11   *Report of the committee appointed by the Local Government Board for Ireland to inquire into the public health of the city of Dublin* [Cd.243] H.C. 1900, p. xxxix.

12   Jones, *Captain of all these men of death*, p. 11.

13   *Report of the Local Government Board for Ireland for the year ended 31 March 1914* [Cd.7561] H.C. 1914, xxxix, p. xxxvii.

14   Ibid., p. 68.

15   *Medical directory for Ireland* (London, 1913), pp 1541-3.

16   Geary, *Medicine and charity,* p. 2.

17   Royal City of Dublin Hospital (hereafter RCDH), *Annual report* (NAI, 2D/38/52, p. 26).

18   Geary, *Medicine and charity,* p. 3.

19   RCDH, *Annual report* (NAI, 2D/38/52 p. 17).

20   For a study on British hospitals, see Lindsay Granshaw, 'The hospital' in W. F. Bynum and Roy Porter (eds), *Companion encyclopaedia of the history of medicine,* vol. II (London, 1993), pp 1180-203; Hilary Marland, 'The changing role of the hospital, 1800-1900', in Deborah Brunton (ed.), *Medicine transformed: health, disease and society in Europe, 1800-1930* (Manchester, 2004), pp 31-58.

21   *Fifty-sixth annual report of the Board of Superintendence of the Dublin hospitals, 1913-1914,* [Cd.7576], H.C. 1914, xix, 44, p. 43.

22   W. F. Bynum, 'Medical philanthropy after 1850', in *Companion encyclopaedia of the history of medicine*, p. 1485.

23   Vaughan and Fitzpatrick, *Irish historical statistics*, p. 5.

24   *Medical directory: 1913*, p. 1541.

25   RCDH, *Annual report* (NAI, 2D/38/52, p. 8).

26   Ibid., p. 9.

27   *Irish Independent*, 17 Dec. 1913.

28   Ibid.

29   *Fifty-sixth annual report of the Board of Superintendence of the Dublin hospitals, 1913-1914,* [Cd.7576], H.C. 1914, xix, 44.

30   Meath Hospital Minute Book, 13 January 1913 (NAI, 2007/128, 5-3, p. 286).

31   Ibid., p. 288

32   *Irish Times*, 6 Sept. 1913.

33   Ibid.

34   *Irish Times*, 27 Sept. 1913.

35   Anon, 'The Dublin hospitals and the coal strikes', *British Medical Journal,* no. 2 (1913), p. 766.

36   Fees for students and apprentices were set at 12 guineas for nine months, eight guineas for six months and five guineas for three months. For more information on the Dublin Clinical Hospitals Standing Committee and student fees (RCPI Archive, DCHC/1; DCHC/2/2).

37   C. H. Holland, *Trinity College Dublin and the idea of a university* (Dublin, 1991), p. 20.

38   F. O. C. Meenan, *Cecilia Street: the Catholic University School of Medicine, 1855-1931* (Dublin, 1987).

39   *Medical directory: 1913*, p. 1541.

40   Anon, 'Ireland', *British Medical Journal*, no. 2 (1913), p. 618.

41   Dublin Clinical Hospitals Standing Committee correspondence, January 1913 (RCPI, DCHC/2/9).

42   Ibid.

43   Gerard Fealy, *A history of apprenticeship nurse training in Ireland* (London, 2005), p. 21.

44   *Irish Times*, 28 Mar. 1914.

45   Ibid.

46   *Irish Times*, 24 Aug. 1912.

47   Geary, *Medicine and charity,* p. 4.

48   Meath Hospital Minute Book, 13 January 1913 (NAI, 2007/128, 5-3, p. 292).

49   *Appendices to the report of the committee appointed to inquire into the extension of Medical Benefit under the National Insurance Act to Ireland* [Cd.7039] H.C. 1913, xxxvii, p. 64.

50   Mercer's Hospital Minute Book, 2 December 1913 (NAI, 2D/36/36).

51   RCDH Minute Book, 8 January 1914 (NAI, 2006/98).

52   Barrington, *Health, medicine and politics in Ireland*, p. 35.

53   Ibid.

54   Ibid., p. 68.

55   Irish doctors were often members of both the British Medical Association and Irish Medical Association. The BMA established a Dublin Branch in 1877. For information and records (RCPI, BMA/1/1).

56   *Report for 1912-13 on the Administration of National Insurance Act* [Cd. 6907] H.C. (1913) xxxvi, p. 451.

57   Anon, 'Manchester and District', *British Medical Journal*, no. 1 (1913), p. 363.

58   Anon, 'Funds of Dublin hospitals', *British Medical Journal*, no. 1 (1913), p. 1082.

59   Geary, *Medicine and charity*, p. 39.

60   RCDH *Annual report* (NAI, 2D/38/52, p. 8).

61   Ibid., p. 9.

62   Ibid., p. 8

63   Mercer's Hospital Minute Book, 2 Dec. 1913 (NAI, 2D/36/36).

64   For a discussion of maternity and child welfare in 20th-century Dublin, see Lindsey Earner-Byrne, *Mother and child: maternity and child welfare in Dublin, 1922-60* (Manchester, 2007).

65   Anon, 'Infant mortality in Dublin', *British Medical Journal*, no. 1 (1913), p. 258.

66   Earner-Byrne, *Mother and child*, p. 11.

67   Anon, 'Dublin hospitals and maternity benefit', *British Medical Journal*, no. 1 (1913), p. 79.

68   *Fifty-sixth annual report of the Board of Superintendence of the Dublin Hospitals, 1913-1914,* [Cd.7576], H.C. 1914, xix, 44, p. 43.

69   Anon, 'Maternity benefits', *British Medical Journal*, no. 1 (1913), p. 243.

70   *Irish Times*, 20 Mar. 1913.

71   *Irish Times*, 12 Apr. 1913.

72   *Appendices to the Report of the Committee appointed to inquire into the Extension of Medical Benefit under the National Insurance Act to Ireland* [Cd.7039] H.C. 1913, xxxvii, p.48.

73   Anon, 'Dublin Insurance Committee, *British Medical Journal*, no.2 (1913), p.460.

74   Barrington, *Health, Mmedicine and politics*, p. 36.

75   Jones, *'Captain of all these men of death'*, p. 35.

76   Ibid., p. 112.

77   Jones, *'Captain all of these men to death'*, p. 111.

78   Meath Hospital Minute Book, 13 January 1913 (NAI, 2007/128, 5-3, p. 283).

79   Meath Hospital Minute Book, 13 January 1913 (NAI, 2007/128, 5-3, p. 288); County Councils took charge as a result of Tuberculosis Prevention Act (1913), See Jones, *'Captain all of these men to death'*, p. 112.

80   See Barrington, *Health, medicine and politics.*

81   *Report of the committee appointed to consider the extension of Medical Benefit under the National Insurance Act to Ireland* [Cd.6963] H.C. 1913, xxxvii.

82   For full list of those interviewed during the Dublin session, see Appendix, Table 2.

83   Richard O'Carroll, 1876-1916, was general secretary, Ancient Guild of Incorporated Brick and Stone Layers' Trade Union from 1906; served on the Irish Trade Union Congress parliamentary committee from 1911; and was a city councillor, Mansion House Ward, from 1907. He moved from Sinn Féin to Dublin Trades Council Labour Representation Committee and Dublin Labour Party and served on the Trades Council executive and South Dublin Board of Poor Law Guardians. Badly beaten during the Lockout, O'Carroll was a member of the IRB and Irish Volunteers and was shot by Captain J. C. Bowen-Colthurst on 26 April 1916, dying on 5 May. Lawrence William White, 'O'Carroll, Richard' in *Dictionary of Irish biography* (Cambridge, 2009).

84   *Appendices to the report of the committee appointed to inquire into the extension of Medical Benefit under the National Insurance Act to Ireland* [Cd.7039] H.C. 1913, xxxvii, p. 44.

85   Ibid., p. 60.

86   Ibid.

87   Ibid., p. 56.
88   Ibid., p. 49.
89   Barrington, *Health, medicine and politics*, p. 61
90   Ibid., p. 60.
91   Ibid., p. 63.
92   Marie Coleman, *The Irish Sweep: a history of the Irish hospitals Sweepstake, 1930-87* (Dublin, 2009).

5.

Women, solidarity and the 1913 Dublin Lockout: Dora Montefiore and the 'Save the Kiddies' scheme

....

Karen Hunt

When Dora Montefiore, Lucille Rand and Grace Neal arrived in Dublin on 18 October 1913, the employers' Lockout was already well-established. These three rather different women had come from London with a specific task – to provide some respite for workers' children from the hardship of the industrial dispute that was paralysing Dublin by providing temporary homes for them with sympathisers in Britain. Dora Montefiore was the most well-known of the three and led the initiative which was sponsored by the radical newspaper, the *Daily Herald*. Montefiore was a 62-year-old middle-class widow and grandmother, an activist in a range of radical causes principally as a socialist and suffragist. Later she was to be a founder member of the Communist Party of Great Britain and the first woman to serve on its executive. Her political journey had begun when she was 40 and, unusually, her politics became more radical as she aged. In particular, she was a determined internationalist, participating in both socialist and women's international organisations, putting her experiences from one part of the world to work in another through her political travels in Europe, the United States and the white Dominions of the British Empire. Her companions had different backgrounds but shared her determination to make a difference. Mrs Lucille Rand was only 21 and had left her young daughter in London.[1] She was well-connected and had recently been married by the highest Roman Catholic prelate in Portugal, where her father had been the American ambassador. Dora Montefiore had met her in Florence earlier that year when she was staying with Professor George Herron, a socialist writer, who was Lucille's uncle by marriage. Rand was described as someone who 'Though quite young … had taken a deep interest in the welfare of the working classes of late years.'[2] The final member of the trio was very different again. She was a former parlour maid in her late 20s who had been the secretary of the short-lived but pioneering Domestic Workers' Union of Great Britain.[3] Like Dora Montefiore she had been a member of the British Socialist Party (BSP), resigning from its Women's Council in July 1913 because of ill-health. Grace and Dora shared other political interests in the growing rebel networks of the pre-war years: they were both adult suffragists and were active in support of the

Daily Herald Leagues. It was as a trade union organiser that Grace Neal was selected to travel to Dublin to make arrangements to enable strikers' children to take up the offer of over 200 temporary homes in Britain.

There are many stories told of what came to be known as the 'Save the Kiddies' episode. Even its origins are contested. The story Dora Montefiore told was that sitting on the platform of the *Daily Herald* League's 'Great Rally of Rebels' on 10 October, she heard Jim Larkin describe the 'straits the Dublin workers were in after seven weeks of slow starvation.'[4] She was determined to do something and while still on the platform she wrote a note to Larkin asking for his backing for her plan of practical solidarity, and then passed his agreement on to another occupant of the platform, the socialist Countess of Warwick, who agreed to become treasurer for the necessary fund.[5] The next day, she said, the *Daily Herald* published her proposal to provide holidays for Dublin strikers' children in the homes of British workers. Yet actually her 'appeal' appeared in the paper on the morning of the rally before she heard Larkin's powerful speech which reinforced what she had already read about the dire distress in Dublin. Even before it was endorsed by Larkin, Dora's proposal had characteristics which meant that it was never the well-meant philanthropic gesture as some have mistakenly represented it.

'Mrs Montefiore's Appeal' drew direct inspiration from the start from earlier examples of industrial solidarity when workers had taken the children of strikers into their homes. 'Cannot', she asked, 'a similar display of working-class solidarity be organised now; and when the next shipload of food is sent by the Trades Unions, cannot it return laden with little Irish lads and lasses, who will find in England mother hearts and hands ready to care for and cherish them, until the Irish workers have won their battle?' She offered to drop all her engagements and go over to Dublin with a batch of *Herald* Leaguers to help organise such a scheme. She called for names of those willing to take 'Irish comrades over 4 years of age' and for funds for the children's travelling expenses, and suggested that it could be discussed at the rally that night.[6] Even at this stage she envisaged direct action for a propagandist purpose: the *Daily Herald* 'could link up our work and publish brief reports from day to day; and I believe the result would be one of the best and most practical answers on the part of the workers to the fifty million fund on the part of the bosses.' This initiative was about the children but it was also about class, solidarity and propaganda.

By 16 October 200 homes had been offered and preparations were being made for Dora and her helpers to travel to Dublin to make arrangements with the strike committee. The *Daily Herald* commented that 'This is the right kind of brotherhood and solidarity.'[7] Dora made preparations at her Earl's Court home with the assistance of a committee of women quickly assembled from her political networks. Supporters were urged to send children's boots and jerseys (in specified sizes and from particular labour movement suppliers) direct to Liberty Hall and cash to the Countess of Warwick at her Essex home. Already practical arrangements were being made such as Plymouth British Socialist Party's offer to house 40 children as well as five of their mothers. The branch offered to pay all the expenses of the journey, board and lodging, while girls on strike at Burns and Co's factory in Hatton Garden offered to overhaul donated second-hand clothing for the Dublin children. Collections were undertaken by trade unionists and socialists from Willesden to Aberfan and Great Yarmouth to Glasgow.

1. Dora Montefiore, 1905.
Courtesy of her grandson, Graham Broad

Just a week after the appeal appeared in the *Herald*, Dora Montefiore travelled on the night mail to Dublin with Lucille Rand, a member of the newly-formed committee, and the 'late organiser for domestic servants' Grace Neal who it was intended should accompany the Plymouth- and London-bound children.[8] They quickly got to work in what Montefiore described as 'A City of Grey Shadows'. At Liberty Hall, they found many friends who were anxious to help, particularly Delia Larkin who Dora said was 'just as fine as her brother, if not finer.' Mrs Rand was soon at work in the kitchen ladling out hot Irish stew to mothers and children while Grace Neal 'surrounded by locked-out colleens', sat on a box peeling potatoes.[9] The offers of homes for the Dublin children continued to rise while Dora sent back to London descriptions of bare-foot ragged children rooting through dustbins for scraps of food. But this was not just about galvanising pity: there was a lesson to be learnt. *Daily Herald* readers were informed:

> Miss Grace Neal and I have both seen something of slums, but Dublin slums just beggar description. They have to be seen and smelt to be realised: and remember these conditions are not due to the strike nor to the Lockout of 3,000 women workers. They are due to callous exploitation and landlordism.[10]

Meanwhile, the business of organising the children's holiday scheme was underway. On the evening of 19 October a meeting was held for mothers in the largest room at Liberty Hall. The room was full to overflowing with mothers and babies and they spilt out into the street. The message was given 'from the workers of England to the wives of the strikers in Dublin.' 'We told them of the offer of 300 working-class homes, and of the love and welcome offered by 600 working-class parents to the Dublin kiddies, and they cheered, and cheered again, only stopping now and then to boo Murphy or to shout gladly as we showed them samples of the warm clothing already sent.' In Dora's report the visceral power of solidarity is felt: 'The meeting was undoubtedly an unconventional and unusual meeting, and it was choked with Celtic emotion, but the main fact stood out that the Dublin mothers were prepared to trust the English mothers.'[11]

On the Monday and Tuesday, Grace Neal worked at Liberty Hall taking the details of children whose mothers wished to take advantage of the scheme. The queues were long. Those who were not wives of strikers or locked-out men were rejected and all were told to ensure that the children's fathers also agreed to the scheme. A group of 50 children was asked to attend the Tara Street Baths on Wednesday morning where they would be washed and re-clothed in preparation for their journey.[12] However on Tuesday 21 October, a letter was published in the local press from Dr Walsh, archbishop of Dublin, who denounced the 'Save the Kiddies' scheme as a 'most mischievous development' which Catholic parents should eschew 'inasmuch as they have no guarantee that the persons to whom the children will be sent are Catholics; or, indeed, persons of any faith at all.'[13] At first, this did not seem to make any difference to the preparations being made at Liberty Hall. Although Dora reported that the scheme had been 'banned with book, bell and candle', she continued that 'in spite of ecclesiastical frowns, the mothers and fathers come one after another this morning to register their children on our lists, and Miss Neal has already reported to me that over 100 are already registered.' She asked whether the archbishop took the homeless and starving children in to his palace. 'If not, we have no time for them or their criticisms, or their excommunications. For, by Heaven, if they will not remove the naked children from the streets we will, with the help of the workers.' Her letter to this effect is to be found in the archbishop's archives and she included it in her pamphlet published later in 1913 about the episode. Here she underlined the purpose of the scheme was industrial solidarity and that many of the homes had been offered by Catholics, a significant number of whom were Irish. Plans were also outlined of arrangements for Catholic schooling for the children and for visits from local priests.[14]

On Wednesday, Dora wired the editor of the *Daily Herald* to expect 50 Dublin children at Euston that evening. However, the staff and students of the Central Labour College and of Bebel House (the working women's college) who waited to meet the boat train were to be disappointed. As Dora reported, since sending the telegram 'we three women have been through a series of scenes that we shall never forget.'[15] From this moment the 'Save the Kiddies' scheme burst into the Irish press of various political colours, the mainstream British press and it rippled out across the world. The stories told served a range of interests and made many claims. Soon it became hard to tell what had or hadn't happened as a variety of different audiences had their prejudices pandered to.

From the point of view of the three women who had travelled from London to carry out the *Daily Herald* scheme, all was going to plan. On Wednesday morning, Grace Neal worked at Liberty Hall, clothing and taking children's names while Lucille Rand was at the baths with a woman helper organising the cleaning of the children. Dora Montefiore was out getting the tickets and the food for the journey. On her return to Liberty Hall, she was told that priests had forced their way into the baths and were hustling the children away. In her report published the following day in the *Herald*, Dora described what happened next:

> I went down to the baths and found an indescribable scene going on in the street, a surging crowd, some with us, some against us, beat up against the steps of the baths and was again and again pushed back by two red-faced, brutal looking constables. Right inside the girls' side of the baths, where he had no business to be, stood a priest, who asked me what I was doing there?

I told him I had come to help Mrs Rand with the children. He replied we should not have the children, and that he was there to prevent their going. When I met Mrs Rand I found that he had already threatened and hustled her, and she had to warn him not to touch her again.[16]

PRIESTS TO THE RESCUE.

MORE CHILDREN SAVED.

SCENE AT AMIENS STREET

WATCHING THE BOATS.

HUGE PROCESSION.

AN ATTEMPT TO DEPORT ANOTHER BATCH OF CATHOLIC CHILDREN TO ENGLAND OR SCOTLAND WAS FRUSTRATED LAST EVENING AT AMIENS STREET STATION OWING TO THE INTERVENTION OF THE CLERGY AND CATHOLIC LAITY, WHO RECEIVED TIMELY INTIMATION OF THE INTENDED DEPORTATION.

MISS DELIA LARKIN, SISTER OF MR. JAMES LARKIN, WAS IN CHARGE OF THE CHILDREN, WHOM IT WAS INTENDED TO SEND AWAY, BUT OWING TO THE DETERMINED SPIRIT EXHIBITED BY THE ASSEMBLY HER DESIGN WAS DEFEATED AND THE CHILDREN WERE BROUGHT BACK TO LIBERTY HALL.

of the City of Dublin Company's and Glasgow boats' sheds prior to their departure, and many priests who were amongst the assembly kept a vigilant look-out for likely victims of the deporting campaign. There was no indication of any arrangement to bring children to either boats.

The crowd afterwards directed their attention to the precincts of the London and North-Western Company's boat, which was the last to leave the North Wall. Amongst the priests present were:— Very Rev. Father Fottrell, S.J.; Father Grimley, P.P., Halston street; Rev. Father Doyle, C.C.; Father J. Hickey, C.C., Halston street; Father Landers, C.C., High street; Father Costello, St. Michael and John's; Father O'Byrne, Halston street. There were large numbers of members of the A.O.H. and city confraternities, and a considerable number of ladies and the general public. Several members of the Girls' Protection Society were also present. In all several thousand people had assembled in the vicinity of the landing stage, and did not leave until the boat had departed.

SPEECH OF FR. FOTTRELL, S.J.

2. *Freeman's Journal*, 25 Oct. 1913.
DCLA

The children that the women got back to Liberty Hall were then provided with bodyguards by Jim Larkin in order that they and the accompanying adults could get to the station to catch the train to Kingstown and the waiting steamer. However more priests were waiting on the platform. Dora was in the centre of the *melée*:

They pulled the children out of the carriages and hustled us and pushed us back violently with their hands. When I told a priest he was assaulting me he told me I was 'insulting Ireland' with my charity. They threatened reprisals on the parents, and finally they got into the carriages, and by the time we reached Kingstown had bullied two women into hysterics, all the children in the carriage were howling.[17]

One witness described what he saw as he attempted to accompany the children and the women workers to the dock side:

Honestly and truthfully, without any exaggeration, I did not expect to get back to Dublin alive. That's the truth. The priests were simply insane, the women were terrified by the threats made by the priests, they were kneeling down in the carriage calling upon Jesus to remove the ban upon them; the children were crying, and naturally the public thought we were kidnappers, as the priests were calling us. They were telling the people that we were taking them away for the white slave traffic, and so on, and I really expected the whole crowd to lynch us. It is no fault of the priests that they didn't.[18]

Of course, others saw something rather different happening, hence the language of deportation, kidnapping and white slavery that now entered the competing narratives.

On this occasion, although Lucille Rand and a few of her charges actually managed to get on to the boat, in all the confusion she seems to have thought better of sailing with the remaining children. However, on disembarking she was arrested and charged with kidnapping a child. Meanwhile Dora had returned to Liberty Hall, assuming that at least some children had got away with Lucille Rand. Her report of the scenes at the station and at the docks, persuaded Jim Larkin to suggest that another group of children should be taken that evening to Liverpool by Grace Neal. Another 15 children were selected who had written consent from their parents for the journey. While Larkin addressed the crowd of transport workers from the windows of Liberty Hall, the children were quickly prepared for the journey in warm clothes. Larkin called on some of the strikers to act as bodyguards to ensure that the party of women and children got through to the boat. This turned out to be a necessary precaution, as Dora reported in the *Herald*, 'the procession had a hot time of it from the priests.'[19] In the end 18 children, two Irish young women helpers and Miss Neal got away to Liverpool where they were met by 'warm-hearted comrades', police, local priests who attempted to intervene, and the photographer from *The Liverpool Weekly Mercury* who captured an image of the group.[20] The Wallasey Socialist Society provided homes for the Dublin children from amongst their members and ensured that local priests had access to the children. One of these, Fr Leech, protested to Dublin about the 'anything but Catholic' atmosphere that the children had been taken to and he was particularly critical of the parents of the children, who by giving their permission had, he said, tied his hands in terms of intervening. 'Where', he added, 'is the old spirit of the famine days?'[21] This was another salvo in the polemical battle which was now raging over the Dublin 'Kiddies', awakening memories of Catholic resistance in the famine to Protestant proselytisers who it was said could prise away hungry Catholics from their faith in exchange for a bowl of soup.

Meanwhile in Dublin, the scheme continued. Lucille Rand was remanded on Thursday although Dora Montefiore had asked for the charge of kidnapping to be transferred to her, as she was responsible for the whole scheme. The magistrate advised her to abandon what he now called 'the deportation movement'. The *Herald* pointed out in response to the widespread accusation of proselytising, that Mrs Rand was a Roman Catholic.[22] On Thursday night another large crowd gathered at the North Wall in Dublin to prevent any more children leaving and there were clashes outside Liberty Hall. Later that same evening the police arrived at Dora's hotel to arrest her on the same charge of kidnapping. Taken to the Bridewell, her account of her treatment there was then published in Saturday's *Herald* and was picked up by newspapers across the world. Although willing to spend the night in the cells, provided a friend might be allowed to bring her a pillow and a rug, she was finally released on the surety of, among others, Constance Markievicz. On Friday morning Grace Neal arrived back in Dublin with news that the first batch of children was settled 'in the houses of friends'.[23] Although Dora now asked people to cease offering new homes but rather to send funds, she commented, 'Every moment seems to bring a new situation and a new demand, but we know that we are shaking the very foundations of Murphyism, so we are content to go on and force someone to feed and care for the Dublin kiddies.'[24]

Now the emphasis of the scheme changed in response to the developing circumstances. The *Herald* advised 'the urgent thing is to feed the kiddies' and proposed to send food and clothing from the co-operative stores to Archbishop Walsh, or his nominee, provided that he undertook to distribute the goods among the starving children of the locked-out Dublin workers. As they knew, this was unlikely as the church did not want to be seen to support the strikers. This was one way to expose the contradictions in the church's position. Similarly, the final attempt to get strikers' children out of Dublin attempted to meet some of the ostensible justifications for what Dora called 'the disgraceful scene which took place on Wednesday.' These were that the children were travelling alone to England and possibly to Protestant homes. It was therefore proposed to send a group of children with their parents to Catholic homes in Belfast. Grace Neal was to take them, and both Dora Montefiore and Delia Larkin went to see the group off at the station. There Dora said she was 'witness of a scene which I should have not thought possible in any part of the United Kingdom.'

> In front of the compartment into which the parents were attempting to get their children, there was a compact, shouting, gesticulating crowd of Hibernians … scattered among them were the priests, who were talking, uttering threats against the parents, and forbidding them to send their children to Protestant homes. Some of the women were upbraiding the priests for allowing the children to starve in Dublin … As a climax to this disgraceful scene … they telephoned to the Castle for more police, and I watched the reinforcement of twenty spike-helmeted destroyers of law and order march on to the platform … and prevented the children leaving for Belfast … leaving the now infuriated parents to take their children back to the slum homes which capitalist conditions in Dublin provide for the workers and their children.[25]

On Monday, Dora was in Liberty Hall talking with Delia Larkin about the future of 'our temporarily frustrated scheme.' Delia was now in charge of all the relief work at Liberty Hall as her brother had been imprisoned, found guilty of using seditious language. At this point Dora observed, 'Some day the real history of this strike and lock-out will be written, and on that day clericalism and all the noxious weeds it nurtures will be swept and scorched and for all time blackened with the leaping, lambent flames of truth!'[26] The story of the 'Save the Kiddies' scheme was almost at an end. The case against Lucille Rand and Dora Montefiore for kidnapping was heard on Wednesday, 29 October. Their defence counsel argued that the work of these two ladies was at an end in Dublin. 'The ladies had come on a mission of charity, and that they should be subjected to such charges rather savoured of Gilbertian humour.' Although the case was technically held over for a month both women were released and, commented the *Herald*, 'thus ended the ridiculous farce.'[27] Dora's account does not sound so amusing, with the continual air of intimidation such as the nightly meetings outside the women's hotel where 'inflammatory speeches' were made by priests to the crowd which 'unchecked by the police, proceeded night after night to 'boo' us women in our hotel.'[28] Both women left Dublin, with Dora returning to London in time to address the Albert Hall Rally to the Dublin rebels on 1 November. Grace Neal remained at Liberty Hall into 1914 working with Delia Larkin to organise the distribution of the aid that continued to arrive in solidarity with the locked-out workers. The Dublin 'Kiddies' scheme had lasted three weeks from Montefiore's original appeal to her return to London, while she and Rand were in Dublin for barely a fortnight. The fund continued to operate and Montefiore made a further visit to Dublin just before Christmas 1913 to report to her readers the continuing effect of these expressions of solidarity once the spotlight had moved on.[29] In the end, only a few Dublin children got the holiday that British workers were offering them in solidarity with their striking and locked-out parents. Yet the reverberations of the Dublin 'Kiddies' scheme were extensive and revealing.

The many stories of the 'Save the Kiddies' scheme

The 'Save the Kiddies' episode of the Dublin Lockout reveals the range of narratives that were produced at the time, and subsequently. Some of the narrators were more conscious of this than others. Dora Montefiore wished for 'the real history' of the Lockout to be written while it was observed in the *Daily Herald* that 'A different story, of course, is told by the other side.' It complained that although the cases against Mrs Rand and Mrs Montefiore made matters sub-judice, 'this does not prevent the Murphy press from filling column after column with violent vituperation against 'Atheists' and 'Socialist kidnappers".[30] Meanwhile the *Irish Independent* reprinted selections from Montefiore's reports in the *Herald* under the headline 'Mrs Montefiore's Abuse' and *The Freeman's Journal* undertook a similar exercise under the heading 'For English Palates'.[31] There was much selective reprinting of rival presses whether it was the *Daily Mail* quoted in the *Daily Herald* or *The Times* in *The Freeman's Journal.*[32] No wonder Dora Montefiore wanted to tell her own version of the story because of what she saw as misleading reports circulating in the capitalist press.[33] Equally, the employers, the church and all the other interested parties wanted to ensure that their accounts drowned out all other versions as they competed for the moral high ground.

By comparing various different kinds of presses (the Irish, the British, and the women's) one can see the rhetorical battle that swirled around the 'Save the Kiddies' scheme. Some in Ireland were alarmed by the wider effects on the country's reputation, thus 'With the help of touring philanthropists, [Larkin] paraded our city's misery and destitution before the eyes of Europe.'[34] In damning Larkin, the primary purpose here, the author also misrepresented Montefiore and the purpose of the scheme. But the language within the Irish press grew wilder as the scheme was variously and often described as deportation, attempted kidnapping and an emigration scheme as well a means to 'capture' children to 'impregnate … [them] with Socialism.'[35] The latter was part of an extreme assessment of the scheme which saw it as an 'abhorrent and un-natural idea' which 'has done more injury to the Socialist leaders, and awakened a fiercer hostility among the Irish people to the whole teachings of Godless Socialism than have any other of the peculiar tactics in which the ribald leaders of Larkinism have indulged.' It was 'so eminently English and silly in its conception, that like all their attempts to proselyse [sic] and pervert the Irish people from the faith of Patrick it proved a grotesque failure.'[36] However exaggerated the language, this extract actually raises most of the anxieties that other parts of the Irish press had also worried away at: the various linked evils of Protestant proselytising, socialism, Larkinism, and the interfering English. An acute sense of the power of Irish history meant that analogies were drawn to reveal what underlay an apparently humanitarian gesture. So the *Irish Independent* claimed that 'Not since the days when Cromwell forcibly deported Irish children to the Barbadoes has such a determined effort been made to deprive Ireland of her little ones.'[37] What is also apparent is that this language inflated very quickly. Thus when *The Freeman's Journal* reported another unconnected successful 'rescue' of Dublin children undertaken for the English suffragette Emmeline Pethick-Lawrence by her friend Mary Neal (no relation to Grace Neal), there was no anxiety expressed about the endangering of the children's Catholicism.[38] Yet it judged the 'Save the Kiddies' scheme, which it saw as deporting Irish Catholic children to English homes, to be 'so stupendous a blunder' by Larkin.[39]

Catholicism was also an issue for the British press. *The Times* noted the surprise in England at the response in Dublin to the scheme. This could be explained by the power of the Catholic church in Ireland, which was notable for its 'extraordinary jealousy' in response to 'any intrusion in its own social and spiritual field.' This was combined, it was argued, with a widespread belief in Dublin that all English trade unionists were socialists and that socialism and atheism were identical. 'The Church here is horrified at the suggestion that young Roman Catholic children should be entrusted to the charge of persons who, if not Socialists and Atheists, may, at least, in the majority of cases be Protestants.'[40] For the *Manchester Guardian*, the scheme was a 'well-meant proposal'. Their own correspondent judged that 'There is no truth in the assertions that this struggle over the children has weakened Mr Larkin's position' but the paper also printed in the same edition a Press Association report from Dublin which came to the opposite conclusion.[41]

The mainstream British press gave extensive coverage to this episode, but the greatest attention was given by the radical *Daily Herald* which had sponsored the intervention. Its coverage was by no means limited to Dora Montefiore's reports. Some of the comment could be vicious, such as Will Dyson's cartoons – a later cartoon about the dispute brought a libel action against the paper from the Dublin employer W. R. Jacob.[42] These powerful images were replicated in the paper's text by a rhetoric which portrayed capitalists as 'the Fat', as in the headline 'Fat on the run in Dublin' or publishing extracts from the 'Fat Press'.[43] The paper gave measured descriptions of the scheme but saw it as part of 'The Capitalist Game'.[44] Although, it was 'never dreamed that they would raise such a hornet's nest', the *Herald* reported that 'whether it was with the Archbishop's consent or knowledge we know not, but some of the rank and file of the Dublin clergy went to extreme lengths, even to the use of physical force, against two or three defenceless women, in order to prevent any of the strikers children leaving for England.'[45] The *Herald*'s language was often one of class war, both in terms of their understanding of the

Lockout itself but also in relation to the ways in which the press responded to the 'Save the Kiddies' episode. For the paper 'The campaign against Mrs Montefiore and Mrs Rand was deliberately planned to rob Larkin of popular support'[46] and it was explained to their readers how the collective memory of the scourge of 'Soupers' – food in exchange for renouncing your faith – was mobilised by Murphyism (the collective term for the employers, led by the powerful William Martin Murphy, chairman of the Dublin United Tramways Company).[47] *The Freeman's Journal* published a supposed quote from Montefiore: 'The English workers feel that the Irish workers are in the soup to-day, and that they themselves may be in the soup tomorrow.'[48] Given so many other inaccuracies in the Dublin press and the politically charged context, the provenance of the quote is debateable. That it would be seen as damaging is undeniable.

ABDUCTION CHARGE

AGAINST MRS. MONTEFIORE.

LARKIN'S TRIAL FIXED.

CARRYING CO. CHARGED.

COMMISSION CASES.

AT THE NORTHERN POLICE COURT YESTERDAY, MRS. MONTEFIORE WAS CHARGED WITH KIDNAPPING A LITTLE BOY NAMED GEORGE BURKE, 3 NORTH ANNE STREET. EVIDENCE WAS GIVEN IN SUPPORT OF THE CHARGE AND THE ACCUSED WAS REMANDED TO WEDNESDAY NEXT, BEING ALLOWED OUT ON HER OWN BAIL.

THE TRIAL OF MESSRS. JAMES LARKIN, P. T. DALY, WILLIAM PARTRIDGE, T.C.; T. LAWLOR, T.C., AND WILLIAM O'BRIEN HAS BEEN

case; but, I am bound by what Mr. Tobias has said. Is there any fear of her going away before Wednesday?

Superintendent Flynn said he had no fear as to that.

Mr. Macinerney—I suppose you would not have any objection if she aid (laughter).

Superintendent Flynn suggested that the evidence of the witness could be taken down just then.

Mr. Macinerney—How would that assist you? I am not trying the case. I am simply doing what Mr. Mahony did. I am not exercising my own discretion at all.

Mrs. Montefiore was accordingly remanded on her own bail till Wednesday.

MRS. MONTEFIORE'S ACCOUNT

OF HOW CHILDREN WERE DEPORTED

Yesterday's "Daily Herald" contains the following account of the deportation proceedings, under the heading, "A Reign of Terror," from the pen of Mrs. Montefiore:—

3. *Freeman's Journal,* 25 Oct. 1913.
DCLA

The *Herald* also was sensitive to a charge made in Dublin which was equally explosive to their own readers – white slavery. A moral panic that young women were being kidnapped off city streets and forced into prostitution had been raging since 1912 in Britain and from the previous year in the United States – the home of Mrs Rand.[49] The abductors were understood to be foreign, particularly Jewish. This anxiety was then connected to Montefiore's married name and mobilised as a means to attack the scheme. The *Irish Independent* carried the headline 'Charged with Kidnapping: Bailed by Dublin Jews' while G. K. Chesterton responded to the Dublin events with an anti-semitic attack on Dora Montefiore.[50] It was the smear of white-slavery, rather than proselytising, that so upset Montefiore and Rand. Dora's account of the priests at the Tara Street Baths is suggestive of what we would now read as inappropriate sexualised behaviour – voyeurism, touching, violence. The *Daily Herald* reported that the rousing of the passions of the crowd against Mrs Rand was through the accusation of white slavery and that this was 'not the least disgraceful aspect of the affair'. This was 'sinister intimidation'. Montefiore complained, 'We have been called in the streets "White Slavers", and there is no end to the lying imputations that have been put upon our actions.'[51] Anonymous postcards were received which slandered Rand and Montefiore as white slavers and blessed the priests for saving the children from white slavery.[52] Indeed when she summed up the whole episode Dora described the sinister rumours, a phrase used in Walsh's letter to her, that were, she claimed, 'set about purposely by the priests and Hibernians that we three women were agents of the White Slave Traffic. The foul suggestion was breathed in our ears as we walked daily between our hotel and Liberty Hall; and finally materialised in filthy postcards sent to our Dublin friends.'[53]

Yet this was not the aspect of the 'Save the Kiddies' episode that was seized upon by the British women's suffrage press. There is surprisingly little coverage of these events by either suffragettes or suffragists, possibly because of the particularity of Montefiore's suffrage politics.[54] Having been an early member of the Women's Social and Political Union (WSPU) and an imprisoned suffragette in 1906, she subsequently became prominent in arguing for adult suffrage and was increasingly critical of the limitations of the demand and tactics of the 'limiteds' – the constitutionalists and militants who campaigned for votes for women on the same terms as men, that is a property franchise. However, suffragette support for the 'Save the Kiddies' scheme is evident in the *Herald* with a cameo appearance from the son of a WSPU member, Rose Lamartine Yates, who made a heart-rending plea on behalf of the Dublin children and a self-styled 'poor suffragette' who expressed her gratitude to the *Herald*'s scheme.[55] The Women's Freedom League's *The Vote* advertised and then covered the 1 November Albert Hall Rally at which their leader Charlotte Despard was a particularly well-received speaker. Her key point was the one that many suffrage activists drew from the Lockout. This was the difference between the government's treatment of rebellious Irish men (Carson and Larkin) compared to rebellious women, that is militant suffragettes.[56] This comparison centred on the observation that Carson was free from arrest despite calling the men of Ulster to arms and that Larkin when imprisoned was placed in the first division, with all its attendant privileges, which suffragette prisoners had been denied for years. Larkin's treatment was contrasted with the 'torture' of the Cat and Mouse Act with the continual re-arresting of hunger-striking suffragette prisoners when they were deemed healthy enough to return to serve a little more of their sentence. Larkin was expected to be released shortly with no fear of re-arrest, for that offence at least. For Despard, and many other suffragettes, this was all part of the double standards of a patriarchal politics, what many saw as a 'sex war'. The only direct reference to the 'Save the Kiddies' episode acknowledged 'the preposterous charges' against Montefiore and Rand 'and the other charitable folk who tried to remove the hapless Dublin strike waifs from the scenes of violence and brutality in which they are wilting.'[57] In *Votes for Women*, now run by the Pethick-Lawrences after their expulsion from the WSPU, there were also advertisements for the various demonstrations held to rally support for the Dublin locked-out workers. They also made their own collection for Dublin children, which they handed over to the *Daily Herald*. Mary Neal, who had 'rescued' six Dublin girls and brought them to the Pethick-Lawrence's Surrey home, gave her impressions of the Lockout. She claimed it would be 'memorable for the heroic part which women have taken in it.' Women workers had been locked-out for wearing a

READ
The
"Daily Herald"
The
Fighting Labour Paper
ALIVE ALL OVER!

$\frac{1}{2}$ D.   Buy it and Recommend it NOW. $\frac{1}{2}$ D.

For all information about the "Daily Herald" League, apply—
"D.H." League Secretary, 21, Tudor Street, E.C.

4. Advertisement for the *Daily Herald* in W. P. Ryan, *The labour revolt and Larkinism* (London, 1913).
Private Collection

union badge, and it was Delia Larkin who she singled out for praise: 'I consider the work which Miss Larkin has done in organising the women workers one of the most important pieces of work ever accomplished for women, and it is a great honour to be allowed to help her by easing the strain which their loyal adhesion to her teaching has put upon the women who have children to keep on their slender strike pay.' For Mary Neal, it was the trust of the women in letting their children go so far which touched her. But in the end her focus was on the Dublin women as workers rather than just as suffering mothers: 'For a new spirit is abroad, and women are realising as never before that in union, in fellowship, is the only hope of the future, that only as we stand together, refusing to be made 'blacklegs', but demanding equally with men a fair wage for fair work, shall we gain the economic freedom on which the future welfare of the race so largely depends.'[58] *Votes for Women* reprinted the *Daily Mirror*'s pictures of the Dublin girls at Sundial Cottage in Dorking and stressed that their religious needs were being met by local priests.[59] There was no mention of the Montefiore initiative.

This pattern continues with the National Union of Women's Suffrage Societies' *Common Cause*. The only reference to the Lockout comes in the 21 November edition when another scheme was highlighted. Dr Barbara Tchaykovski's appeal concerned alleviating the suffering of women and children in Dublin. It seems to have been purely philanthropic in motive. Interestingly though not framed in terms of solidarity, the link was drawn with support that *Common Cause* readers had given to victims of the Dock Strike in 1912.[60] The WSPU also showed little interest in any aspect of the Lockout. In their paper *The Suffragette*, edited by Christabel Pankhurst, the focus was much more on another part of Ireland, Ulster, and the possibilities for women's enfranchisement to be included in any solution to the Irish Question. There are no references to the 'Save the Kiddies' episode but there are weekly reports of the new Dublin branch of the WSPU. Nowhere in the detail of local campaigns and meetings is there any reference to the Lockout and local experiences of it or attitudes to it. However, the Lockout was to have an indirect effect of some significance for the WSPU. *The Suffragette* also contained comparisons between the treatment of Carson and their own members, and some references to the speeches at the 1 November Albert Hall rally. Initially they reported Sylvia Pankhurst's participation in the meeting in terms of exposing government hypocrisy: 'In order to test whether the Government would arrest her and let Mr Larkin go free, Miss Sylvia Pankhurst appeared on the platform at the Albert Hall meeting, but was not arrested … This looks uncommonly like a triumph and breakdown of the 'Cat and Mouse' Act where she is concerned.'[61] The following week they noted that 'the Government have cheated women, and have cheated all concerned by simply releasing Mr Larkin and nothing more.' But Christabel now outlined the sheer incompatibility of the WSPU not only with the *Daily Herald* League, which had organised the Albert

Hall rally, but also with any other men's political organisation, as she characterised the entire labour and socialist movement.[62] Sylvia was forced to deny that she sought such an alliance and to explain her presence at the Albert Hall. Her days in the WSPU were now numbered and the rally for the Dublin rebels, indeed the Lockout itself, had become the means to finally and formally divide the WSPU from its many supporters in the rebel networks, on the grounds that the sex war trumped the class war. Yet for many, then and subsequently, the work of solidarity with the locked-out workers of Dublin illustrated the strength of the bonds between the labour and women's movements.

When in Dublin, Dora Montefiore seemed to illustrate the interconnections between the struggles of labour and of women. She spoke at a Dublin meeting of the Irish Women's Franchise League (IWFL). She apologised as she said she was exhausted from her efforts in the cause of the starving children of Dublin. However, even this was a contentious matter. One woman reportedly said that there were no starving children in Dublin, but she was ignored. Dora explained that the keynote of the struggle was equality between the sexes. The enfranchisement of women was not an isolated movement. Instead, she said, they should look upon their movement as a human movement where men and women stood together in the struggle. 'We feel that that power and responsibility which men possess should be shared by women, and we want to use the industrial weapon for the emancipation of the workers. We know there is value in both, and until we can get hold of that political weapon, we are fighting with one arm tied behind our backs.'[63] These were not the words of a Lady Bountiful charitable social worker, as she was characterised at the time and subsequently:[64] so what was Dora Montefiore's view of the purpose of the 'Save the Kiddies' scheme? From her original appeal in the *Daily Herald* for practical support, Dora Montefiore's intentions were clear: working-class solidarity. As she explained in her 1913 pamphlet:

> if we could give the children a holiday and fill them with a vision of what life might hold in the way of a cleaner and more hopeful environment, my colleagues and I might be the means not only of saving some of the children, who should be the hope of the race, but also of doing some constructive work for the future of organised industrialism.[65]

Her inspiration was the efforts of New York socialists to evacuate children ('strike waifs', according to the *New York Times*) from the violent industrial dispute in Lawrence, Massachusetts in 1912.[66] This act of practical solidarity, she felt,

> focussed the attention of the whole world upon a particularly intense exhibition of the class struggle … The Socialists' care of the kiddies put heart into the Lawrence strikers and made mad the mill bosses … 'The kiddies must stay behind

and starve,' was the capitalist fiat. And this brutal order aroused the indignation of all classes all over America and brought greater sympathy and practical support to the strikers.[67]

Here was the clear politics that motivated the 'Save the Kiddies' scheme and which she hoped would bring the same benefits not only for the Dublin children but also for the strikers and the wider industrial struggle. It was, she said, a 'humanitarian cause', but she was absolutely clear that this was not philanthropy: 'We are not sentimentalists.'[68] When she spoke to the Albert Hall rally alongside James Connolly and Bernard Shaw among others, she was unequivocal: 'the new principle her action had endeavoured to teach was that when industrial war became acute at one spot it was the duty of the workers in safer parts to remove all the children from the danger zone.'

There were, and are, different ways of reading the solidarity work that 'Save the Kiddies' exemplified. At moments even Dora choose strategically to represent the scheme as a charitable endeavour as when her case was heard in the magistrate's court. However, generally she made clear that the shocking poverty of Dublin was caused by 'callous exploitation and landlordism' and that what she was engaged in could not be described as philanthropic or as 'relief work'. Nevertheless, Yeates in his encyclopaedic *Lockout: Dublin 1913* seems to lump her with all the other 'valiant middle-class women who provided relief work – be it as sanitary visitors, socially concerned suffragists, nuns, members of St Vincent de Paul ladies' committees, union organisers, or indeed professional revolutionaries.'[69]

If not philanthropic, this was undoubtedly seen as working-class solidarity. The context for this was the much larger TUC's Dublin Strike Fund, which raised £106,000 which funded food ships on which the locked-out workers survival was heavily dependent.[70] The scale of the 'Save the Kiddies' scheme was much more modest and during its lifetime additional funds were always being requested. Instead Montefiore felt that a by-product of such class-based solidarity would be 'implanting in the minds of the workers the sense that they are gradually evolving a workers' state within the capitalist state – a state of efficient and co-operative administration of things as opposed to a state for the government of persons.'[71] More practically what the organisation of such solidarity showed was that it was possible to work purposely across sectarian divides. Dora drew attention to the way in which the scheme was taken up by official sections of the British Socialist Party, Independent Labour Party, Trades Councils, the WSPU and Clarionettes.[72]

However, this was also a solidarity which self-consciously had a gender dimension. The first meeting at Liberty Hall had noted that Dublin mothers were prepared to trust the English mothers. Despite Christabel Pankhurst's later response, there was also evidence of support from the women's movement to the workers' movement. A 'suffragist rebel' paid the £25 hire of the Albert Hall so that all of the collection at the 1 November rally could go to Dublin. The same meeting was addressed by suffrage speakers, such as Charlotte Despard and Sylvia Pankhurst, as well as the women activists Delia Larkin and Dora Montefiore. Other speakers made the connection too. George Lansbury said, 'I see no difference between the upheaval of the workers and the upheaval of their wives and sisters.' Connolly had a slightly different emphasis when he spoke of 'the heroic manner in which the poorest women had joined in the strike ... They would rather starve to death than be untrue to their class.' The symbolism of unity across the women's and industrial movement continued with a hundred women collectors at the meeting and with all the stewarding done by women in suffragette colours.[73] However, rhetorical rather than practical connections seemed easier to sustain. The involvement of Irish suffragists, who wore their green and orange IWFL badges as they laboured in the soup kitchens of Liberty Hall, was not mentioned in the English radical or suffrage press.[74] But the gendering of this solidarity and indeed of the Lockout itself is often taken for granted. Although women seem to have served the food, Dora for example noted a sexual division of labour at work at Liberty Hall when she visited in December 1913: 'Employed in various capacities are the locked out and victimised girl Unionists; while a tramway man cooks the daily dinners for the mothers and another transport worker prepares the 3,000 children's breakfasts.'[75] Sue Bruley has noted a similar sexual division of labour in the soup kitchens of the 1926 Miners' Lockout in South Wales.[76] There also seems to have been some gendering of the funds themselves. This 'women's' solidarity was funded separately to the male trade union relief funds, indeed at one point the 'Save the Kiddies' committee asked to have 5% of the larger collections earmarked for 'Dublin Kiddies'.[77] Finally, a gendered reading of the solidarity work undertaken in relation to the Dublin Lockout necessarily pushes Delia Larkin far further forward in the story than is usual.[78]

There is also a case for seeing the 'Save the Kiddies' intervention as a militant or suffragette form of solidarity. This is not because it was undertaken by suffragettes – it was not. Rather, it is because it seems to respond to the rebellious spirit of the time and fits with the WSPU's slogan of 'Deeds not Words'. Did the women contribute to the Lockout through their stoicism or through direct action? The stoicism of the Dublin women was commented on at the time, but other women saw the issue differently. Charlotte Despard at the Albert Hall meeting said, 'Women were in industry and would have to be considered. When you said that men made this, men made that, you should remember who it was that made the men. The time was passed for speaking, for thinking – the time for action had come.'[79] In a similar spirit *Votes for Women* claimed 'that the whole Larkin agitation itself would never have reached its present proportions if the militant woman suffragists had not, by their example, pointed out the pathway of rebellion.'[80] It did not occur to Dora Montefiore to stay in London and merely administer a fund, she was determined to knit together the contemporary politics of direct action with practical solidarity.

Montefiore had also noted that the power of past examples of industrial solidarity had been that they had acted as a form of propaganda. She may have got more publicity than she had anticipated but the intention had always been to publicise what they were doing in Dublin, as all her reports in the *Herald* make clear. It was also to ensure that the cause echoed around the world and beyond the usual audiences. Her experience working with radicals in her international travels had demonstrated the reach of the radical press and the socialist propagandist.[81] Here the purpose was not just to reiterate the justice of the strikers' cause but to go further and expose the nature of the broader forces shaping daily life. For Montefiore this was capitalism, now in the shape of Murphyism but also 'clericalism and all the noxious weeds it nurtures.' For others solidarity with those affected by the Lockout served as a means to make their own propaganda, thus Sylvia Pankhurst said that she was glad to speak on behalf of the Dublin strikers with a fellow hunger-striker, James Connolly, but she asked the Albert Hall audience to remember Rachel Peace who was at that moment being force-fed three times a day. For her, 'Revolt was imperative ... Women had no votes, and could not strike; the only thing they could do was fight.'[82] All these activists seized the opportunity to make propaganda for their cause, and 'Save the Kiddies' was one such opportunity.

So, finally, what was the significance of the 'Save the Kiddies' episode? It certainly shows that the Lockout is open to a gendered reading. In one way this episode illustrates traditional gender roles: women cared; they changed their minds (some of the Dublin mothers); they were seen principally as mothers; they were easily manipulated; they were tenacious (e.g. Delia Larkin). In contrast men intervened; they attempted to impose authority; they were violent; they were protective (as bodyguards). Yet gender roles were also subverted, principally through women showing that they could organise this project themselves.

'Save the Kiddies' demonstrated cross-class solidarities, both in the team of Montefiore, Rand and Neal, but also in the London-based organising committee for the scheme. The scheme subverted apparent political divisions, showing that suffragists, suffragettes, socialists and trade unionists could work together, particularly through the new rebel networks centring on the *Daily Herald*. However, it was not a simple unity of interests between radicals. There was, for example, a complicated relationship between suffragettes and the Lockout. 'Save the Kiddies' also shows clear international resonances not only in the way it drew on earlier international examples of solidarity such as at Lawrence, but also that it in turn was covered in presses across the world. A smaller but more practical form of international solidarity was that between women workers across the Irish Sea, when women strikers in London offered to mend clothes to send on to their Dublin sisters and brothers. However, the scheme also prefigured some of the tensions that become apparent for many progressives about the politics of relief work once the First World War began. The power of the event was that networks were sustained and extended through solidarity. There was, for example, a continuing relationship between Montefiore and both Larkins. In many ways Dora's reporting from Dublin introduced Delia Larkin to a wider radical public. Lastly, at the outset of the scheme it had been observed that 'As the industrial warfare becomes keener, and the workers get stronger in their fighting industrial organisations, this aspect of the campaign will become more and more important, and we hope that some permanent, not red cross, but red flag, organisation will grow up to take care of the dependent non-combatants.'[83] Although described by many as a failure, the 'Save the Kiddies' scheme was an act of working-class solidarity organised by women which sought to show why a transnational red flag solidarity organisation was a necessity as conflicts intensified as the world wandered to war.[84]

Notes

1   *Freeman's Journal,* 24 Oct. 1913.
2   Ibid.
3   For the Domestic Workers' Union of Great Britain, see Arthur Marsh and John B. Smethurst, *Historical directory of trade unions,* vol. 5 (Aldershot, 2006), p. 227.
4   Advertisement in *Votes for Women,* 3 Oct. 1913; Dora B. Montefiore, *From a Victorian to a modern* (London, 1927), p. 156.
5   For the Countess of Warwick, see K. D. Reynolds, 'Greville, Frances Evelyn' in *Oxford dictionary of national biography.*
6   *Daily Herald,* 10 Oct. 1913.
7   *Daily Herald,* 16 Oct. 1913.
8   *Daily Herald,* 17 Oct. 1913; 18 Oct. 1913.
9   *Daily Herald,* 20 Oct. 1913.
10   *Daily Herald,* 21 Oct. 1913
11   *Daily Herald,* 21 Oct. 1913.
12   Dora B. Montefiore, *Our fight to save the kiddies* (London, [1913]), p. 6.
13   *Daily Herald,* 22 Oct. 1913.
14   Dora B. Montefiore to the archbishop of Dublin, 21 Oct. 1913, reprinted in Montefiore, *Our fight,* p. 8.
15   *Daily Herald,* 23 Oct. 1913.
16   Ibid.
17   Ibid.
18   *Daily Herald,* 24 Oct. 1913.

19   Ibid.

20   *Liverpool Weekly Mercury,* 25 Oct. 1913.

21   Ibid.

22   *Daily Herald,* 24 Oct. 1913.

23   Montefiore, *Our fight,* p. 12.

24   *Daily Herald,* 25 Oct. 1913.

25   Montefiore, *Our fight,* p. 12. The 'Hibernanians' refers to the Ancient Order of Hibernians, an Irish
      Catholic organisation.

26   *Daily Herald,* 29 Oct. 1913.

27   *Daily Herald,* 30 Oct. 1913.

28   Montefiore, *Our fight,* p. 13.

29   *Daily Herald,* 24 Dec. 1913; 2 Jan. 1914.

30   *Daily Herald,* 29 Oct. 1913; 24 Oct. 1913; 27 Oct. 1913.

31   *Irish Independent,* 24 Oct. 1913; *Freeman's Journal,* 24 Oct. 1913.

32   *Daily Herald,* 24 Oct. 1913; *Freeman's Journal,* 23 Oct. 1913.

33   *Daily Herald,* 1 Nov. 1913.

34   *Irish Times* quoted in *Daily Herald,* 27 Oct. 1913.

35   *Butte Independent,* 15 Nov. 1913.

36   Ibid.

37   *Irish Independent,* 23 Oct. 1913.

38   *Freeman's Journal,* 22 Oct. 1913.

39   *Freeman's Journal,* 23 Oct. 1913.

40   *The Times,* 22 Oct. 1913.

41   *Manchester Guardian,* 23 Oct. 1913; 25 Oct. 1913.

42   John Shepherd, *George Lansbury* (Oxford, 2002), p. 145.

43   *Daily Herald,* 30 Oct. 1913; 25 Oct. 1913.

44   *Daily Herald,* 23 Oct. 1913.

45   *Daily Herald,* 24 Oct. 1913.

46   *Daily Herald,* 27 Oct. 1913.

47   *Daily Herald,* 26 Oct. 1913.

48   *Freeman's Journal,* 21 Oct. 1913.

49   See Lucy Bland, *Banishing the beast* (London, 1995), pp 297-302.

50   *Irish Independent,* 23 Oct. 1913; Rebecca West, 'Mr Chesterton in hysterics: a study in prejudice'
      Clarion, 14 Nov. 1913.

51   *Daily Herald,* 24 Oct. 1913.

52   *Daily Herald,* 27 Oct. 1913.

53   Montefiore, *Our fight,* p. 10.

54   See K. Hunt, 'Journeying through suffrage: the politics of Dora Montefiore' in C. Eustance et al. (eds), *A
      Suffrage reader* (Leicester, 2000). For an introduction to British suffrage organisations, see Harold L.
      Smith, *The British women's suffrage campaign 1866-1928* (London, 2007).

55   *Daily Herald,* 23 Oct. 1913; 26 Oct. 1913.

56   *The Vote,* 7 Nov. 1913.

57   *The Vote,* 21 Nov. 1913.

58   *Votes for Women,* 24 Oct. 1913.

59   *Votes for Women,* 31 Oct. 1913.

60   *Common Cause,* 21 Nov. 1913.

61   *The Suffragette,* 7 Nov. 1913.

62   *The Suffragette,* 21 Nov. 1913; Barbara Winslow, *Sylvia Pankhurst: sexual politics and political activism* (London, 1996), pp 63-6.

63   *Freeman's Journal,* 22 Oct. 1913.

64   See, for example *Freeman's Journal,* 21 Oct. 1913; *Irish Independent,* 23 Oct. 1913; Arnold Wright, *Disturbed Dublin: the story of the great strike of 1913-1914* (London, 1914), p. 220; Emmet Larkin, *James Larkin* (London, 1968), p. 124.

65   Montefiore, *Our fight,* p. 4.

66   *New York Times,* 2. Feb. 1912. For the Lawrence Strike, 1912, see Ardis Cameron, *Radicals of the worst sort* (Chicago, 1995).

67   Montefiore, *Our fight,* pp 4-5.

68   Ibid., p. 6.

69   Pádraig Yeates, *Lockout: Dublin 1913* (Dublin, 2000), p. 341.

70   See Pádraig Yeates, 'The Dublin 1913 Lockout', *History Ireland*, vol. 9, no. 2 (2001), p. 33; Yeates, *Lockout,* ch. 27.

71   *Daily Herald,* 17 Oct. 1913.

72   Ibid. Clarionettes were groups associated with socialist newspaper, *The Clarion.*

73   *Daily Herald,* 3 Nov. 1913; *Irish Independent,* 3 Nov. 1913.

74   Margaret Ward, *Hanna Sheehy Skeffington: a life* (Dublin, 1997), p. 116; Yeates, *Lockout,* p. 331.

75   *Daily Herald,* 24 Dec. 1913.

76   Sue Bruley, *The women and men of 1926* (Cardiff, 2010).

77   *Daily Herald,* 18 Oct. 1913.

78   For an exception see Theresa Moriarty, 'Delia Larkin: relative obscurity' in Donal Nevin (ed.), *James Larkin: lion of the fold* (Dublin, 1998).

79   *Daily Herald,* 3 Nov. 1913.

80   *Votes for Women,* 14 Nov. 1913.

81   See for example Karen Hunt, ''Whirl'd through the World': the role of travel in the making of Dora Montefiore, 1851-1933' in *Österreichische Zeitschrift für Geschichtswissenschaften,* 22, no. 1 (2011).

82   *Daily Herald,* 3 Nov. 1913.

83   *Daily Herald,* 16 Oct. 1913.

84   See, for example, George Dangerfield, *The strange death of liberal England* (London, 2008, original edition, 1935).

6.

'The children have such freedom, I might say, such possession of the streets.' The children of Dublin 1913

....

Kate Cowan

On 2 September 1913, two tenement houses collapsed on Church Street in Dublin. These tenements buildings held shops and were also the homes of over 40 people. *The Irish Times* reported that 29 people were removed from the rubble, seven of them dead, ranging from small children to sole family earners. One of those who died while saving his younger siblings was Eugene Salmon.[1] Salmon became a young martyr for his actions but this tragedy also highlighted the dangers of slum housing conditions in 1913.

This essay will explore the events of the 1913 Lockout, with reference to the lives of the children affected. It will do this by exploring the life of the working class family, through housing, health, education and employment, especially of children. It will look at the role played by minors during this period, examining the violence against them. It will discuss the strikes of school children and evaluate youth begging on the streets. It will also look at the charitable and official responses concerning the welfare of the children in the city. Lastly it will examine and evaluate the 'Save the Kiddies' scheme that Dora Montefiore, along with several other women, ran to help the children affected by the Lockout, and the failure of that scheme. The 1908 Children Act defined a child as someone under 16 years of age, but this discussion will include references to young people up to 17 years of age. For example Eugene Salmon was 17 years old, and was a locked out worker of Jacob's biscuit factory.

The Church Street disaster

The Church Street disaster exposed the living conditions of the Dublin tenements to media scrutiny.[2] As mentioned above, many families lost their sole earner or breadwinner in the disaster so a fund was set up in aid of the families involved and the injured. This was dubbed in the newspapers as the Church Street Tenement Housing Disaster Fund and by the end of September it had close to a £1,000 in it. The Mansion House co-ordinated the appeal, with many different bodies, such as the Lord Mayor of London, sending large amounts of money for this fund.[3]

Church Street was just one of many locations where housing conditions were deemed a concern, as indicated by a Local Government Board inquiry 1900.[4] The 1911 census showed that 301,802 people, or 28% of the population lived in this type of housing in Dublin. With the collapse of the buildings in Church Street, another report was produced and published in 1914.[5] This second report classified housing in three sections; third class was unfit for human habitation, second class was so decayed that it was on the borderline of being unfit for human habitation and first class was structurally sound. The following table shows the recorded family units and people living in these conditions at the end of 1913.

Table 1. Housing in Dublin 1913

Tenements	Family units, (number of people)
First class	8,295 (27,052 people)
Second class	10,696 (37,552 people)
Third	6,831 (22,701 people)

Source: *Report of the committee appointed by the Local Government Board for Ireland to inquire into the public health of the city of Dublin* **(Dublin, 1900), p. 3.**

1. Morgan's Cottages.
DCLA, Dublin in Decay: images from 1913

Lives of children

The child mortality rate in Dublin was high in 1911 with 1,808 infants recorded dying in their first year. In 1913, a public health report showed that 4,642 adults and children died of respiratory and digestive diseases such as pneumonia and diarrhoeal diseases. Other infectious diseases like influenza and tuberculosis caused death of 93 and 1,444 respectively.[6] *The Irish Worker* in 1913 stated: 'the unfortunate infant brought into being in the Dublin underworld is cruelly handicapped from the day of his birth; the land that varies (sic) him denies him sufficient food, sends him adrift when he can scarcely toddle to swell the ranks of the homeless, ragged, half starved.'[7] As Arnold Wright said in *Disturbed Dublin* published 1914: 'if a child lives past infancy, life is bound to be difficult. Being ill-fed, ill-taught, ill-disciplined, rushed into matrimony and the old process starts to repeat itself … numbers never rise of slum life.'[8] Both quotations help to explain the situation for working-class children and their prospects.

While the census reports provide a lot of information on health, occupation and education of minors, there is no breakdown of family size. The 1911 census recorded that 1,503 children between the ages of nine and 17 living in the city were illiterate.[9] In the same year, in the city of Dublin, the census recorded that 65,856 minors between the ages of seven and 17 were attending school, though in practice school ended at primary level for nearly all working-class children.[10] In terms of occupation, the 1911 census indicates that 883 children under the age of 15 were working, though it does not give the figures for those children working who fell into the age category of 15 to 17.

Table 2. Occupations of minors 1911

Occupation/company	Number	Age
Dublin United Tramways Company	15 boys	14-17
Newspaper vendors	98 boys and girls	13-17
Labourers	270 boys and girls	7- 17

Source: NAI, 1911 census (http://www.census.nationalarchives.ie/search/) (1 Sept. 2012)

There is no way of knowing and the figures cannot establish how many of these took part in the strike of 1913 or were locked out of their place of employment.

Lockout

The Lockout began on 26 August 1913 at 10 a.m., trams stopped working all over Dublin as both drivers and conductors walked off the job. William Martin Murphy, owner of the Dublin United Tramway Company, also owned the *Irish Independent* and *Evening Herald* newspapers. Soon after the initial strike, a boycott of both papers commenced, encouraged by James Larkin, who asked vendors not to sell either publication. Many younger newspaper vendors joined the strike in 1913, which is not surprising, because Desmond Greaves has shown that Larkin had unionised some of the vendors two years earlier.[11] Newsvendors appeared to be spilt on the issue of striking and in an interview in one of his newspapers, William Martin Murphy said that his newsboys had been attacked several times since the strike begun. The *Weekly Irish Times* reported that Christopher Crosbie (aged 18) and four boys, one being Patrick Cleary (aged 13) had assaulted *Evening Herald* newsboy, Matthew Mahon. Mahon had been told by his attackers to put his papers down or they would keep beating him. This was not an isolated incident, on 6 September, James Quinn who was described as a 'little boy', was confronted at Nelson's Pillar but managed to escape from his attackers.[12]

2. Tyndall's Alley, Bridgefoot Street.
DCLA, Dublin in Decay: images from 1913

The Lockout caused widespread distress as labourers everywhere began to get locked out of work. Though not all workers were locked out or striking, their work environment would have been heavily affected. In one case, Mary Murphy, a factory worker, aged 14, was charged with attacking another girl from her factory, Messrs. W. & R. Jacob's, as she went into work.[13] Trying to continue working amidst the Lockout was made harder by the continuous update to their 'scabs' list, published in *The Irish Worker*. The scab list was a list of people still working for companies that had locked out employees. The 27 October issue gives an example of this as the papers mention both companies and people who were 'scabs', giving full addresses for most. It is surprising with lists such as this that more beatings were not reported in the newspapers, like for instance, that of James Reilly who was harassed at his home by locked-out workers of the same company for which he worked.[14]

3. Thomas Pender, injured during the baton charge on 31 August 1913.
Freeman's Journal, 4 Sept. 1913.
DCLA

Working during this chaotic period was not the only way of getting hurt; the infamous large-scale riots had thousands of casualties and a number of deaths. On 2 September, *The Freeman's Journal* reported that 400 people had been injured over two days of rioting in the city, these riots also led to the loss of two lives, James Nolan and James Byrne.[15] Large numbers of people were arrested during the following days, and by 3 September several minors were facing charges for throwing missiles at police. James Doyle was arrested on Winetavern Street and had his head bandaged when he was arrested. James Brady was also in the same state when he was arrested on Mary Street for the same crime.[16] This was the first of many riots that took place throughout this period until December. Dublin Castle's intelligence report gave an account of rioting in Finglas on 16 September, in which Patrick Daly was shot in the back by a police constable. Patrick Daly, who was 17 years old, was described as a quiet boy and employed in the local village. He recovered from his wound, as the bullet had hit his shoulder.[17]

By 23 September the state of the city had become very dangerous for civilians and police and the commissioner of the police reported that he did not have enough uniformed police to perform all the necessary duties. Strangely, the intelligence report does not record if he received extra men to help with the situation, as he already had use of military stations in Dublin.[18] The Dublin Scout Association, also known as the Baden Powell scouts, asked its members to stop wearing uniforms in the city until further notice, and this can be assumed to be for the boy scouts' safety.[19]

A martyr and victim of the violence during this period was Alice Brady. Brady was 16 years old; a member of the Irish Women Workers' Union (IWWU) who was shot in the hand during a minor riot in Great Brunswick Street. She died a month later from tetanus.[20] The riot had been caused when a group of women screamed at coal workers, who apparently broke the strike; one worker panicked and set off his revolver. In the court case it was argued that the man, Patrick Traynor, did not mean to shoot at anyone and did not aim at Brady.

Alice Brady's funeral took place in January 1914 and was used for propaganda. *The Freeman's Journal* noted that the procession was large, with 500 IWWU in attendance along with several other bodies represented. James Larkin, James Connolly, Delia Larkin and Countess Markievicz walked behind the parents in the procession, with graveside orations given by both Larkin and Connolly. Larkin said that their sister had been sacrificed at the altar of sweating misery and degradation; with her great strength of character she would have been a great woman. When giving sympathies to the parents, he also gave his sympathies to the IWWU on their loss. He finished by saying that they would leave her graveside more determined than ever to have an Ireland free from slavery thraldom, while James Connolly stated that her death was on every 'scab' and employer of a 'scab'.[21]

School strikes

Working minors were not alone in taking part in the strike during this period, as strike fever seemed to have gripped the city and many schools reported to have a problem with school children going on strike. A precedent was set in 1911 when the boys of the East Wall Primary School went on strike. It has been said that there was obvious evidence that the boys were well versed in the tactics of 'Larkinism' and articulate about their demands.[22] Their demands were logical: cheaper books, shorter hours and less caning. Teachers interviewed in *The Irish Times*, speculated that boys who had recently left school to work were behind it. Over all it does not seem to have been taken seriously by the adults or some of the children who were reported to be 'cheering and shouting and amusing themselves with some mischievousness as throwing cabbage stumps at doors.'[23] In 1913, the boys in the Pro-Cathedral National Schools went on strike, which turned violent when they started throwing stones at the windows and scaling the wall, police then came to disperse them. It was stated that around 60 boys were involved in this 'strike' and the school principal believed they did it because it was 'in the air'. At Inchicore, schoolboys went on strike because they were deprived of their rights (not explained), *The Irish Times* described their 'strike as parading around the neighbourhood and singing ragtime songs.'[24]

Street begging

Not all of the working-class children of Dublin were at work or at school. Street begging was common, and during the Lockout, it spiralled out of control. Many different people from Dublin and visitors recorded a huge number of children on the streets begging and searching for food. John Cooke, of the National Society for the Prevention of Cruelty to Children (NSPCC), said in his testimony to the Dublin Housing Inquiry that:

> The children have such freedom, I might say, such possession of the streets as Dublin. Many thousands of little ones throng the thoroughfare under no control, running moral and physical risks.[25]

Through interviews like the above, and letters to editors of newspapers, the situation of children on the streets was continuously mentioned in the media. *The Freeman's Journal* reported that the Children's Court saw increases in number of child beggars, which was partly due to the charitable public. This was said in the context of a case of two 14-year-old boys charged with late night begging; the fact that the police were distracted from their normal duties was also cited as a factor in this increase.[26]

An inspector from the NSPCC in an article for *The Irish Times* discussed the increase of child begging in detail, but asked not to be named. He said there was a change in the type of children on the street and that 'a new crowd that had come on their own to beg, dropping school and making friends with [the] dregs of society.'[27] He said that he 'recognised a child dressed in rags as the son of a wealthy tradesman, who earned 30 shillings a week' and that the father had not seen his son for a month. *The Irish Citizen* complained that begging was the 'hardest obstacle confronting decent people today.'[28] Pádraig Yeates attributes the increase in child begging to the Dublin Children's Street Trading courts, that show an unseasonal increase in the number of street trading licenses issued to minors at the end of 1913.[29]

Though some children might have been out on the streets of their own accord, there was a history of children being used for begging purposes by adults. An *Irish Times* article, published in May 1914, shows that 465 cases of neglect in the form of using children for the purposes of begging came in front of the NSPCC and the courts in the previous year.[30] The annual reports from the NSPCC actually suggested that children were better off during this period in Ireland than previous years, because they record fewer complaints received than in either 1912 or 1914. The report stated there was also a decline in the number of adults charged with cruelty to children.[31]

One reason for the rise in street begging was the many evictions in late 1913. With wage earners out of work, many could not afford to pay the rent. Some companies started to evict employees. For instance, when the union members at Merchants Warehousing refused to handle flour, the company reacted by obtaining eviction orders against 60 employees and families who lived in company houses in East Wall. By the end of September Dublin United Tramways Company was evicting strikers and their families from the company cottages.[32] On 4 December *The Irish Times* reported that the Guardians of the North Dublin Union had started to look into the evictions of East Wall to see if they could have been prevented or postponed.[33] Though there was discussion about getting canvas tents for evicted families in time for Christmas, evictions were causing many men to try and get reinstated in work. The Dublin United Tramways Company started to take back employees with a good record but only on condition of a pay cut of three or four shillings per week.[34]

Relief measures

There were some charitable responses in the city at the time. Starting in September, ships from England were sent to Dublin Port carrying food. The first ship arrived on the weekend of the 28 September 1913. The main issue with this relief was that only workers with food tickets from their trade union could access these supplies. Food ships continued to arrive until late November, bringing huge amounts of tea, sugar, margarine, bread loaves, potatoes, biscuits, jam, tins of fish, cheese, coal and also clothing. Though the *Sunday Independent* reported 'pitiable spectacles' and scenes of women pushing and shoving with their children in their arms, other accounts give a different scenario.[35] One reporter describes an incident he witnessed of a woman dividing her tea with another woman who wasn't as lucky as her to have food tickets. Many of the poor who were around were not entitled to this food, as they were not members of a trade union.[36]

The St Vincent de Paul Society was one of many charitable organisations that ran a programme for Dublin children. The Catholic archbishop of Dublin, Dr William Walsh, stated that 2,450 meals were given out daily in Catholic schools within the three parishes most affected by the Lockout. Later on he describes four different parishes that collectively had 2,045 of their children clothed by the society. The archbishop further remarked that many more children could be helped if 'money expended foolishly on, to say the least of it, sending children away from their homes … [could] instead strengthen those hands [which] are already working.'[37] Archbishop Walsh was of course referring to the 'Save The Kiddies' scheme, but his point was valid; the St Vincent de Paul Society was working on long-term relief projects, while Dora Montefiore's scheme was a short-term solution for a long-term problem.

Councillors on both sides of politics called for the Lord Mayor of Dublin to establish a fund for the women and children of workers affected by this unfortunate disturbance. Unionist councillor, David Crozier (who was a substantial slum landlord) stated that the situation was becoming desperate and that the children in the slums were neglected and it would be a bad job for Dublin.[38] The Lord Mayor himself, Lorcan Sherlock, offered the opinion that finding extra shillings for such a fund would be difficult. Two weeks later his wife, Catherine Marie Sherlock, set up the Women and Children Fund at the Mansion House, which raised money for distribution to the 15 known institutions targeting help to the poor and struggling workers' families. This was mostly done through schemes already operating in Dublin and run by the Catholic Church. In a letter to the press, it was stated that in the case of schools that weren't run by nuns, money would be given to charitable committees who were already established to feed the children.[39]

Just like most philanthropic societies at the time, money was raised for this fund mostly through subscriptions; the acknowledgement for donors was a list of their names with a letter of appreciation published in the newspapers. These thank you letters can be seen in *The Irish Times, Irish Independent, The Irish Worker* and *The Freeman's Journal*. For instance in *The Freeman's Journal*, the Lady Mayoress wrote a letter thanking over 28 people, although half of these were anonymous.[40] Subscriptions to this fund came in from different countries and counties, the *Irish Independent* noted that the Lord Mayor of Cork contributed to the fund by raising funds at a public meeting in his county.[41]

Another Women and Children Fund was started by *The Irish Worker* specifically to support dependants of the ITGWU. This fund raised money from concerts and benefit performances. In letters published by the newspaper, there were acknowledgements to a number of different theatres and performers, who conducted the benefits. Looking at the continuous number of them over late November and most of December, the fund-raisers must have been popular.[42]

With Christmas approaching, the *Daily Sketch* had appealed to its readers to send dolls to them to be given to children of poor families in Britain. The Lord Mayor requested to the newspaper that the dolls be sent to Dublin and 5,000 dolls were sent for distribution. *The Irish Worker* recorded that little girls queued all along Dawson Street to receive their dolls at the Mansion House. These girls would have been chosen by clergy and lay friends of the Lord Mayor, from the poorer districts of the city. As Pádraig Yeates points out, this would have helped Lorcan Sherlock in his re-election campaign in January, which he won and served another year as Lord Mayor of Dublin.[43]

The St Vincent de Paul Society was also given credit for maximising its help for families during the Christmas period. Reported several times during the Lockout months, for their committee being heavily involved in the distribution of relief funds, an article that stood out among them all was published on the 31 December in *The Freeman's Journal*. It credited the society with sheltering 1,700 families in December 1913, which is an increase of 310 families since the previous year. Giving shelter to families was just one of the many things this society did for the poor of Dublin, also mentioned in this chapter is their involvement in providing children's meals in schools.[44]

Save the Kiddies

In October 1913, Larkin agreed to the temporary evacuation of children of locked-out workers to English families in England. This was dubbed the 'Save the Kiddies' scheme in newspapers and was organised by Dora Montefiore, an English-Australian suffragist. Montefiore and a committee based in London laid plans to find willing families and homes for children in England affected by the Dublin Lockout, until all striking issues had been resolved.[45] Looking at the basic idea of the scheme it appeared that it would be extreme, but helpful for families who were struggling to provide for their children. From reading Dora Montefiore's memoirs and newspaper articles, it was well planned and could have possibly been a success, but sadly this scheme is nearly exclusively remembered for its failure.

After weeks of collecting clothes, getting second-hand boots fixed, organising over 100 homes to take Dublin children to England and raising money to cover transport, a three-woman delegation arrived in Dublin. This consisted of Grace Neal, Lucille Rand and Montefiore. Grace Neal was a well-known figure in the labour and suffrage movement in England; she was also heavily involved in the organisation of the Domestic Workers' Union of Great Britain in London. Lucille Rand was different as she was a newly married daughter of a wealthy American lawyer and former Californian Governor, Henry Gage. Montefiore described her briefly by saying her social and religious credentials were impeccable.[46]

Immediately after their arrival in Dublin, they began to receive attention from the press. At first this helped to get word out about their project but soon became inimical to their cause. On the day they took names for children for the scheme, Montefiore described the scene at Liberty Hall as chaotic, saying women were pushing each other to get through the door to sign up their children. She also mentioned having to turn away a mass of mothers who had not got striking husbands but wanted to take advantage of the opportunity.[47] This contradicts *The Freeman's Journal*, which published interviews with mothers who were eligible for this scheme. Most of these were curious but doubtful of the project, one woman said with reassurance of proper care, they would consider it but some others went as far to state that:

> though they were homeless, and had not a roof over their heads, they would not part with them. They would rather see them dead in their arms than give them up to a stranger.[48]

This is not the only strong opposition to what Montefiore was trying to do. The archbishop of Dublin, Dr William Walsh, wrote on a number of occasions to Save the Kiddies condemning it, calling the scheme 'a most mischievous development in our labour troubles.'[49] Archbishop Walsh condemned it by stating that there was no security as to whom they were handing their children over or whether they would be Catholic or even a person of any faith. On other occasions clergymen went as far to say it was a scheme to convert Catholic children to Protestantism, and these sentiments can also be seen in the way *The Freeman's Journal* covered the numerous attempts which the delegation made to proceed with their plan.[50]

The Catholic Church was not alone with these extreme views. Hilda Minchin mentions that Walsh received letters of support from England, America and France.[51] These came from businessmen, scholars and priests. Maud Gonne wrote from France to *The Irish Times* in support of Archbishop Walsh, stating it was a 'terribly dangerous thing to send children away like that but the facts still remained unchanged, and is a disgrace to us all, that there are always starving children in Dublin.'[52] While Gonne's stance on the merit of sending children away is debatable, her comment on the existence of starving children was correct. When discussing the plight of Dublin children and her scheme Dora Montefiore described street children she saw from her hotel window in Dublin:

> I saw three nippers, about four or five years of age, turning over the garbage, wolfing down pieces of bread and meat that they got mixed up in the refuse. That's an incredible state of things. It is a disgrace for any civilised country.[53]

The first batch of children tried to leave the Tara Streets Baths on 22 October. The group found this difficult due to two local priests, Fr Fleming and Fr Landers, from the parish of St Andrews in Westland Row blocking the way with their supporters.[54] As the group made its way to the train station, en route to the ferry at Kingstown, the crowd opposed to the scheme grew larger. Montefiore described in her memoirs, that as the crowd grew they became 'more hysterical' which forced the group to retreat to Liberty Hall.[55] At this point they were down to 16 children, and with the help of Larkin attempted again to travel to the ferry that evening. Two priests, Fr Thomas McNevin and Fr Thomas Ryan, followed on the train and even onto the ferry, continuously hounding them as they travelled. The group of 16 children successfully arrived in Surrey, to the outrage of many, but Lucille Rand, who was in charge of this group, was arrested for kidnapping.[56] As Pádraig Yeates suggests, a kidnap mania had settled on the city after the first successful group emigrated. People began to watch the ferries to make sure that no groups of children were leaving, which made the second attempt harder to organise.[57] One instance of this mania was that of a grandfather who, with his grandson and daughter, were stopped and surrounded at Kingsbridge Station. The crowd would not let him go with the child unless he agreed to a policeman and a priest accompanying them even though he was just taking them to Galway.[58] This hysteria around kidnapping made planning for another group of children to travel harder to organise.

DEPORTING CHILDREN---DUBLIN CASES.

4. Fr Fleming and Fr McNevin with the boy George Burke. Brothers Thomas and James McMahon. *Freeman's Journal*, 25 Oct. 1913.
DCLA

On 24 October, another group of 15 children attempted to travel, and this time Larkin spoke to the crowd gathered outside Liberty Hall and asked for help to get them to the train station. Montefiore records that all 15 children were carried on dock workers' shoulders the whole way.[59] The attempt to stop this group of children was led by the Ancient Order of Hibernians (Catholic fraternal organisation), followed by members of Irish National Foresters (Friendly Society), both strongly nationalist, and again by a large group of Catholic priests. The scene was described as great 'excitement', which turned to anger as the women were tackled for taking the children away.[60]

In the end a group of 18 children travelled and arrived safely in Liverpool. Yeates discussed how the newspapers, especially *The Freeman's Journal* said that the children didn't succeed in departing and then a few days later having reported that only 15 went. Both letters from Canon William Pinnington in England to Fr Flavin from the period and Montefiore in her own memoir state otherwise from what was reported originally in *The Freeman's Journal*.[61] It is logical to assume that as Canon William Pinnington and Montefiore were dealing with the group first hand in Liverpool, it is most likely that they are correct.

In the many letters that were published in opposition to the Montefiore scheme, there were several interesting points made. In many of Archbishop Walsh's letters to *The Freeman's Journal*, he mentioned schemes that the diocese was running, commenting that the money for Montefiore's scheme would have been better put into helping what is already in action to run more successfully. The aforementioned schemes match the descriptions of the work of the St Vincent de Paul Society. Larkin objected to the archbishop's claims and in *The Irish Worker* stated that the church provided no effort at all for the children until the last minute, which can be seen as untrue.[62] On 23 October, Montefiore was arrested from her hotel in Dublin on the same abduction charges as Rand. Countess Markievicz later that night made her bail, as she was a supporter of the scheme.[63]

Hilda Minchin suggests in her thesis that this scheme would have been successful if it had the full backing of the public and that it had the possibility of benefiting the situation. However, from all the evidence and Yeates' commentary, it would seem that the scheme was not viable and perhaps the money could have been used successfully by many charities in operation in Dublin at the time. From Minchin's evaluation of the 'Save the Kiddies' scheme, it is clear that there were influential forces working to make this scheme unsuccessful, notably the Dublin Catholic Church.[64] It was also opposed by many in the nationalist movement.

By December, many of the strikers and locked-out workers, had slowly started returning to work and by January anyone who still had a job had returned to work, but without any improvement in conditions. With the strike and the Church Street disaster, the situation in the Dublin slums, especially the lives of children living there were highlighted in the media. Sadly, though the charities, such as St Vincent de Paul Society, kept up their work of helping the poor, nothing serious was done by the government to improve working-class housing in these areas except for Church Street, where the number of houses was reduced from 73 tenement houses to 28 newly-built houses by 1918. Many other districts required urgent attention, but this was delayed until nearly a decade after.[65]

Conclusion

This essay explored the events of the 1913 Lockout, with reference to the lives of the children affected by the event. In evaluating the life of the working-class family, through housing, health, education and employment, a clear picture emerges of what a working-class minor's life would have entailed in 1913. It is clear that the life of the working-class child was a difficult one and shows that many repeated the life cycle of their parents. This chapter looked at the role played by minors during this period, striking in both work and school settings and examined the violence against them. In work, many children who stayed in their jobs were under threat to their safety. In school it can be seen that the student strikes were not taken seriously by the newspapers or school staff. The threat of violence was high in Dublin, there was evidence of many children getting hurt in various scenarios, an example of this being the tragic death of Alice Brady. In some instances, violence was also caused by children, for example the assault on Matthew Mahon, an *Evening Herald* newsboy. In evaluating children begging on the streets, there were many possible reasons given for the rise in numbers, which included sympathetic donations from the charitable public, an increase in vendor licences and the eviction of workers. Looking at the charitable and official responses concerning the welfare of the children in the city, it is clear that some were temporary and exclusive, such as the food ships and the doll distribution for Christmas, while others were long running schemes, such as those of the St Vincent de Paul Society. In studying past societies the lives of children often remain hidden, but due to the particular circumstances surrounding the Lockout, children's lives are highlighted from a number of different perspectives. Charitable organisations reported on children in relation to food, shelter and clothing; the newspapers reported on incidents in the streets, or instances of begging; Dora Montefiore's 'Save the Kiddies' scheme generated documentation from the Dublin Diocesan Archives, and reports in the Irish and British newspapers; visitors and observers reported on the condition of poorer children, while official reports detailed living conditions for adults and their children. This abundance of source material allows the researcher to document in some detail the lives of children in Dublin at this period.

Notes

1   *Irish Times*, 6 Sept. 1913; *Freeman's Journal*, 6 Sept. 1913; Pádraig Yeates, *Lockout: Dublin 1913* (Dublin, 2000), p. 106.

2   *Freeman's* Journal, 21 Oct. 1913; *Irish Times*, 15 Sept. 1913.

3   *Irish Times*, 27 Oct. 1913; *Freeman's Journal*, 16 Sept. 1913.

4   *Report of the committee appointed by the Local Government Board for Ireland to inquire into the public health of the city of Dublin (Dublin, 1900)*, p. 3.

5   *Report of the departmental committee appointed by the Local Government Board for Ireland to inquire into the housing conditions of the working classes in the city of Dublin (London, 1914)*, p. 2.

6   Curriculum Development Unit, *Dublin 1913: a divided city* (Dublin, 1989), p. 42.

7   *Irish Worker*, 18 Oct. 1913.

8   Arnold Wright, *Disturbed Dublin* (London, 1914), p. 31.

9   Census of Ireland, 1911. 'Area, houses, and population: Also the ages, civil or conjugal condition, occupations, birthplaces, religion, and education of the people. Province of Leinster' [CD. 6049], H.C. 1912-13, p. 253.

10   Ibid., p. 265.

11   Desmond Greaves, *The Irish Transport and General Workers Union: the formative years* (Dublin, 1982), p. 95.

12   *Irish Times*, 6 Sept. 1913. Attacks on newspaper vendors recorded also in *Freeman's Journal*, 21 Sept. 1913.

13   *Intelligence notes 1913-1916, preserved in the State Paper Office* (Dublin, 1966), p. 56.

14   *Irish Worker, 27 Oct. 1913; Irish Times,* 26 Nov. 1913.

15   *Freeman's Journal,* 2 Sept. 1913.

16   Both described as young, no ages given. *Freeman's Journal,* 3 Sept. 1913.

17   *Intelligence notes, 1913,* p. 51; *Freeman's Journal,* 18, 19 Sept. 1913.

18   *Intelligence notes, 1913,* p. 51.

19   *Dublin Evening Mail,* 13 Sept. 1913.

20   Yeates, *Lockout*, pp 487,497; *Irish Times* 1 Jan. 1914; 7 Jan. 1914.

21   *Irish Times*, 5 Jan. 1914.

22   Joe Mooney, 'Dublin's East Wall celebrates centenary of 1911 school strike' (http://1913committee.ie/blog/?p=370) (29 Nov. 2012).

23   *Irish Times*, 15 Sept. 1911.

24   *Irish Times,* 27 Sept. 1913; Yeates, *Lockout,* p. 161.

25   Wright, *Disturbed Dublin,* p. 30.

26   *Freeman's Journal,* 6 Dec. 1913; *Irish Independent* 5, Dec. 1913.

27   *Irish Times*, 28 Oct. 1913.

28   *Irish Citizen,* 3 Dec. 1913.

29   Yeates, *Lockout*, p. 314.

30   *Irish Times*, 25 May 1914.

31   Yeates, *Lockout*, pp 313-14.

32   Yeates, *Lockout*, pp 163, 446.

33   *Irish Times*, 4 Dec. 1913.

34   *Freeman's Journal*, 11 Oct. 1913; Yeates, *Lockout*, p. 251.

35   *Sunday Independent*, 28 Sept. 1913.

36   Yeates, *Lockout*, p. 185.

37   *Freeman's Journal,* 28 Oct. 1913; *Irish Independent,* 28 Oct. 1913.

38   Yeates, *Lockout,* p. 286; *Irish Times,* 27 Sept. 1913.

39   *Irish Times,* 8 Sept. 1913; *Freeman's Journal,* 8 Oct. 1913.

40   *Freeman's Journal,* 26 Sept. 1913.

41   *Irish Independent,* 31 Oct. 1913.

42   *Irish Independent,* 31 Oct. 1913; *Irish Worker,* 22 Nov. 1913; 29 Nov. 1913; 20 Dec. 1913.

43   *Irish Worker,* 20 Dec. 1913; *Yeates, Lockout,* p. 493.

44   *Freeman's Journal,* 31 Dec. 1913.

45   Dora Montefiore, *From a Victorian to a modern* (London, 1927), p. 157.

46   Yeates, *Lockout*, p. 249; Montefiore, *From a Victorian to a modern,* p. 159.

47   Montefiore, *From a Victorian to a modern,* p. 160; *Freeman's Journal,* 23 Oct. 1913.

48   *Freeman's Journal,* 21 Oct. 1913.

49   *Freeman's Journal,* 21 Oct. 1913.

50   This can be seen in numerous articles in the *Freeman's Journal* between 22 and 26 Oct. 1913.

51   Hilda Minchin 'Dora Montefiore and the plan to evacuate children during the 1913 Lockout' (M.A. thesis, NUI, Maynooth, 1998), p. 45.

52   *Irish Times,* 23 Oct. 1913; Yeates, *Lockout,* p. 309.

53   *Freeman's Journal,* 21 Oct. 1913.

54   *Freeman's Journal,* 23 Oct. 1913.

55   Montefiore, *From a Victorian to a modern,* p. 161.

56   *Freeman's Journal,* 23 Oct. 1913.

57   Yeates, *Lockout,* p. 286; *Freeman's Journal,* 25 Oct. 1913.

58   Yeates, *Lockout,* p. 286.

59   Montefiore, *From a Victorian to a modern,* p. 162.

60   *Freeman's Journal,* 25 Oct. 1913.

61   Yeates goes on to explain why he believes Montefiore over the newspapers in this particular account. Yeates, *Lockout,* pp 269, 609.

62   *Irish Worker,* 8 Nov. 1913.

63   Dora Montefiore, *From a Victorian to a modern*, pp 169-70.

64   Minchin 'Dora Montefiore and the plan to evacuate children', p. 43.

65   Jacinta Prunty, *Dublin slums, 1800-1925: a study of urban geography* (Dublin, 1998), p. 320.

7.

'Infernos of degradation': a visual record of tenement life in Dublin

....

Enda Leaney

On the evening of Tuesday 2 September 1913, two tenement houses at 66 and 67 Church Street collapsed. Seven people were killed. Three of the dead were children. One of the men who died was Eugene Salmon who was on strike from his job at Jacob's. The Church Street tragedy took place two days after 'Bloody Sunday' when the Dublin Metropolitan Police baton-charged members of the public after a trade union meeting on Sackville (O'Connell) Street. The ensuing riot left two dead and many injured. Violence spread throughout the rookeries of Foley Street, Townsend Street, Chancery Street, and Mary's Place. The bloodshed, beatings, and mayhem of September 1913 testified to a city that was coming apart at the seams. One contemporary commentator saw the widespread poverty of the city at the root of revolution: 'It is beyond serious cavil that the evil social conditions of Dublin were a cause, possibly the primary cause, of the Larkinite movement obtaining the hold it did.'[1]

The Church Street collapse instigated a significant inquiry into the state of housing in Dublin. The inquiry was held during the Lockout in November and December 1913. As part of this inquiry, John Cooke (honorary treasurer of the National Society for the Prevention of Cruelty to Children) and his colleague W. J. Joyce took a number of photographs to illustrate the horrific conditions endured by almost one-third of Dubliners.[2] The personal and uniquely visual nature of these photographs ensures that they are the most shocking records of Dublin's 'infernos of degradation'.[3] If it is true that chronic poverty lay at the root of urban unrest in 1913, then it follows that any consideration of the legacy of the Lockout must include these images.

In the early years of the 20th century, Dublin was the one of the worst places to live in Western Europe. Dublin had a death rate comparable to Calcutta and Moscow, and consistently had the highest infant mortality rates for the United Kingdom.[4] The totems of this degradation were the city's infamous tenements.

145

1. Tenement buildings in Dublin, 1913.

The tenement system arose from the migration of Dublin's upper and middle classes from the city centre to the suburbs in the middle of the 19th century. The mansions they left behind in Gardiner Street, Gloucester Street, Mount Street, and Merrion Square were broken up into tenements. Dublin's labouring poor, unable to afford rents beyond those of one or two rooms, transformed these tenements into over-crowded hives of dirt and disease. The 1901 census showed that 36.6% of families in Dublin lived in one room. This far exceeded other major cities in the United Kingdom: Glasgow (24%), Edinburgh (14.2%), and London (14.7%).[5] The Chief Medical Officer for Dublin, Sir Charles Cameron, noted: 'I know of no other city in which so large a proportion of the population reside in houses originally meant for higher classes of society.'[6]

2. Kennedy's Cottages, off Sandwith Street, 1913.

3. Ruinous stable at the rear of South Cumberland Street, 1913.

The adjoining coach-houses and stables of Dublin's Georgian mansions were sometimes converted into ramshackle 'courts' and 'cottages'. These transient structures often bore the name of current or previous landlords. They were notorious for over-crowding and poor sanitation. Examples of this 'forgotten Dublin' include Saul's Cottages (near Power's Court), Latimer's Cottages (near Newfoundland Street), and Murphy's Cottages (near St Mary's Place).

A family lived in the loft while the ground floor was used as a stable. Converted stables and coach-houses were especially common at the rear of fashionable squares and streets as Merrion Square, Fitzwilliam Square, St Stephen's Green, and Upper Mount Street.[7]

4. Entrance to Tickell's Court, Beresford Street, North King Street, 1913.

Tickell's Court is an example of one of the many 'courts' hidden behind the main streets of the city and often built on the gardens of formerly grand Georgian houses. The families living in these courts – sometimes two families to a single cottage – often shared a single toilet and tap. The warren of lanes and alleys bounded by North King Street, Church Street, and Beresford Street in the North Inner City was notorious for its deprivation. Tickell's Court was one of the many courts and alleys in this area.

The housing problem

The problem stemmed from a lack of adequate housing rather than over-population. For example, in Belfast there was one house for every five people yet in Dublin there was one house for every nine people.[8] Scarcity of housing created the tenement problem as sometimes up to 30 families moved into the buildings that were never intended to house more than one family. In 1903 more than one third of the population of Dublin (est. 293,385) lived in 6,195 registered tenement houses.[9]

5. Storey's Buildings, off Thomas Street, 1913.

6. Forbes' Cottages, off Marrowbone Lane, 1913.

Poor families could rarely afford to rent more than one or two rooms. Over-crowding and its concomitants of lack of privacy, sanitation, and adequate light were everyday hardships for thousands of Dubliners. For example, the 1911 census lists Thomas Murphy, a coal porter, living with his wife Ellen and seven children at Storey's Buildings.

A widow named Elizabeth Kearney lived with her seven children in two rooms at Forbes' Cottages. Over 50 people lived here. The Dubliners who lived in these slums had a degraded existence. An investigation into the conditions of 1,254 working class families in 1904 found that 60% were living in one room tenements. 12% lived in buildings that were conducive to health. Only six families enjoyed satisfactory sanitation.[10]

7. Nerney's Court, 1908.

Nerney's Court was typical of the living conditions of Dublin's poor. The house at 1 Nerney's Court, was divided into six rooms, each room housing a family. A total of 21 people lived in the house. The following lists the entire worldly goods of a family consisting of a husband, his wife, and three children that lived in a room at 1 Nerney's Court: 'no bed, sacks thrown on floor; pan, 2 buckets, 2 cans, 4 mugs, 2 tin canisters, tumbler, 4 bottles, small milk jug, statue, 5 pictures (frameless), 2 shawls, quilt, comb, bad clothes brush.' Their diet consisted entirely of bread and tea (no butter), bacon occasionally, and 'cabbage on Sundays'.[11]

Disease

It had been long been recognised by observers that the one room tenement was a death trap. Before the Public Health Inquiry of 1900 Sir Francis McCabe identified 'the tenement dwellings of Dublin as the prime source and cause of the high death rate.'[12] Contagious diseases such as typhus, TB, and whooping cough, flourished where people were in such close proximity to each other '... it is almost exclusively the homes of the very poorest – nearly one fourth of the population – that prove the hotbeds of disease, in which germs and microbes flourish, and from these places they speed out into other houses.'[13] Children went to bed in filthy sheets and slept on disease-ridden rags. In 1903 one of the vectors of the smallpox epidemic (the last of its kind in Ireland) was infected clothing.[14] Washing clothes in poorly-ventilated buildings created a different hazard as dampness was the ideal environment for colds and fevers to spread.[15] Statistics compiled by Dublin Corporation's Public Health Committee put beyond question the direct causal relationship between poverty and death. The death rate of people living in one or two room tenements was 27.74 per 1,000 compared with the rate for those in three or four room tenements (19.45 per 1,000) and those in five rooms or more (11.23 per 1,000).[16]

8. Tyrone Street, 1913.

In 1907 an outbreak of typhus was traced to houses in Tyrone Street ('and its immediate neighbourhood') and Chancery Lane: 'In nearly all the houses in which the disease occurred there was poverty and its usual concomitant – filth.'[17] It was discovered in 1909 that typhus was a disease of dirt transmitted by the human body louse. In 1913 a total of 13 people died from typhus in Dublin while only two deaths were recorded in the whole of England and Wales.[18]

9. Church Street, 1913.

In 1903 a smallpox epidemic was traced to a number of locations including 56 Church Street, which housed 13 families and 42 persons: 'All were poor, some in absolute want.'[19]

10. Engine Alley, 1913.

In 1913 a family of six people from 17 Engine Alley were admitted to the Cork Street Fever Hospital with typhoid fever. The infection was traced to a faulty drainage system. Two of the family subsequently died.[20]

11. Common water fountain at Angle Court, off Beresford Street, 1913.

12. Kean's Court, off Church Street, 1913.

Sanitation

The mansions of ascendancy Dublin were not intended for the use of multiple families. Observers noted that excrement covered the hallways of some tenements because of a lack of adequate toilet facilities.[21] One tenement had 95 inmates sharing three water closets. A house in Francis Street had 107 people sharing two water closets. Over 1,000 tenements having 20 or more inhabitants had a single water closet per building. Common water fountains – a health risk in themselves – were often found close to sewers.[22]

A house near Kean's Court containing 11 rooms housed 50 people with one available closet in the yard. One family of 11 people 'were in a very bad way' – the father, a tradesman, was long out of employment. Another court in the area contained nine houses with four rooms in each, holding 36 women. There were three open closets for the area.[23]

13. Crabbe Lane, off Mercer Street, 1910.

Lanes not owned by Dublin Corporation were not cleaned and became dumping grounds for refuse and sewage. They were synonymous with filth and disease. In 1910 there were 900 streets, lanes, streets, courts, passages, and open yards not in charge of the Corporation. The dwellings in these lanes were occupied by 16,000 people. Crabbe Lane, off Mercer Street, was one of the very worst parts of the city in this regard. Rotting meat and vegetable matter created swarms of flies and noxious vapours. In 1909 Public Health Inspectors discovered a pile of refuse weighing over five tons in a lane off Richmond Road.[24]

14. Magennis Court, off Townsend Street, 1913.

15. Brady's Cottages, off Lime Street, 1913.

Dry toilets were a particular problem. There were at least 17,200 houses in Dublin relying on outdoor dry closets or privies (a simple hole in the ground with limited water for flushing). These were rarely emptied. In the late 19th century Charles Cameron found 'an ashpit containing certainly not less than a ton-weight of semi-fluid filth' at Magennis Court. The odour was so disgusting that residents could not open their windows.[25]

Unemployment

The 1911 census showed that there was little economic growth in Dublin. The numbers employed in manufacturing had fallen from 33% (1841) to 20% (1911). Over 24,000 men – one quarter of adult males in the city – worked as unskilled or 'general' labourers. The commonest occupations listed for tenement dwellers were 'labourer' and 'charwoman'. The only equipment they had was their muscle and they were reduced to eking out an existence on the wharves or doing odd jobs. For example, eight of the 13 men living at Brady's Cottages, off Lime Street in 1911, worked as 'general labourers'. The supply of unskilled labourers greatly exceeded demand and drove wages down. The housing inquiry of 1913 found that of the 21,000 heads of families that occupied the tenements, only 12% earned over 30s. per week. It was generally agreed that a weekly income of 21s. was necessary to remain above subsistence levels.

16. Cook Street, 1913.

For most of Dublin's unskilled workforce, their day-to-day existence was an eternal grind to keep their families fed and sheltered. It was impossible for families to have sufficient nourishment from their diet. The entire diet of one coal labourer's family from South Gloucester Street, with a weekly and infrequent income of 14s. per week, consisted of bread, butter, and tea. Another labourer's family of five from Great Clarence Street fared even worse living on 'tea and dry bread … and sometimes a rasher of bacon and an onion.' A labourer's family of six from Thunder's Court existed on 'bread, butter, and tea for all meals' with 'occasionally meat or a rasher and egg for dinner.'[26]

A popular occupation for young men, especially teenagers, was as 'messengers'. One such messenger lived at Bride Street with his wife, and four children. He earned 11s. per week. The rent was three shillings a week, leaving eight shillings for food, fuel, light, clothes, bedding, etc. His wife and youngest child were consumptives. Their diet consisted entirely of bread and tea.[27]

17. Hackett's Court, 1913

Children

Dublin had the highest rate of infant mortality in the United Kingdom from 1899 to 1913. For example, the death rate of infants in 1913 for Dublin county (160 per 1,000) and Dublin city (153 per 1,000) were far higher than Liverpool (133 per 1,000), London (106 per 1,000), and Glasgow (129 per 1,000).[28] It was the high mortality of the children of the poor which greatly raised the general rate. The principal killers of children were measles, whooping cough, and diarrhoea. The contrast between the life expectancies of the rich and poor was at its most pronounced when one considered infant mortalities (i.e. deaths of infants under one year old): the death rate of children of 'independent, professional, and middle classes' was 2.5 per 1,000 in 1903. The death rate for children of 'hawkers, porters, labourers, etc.' was 14.2 per 1,000.[29] Poor clothing, malnourishment, and squalid environments caused pneumonia, bronchitis, and gastric illness. As Charles Cameron noted: 'Infants are to be seen in the arms of adults or children seated on the door steps in cold weather and exposing the tender infants to cold and even damp; want of cleanliness, irregularity of feeding ...'[30] In 1907 tuberculosis in other organs of the body (excluding the lungs) killed 474 people, the majority of whom were children. The disease was spread by coughing or spitting or through drinking milk from TB-ridden cattle. Weakened children were especially susceptible to diseases like measles that rarely caused fatalities in the middle and upper classes.[31]

The character of the working classes

The notoriously run down Ash Street in the Coombe area was a haven for prostitutes. 'I think that each and every house in that street ought to be levelled to the ground' said a priest from the Francis Street Parish.[32] The social habits of the poor were a source of morbid fascination for observers. For Arnold Wright, an apologist for Dublin's merchant class, the Dublin slum was 'a thing apart in the inferno of social degradation. To say that men and women live like beasts of the field is in fact the merest truth.'[33] The sexual mores of Dublin's poor are hard to quantify although the city boasted a thriving prostitution industry and startlingly high rates of gonorrhoea and (until 1910 at least) syphilis.[34]

18. The Coombe area, 1913.

Rev. William Farrell of the Westland Row Parish complained of 'orgies' taking place at a tenement in Fitzwilliam Lane, off Baggot Street. Fitzwilliam Lane had a particularly poor reputation and was regarded as a half-way house before the workhouse and probable death. The mortality rates for Dublin's public institutions were truly shocking. In 1910 44.1% of the total number of deaths in Dublin were in workhouses. In the larger English towns, this figure was usually around 18%.[35] The houses that collapsed in Church Street were said to be 'palaces' in comparison to the dens of Fitzwilliam Lane.[36]

For many, the attractions of the public house provided a respite from the horrors of home. There was some debate about whether the pub or the tenement was the greater

19. The Tower Bar, Henry Street, not dated.

influence on the character of the poor. There are varying accounts of the drinking habits of Dublin's poor from those who had direct experience of the slums. Some such as Rev W. J. McCreery of the Parish of St Kevin's, St Werburgh's, and St Anne's held 'that the slums are the results, not of the high rents and of the low wages, but … of the unfortunate habits of the people.'[37] McCreery opined that 'a man would not live in the slums at all if he was a sober and industrious man.'[38] For John Cooke, drinking was the primary cause of the neglect of children: 'All through the twenty-four years work of the Children's Society the dominating cause of the misery, destitution of the working classes, and the consequent neglect and cruelty to children is drink.'[39] One woman who kept a very tidy room in a tenement informed Cooke that 'the froth of porter is never blown to the floor of this room.'[40] Others such as Fr Costello of the Parish of St Michael's and St John's were less inclined to moralise and believed that the 'conditions of life which [the poor] lead [were] calculated to drive them to drink.'[41] Fr Aloysius of Church Street concurred that 'the condition of the houses is largely responsible for the drinking habits of the people.'[42] Walter Carpenter of the Independent Labour Party emphasised the utter lack of comfort in the homes of the poor who 'were driven from that house to the street, and from the street to the public house.'[43] Even Sir Charles Cameron – a man not noted for his moderate opinions – detected a touch of hypocrisy in those who painted Dublin's poor as *causa sui* degenerates: 'the workman is blamed for visiting the public house, but it is to him what the club is to the rich man. His home is rarely a comfortable one, and in winter the bright light, the warm fire, and the gaiety of the public house are attractions which he finds difficult to resist.'[44] Rev. P. J. Monahan of the Parish of St Francis noted that men who were removed from the slums to a 'week house' in the Dublin Artisans' Dwellings Company had an improved 'tone and respectability' and had no interest in the attractions of the pub.[45]

20. St Mark's Court, off Mark's Lane, off Mark Street, 1913.

The plight of Dublin's poor at the beginning of the 20th century is barely comprehensible for Dubliners today. For many, life was a relentless treadmill of dirt, disease, and death. Most damning of all, there was an absence of hope in their lives.

Arguably the most chilling statement to the 1914 housing inquiry was made by John Cooke, the man whose photographs do more than anything else to remind us of the terrible conditions our predecessors endured. The poor, Cooke told the Committee of Inquiry, had a fatalistic perspective on their situation: 'Nowhere did I find a revolt against the housing conditions; on the contrary, I found expressions of fear that anything was going to be done which would limit the tenements by the destruction of houses, and that they would be rendered homeless.'[46]

A note on the photographs:

The following images originally appear in the 1914 Housing Report and are available to view online at http://dublincitypubliclibraries.com/image-galleries/digital-collections/derelict-dublin-1913 (Nos. 1, 2, 3, 4, 5, 6, 8, 10, 11, 12, 16, 19). Image No. 7 appears in the *Report upon the state of public health and the sanitary work, etc. performed in Dublin during the year 1908, also forty-sixth annual report upon the analysis of food, drugs, water etc.* (Dublin, 1909). Image No. 13 appears in *Report upon the state of public health and the sanitary work, etc.* performed in Dublin during the year 1910, also forty-ninth annual report upon the analysis of food, drugs, water etc. (Dublin, 1911). Images Nos. 7 and 13 are available to view online at http://dublincitypubliclibraries.com/image-galleries/digital-collections/dirt-and-disease-public-health-dublin-1903-1917. Image No. 18 is part of the Dublin City Council Photographic Collection.

Notes

1 Arnold Wright, *Disturbed Dublin, the story of the great strike of 1913-1914, with a description of the Irish capital* (London, 1914), p. 250.

2 See Christiaan Corlett, *Darkest Dublin, the story of the Church Street disaster and a pictorial account of the slums of Dublin in 1913* (Dublin, 2008) for the definitive account of the Church Street disaster and the photographs taken of Dublin's slums in 1913.

3 Wright, *Disturbed Dublin*, p. 29.

4 James Connolly, *Labour in Ireland, Labour in Irish history, The re-conquest of Ireland* (Dublin and London, 1922), pp 254-5.

5 Sir Charles A. Cameron, *Report upon the state of public health and the sanitary work, etc. performed in Dublin during the year 1903, also forty-second annual report upon the analysis of food, drugs, water etc.* (Dublin, 1904), p. 100.

6 Cameron, *Report upon the state of public health and the sanitary work, etc. performed in Dublin during the year 1908, also forty-sixth annual report upon the analysis of food, drugs, water etc.* (Dublin 1909), p. 111.

7   Cameron, *Report upon the state of public health 1903,* p. 101.

8   Ibid., p. 100.

9   Ibid., p. 106.

10   See the testimony of Mr J. B. Hughes who had 13 years experience of social work in Dublin to the 1914 housing inquiry. *Report of the Departmental Committee appointed by the Local Government Board for Ireland to inquire into the housing conditions of the working classes in the city of Dublin, presented to parliament by command of His Majesty, with, Appendix to the Report of the Departmental Committee appointed by the Local Government Board for Ireland to inquire into the housing conditions of the working classes of the city of Dublin, minutes of evidence, with appendices* (London, 1914), p. 187.

11   Cameron, *Report upon the state of public health 1908,* p. 113.

12   Quoted in Joseph V. O'Brien, *Dear dirty Dublin, a city in distress, 1899-1916* (Berkeley, CA, 1982), p. 125.

13   Charles Cameron, quoted in *Report of the Departmental Committee appointed by the Local Government Board for Ireland to inquire into the housing conditions of the working classes,* p. 231.

14   Cameron, *Report upon the state of public health 1903,* p. 67.

15   Sir Charles A. Cameron, *Report upon the state of public health and the sanitary work, etc. performed in Dublin during the year 1907, also forty-fifth annual report upon the analysis of food, drugs, water etc.* (Dublin, 1908), p. 120.

16   Cameron, *Report upon the state of public health 1903,* p. 100.

17   Cameron, *Report upon the state of public health 1908,* p. 39.

18   O'Brien, *Dear dirty Dublin,* p. 109.

19   Sir Charles A. Cameron, *Report upon the state of public health and the sanitary work, etc. performed in Dublin during the year 1902, also forty-first annual report upon the analysis of food, drugs, water etc.* (Dublin, 1903), p. 42.

20   *Report of the Departmental Committee appointed by the Local Government Board for Ireland to inquire into the housing conditions of the working classes,* p. 101.

21   Ibid., p. 200.

22   Ibid., p. 118.

23   Ibid., p. 103.

24   Sir Charles A. Cameron, *Report upon the state of public health and the sanitary work, etc. performed in Dublin during the year 1909, also forty-seventh annual report upon the analysis of food, drugs, water etc.* (Dublin, 1910), p. 98.

25   Quoted in Jacinta Prunty, *Dublin slums, 1800-1925: a study in urban geography* (Dublin, 1998), p. 68.

26   Ibid., pp. 114-115.

27   Cameron, *Report upon the state of public health 1907,* p. 113.

28   O'Brien, *Dear dirty Dublin,* p. 107.

29   Cameron, *Report upon the state of public health 1903,* p. 100.

30   *Report upon the state of public health and the sanitary work, etc. performed in Dublin during the year 1910, also forty-ninth annual report upon the analysis of food, drugs, water etc.* (Dublin 1911), p. 54.

31   Cameron, *Report upon the state of public health 1903,* p. 109.

32   *Report of the Departmental Committee appointed by the Local Government Board for Ireland to inquire into the housing conditions of the working classes,* p. 118.

33   Wright, *Disturbed Dublin,* p. 29.

34   O'Brien, *Dear dirty Dublin,* pp 119-20.

35   See Cameron, *Report upon the state of public health 1909,* p. 34.

36   *Report of the Departmental Committee appointed by the Local Government Board for Ireland to inquire into the housing conditions of the working classes,* p. 126.

37   Ibid., p. 199.

38   Ibid., p. 200.

39   Ibid., p. 102.

40   Ibid., p. 102.

41   Ibid., p. 97.

42   Ibid., p. 124.

43   Ibid., p. 237.

44   Cameron, *Report upon the state of public health 1903*, p. 120.

45   See Monahan's testimony in the *Report of the Departmental Committee appointed by the Local Government Board for Ireland to inquire into the housing conditions of the working classes*, p. 120.

46   Ibid., p. 102.

21. Michael J. F. McCarthy, *Priests and people in Ireland* (Dublin, 1903).

8.

William Martin Murphy, the employers and 1913

Thomas J. Morrissey

The early years

It is a truism that to understand a person one must view him/her in context. This is particularly so of a man as complex as William Martin Murphy.

He was born near Castletownbere, Co. Cork, on 6 January 1845, the only child of Denis Murphy, building contractor, and his wife, Mary Anne Martin. The next year the family and business moved to Bantry, Co. Cork. When William was four years of age his mother died. His father was away a good deal on business; William received much support from relatives and family friends, especially the Sullivan family. T. D. Sullivan (author of 'God Save Ireland', the anthem of the Irish Parliamentary Party) and A. M. Sullivan (proprietor of *The Nation* newspaper) were close friends of his father.

William became self-reliant from an early age. A smallish, quiet, but intelligent boy, he felt at home in Bantry; and he returned there each year throughout his life, remaining 'Willie Murphy' to the local people despite his business success. He was to describe himself as belonging 'to the people, belonging to the common clay of Ireland. It is in my nature and my bones'.[1]

He attended the local national school and then, aged 13, was sent to Dublin to attend Belvedere College. He lived in lodgings with two of the Sullivan boys. His self-reliant, determinedly independent personality was already evident. In later years, he recalled two indications of this with some pride. When he left home, his father arranged that on the 40 mile coach journey from Bantry to Cork he would sit beside Mick Sullivan, the driver of the horse-drawn vehicle, a 'whip' of local fame. During the journey, a Captain Walker came on board and put pressure on young Murphy to vacate his seat to him, but he remained unyielding, showing 'scant respect for age and rank.' Again, on his first day in Belvedere he experienced bullying from a bigger boy sitting behind him. He tried to ignore it, but 'on receiving a more severe assault' he reached out and gave his tormentor 'a back-hander across the face.' To his relief, his teacher, who was the rector of the college, exonerated him, saying: 'That's right. He deserved that. I was watching him.'[2] Throughout his life Murphy would refuse to be bullied.

After school, he and the Sullivan boys spent time assisting at *The Nation* offices. On leaving Belvedere he was apprenticed to a well known Dublin architect, John Lyons, owner and editor of *The Irish Builder*. He obtained further newspaper knowledge doing sub-editing and other work on *The Irish Builder*. Then, in his 18th year, his father died, and he had to return home to run the business.[3]

1. Portrait of William Martin Murphy.
E. MacDowel Cosgrave, *Dublin and County Dublin in the twentieth century* (Dublin, 1907).
DCLA

The successful business man

Murphy related easily with the work force, and soon expanded the enterprise to the point of moving his headquarters to Cork city. He branched into light rail construction. He soon made a mark in Cork society. He was a sober young man, a practising Catholic, with a social conscience (he was an active member of the St Vincent de Paul Society), and in an age which valued good conversation he could converse knowledgeably on many subjects – he was widely read in history, to a lesser degree in literature, as well as in engineering, architecture and law. He was far from Yeats's association of business with philistine fumbling 'in a greasy till'. He married Mary Julia Lombard, from one of Cork's oldest business families, by whom he had five sons and three daughters.

In 1875 business prospects led him to move headquarters to Dublin, where he developed interests in railways and tramways in conjunction with his influential father-in-law, James Fitzgerald Lombard, and in Clery's department store and the Imperial Hotel. He bought a large house and property at Dartry, known as Dartry Hall, and participated in local activities. He set up a branch of the St Vincent de Paul Society at Terenure and acted as its president for many years. He involved himself in unostentatious works of charity,[4] and also acted as president of the Rathmines and Rathgar Musical Society, and as captain of Milltown Golf Club.[5] At Kingstown (Dún Laoghaire) he continued his life long acquaintance with the sea and with sailing.

Member of Parliament

Murphy's home area of Bantry provided a number of prominent politicians to the Irish Parliamentary Party. Among them were T. M. Healy and his brother Maurice, T. D. Sullivan, A. M. Sullivan, and Dónal Sullivan. They were related and were known as the 'Bantry Band'. Young Murphy grew up with a strong sense of patriotism and an interest in politics. His patriotism found practical expression, as his business expanded. Although he built tramways and/or light rail in Britain, Portugal, South America, and Africa, he retained his headquarters in Dublin rather than in London, invested his money in Ireland rather than overseas, retained his belief in the country's possibilities and felt a sense of obligation to provide employment. He also took pride in being, what was then a rare phenomenon, a successful Irish Catholic businessman. His interest in politics found expression in his seeking and winning election to parliament for St Patrick's Division, Dublin, in 1885. He became one of the 'Bantry Band' and a respected member of parliament, speaking up for workers on social issues. On 24 March 1890, he pointed out, in *The Freeman's Journal*, with respect to the building labourers' strike in Dublin, that the employers had no case, that the sum sought by the workers he had been paying as the going rate ten years previously. Subsequently, he was invited by the union's secretary to chair the public meeting which announced the arbitration settlement. At the meeting, he, together with the arbitrators, Archbishop William Walsh, Michael Davitt, and Charles Dawson, was loudly cheered by the assembled workers. His presence in politics also widened his social and business contacts in Britain.

Murphy's popularity with his constituents changed to vituperation following the Parnell split. He sided with the majority of the Irish Parliamentary Party and founded the *National Press*, which was critical of Parnell. The Dublin working class remained intensely loyal to Parnell, and in 1892 Murphy was defeated by a Parnellite candidate, William Field, a Dublin victualler, and was portrayed as an unscrupulous betrayer and destroyer of the 'martyred Chief'.[6] The hostile image was set in the workers' memory before Larkin added his weight of invective to it.

Knighthood refused

In 1907 Murphy played a major part in the highly successful Irish International Exhibition. There was talk of his being knighted for his work. He made it clear to the Lord Lieutenant, the Marquis of Aberdeen, that he would not accept the honour. The Lord Lieutenant did not pass on the message to King Edward VII, who arrived at the exhibition with a schedule that included the knighting of William Martin Murphy. When the time came for His Majesty to call for the ceremonial sword, Aberdeen looked at Murphy. The latter refused to budge, and the Lord Lieutenant was obliged to step forward to explain that this part of the proceedings was being omitted.[7] The stubbornness and strength of character that could refuse a Lord Lieutenant and inconvenience a king made a considerable impression. The *Daily Chronicle*, in its 'Office Window', seeking to grasp Murphy's elusive personality, observed that when one met him one 'got the impression of an ascetic, kindly man of the diplomatic class, exceedingly well dressed, quiet spoken with a humorous twinkle in his eye, and no trace of a Dublin accent. His was a case of the iron hand in the velvet glove.'[8]

Attitude as employer

Murphy had the reputation of being a demanding but fair employer. He operated a family business and he had a paternal sense of his role as an employer. He made his views clear to fellow employers:

> Apart from its justice, the policy of looking after the conditions of your labour, particularly low paid labour, without waiting to be asked, will be found to pay from a business point of view. A voluntary advance of wages to meet the increased cost of living will be far more highly valued than anything extracted in times of social welfare ... It is not possible in large undertakings that employers can come into personal contact with many of their workmen, but the latter are quick to discern when they are looked upon as something more than mere machines, and

where an interest in them and their welfare exists beyond the mere exchange of labour and wages.[9]

He felt he could look after his own workers, that unions were not necessary. Like many employers he viewed trade unions as a constraint, something to be accepted only as a necessary evil. He came to be more amenable to traditional unions when confronted with Larkin's more aggressive and unstable form of combination.

Larkin's impact

The Irish Transport and General Workers' Union (ITGWU) came into existence in 1909. James Larkin was General Secretary, and the union's ultimate aim was 'the realisation of an industrial commonwealth' in which 'all children, all women and all men shall work and rejoice in the deeds of their hand.'[10] In Murphy's view, what Larkin sought was the destruction of capitalists and the establishment of a co-operative commonwealth 'in which he, no doubt, was to be Cromwell.'[11]

The reference to 'Cromwell' indicated the fear generated by Larkin's intimidating stature, assertive personality, and a power of rhetoric and invective that stirred up and won the loyalty of very many of the Dublin working class. 'It was strange enough', Murphy observed, 'that even the most ignorant labourers should be caught up by this claptrap, but it is amazing to think how the skilled tradesmen of the city, as represented by the Trades Council, came under the domination of Mr Larkin, and allowed themselves to be dragged at his tail.'[12]

Larkin's main weapon, both to undermine employers and to unite workers, was the system of 'sympathetic strikes'. His influence was furthered by his newspaper, *The Irish Worker*, which had a wide circulation, taught workers their rights, and was remarkable, in an age of abusive journalism, for its scurrilous, libellous comments and character assassination. Nobody or no organisation was safe from the vitriol of Larkin's pen. Murphy became a particular target.

Employers' response

Trade union unrest extended far beyond the bounds of 'Larkinism'. There was strike fever in Dublin in 1911. Workers faced violence if they crossed picket lines. Many employers gave way to worker demands. A carters' strike in June proved the last straw for affected employers. The carters had gone on strike without notice, and then prevented other workers from working 'by intimidation and violence'. The Dublin Employers' Federation

Limited (DEF) was founded, which had as its objectives the 'mutual protection and indemnity of all employers of labour in Dublin who join the federation, and to promote freedom of contract between employers and employees.'[13]

Hardly had the DEF been formed than a new wave of strikes, including rail strikes, paralysed trade and infuriated the impotent managers and directors. *The Irish Times* of 24 August, 1911, commented:

> We are getting into a position in which the fight between capital and labour will have to be fought out to the bitter end ... Anything is better than these constant strikes and threats of strikes, which dislocate business in all directions and (cause) an infinity of harm ... The strikers must be taught that they are not omnipotent.

On 21 September a resolution was sent to Dublin Castle from the local branch of the Chamber of Commerce criticising 'the apathy displayed by the authorities (in the railway strike) and their apparent disregard of the people.'[14] Six days later, at a militant Chamber of Commerce meeting, P. O'Reilly, owner of a large drapery store, warned that 'the workman of this country had been brought under the influence of that continental socialistic plague which had its origins in Russia and had spread into France and England ...' Edward H. Andrews, a prominent member of the Chamber of Commerce and a future president (1918), had no objection to strikes in the normal sense, when workers had no other course open to them, but the present run of strikes was different. They marked 'the beginning of a social war – a revolution – in the sense of setting class against class ... A small party of agitators have thought well to make Ireland the cockpit for their experiments ... The present is only the beginning of the trouble.'[15]

William Crowe, one of the timber merchants affected by the rail strike, was of the view that the ITGWU was 'permeating the whole country like a plague' and that 'the present offered an opportunity which might not come again to get rid of the pestilence which had come into their land ...'[16] As a counter, the Dublin Chamber of Commerce, on 27 September, set up an all-Ireland employers' organisation, which would advise its members on labour troubles and protect their interests in strike situations.[17] Edward H. Andrews assured the members: 'the country and the press are at our back, all religious denominations are with us, we must not falter in our duty, nor stand at ease until full liberty is restored to us.' This they could not expect to see, however, unless they were united throughout the whole country, and united also with those who thought like them in other countries.[18]

Larkin was seen as bearing the blame for all the industrial unrest, even though the major strike in the Great Southern and Western Railway was led by a large British union, the Amalgamated Society of Railway Servants (ASRS), which from 29 March 1913 became the National Union of Railwaymen (NUR). He was the *agent provocateur* who caused disorder and havoc wherever he went, in Belfast, Newry, Cork, and now in Dublin. Whether or not Larkin believed in class war, he ensured that the employers of Dublin did. What many of them failed to recognise was that without widespread grievance agitation would not be successful.

Curbing extreme reaction

Murphy, it would seem from his reminders to fellow employers, was conscious of the grounds for grievance. He was also aware of the need to curb the militancy of many of the members of the Chamber of Commerce. This last became evident in November 1911, when members, exasperated by the abuse of 'peaceful picketing', expressed their grievance against the government 'for conspicuously neglecting, in a crisis of great gravity, their obvious duty as defined by Mr Churchill.' In such circumstances, the Home Secretary, Winston Churchill would have brought in the military. The censure against the government was proposed by Mr Shanks, and seconded by a Mr Bennett. William Martin Murphy, one of the elders of the chamber, observed acidly that those who proposed the motion of censure were evidently distinguished by altruism, since they had not suffered at all in the strikes and offered absolutely no evidence to substantiate their assertions. He then proceeded with unaccustomed vigour to remind the members that while in the past the gathering of three or four people could be treated as an unlawful assembly, this was no longer the case. Peaceful pickets were protected by the Trade Disputes Act, 1906. He agreed that the government could have done more, 'but to suggest that the government should have brought in the army to mow down peaceful pickets was neither possible nor thinkable. What was known as the massacre of Peterloo was not likely to be repeated in their time. As to Mr Churchill, if his administration in England were compared to that of the administration in Ireland the result would be favourable to the latter. There was no bloodshed in Ireland. No people shot down as in England and Wales, and there was no serious rioting.[19] The motion was defeated, but not by much. The desire remained for stronger action leading to the removal of the ITGWU, which was masquerading as a trade union.

The way forward

There was one noteworthy success by management in 1911, which served as a headline for Murphy and the senior council members. On 22 September the executive of the English union, the ASRS, called an all-Ireland railway strike. The directors of the Great Southern and Western Railways (GSWR), under the chairmanship of Sir William Goulding, responded resolutely and relentlessly. Following notice of industrial action, the directors threatened to close their workshops on 28 September, putting a further 1,600 men out of work, if the strikers did not return to work. Meantime, they brought in labour from

England to keep the line going, and even managed to acquire some locomotive men. Subsequently, members of the Royal Engineers were engaged to man the engines. As a result, more and more trains ran and the strikers' morale was undermined. The union, moreover, disappointed them by refusing to bring out its members in Britain. On 27 September, the day before the closure of the workshops, the strikers' representatives sought a meeting with the GSWR board. At the meeting, the company required that the men withdraw their demand concerning 'tainted' or 'blacked goods' and express their regret for striking without notice. As regards reinstatement, each man would have to make application to the head of the respective department and would have to sign an undertaking to accept all traffic offered. The company reserved the right to re-employ. On 4 October, the workers' representatives accepted the company's terms.[20] Thus, within a short time, the members of a major British union, in Murphy's words to his own employees, 'were beaten to the ropes'. The victory gave much needed confidence to the all-Ireland employers' federation.

Fearing confrontation?

Murphy was elected vice-president of the Dublin Chamber of Commerce in 1911. He had been 'a most regular attendant' at meetings of the central council and had the reputation of being 'always foremost in looking after the interests of the commercial community.'[21] During 1911 Larkin made an unsuccessful attempt to organise the Dublin United Tramway Company (DUTC). Murphy was certain he would try again during his term as president. He had no desire to fight, but saw no alternative. Consequently, as was his way, he planned ahead. Speaking at the quarterly meeting of the Chamber of Commerce on 2 September, 1913, he stated that he had not gone into that year's conflict 'in a light-hearted and haphazard way', and that 'no man could go into a fight like this unless he was prepared to take some trouble and lose some money.'[22]

His calm, apparent imperturbability was probably a cover for considerable anxiety. He was laid low by a long, unexplained, but 'serious illness' from the end of February to the beginning of May, 1913. One suspects that it was influenced, at least in part, by the additional demands on him as president of the Chamber of Commerce and the inevitable forthcoming showdown with Larkin. He was almost 68 years of age and, as he later emphasised, he had never previously experienced a strike and an employer in that situation, anticipating a strike, 'got terrified'. Workers were at the strongest before a strike, but once they struck they had fired 'their last cartridge' and the tension was lifted from the employer.[23]

2. Trams on Grafton Street.

National Transport Museum Collection

In Murphy's case, the anticipation was all the more intimidating in that Larkin was obsessed with organising Murphy's companies and, as was his practice when faced with opposition, spewed forth a persistent stream of personalised invective against him. He created an enduring caricature of him in workers' minds as a 'capitalist sweater', a 'demon of death', and even, as in *The Irish Worker* of 7 September, 1912, 'a creature who never hesitated to use the most foul and unscrupulous methods against any man, woman, or child, who, in the opinion of William Martin Murphy stood in William Martin Murphy's way, a soulless, money-grubbing tyrant.' T. M. Healy, representing the employers and especially Murphy before the Askwith Court of Inquiry, observed that Mr Larkin, 'like a skilful general, in order to inflame his troops, had for some years been engaged in abusing Mr Murphy', describing him 'as the greatest ogre, as a monster in human shape, a sweater, and wound up with the statement that he would break his heart.' He also called him 'a low toady, a renegade, an untruthful politician, a false friend … and a whited sepulchre. It was only in Ireland', Healy remarked to loud laughter, 'that one man could fulfil all those conditions.'[24]

Murphy refused to be bullied. Nearly all the other employers, according to Healy, met with Mr Larkin and yielded to him. Murphy never met with him, and Larkin, knowing Murphy's stamp, never applied to see him.[25] He focussed on character assassination, abuse, and building up hatred and hostility. It was a recognised trait in Larkin's behaviour. James Connolly, writing privately to William O'Brien on 23 July 1913, remarked that he found Larkin 'singularly unbearable' as a boss. He 'is consumed with jealousy and hatred of anyone who will not cringe to him and beslaver him all over. He tried to bully me out of the monies due to our branch … I told him that if he was Larkin twenty times over he could not bully me.'[26] Murphy's history indicated a similar response.

An art gallery and criticism

Murphy also faced criticism from a different quarter during 1913; criticism which was to unfairly adhere to his name. He refused to help fund an art gallery to house Sir Hugh Lane's paintings, which the latter wished to have built over the River Liffey. Dublin Corporation turned down the impractical plan, but it was Murphy's dismissal of it as something to satisfy a minority of people when funds were needed for more pressing projects, that greatly angered literary figures such as W. B. Yeats and Æ (George W. Russell). Yeats, who seemed to view business people as devoid of interest in culture, is thought to have bestowed an unwelcome immortality on Murphy in his poem 'September 1913', which was not about the great strike/lockout but was a lament for the loss of a 'romantic Ireland', a loss occasioned by such as those who 'fumble in a greasy till' until they 'have dried the marrow from the bone'. However wide of the mark as a depiction of Murphy, it has continued to be used as criticism of him in the context of the 1913 strike.

Deciding to face down Larkin

Six weeks after his return to work, Murphy decided to face down the transport union. Conscious of renewed attempts to infiltrate the tramways company, he summoned a meeting of the tramway workers after midnight on Saturday, 19 July 1913. More than 700 men attended. Murphy prepared what he had to say very carefully in an attempt to create an atmosphere of reasonableness and friendship, while at the same time making it clear from the start what the company's policy was with respect to the ITGWU. He knew, he declared, that an attempt had been made to seduce men to go on strike. The directors of the company had 'not the smallest objection to men forming a legitimate union', provided they did not ally themselves to 'a disreputable organisation' under 'an unscrupulous man' who sought to use them 'as tools to make him the labour dictator of Dublin.' He was aware of those actively fomenting a strike. It would not take place, and if it did it would prove 'the Waterloo of Mr Larkin'. There were situations when strikes were justified 'and ought to be carried out' if they had any chance of success. But there was no prospect of success in the present circumstances. He drew their attention to what had happened with the Great Southern and Western Railway Company, 18 months earlier, when, despite being funded by a large British union, 'the men were beaten to the ropes in nineteen days and had to sue for peace.' There was even less chance of success against the DUTC, which would 'spend £100,000 or more to put down the terrorism which (was) being imported into the labour conditions of this city.'

Having thus warned his workforce, Murphy moved to more benign and personal matters. In the 50 years since he became an employer, he not only had 'never experienced a strike', but had never had 'any serious friction' with his men, and this was because they knew that he had sympathy with them, helped them when they were in trouble, and was always ready to meet them, 'not as a master to his servant, but as man to man.' (applause) Turning to the benefits of employment in the company, Murphy pointed to the demand for places, and how conditions and pay were more favourable than in other enterprises.[27]

One month later, nevertheless, he discovered that the ITGWU had infiltrated the parcel service of the company. He dismissed 100 men. At the same time he paid off men in the despatch department of the *Irish Independent* and its sister newspaper the *Evening Herald*. Larkin, at a public meeting at Beresford Place,[28] told the assembled workers: 'Mr Murphy says there will be no strike. I tell Mr Murphy that he is a liar. Not only is there to be a strike on the trams … we are going to win this struggle no matter what happens.' The following day, Tuesday 26 August, the first day of the Dublin Horse Show, he carried out his threat. Shortly before 10.00 a.m., as the crowds were making their way to Ballsbridge for the show, some 200 motor men and conductors left their tram cars without warning. The cars driven by men who were not members of the ITGWU were held up, with the result that the entire area from College Green to the General Post Office was lined with trams. Murphy acted immediately. By noon the congestion was cleared, and he claimed that only 150 out of 700 tram men had answered the call from the union, that the trams were running, and the strike broken. He found it easy to get replacements for the strikers and, despite acts of violence, the trams continued to run. The strike seemed definitely to have failed.

At this juncture the authorities made the mistake of arresting three prominent supporters of Larkin, P. T. Daly, William O'Brien, and Councillor Thomas Lawlor, on charges of sedition, and proscribed a labour demonstration planned for Sunday, 31 August. All were Dublin Trades Council executive members and Lawlor secretary of the Irish Municipal Employees' Trade Union. This provided Larkin with the opportunity to charge the authorities with acting 'at the dictates of William Martin Murphy'.[29] He publicly burned the proclamation banning the Sunday meeting scheduled for Sackville (O'Connell) Street, and then found refuge from the police in Countess Markievicz's house. As Sunday approached there were outbreaks of violence at a number of locations and the overstretched police force bludgeoned two men to death. On the Sunday, Larkin made his celebrated appearance at the window of Murphy's Imperial Hotel. The police, it is alleged, fearing a move to rescue Larkin, were given the order to charge. Panic ensued as men and women were beaten indiscriminately and some were trampled underfoot.[30] The police behaviour united the workers more than ever behind Larkin, even though the main newspapers defended the police, who were described as trying to curb the reign of ruffianism being forced on the city under the red flag of anarchy. That evening a series of conflicts broke out between police and people, and several tram cars were attacked. 'Over 400 civilians, including several women and children, were treated in hospitals for injuries received during Saturday and Sunday, while more than 50 police had also to be treated for wounds.'[31]

A critical mistake

To Murphy and the members of the Dublin Chamber of Commerce, at their quarterly meeting on 2 September, Larkin seemed defeated. Murphy informed those present, 'it was time to stop this man, and I think I have stopped him', but he added forthrightly, to applause, 'that some employers in Dublin had bred "Larkinism" by the neglect of their men, and then continued to support Larkin by not having the courage to stand up against him.'[32] Two days later, however, Murphy and the employers made a major blunder. Pressing home their advantage, they decided to shut out their employees from the ITGWU: workers were asked to sign a document which required them 'to carry out all the instructions' given them by or on behalf of their employer, and required them 'to immediately resign' their membership of the ITGWU (if a member) and to undertake that they would 'not join, or in any way support this union.'[33] To be obliged to forfeit one's right to join the union of one's choice violated a basic principle of trade unionists. It brought British unions to the support of the Dublin workers. The first of their food ships arrived before the end of the month. The prospect of a short, sharp struggle, which both Larkin and Murphy had envisaged, was no longer likely.

With the prospect of a long struggle, and the resultant loss of money for employers, there was a temptation to make concessions. Murphy and his council settled themselves to endure and to stiffen the resolve of fellow employers. The workers, for their part, seemed to exude confidence while focussing their enmity on Murphy: 'It's all due to William Martin Murphy, William Martin Murphy!'[34] Despite the generated hate and tangible hostility, Murphy insisted on living his normal life. His severe critic and political opponent, T. P. O'Connor, M.P., acknowledged that 'throughout all this period Mr Murphy conducted himself with characteristic courage; while people were fearing for his life every second of the day, he walked alone and unperturbed through the streets of Dublin with his umbrella under his arm';[35] until, it should be added, the police, much to his indignation, insisted on escorting him.[36]

The Askwith inquiry

On 29 September 1913, the public hearings into the strike commenced in the Court of Inquiry, which had been set up by the Board of Trade with Sir George Askwith, a respected figure in industrial relations in Britain, as chairman. T. M. Healy, M.P., S.C., as mentioned earlier, represented the employers, Larkin the workers. Healy called a number of employers as witnesses to demonstrate that it was impossible to carry on trade in Dublin in face of Larkin and his union's practice of 'sympathetic strike' and boycott of 'tainted goods'. 'Agreements made by the Irish Transport Union', Healy declared, 'had been shamelessly and scandalously broken', and 'the employers had been forced into a combination to preserve whatever little was left of the trade and commerce of Dublin.' Their stand resulted from their experience that there was 'no way by which they could have any guarantee that the sympathetic strike, which had been put down and crushed in England, would be stopped in Ireland.' Larkin, in his turn, subjected many of the employers to severe cross-examination. To Mr Jacob he was deliberately offensive, and was not corrected by the chairman. His aim appeared to be to discredit the statements made by the employers by attempting to prove inaccuracies in matters of detail. As part of the discrediting process, he indulged in personal attacks and seldom kept to the point.[37]

On 3 October he interviewed Murphy, towering over him. It was the first time they met. John Eglinton (W. K. Magee), a well-known literary name in Dublin, who was present on that day, recalled 'the dark inchoate face of Larkin and … his tall ungainly figure, craning forward as he bellowed forth his arraignment; and opposite him the calm handsome face of Murphy, with trim white beard, speaking just above his breath and glancing occasionally at his angry foe.'[38] Larkin went through Murphy's business relations during the previous 35 years and came up with allegations of ill-treatment of employees and protests by them, but Murphy remained unmoved and the allegations unsubstantiated. There was much cut and thrust without Larkin being able to break down his antagonist's seeming imperturbability.[39]

In his final address, Larkin, instead of responding to the employers' arguments, launched into a passionate account of the miserable social conditions in the city for which, he asserted, the employers were responsible. He then made personalised, unsubstantiated attacks on individual employers, particularly Murphy, without them being given a chance to reply. He, and those who thought like him, wanted 'to show the employers that the workers will have to get the same opportunities of enjoying civilised life as they themselves.' He had given the men, he asserted, 'a stimulus, heart and hope which they never had before.'[40]

On 6 October, the report from the tribunal of inquiry was issued. Among its many clauses was one offering a general criticism of the use of the sympathetic strike, and another which stated that the employers, in requiring their employees to sign the anti-union document, were acting 'contrary to individual liberty'. The tribunal urged the setting up of a conciliation board based on a Canadian plan. The employers replied on 14 October criticising the leniency shown to Mr Larkin in his personalised attack on Mr Jacob, and in his concluding speech, and then announced that, while it was not in their province to interfere with the internal management of trade unions', they were 'compelled' in face of the court's conclusions regarding the sympathetic strike, broken agreements, and the further statements recently made in public by the secretary of the Transport Union, including his declaration in London, 'to hell with contracts', not to recognise the Transport Union until, firstly, it was 'reorganised on proper lines', and, secondly, had 'new officials' who 'met with the approval of the British Joint Labour Board'. Meantime, they regretted that 'they would have to insist that workers continue to sign the undertaking against the union as it stood.'[41]

'The Demon of Death spread his wings on the blast,
And spat on the face of the poor as he passed.'
— From Byron (slightly altered)

3. Cartoon by Ernest Kavanagh, *Irish Worker*, 3 Jan. 1913.

The employers' stand evoked criticism from the newspapers not controlled by Murphy. They had, by their attitude, 'played into the hands of the agitator', declared *The Times*, 'and gives substance to the charge that they care for nothing but money'; while *The Irish Times* modified its position of support for the employers. Already on 7 October, indeed, it had published the celebrated letter by Æ (George W. Russell), later republished by *The Freeman's Journal*, in which he praised the striking workers and castigated the employers for their lack of 'unremitting efforts to find a solution' and their determination 'in cold blood to starve out one-third of the population of this city'. Archbishop Walsh, just returned from weeks on the continent, during which he had kept himself informed by having copies of *The Irish Worker* sent to him,[42] sent a reply to a letter of Lord Aberdeen, on 10 October, in which he questioned Sir George Askwith's competence as a chairman in his not giving employers the opportunity 'to rebut the statements made in the speech of the Labour leader.' Lest Aberdeen might misunderstand where his sympathies lay, he hastened to add:

> In any case, the Labour leader has an extraordinarily strong case. Plainly the action of the parties … in their response to Sir G. Askwith's report has strengthened the position of the workers, and cannot fail to bring them abundant help from England. I must say that, on the merits of the case generally, my sympathies are altogether with them, and I trust that the outcome of the present case will be a radical change for the better in the position of the unemployed in Dublin.[43]

On the evening of 6 October, Larkin, at a mass meeting, described the inquiry's report as a victory. 'The employers are beaten to a frazzle', he declared, 'and the workers got a verdict in their favour, even though two members of the court of inquiry were men of the capitalist class.'[44]

Two key decisions

Despite the hyperbole, and his arrest shortly afterwards for seditious language, Larkin had public sympathy with him. Then, two issues swayed popular opinion once more: the decision to send the children of strikers to England to be properly fed and looked after, and James Connolly's closure of Dublin port in his capacity as leader in Larkin's absence. The first, in the light of the extensive practice of proselytism in the Dublin area, gave rise to anxiety for the children's religious beliefs. The press, especially Murphy's papers, whipped up fear of a secularist, anarchist plot. Unseemly scenes occurred at Dublin docks between those seeking to prevent the departure of the children and those facilitating it. The archbishop attributed no false motives to anyone, as Connolly noted,[45] but carried out his obligations as the central pastor. He condemned the 'deportation' of the children. Connolly, towards the end of October, announced the end of the children's scheme because of the hostility it had aroused in Dublin.[46] It had caused division among the strikers themselves, and had alienated many sympathisers.

The employers attempt to import 'blackleg' labour led Connolly to introduce mass picketing on the quays, and when this failed he closed the port of Dublin on 13 November. This immediately affected the City of Dublin Steam Packet Company, the only Irish cross-channel company operating from Dublin. The closure violated an agreement signed between the transport union and the company on 28 May 1913. This provided the employers with fresh ammunition.[47] Dublin's largest employer, Guinness, which had not joined the DEF, now contributed to the federation's contingency fund.[48]

Unavailing steps towards a solution

Nevertheless, there were glimmers of hope of a settlement during November 1913. William Martin Murphy, in a public letter, stated that 'there were not five per cent of the men out of employment who might not safely return, before their places were filled up, without any sacrifice of principle or without any undertaking except to do the job they were paid for doing.' James Connolly announced, in Liberty Hall, that 'he would never consent to abandon the sympathetic strike in industrial warfare, but he would agree to check its operation to the extent that it should not be used recklessly and indiscriminately.' Quoting these statements, Archbishop Walsh questioned – 'Why people should turn their attention away from such significant statements and fasten exclusively upon other statements, recklessly made,' which, if taken literally, 'amounted to so many declarations of implacable and never-ending war.'[49] His appeal was bluntly rejected by the employers. Two previous efforts of his towards mediation had been repulsed by the employer side.[50]

That all was not single-minded on the employer side, however, was signalled towards the end of November. Some members found it difficult to stand over 'the signatories' conditions' which the inquiry report had judged 'contrary to individual liberty'. On 27 November 1913, two employers, Richard Jones and Edward Lee, provided notices of motion for the council of the Chamber of Commerce, with a view to their being raised at the quarterly meeting on 1 December. The key motion proposed that this meeting 'whilst determinedly opposed to the principle of sympathetic strikes with their attendant disastrous effects to employers and workers, are of the opinion that the employers in the interest of peace and goodwill ought to withdraw the agreement they have asked their workers to enter into in respect of the ITGWU, which the workers consider infringes their personal liberty.' The council, after debating the notices of motion, announced that they were 'unanimously of opinion that the discussion of these resolutions at the present time would be undesirable.' The council decided 'not to bring such business before the quarterly meeting to be held on Monday 1 December.' The president (Murphy) was requested 'to announce the substance of the foregoing resolutions to the meeting.'[51]

The undesirability of discussing these resolutions 'at the present time' was probably related to the negotiations that were going on, at the end of November, between the Dublin employers' representatives, British Labour delegates led by Arthur Henderson, M.P., and representatives of the strike committee. The negotiations led to some coming together but broke down on the issue of 'complete reinstatement' of all the men 'now disemployed'. On 9 December, at a special trade union congress in England, Larkin's appeal for sympathetic strike action in Britain was turned down. Thereafter, further negotiations took place between employers and British and Irish labour delegates, but again, and finally, broke down on 'complete reinstatement'. By then it was evident to the employers that the workers could not hold out much longer.[52] Hence, when Archbishop Walsh made a further attempt at a settlement, he was told on 19 December, by J. Oates of the employers' federation, 'don't interfere'.[53]

Christmas proved particularly cold and hungry for strikers and their families. By mid-January, despite Larkin's desire to continue the strike, the union found it impossible to prevent many workers drifting back to work on whatever terms they were offered.[54] By the end of January 1914, all was over.

The aftermath

At the annual general meeting of the Chamber of Commerce on 28 January 1914, the outgoing president, Mr William Martin Murphy, reviewed the year at some length. On the strike, he commented: 'I was not conscious that I was opening a fresh chapter in the history of labour disputes when I took what appeared to be the only and natural course of defending, by every means at my disposal, a wanton attack on properties for which I was responsible. This attack was easily repelled, but it soon became evident that it was but part of a plot to plunge the city into a state of anarchy and to make all business impossible' by means of 'a system known as "syndicalism" or "sympathetic strikes"'. The whole attempt to undermine the trade of Dublin would have been short lived, were it not for 'the intervention of certain leaders of the English Labour party', who kept the struggle going for five months 'by doles of money and food'. In future, when the question arose of giving support to a particular trade union, he suspected they would 'have some regard to the manner in which it conducts its business, and take a lesson from the DEF, who' – as he reminded his audience – 'will not support any employer who does not agree to give his work people the full standard condition of employment and wages current in his trade.' (applause) He then observed that what workers frequently failed to understand was 'that in ninety-nine cases out of a hundred they will get more out of their employers in anticipation of a strike, than after it takes place. The threat of a strike has more terror for the employer than the strike itself.' In conclusion, the alleged 'money-grubbing tyrant' and 'sweater' reminded his colleagues once again that 'the events through which they have passed and the victory they have won, should not absolve employers from the obligation from seeing that their work people receive a wage which will enable them to live in frugal comfort. Let us not be deterred from our recent experience from acting on this principle and from doing our best to develop the industries and trade of this city.'[55]

At the annual meeting the following year, 'expressions of esteem' for Mr Murphy were received from all parts of Ireland. It was decided that a testimonial in his honour 'should take the form of a portrait by the Irish artist, Mr William Orpen.'[56] In February 1915, Murphy was presented with the portrait and with an inscribed address 'bearing the signatures of 410 noblemen and gentlemen, representatives of trade, commerce, and the professions, not only in Dublin but throughout the country.' In his address, the normally restrained Murphy allowed himself to bask in the esteem of his colleagues and to look with a benign gaze on past years.

> There are things I will claim for myself, namely, that any part I have taken in the public life of Dublin has been free from self-seeking, and I am inclined to think that it is a recognition of this fact more than anything else that has brought together an array of more than 400 signatories of distinguished men and leading firms to an appreciation of my services, of which any citizen might feel proud … With regard to the commercial undertakings … to which you so generously refer, they were, of course, embarked upon primarily with the object of making profit … At the same time I may claim that the making of profits has never been my leading idea in the various undertakings that I have projected. To achieve something and to overcome obstacles in reaching my goal has always had a more stimulating effect on me than mere profit-seeking. To me and many others, though perhaps they do not see it in that light, the game of business and the striving towards success in commerce is more fascinating than any form of sport.

'As you know', he added, drawing to a conclusion:

> I have carried the Irish flag far afield in commercial undertakings, and I have proved that an Irishman, making his headquarters and spending his life in his native land is not handicapped to such an extent as to prevent him from successfully extending his interests to Great Britain and abroad.[57]

William Martin Murphy's remaining years were mainly exercised in combating partition and conscription. To his friend, T. M. Healy, he remarked that he slept soundly during the great strike, but that he had sleepless nights at the prospect of the partition of his country. In opposition to it, he brought to bear all the power of his newspapers, as well as personally endeavouring to influence his British contacts, including the Prime Minister, Lloyd George. The redoubtable Lord Mayor of Dublin, Laurence O'Neill (1917-24), who had led the anti-conscription movement, and had supported Larkin and defended the union in its darkest days, described Murphy as the man who impressed him most among 'so many great personalities' in the National Convention in 1917. 'A man of quiet demeanour, enthusiastic without showing it, a hard business man, as he had need to be, his arguments were sound, logical and full of common sense ... One could plainly see that his whole desire was a settlement, as he was in a position to gauge, and realise what would happen if the convention failed.'[58] He bent all his ability to bring unionists and nationalists together in a united Ireland.

Murphy died unexpectedly of a heart attack on 26 June 1919, aged 74 years. He left a personal estate of over a quarter of a million pounds. He also left to posterity his highly organised tramway system, later short-sightedly destroyed, and his *Independent* newspapers. He was laid to rest in Glasnevin cemetery in the privileged circle around the great cenotaph commemorating Daniel O'Connell. The Dublin City Council, on 27 June 1919, expressed its deepest sympathy at the passing of one 'whom we always regarded as one of our ablest and best citizens, and whose loss – commercially, intellectually, and personal – will long be felt by the community and by our country generally.'[59] The editorial in the main rival newspaper, *The Freeman's Journal*, on Friday 27 June, endeavoured to summarise his career and influence.

> Once upon a time, when Ireland was being assailed as a bankrupt and dependent, ... he proved that Ireland was one of the most solvent countries in the world, and boasted that for his work in Irish enterprises he was able to obtain in Ireland itself all the capital necessary, and at rates that enabled him successfully to meet and beat the outside exploiter ... He was the leading figure and the organiser of the employers' victory in the strike of 1913. Perhaps, his peace was too much of the victor's peace, and a less sweeping victory might have had more satisfactory results in the years that have followed. But it is due to him to acknowledge that it was not so much the pecuniary profits of the success that interested him as his desire to safeguard those powers of independent management which he regarded as indispensable for the prosperity of Irish industry.

Where the greater body of Dublin workers were concerned, however, Larkin's propaganda and their memories of months of deprivation ensured the fulfilment of Æ's prediction – 'You may succeed in your policy' but 'the men whose manhood you have broken will loathe you … the children will be taught to curse you … the infant being moulded in the womb will have breathed into its starved body the vitality of hate …'[60]

It was not until the reality of a European Union and the exaltation of business and entrepreneurship, and the experience of business corruption, that a renewed interest began to emerge in William Martin Murphy, his practical patriotism, forthrightness, and the range of his international business achievements.

Larkin, for his part, long outlived his senior antagonist. He went to the United States of America in October 1914, and was imprisoned there. On his return to Dublin in 1923, he split his own union and caused industrial havoc. He proclaimed himself a communist [his son, young Jim, was educated at the International Lenin School in Moscow], and subsequently mellowed and played an active role in Dublin City Council. Over the years, he became an institutional figure; and on his death, on 30 January 1947, as he lay in state in St Mary's Church, Haddington Road, in his hands brown rosary beads, given him by the archbishop of Dublin, a multitude passed his coffin, those who loved him, and some who did not. Next day, despite the cold and snow of one of the country's severest winters, a cortege of thousands marched or thronged the streets for his final journey.

His left-wing friend from his American years, the well-known author, Bertram D. Woolfe, commented graphically in *Strange Communists I have known*: 'Big Jim Larkin had never really fitted into the Communist party, but in the Catholic Church as in the hearts of humble Irishmen, he remained to the end.' Despite 'all the tumult in his temperament and chaos in his actions', he brought to the labour movement, in Seán O'Casey's evocative words, 'not only the loaf of bread but the flask of wine.'[61]

Notes

1   *Freeman's Journal*, 23 May 1895.

2   *The Belvederian* (1909), pp 34-6.

3   Ibid., p. 38.

4   T. P. O'Connor, *Memoirs of an old parliamentarian* (2 vols., London, 1929), ii., p. 58; *Irish Independent*, 29 June 1919.

5   T. J. Morrissey, *William Martin Murphy* (2nd ed., Dublin, 2011), pp 6-7.

6   Ibid., pp 25-6. William Field, 1843-1935, was a highly successful politician who retained his seat until the collapse of the Irish Parliamentary Party in 1918.

7   Arnold Wright. *Disturbed Dublin: the story of the great strike of 1913-1914* (London, 1914), p. 77.

8   *Daily Chronicle*, 27 June 1919.

9   Dermot Keogh. *The rise of the Irish working class* (Belfast, 1982), p. 16, citing W. M. Murphy, *Wood Quay National Registration Club Speech* (1887), TCD pamphlet, p. 12.

10   *ITGWU rules*, 1909.

11   Dublin Chamber of Commerce (DCC). *Report of annual meeting*, 28 Jan. 1914, p. 404 (NAI, 1064/2/1-2). See also *Irish Catholic,* 28 Jan. 1914.

12   DCC, *Report*, 28 Jan. 1914, p. 404; and see T. J. Morrissey, op. cit., p. 65.

13   *Irish Worker,* 29 July 1911.

14   DCC, *Minutes*, 21 Sept. 1911.

15   Ibid, 27 Sept. 1911.

16   Ibid.

17   Keogh, *Rise of the Irish working class*, p. 177.

18   DCC, *Minutes*, 27 Sept. 1911

19   Ibid., 3 Nov. 1911. "Peterloo" referred to an incident on 16 Aug. 1819, when the magistrates sent a body of cavalry to disperse a peaceable crowd. Eleven civilians were killed and over 500 injured. The reference to Churchill concerned his action, as Home Secretary in sending in the military in 1911 to curb strikes and riots. Some workers were shot dead.

20   Transcript of GSWR company minutes of 27 Sept. 1911 in Peter Rigney. 'Trade Unionism and the Great Southern and Western Railway, 1890-1911' (B.A. thesis, Trinity College, Dublin), pp 53, 63. Much of the account of the strike comes from this source. Conor McCabe, 'The context and course of the Irish railway disputes of 1911', *Saothar* 30 (2005), pp 21-31; Conor McCabe, 'The 1911 rail strikes' (http/1913committee.ie/blog/?p=80); Francis Devine, 'The Irish Transport & General Workers' Union and labour unrest in Ireland, 1911', *Historical Studies in Industrial Relations,* 33 (2012), pp 169-88.

21   DCC, *Report of council*, 30 Jan. 1920 (NAI, i.380.944. D.4).

22   DCC, *Report of quarterly meeting*, 2 Sept. 1913, p. 398 (NAI, 1064/2/1-2).

23   Ibid. See also DCC, *Report of annual meeting*, 28 Jan. 1914. As regards Murphy's illness during 1913, he was missing from the meetings of 10 March and 14 April, and the council's minutes of 5 May record Mr Pim expressing the pleasure of all 'to see the president back again after his severe illness' (NAI, 1064/3/16).

24   'Dublin Strike 1913', pamphlet giving T. M. Healy's speech at the court of inquiry, p. 20.

25   Wright, *Disturbed Dublin*, p. 195.

26   Connolly-O'Brien, 25 July 1913 (NLI, O'Brien MSS 13908 (2)).

27   *Dublin United Tramway Co. Ltd., Meeting of Motor Men, Conductors etc. held in the Antient Concert Rooms at the invitation of the Chairman, soon after midnight of Saturday19 July 1913*, p. 83. (NLI, LO).

28   *Daily Express*, 25 Aug. 1913.

29   Ibid, 30 Aug. 1913.

30   *Evening Telegraph*, 31 Aug. 1913. See Keogh, *Rise of the Irish working class*, p. 199.

31   *Intelligence notes 1913-1916, preserved in the State Paper Office* (Dublin, 1966).

32   DCC, *Minutes*, 2 Sept. 1913.

33   *Freeman's Journal*, 5 Sept. 1913.

34   Fr Michael Curran - Abp. Walsh, 12 Sept. 1913 (DDA, Priests' file).

35   O'Connor, *Memoirs*, vol. 2, p. 57.

36   Wright, *Disturbed Dublin*, p. 161.

37   Ibid., pp 195f.

38   John Eglinton. *A memoir of Æ - George William Russell* (London, 1937), p. 86.

39   Wright, *Disturbed Dublin*, pp 198-9.

40   'Labour's Scathing Indictment of Dublin Sweaters', pamphlet. Larkin's address before the Askwith Inquiry. National Labour Press, no date.

41   'Court of Inquiry into Disputes in Dublin. Employers Reply to Sir George Askwith's Findings' (DDA, Walsh papers, Laity file, 14 Oct. 1913).

42   T. J. Morrissey. *William J. Walsh, Archbishop of Dublin, 1841-1921* (Dublin, 2000), p. 245.

43   Walsh - Aberdeen, 10 Oct. 1913 (DDA, Walsh Papers, Laity file).

44   Cited in Donal Nevin. *James Connolly: a full life* (Dublin, 2005), pp 458-9.

45   *Forward,* 1 Nov. 1913.

46   *Freeman's Journal,* 29 Oct. 1913

47   Emmet Larkin. *James Larkin: Irish labour leader* (London, 1989 ed.), pp 142-3.

48   Nevin, *James Connolly*, p. 468.

49   *Irish Catholic directory* (ICD) 1914, report on events in 1913, under 24 Nov., p. 493.

50   Mr McGloughin - Abp. Walsh, 23 Oct. 1913; Chas. D. Coghlan, secretary of the employers - Abp. Walsh, 27 Oct. 1913 (DDA, Box 385, 1. f. 377/3).

51   DCC, *Minutes of council*, 27 Nov. 1913 (NAI. 1064/3/16).

52   Larkin, *James Larkin*, pp 155-6.

53   J. Oates - Abp. Walsh (DDA. Box 385. 11. f.385.1).

54   T. J. Morrissey, *A man called Hughes* (Dublin, 1991), p. 43.

55   DCC, *Annual meeting*, 28 Jan. 1914, p. 404; *Irish Catholic*, 28 Jan. 1914. The term "frugal comfort" was much used in Catholic social teaching at the time, having been used in Pope Leo XIII's celebrated social-rights encyclical, *Rerum Novarum* in 1891.

56   DCC, *Report of council* for 1914 at AGM, 29 Jan. 1915, pp 9-10 (NAI, 10645/1/9-17).

57   *Irish Independent*, 27 June 1919. Italics mine.

58   A brief profile 'William Martin Murphy'; and see T. J. Morrissey, *William Martin Murphy*, p. 86. In the O'Neill Family papers there is a letter from Wm. O'Brien, 1923, stating that the Transport Union would never forget his support for them when they were on their own. (Laurence O'Neill family papers (private)). A biography of Laurence O'Neill is being prepared by the author.

59   Dublin Municipal Council, *Minutes*, 27 June 1919, no. 553, pp 351-2.

60   *1913: Jim Larkin and the Dublin Lockout* (Workers' Union of Ireland booklet, 1964), p. 5.

61   B. D. Woulfe. *Strange Communists I have known* (London, 1966), p. 71.

Image printed on fabric issued by the Irish Players to raise money for a building to house the Hugh Lane bequest. (pp 255-74)
DCLA

Watercolour drawing of Edwin Lutyens' proposed new art gallery on the River Liffey by R. Walcot.
(p. 262)
Collection: Dublin City Gallery The Hugh Lane

Oróce (Night)	An t-am (Time)	Ṡṙáo: Feiṙ Ḃaile Áta Cliaṫ (Standard based on Dublin Feis)	Máinteóiṙ (Teacher)	Seomṙa (Class Room)
Dia Luain	8 to 10.30	Choir and Singing Classes in Lecture Hall.		
Dia Máiṙt (Tuesday)	8 to 9.30	An Céao Ḃliaḋam (for Beginners)	Éamonn ve Veléara, Ḃ.É.	8
	8 ,, 9.30	An Oaṙa ,, (Intermediate)	Ḃriġio Ní Flannaġáin	9
	8 ,, 9.30	An 3aḋ ,, (Adv. Inter.)	Tomáṙ Mac Vomnaill	6
			(Connaċt College)	
DiaĊéaovaoin (Wednesday)	8 to 9.30	An 3aḋ Ḃliaḋam (Adv. Inter.)		8
	8 ,, 9.30	An 4aḋ ,, (Advanced)	Miċeál Ó Ḃriain	9
	8 ,, 9.30	An 5aḋ ,, (Advanced Grammar, Phonetics, etc.)	Vomnall Ua Murċaḋa	6
			(Leinster College)	
Diaṙoaoin	8.15 to 10	Léiġeaċt i nṠaeoilis nó i mḂéaṙla. Lecture Hall*		—
Dia h-Aoine (Friday)	8 to 9.30	An Céao Ḃliaḋam (Beginners)	Páoṙaig Ó Séaċáin	9
	8 ,, 9.30	An 2aḋ ,, (Intermediate)	Cṙioṙtóiṙ Ua Monaċáin	8
	8 ,, 9.30	An 4aḋ ,, (Advanced)	Liam Ua Vomnaill	6
Dia Saṫaiṙn (Saturday)	8 to 9.30	Seanċaṙ. Tiocṙaḋ comaltaí na Cṙaoiḃe le céile cum an Ṡaeoilis vo cleaċtaḋ. Ḃeiḋ buṙoean ṙinnceoiṙeaċta, Oṙámanna ꞵ Céiṙóṫe aġainn ṙeiṙin.		

* Tionólṙaṙ Cṙuinniuġaḋ Puiḃliḋe ṙan halla ġaċ oṙóce Diaṙoaoine. Léiġṙaṙ airte Ṡaeoilse nó Ḃéaṙla ann iṙ cuiṙṙeaṙ oíoṙṗóiṙeaċt aṙ bun ṙá n-a ḃṙuil ṙan airte. Comairliġteaṙ vo ġaċ n-aon ḃeiṫ vo lataiṙ. A Public Meeting will be held every Thursday evening in the Hall at 25 Rutland Square. Lectures in Irish on Interesting Subjects will be delivered twice monthly, and a discussion will follow. A History Lecture and a Lecture in English will also be given each month.

N.B.—ANNUAL SUBSCRIPTION, 5s., payable in OCTOBER. CLASSES AND LECTURES ARE FREE TO MEMBERS.

an ÁRO-ĊRAOḂ. CLÁR na mḃuiṙḃean Ṡaeoilse. (Programme of Irish Classes.). 1910-11.

Flier for Irish classes, 1910-11, issued by the Gaelic League. (p. 304)
DCLA (BOR 14/04)

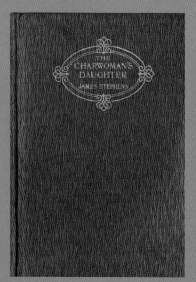

First edition of James Stephens'
The charwoman's daughter
(London, 1912). (p. 340)
DCLA

Sackville Street and O'Connell Bridge
DCLA, Dixon postcards (FED 12)

James Larkin in Belfast, 1907
Private Collection

Portrait of William Martin Murphy *after*
Sir William Orpen
© Dublin Chamber of Commerce
Photography: Alastair Smeaton

The John Shillito Co-operative CWS
Medal was issued to celebrate the CWS
Jubilee in 1913. When the captain,
officers and crew of the food ship,
SS Hare, returned from Dublin, the
CWS president, John Shillito, made
a presentation to them.
© National Co-operative Archive

1. ITGWU Red Hand badge, 1913

2. TUC delegate badge, Manchester, 1913, chairman W. J. Davis (Amalgamated Society of Brassworkers)

3. Workers' Union of Ireland, 50th anniversary of Lockout 1913-1963

4. FWUI, 75th anniversary of 1913 Lockout, 1988

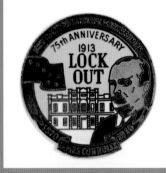

5. ITGWU, 75th anniversary of 1913 Lockout, 1988

6. SIPTU, 90th anniversary of 1913 Lockout, 2003

Private Collection

9.

Jim Larkin and *The Irish Worker*

....

John Newsinger

To the working class of Ireland the Editor of the Irish Worker makes his bow – not in any humble manner, however, but as one who desires to speak to you and of you with honour and pride. Too long, aye! For too long have we the Irish working people been humble and inarticulate ... The Irish Working Class (capital letters good Mr Printer) are beginning to awaken. They are coming to realise the truth of the old saying: 'He who would be free must strike the blow.'

With these words Jim Larkin introduced *The Irish Worker and People's Advocate* ('the *Worker*' as it was popularly known) to the Dublin working class. This first issue (27 May 1911) sold some 5,000 copies. The following week sales increased to 8,000, the week after to 15,000, peaking the following week at 20,000 copies. Thereafter circulation fluctuated around 20,000 copies. Many more people would have read it than bought it. The new paper had a tremendous impact. It was to become the voice of the Dublin working class. According to the historian, Emmet Larkin, 'Nothing like it has ever been seen since ... It was less a newspaper than the spirit of four glorious years.' To read it, he wrote, was to feel 'the quickening pulse of Dublin'.[1] Robert Lowery, in his account of Seán O'Casey's involvement with the paper, described the *Worker* as 'an extraordinary newspaper, a milestone in the history of working class journalism.' He went on to pay tribute to Jim Larkin himself, pointing out that over a 41 month period, as well as editing the paper, Larkin had personally written nearly 400 articles.[2] He combined this journalistic activity with the leadership of the Irish Transport and General Workers Union (ITGWU) at a time of escalating industrial conflict, with active involvement in the affairs of the wider labour movement and with campaigning to build an Irish Labour Party. The man's energy was astonishing. His larger than life presence earned him many enemies, but he gave his name, Larkinism, to the great wave of working class revolt that swept over Ireland in the years before the First World War.

'These Soulless Bloodsuckers'

What of the *Worker's* social vision? The ITGWU's 1912 rules committed the union to 'the realisation of the Industrial Commonwealth' as its 'ultimate ideal'. The union looked forward to 'the glorious time spoken of and sung by the Thinkers, the Prophets and the

Poets, when all children, all women and all men ... become entitled to the fullness of the earth and the abundance thereof.'[3] To this end, from the very beginning, the *Worker* preached discontent and rebellion, condemning the existing capitalist social order in the most ferocious terms and urging its readers to rise up and fight for a new social order, for the establishment of 'a mutual Commonwealth', in a free Ireland. The way to achieve this transformation was through the establishment of the One Big Union (OBU) as a power in the land, although the paper combined this syndicalist approach with enthusiastic support for an Irish Labour Party and an electoral challenge to John Redmond's Home Rule party.[4]

Week after week, the paper exposed the appalling working and living conditions that were the lot of the Dublin working class. On 11 November 1911, the whole front page was devoted to R. J. P. Mortished's 'Facts about Dublin', a statistical account of poverty in the city.[5] Over five weeks in August and September 1912, it carried a series of articles, 'Labour and Frugality' by 'Euchan', the pseudonym of Andrew Patrick Wilson, one of the paper's journalistic mainstays.[6] These demonstrated that no matter how careful a family was, the wages of the unskilled were not enough to live on. And in May 1912 the paper began the serialisation of James Connolly's *Labour and the Reconquest of Ireland* (it ran on the front page from 4 May through to 15 June). This sort of closely argued, well-researched social commentary was accompanied by more passionate responses to specific examples of exploitation. On 24 May 1913, Larkin himself told the paper's readers of how:

> While we write, two children accompanied by their poor, hungry, ill-dressed mother are telling their tale of woe. Two children-girls of 14 and 16 years-were slaving for Somersets of Golden Lane, embroiderers and linen manufacturers. They supply finished goods to Roberts of Grafton Street. These two hungry children worked 12 days for 10*d*-twelve days for ten pence! This is no exaggeration or mis-statement. They produced their dockets issued by these soulless bloodsuckers.

Larkin warned such employers that the time 'is rapidly arriving when you will be called to a halt!' The *Irish Worker* was educating 'the working class to their own want of knowledge, want of class loyalty, want of solidarity, want of earnestness, want of spirit, and their rights, which they have forgotten to demand.' He warned them that a new era was dawning as 'a new type of man and woman is being formed among the working class.' Increasingly, they were looking forward to the establishment of:

> A mutual Commonwealth built on service, a broadening out of the perspective of life, a fuller and more complete life, the obliterating of class rule and the distinction of caste – a day when work, useful and beautiful, will be the test; when the idler, the wastrel, the fop, the creature of an hour shall cease to be, and

the builder, the beautifier shall take their rightful place in the land and among the nations, there will be no child slaves in those good days to be working twelve days for tenpence.

1. Jacob's women workers paid off.
Freeman's Journal, 8 Sept. 1913.
DCLA

This was Larkin's journalism at its most powerful, moving from a specific, heartbreaking injustice to a vision of a new and better world that a remade working class was going to establish for itself.

The *Worker* exposed and condemned the conditions in Dublin workplaces week after week. The biscuit firm, Jacobs, was a favourite target. In June 1911, Larkin asked:

If a girl who makes a collection for another work girl, either in the way of a wedding present or for some other purpose, deserves instant dismissal according to the firm's rules, what do the snivellers who terrorise the employees into giving a donation (voluntary, moryah!) for a wedding present to Miss G M Jacob deserve – the snivellers think promotion, I think a summons under the Truck Act.[7]

The grateful employees presented Miss Jacob with a clock, a clock to which Larkin was to return in December of that year when he devoted an editorial to the firm, 'Peace on Earth: Good Will to all Men':

Let us take the philanthropic firm of Jacobs. Here on the eve of Christmas, so to speak, a large number of men, boys and girls have been dismissed, and a still larger number under notice of dismissal this week. The excuse is slackness of trade and the shutting down of plant, the night shift having been dispensed with. One would naturally expect that the last persons employed would be dispensed with first. Not so in Jacobs. Men and youths, with from 6 to 12 years service have been discharged at a few minutes notice ... we ask George Jacob has his daughter's clock ticked; for if so, she must be reminded that a number of employees of Jacob and Co. who kept her and her family in affluence and luxury and who provided her dowry – aye, even the clock that ticked – are now sacked on the eve of Christmas ... We wonder did Mr George Jacob ever read Charles Dickens' *Christmas Carol* – we wonder.[8]

George Jacob was later to be one of the leading lights of the Dublin Employers' Federation (DEF) and the mass sackings he carried out in 1913 were to be one of the decisive moments in launching the Great Lockout.

The employer who most excited the *Worker's* hatred, however, was, William Martin Murphy or 'Murder' Murphy as he was often called. He was 'the most foul and vicious blackguard that ever polluted any country' and this was when the paper was feeling generous![9] Murphy was a former Home Rule M.P., who had lost his Dublin seat to a Parnellite in 1892. His opponent, William Field, was, at the time, sympathetic to labour. Murphy remained a Home Ruler, but was critical of the party leadership. He was also Catholic Ireland's most successful capitalist with extensive business interests in Ireland and Britain. He controlled the Dublin United Tramway Company (DUTC) and owned the city's largest hotel, the Imperial along with Clery's department store and the *Irish Independent* newspaper group. As the ITGWU increasingly came into conflict with Murphy in the weeks before the Great Lockout, so its attacks became increasingly vitriolic. On 26 July 1913, the paper responded to claims that Murphy was a good employer, always prepared to deal with 'a respectable Union'. Murphy claimed that no one who worked for him had ever even thought about going on strike until Larkin came along. Larkin replied in an editorial, 'Napoleon Murphy (Moryah!)':

For fifty years as an employer, he has had no strike. What a lie. What a damned lie. There is not a company or industry that you are connected with, directly or indirectly, that has not had disputes prolonged or otherwise. What about the Clare railway strike, you Christian? You were a Member of Parliament; yes, but they found you out. You have been driven from public life as a toady, a renegade, and untruthful and dishonest politician; a false friend, a sweating employer, a weak-kneed tyrant. Witness the funk you are in now, you whited sepulchre.

Larkin urged Murphy to repent his sins against the working class now or face having 'an eternity to expiate the crimes, public and private, you have been guilty of.' Murphy was 'a renegade to your Creator' because he only worshipped 'one god – that god profit'.

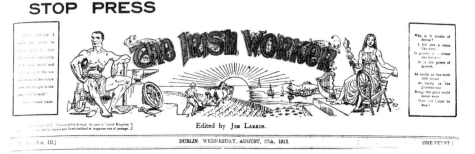

2. Masthead of *The Irish Worker* 1913.
DCLA

A week later, Wilson continued the assault when he revealed on the front page how Murphy's mother had long ago despaired of her son. When he was a lad, she had a dream of him as 'an old man with a scraggy white beard and hard cruel lines marked on every feature of his face ... he was on the verge of his second childhood, but 'old and feeble-looking as he was he still stood on the neck of a man dressed in the garments of a toiler.' She saw that as her son 'watched the sufferings of his writhing victim an unholy smile played around his vicious mouth.' Suddenly, 'a large red hand, belonging not to one worker, but to a huge army of them, had seized her son and dragged him from his prey.' He appealed to her for sympathy, 'but she turned away with a shudder of revulsion.'[10] The ITGWU's Red Hand badge was the central emblem of 1913.

Larkin took particular exception to the journalists employed on the newspapers owned by Murphy, 'this modern capitalistic vampire'. 'This Murphy', he wrote, 'employs a group of journalistic renegades, whose bodies and souls he controls. They write the most foul, vicious and lying tirades against the working class at so much a column.'[11] These people 'sell your talent for a miserable thirty pieces of silver', but, he warned them, 'ye paid blacklegs of the press will be remembered ... and the men ye lied about will not forget.'[12]

The ferocity of the *Worker's* journalism was quite deliberate. Larkin was concerned to make the working class aware of its potential and this involved abusing and diminishing its enemies. He set out to expose sweatshop employers, slum landlords, lying journalists, corrupt politicians, and, of course, William Martin Murphy, as moral pygmies. They made their money out of the exploitation of working people, their profit was squeezed out of working-class misery, and, moreover, they actually despised the people who made their affluent lifestyles possible. Far from being better than the poor, they were worse, much worse. His attacks attempted to turn these people from being seen as worthy of respect because of their position in society to being seen as deserving of contempt because of their hard-hearted hypocrisy. The *Worker's* journalism was intended to rally the working class, to bolster its self-confidence, in the face of ruthless employers who would destroy the trade union movement if they could. Larkin was out to turn the world upside down and this would involve, among other things, some harsh words.

Mention should be made here of the part that the *Worker's* cartoons played in propagating its message. Of particular importance were the cartoons of Ernest Kavanagh. These were, as far as its readers were concerned, 'likely one of the paper's most widely appreciated features.'[13] Kavanagh's cartoon image of Murphy was to do the man great damage at the time and has pursued his reputation ever since. The role of cartoons in socialist and trade union propaganda is often acknowledged but less often explored.

'The Dream of the Workers'

In a powerful article, 'The Time of Dreams and the Virtues of Discontent' that appeared at Easter 1913, Wilson proclaimed that the workers' struggle for a new world was a holy struggle, sanctified by God. Indeed:

> Just as the stone was rolled away on that first Easter morning, so, too are the stones which veil our eyes rolled away with the coming of spring, and we who are not yet grey of heart see visions and dreams – dreams, too, which we believe can be realised.

The working class, he went on:

> are beginning to understand that when they dream of freedom and when they grow discontented with their chains, they are becoming real men and real women, real images of God, and not the beasts of burden they have hitherto been content to remain ... it was the rolling away of the stone on that first Easter dawn that gave the workers the right to be discontented, for then, indeed, had the old order passed and the new order of Christian Brotherhood had become the world's ideal ... it is the dream of the workers that this era of wage slavery shall cease, and this dream shall be realised, too, for its realisation depends upon the workers themselves, their combination and their solidarity; and they are already working for these things and working hard. The workers have awakened.[14]

We shall return to the *Worker's* attitude towards religion and the Catholic Church (although it is worth noticing here that Murphy, for example, was to be attacked in the paper for not being 'a good Catholic'[15]), but what of the paper's vision of a better world?

The *Worker* sought to uplift the Dublin working class, not just economically and politically, but in every aspect of social and cultural life as well. Early in January 1912, 'O'F' had asked, in its pages:

> Is it because a man joins a trade union he is never to think of anything but committee meetings; never to wish for anything but strikes; never to hope for anything better than a rise of a few shillings in his pay? Should he not love good books and plays, and the sun and the stars and the fields and the flowers? Ought he not to love his wife and children, and to teach them all he can? Is he allowed to have a home, is he not entitled to learn how best to keep it? If he is expected to rear children, why is he not to seek all the information he needs on the subject? If home and family are not bad for the working man, then all things that in any way bear on either come within the scope of a Labour paper. There is no topic from stars to strikes in which the worker should not be encouraged to take an interest.[16]

What is striking to today's reader, of course, is the extent to which this vision is addressed to men, to the men who will teach their wives and children all they can. And this was in a paper that vigorously supported women's suffrage and the rights of women workers! Such were the assumptions of the times which the *Worker* never challenged.

The union put considerable effort into providing a social and cultural life for its members.[17] To this end it bought Croydon Park, a house and three acres of land in Clontarf, for the use of union members and their families. When Croydon Park was opened for the use of union members in August 1913, Wilson published an article, 'The Jovial Revolution', celebrating the event in the *Worker*. He proclaimed it the beginning of a social revolution: 'There was no bloodshed and no violence, but nevertheless there had been a revolution.' The working class were, as Wilson had put it earlier that year, becoming 'real men and women, real images of God.' Wilson saw the opening of Croydon Park as a giant step towards this transformation:

> To watch a dock labourer walk into a mansion, saunter into the dining-room and proceed to put a tuppence doorstep-sandwich and a penny bottle of minerals out of sight without the slightest air of surprise at his surroundings struck me as the most revolutionary sight I ever saw in my life ... Not so long ago a mansion was a place which working men were supposed to pass with cap in hand and with a mumbled blessing or curse for the lord of the manor. Nowadays things have changed. Through organisation the workers of Dublin have secured a spirit of

independence and self-reliance which enables them to snap their fingers at the lords of the manor, of the factory and of the workshop.

This 'spirit of independence and self-reliance' had led to the workers realising 'that they require a fuller and more enjoyable life.' They were beginning to want for themselves what the employers took for granted: 'If the employers and their families need lawns and gardens to sport in, then the workers and their families need them also ... The idea may be revolutionary, but it was merely bare justice nevertheless.'[18] Even as Wilson wrote this celebration of 'the Jovial Revolution', the employers were readying themselves to roll back the tide of working class revolt and destroy the ITGWU.

'First nationalise the People'

One aspect of the *Worker*'s social vision that is often underestimated is its wholehearted commitment to Irish independence and to the establishment of an Irish Republic. This commitment is usually associated with James Connolly, but, in fact, the paper was committed to the republican cause from the very beginning. The first issue proclaimed that 'We owe no allegiance to any other nation, nor the king, governors, or representatives of any other nation'. The *Worker* certainly stood for 'National Freedom', but also for 'Individual Freedom', that is freedom 'from a more degraded slavery, economic or wage slavery.' This was Connolly's workers' republic without actually using the phrase. Its social republican credentials were further established when, from the 17 June 1911 issue up to the 12 August issue it carried a series of reprints from James Fintan Lalor's the *Irish Felon*. And just in case there was any doubt, in July 1911 the paper made its position absolutely clear with its front page response to the British King George V's visit to Dublin:

> Over one thousand persons deliberately chose to visit Wolfe Tone's grave on Saturday last in preference to staying in the city to watch the procession. Over one thousand young men and women, in Dublin alone, who cared more for the principles of a man, whom the British Government sentenced to death, than they did for all the tawdry pomp and bloody vengeance of the Pirate Empire. Some may say that this is out of place in a labour paper; that we should not take Sides in politics. We know what we are about. We know that until the workers of Ireland obtain possession of the land of Ireland and make their own laws they can only hope for and obtain partial improvement of their conditions ... Our ambition is nationalise the wealth and production of the country; to do this we must first nationalise the people, then the Government ... The welfare of the people of Ireland is more important to us than the smiles of king or queen. While there is a

hungry man, woman or child in Ireland, while there is even one of our people ill-clad or ill-treated, we will join in no display of hypocritical loyalty. While there is one bare-footed child in this country we cannot afford to buy flags or fireworks, or present royal addresses.

Even while it championed socialism and republicanism, however, the *Worker* was still prepared to support Home Rule, but not as a final settlement. Its reasons for this support were all negative. According to Larkin, the Home Rule Bill would show 'the class for whom we speak that not in Bills nor Acts lies freedom – the only freedom worth enjoying – "economic freedom"'. As far as he was concerned, 'this emasculated measure is not and cannot be a final settlement, and this statement will be supported by the vast majority of the working class in this country.' The only good thing about Home Rule was that it would clear the way for an Irish Labour Party, for 'a conscious working class party' such as had been successfully established in other countries, so that 'no longer will we be the helots of the world-wide working class movement.' Then and only then, he argued, would there be 'a day of reckoning, and then the final settlement.' Larkin ended with an appeal to the 'shades of Michael Davitt, Lalor, Emmet and Tone ... Ever watching, ever waiting ... still pursuing the final settlement.'[19]

Later that same month, in an editorial of 27 April 1912, Larkin brutally satirised the position of John Redmond and the Home Rulers:

> We regret to inform our readers from wireless messages received, signed Tone, Emmet, Russell, Lalor, Mitchel and Davitt, that the old barque 'Erin', struck an iceberg whist bound for the port of Independence. From latest advice to hand, it seems that during the voyage of 800 years bound for the above port numerous skippers had commanded the craft, some of whom had given up the job in despair; others had given up their lives in bad weather in trying to keep her head to the wind; but not one of those who had gone before ever dared to suggest they should alter course. The port of Independence they were bound for – the port Independence they had orders to reach; and if they had dared, we repeat, to go about and alter course by a point the crew who served under them would have keel-hauled them. But times have changed. The present skipper has thought it wise to discharge the crew and depend on the passengers to bring the old craft in ... the boatswain will pipe God Save The King and persuade the crowd in the forecastle it is A Nation Once Again.

The *Worker* often gloried in full-blown republican rhetoric. Larkin provided a good example of this in the editorial, 'Allen, Larkin and O'Brien', he wrote commemorating the Manchester Martyrs in November 1912:

And yet those three humble working men, who gave all for the Irish nation, live on in the hearts of all true men, though dead they truly liveth …Were Allen, O'Brien and Larkin justified in protesting against the brutal power of the English Government, were they right in trying to break the chains that shackled and still shackle their beloved country …? We say emphatically, Yes … Remember, if Esau sold his birthright for a mess of pottage, it is not necessary for us to repeat that foolishness. Better the roadside starvation and Freedom … No to you our dead, lying in the cold clay of England, your bodies burned by the cursed quicklime, if it be our own fate to go through the furnace, we repeat our vow, as true as you were to Kathleen Na Houlihan, so too, we bone of your bone as we are, will never disgrace you nor forget.[20]

It is worth making the point that at this time the *Worker* was the loudest public voice of Irish republicanism. This was a distinctive working class republicanism, however, a working-class republicanism that Connolly was to provide a historical background and a basis in Marxist theory for in his *Labour in Irish history*. The paper urged contemporary republicans to embrace Wolfe Tone's recognition that 'it was useless to appeal to the landed and capitalistic section of the community'. Instead, 'he was forced to realise that there was but one section only who answered his call … the working class.'[21] On another occasion, the paper made the point that while 'the cause of Labour is the same the world over', nevertheless, in Ireland there was 'a clear national issue and one that deserves a clear and distinct answer.' The answer was clear: a wholehearted embrace of Irish republicanism. After all, 'there is not a hill nor a valley that is not sanctified by the blood of her martyrs, and blessed by the footprints of her saints.' The Irish people, the paper insisted 'love their country with a love as passionate and as true as Mitchel and Tone.' Their love for Ireland was 'as pure and holy as maiden ever was honoured by man.' Indeed they 'love the grass of her fields, the pavements of her streets, and the wind that blows across the hills.' And, of course, once again there was the declaration that 'ever in the forefront of the fight for freedom was the working man … the national forces of Ireland were ever composed mainly of working men, and if there is a future for Ireland it is the working men will achieve it.'[22] This combination of romantic nationalism and proletarian politics was one of the *Worker's* hallmarks.

Inevitably, the *Worker* regarded any talk of partition with horror. On 27 July 1912, Larkin responded to the anti-Home Rule riots in Belfast by arguing that 'the unmitigated blackguards of the governing classes' in the North were trying 'the same methods they used one hundred years ago to divide the common people.' It was all about keeping the workers divided. And he made the point that many of those expelled from their workplaces were not Catholics, but 'prominent Labour men', many of them Protestants.

The employers in the North feared Home Rule because they knew that once that question was settled 'the working class would coalesce, and they are determined to keep them divided.' Later when partition was incorporated into the Home Rule bill, the paper condemned the 'pigmy statesmen' who were acquiescing in this attempt 'to stereotype by Act of Parliament, two distinct Irelands.' They were out to reverse what the paper somewhat optimistically referred as 'the fusion of Orange and Green that was rapidly taking place among the workers of Ulster.' It put much of the blame for this on the sectarianism of the Hibernians without whom 'the Orange Society would have long since ceased to exist.' The governing class were ensuring that 'for generations to come ... Irish energy, wit and enterprise will be spent in faction-fighting ... rather than in a combined effort to lift the toilers of all creeds to a position of affluence in the land of their birth.' In that same issue, Larkin editorialised in support of 'a united Ireland, the Ireland of Tone, Emmet and McCracken', an Ireland uniting Catholic, Protestant and Dissenter.[23] On 14 March, Connolly condemned 'the dogs of aristocratic power' that were determined to keep the Irish people divided. If they were successful it would mean 'a carnival of reaction both North and South, would set back the wheels of progress, would destroy the oncoming unity of the Irish Labour movement and paralyse all advanced movements whilst it endured.' 'Labour in Ulster', he concluded' 'should fight even unto the death if necessary, as our fathers fought before us.'

BELFAST STRIKE.—Labour Leaders addressing the Strikers at Queen's Square, Belfast
Messrs M'Keown   Boyd   Larkin   Murray   M'Kessock

3. Labour leaders address Belfast strikers, Jim Larkin is seated in the centre.
Private Collection

'The Gage of Battle is Accepted'

Soon after the launch of the *Worker*, in August 1912, Larkin examined the state of working-class consciousness and the level of class struggle in the country. He wrote:

> The apathy of the workers seemed to stultify all our efforts; it seemed that with the advance of education a spirit of selfishness had been imported and self-sacrifice had died out. The gospel of the materialistic school seemed to have captured the great mass of the working class. Men replied to your appeal for fellowship and brotherly love in the words of Cain: 'Am I my brother's keeper?'... And then suddenly when things seem blackest and dark night enshrouds abroad, lo! Thereunder rises wrath and hope and wonder, and the worker goes marching on.[24]

No matter what the setbacks, the struggle went on.

At the centre of the ITGWU's ethos was the principle of solidarity. The words of Cain were anathema and in their place were inscribed 'fellowship and brotherly love'. Solidarity made everything possible and would usher in the age of 'wrath and hope and wonder'. As far as Larkin and his comrades were concerned the strength of the working class was completely bound up with the notion of solidarity. Any group of workers in dispute had to be able to turn for support to the rest of the working class. Picket lines were to be scrupulously respected (the *Worker* regularly printed the names and addresses of blacklegs) and 'tainted' goods, that is goods handled by blacklegs, were never to be touched. Workers in dispute should be helped financially by the rest of the movement. And the sympathy strike was seen as a crucial weapon for breaking employers' resistance, so that no group of workers was ever to be allowed to be defeated in isolation. For the Larkinites, the ambition was that every section of the working class should be enrolled in the One Big Union. As Wilson put it, 'the workers should stand firmly together shoulder to shoulder ... one union for all the workers, and the capitalist class could not resist.' 'The workers', he went on, 'are not making the class war, for the class war has been forced on them ... Federation! Consolidation! Organisation! These are the watchwords for the workers – the three-leafed Shamrock of Labour growing from one stalk – the one great union for all workers.'[25]

Building the union was a hard struggle. Sometimes the odds seemed all against the militants and activists and the *Worker* reflects these ups and downs. On 4 May 1912, for example, Larkin published a somewhat depressed May Day editorial: 'Another May Day come and gone. Another year passed and the Irish working class stand despairing, despised and inarticulate, while their brothers the world over are gathering together

4. Irish transport workers marching on St Stephen's Green.
An Claidheamh Soluis, 1 Nov. 1913.
DCLA

like the rush of angry waters ... whilst their brothers the world over – in untold millions – raise their voices demanding their due share of God's great gifts to man, the Irish working class remain dumb.' 'Will nothing rouse them?' he asked. The situation was soon to change.

Over the next six months, the ITGWU was able to consolidate its position. By 4 January 1913, Larkin felt able to editorialise that '1913 seems to presage a more hopeful outlook for Labour, but as we believe God helps those who help themselves, we must determine to help ourselves ... success means further success ... Our watchword – the World for Labour.' By the summer, the union leadership believed that it had Dublin in its hands with Larkin telling the Trades Council that it was now the best organised city in the world, something which Desmond Greaves' history of the ITGWU concedes 'was possibly true'.[26]

It was the ITGWU's attempt to organise the tramway men, employees of William Martin Murphy, that was to precipitate the decisive clash. On 23 August 1913, the *Worker* carried a 'Manifesto to the Citizens of Dublin'. Readers were told that the union had 'been compelled to withdraw the men of the DTUC owing to the tyrannical action of Mr William Martin Murphy ... who dismissed some two hundred men from their employment for daring to exercise their God-given rights as freemen in combining with their fellows.' This was merely the opening salvo. The following week, the paper reported 'that the Dublin employers have decided to lock-out all members of the Irish Transport and General Workers Union.' The union will only be 'strengthened by the opposition offered'. Indeed, Larkin predicted that the employers 'are about to raise a Frankenstein that will envelop and destroy them all. Time fights on our side.'[27]

The ITGWU found itself the victim of an all-out attack involving the employers, the Dublin Castle authorities, Home Rule politicians, the police, the clergy and the press. The determination of the authorities to break the union was shown over the weekend of Saturday 30 and Sunday 31 August when the police ran riot, beating two men to death, injuring hundreds of others, including women and children, even breaking into people's homes and wrecking their few possessions. As the *Worker* pointed out this behaviour was hardly a surprise. The Dublin Castle administration was effectively in the hands of the Under Secretary, James Dougherty, whose wife was a shareholder in the DTUC, so that 'the man who is bound to be impartial in the dispute' actually had an indirect financial interest in its 'prosperity'. And as for the magistrate, E. G. Swifte, who banned the Sunday protest meeting in Sackville (O'Connell) Street, 'Well, is it not peculiar that the same name should be in the list of shareholders in the Company.'[28]

When Larkin proclaimed 'Time fights on our side', he underestimated the unity and determination of the employers. In fact, the longer the Lockout went on the greater the hardship for union members and their families. Of crucial importance in assisting the ITGWU in carrying on a protracted fight was the financial assistance that it received from the British trade union movement. British unions made large donations to the Dublin workers that eventually came to some £150,000 (some £11,500,000 in today's money). While this financial and moral support was certainly vital, as Larkin soon realised, if the fight was to be won, then the British unions were going to have to take action in support of the Dublin workers and black 'tainted' Dublin traffic. To this end, Larkin launched his 'Fiery Cross Crusade' to rally the British rank and file to the Dublin workers' cause. The rallies that were held across the country were a great success. On 22 November, Connolly reported on the rally in Manchester in the *Worker*. He compared the reception Larkin had received with the fate of the Manchester Martyrs. Larkin had spoken to a great 'gathering of Manchester democracy ... over 25,000 people' that 'roared out to welcome the Irish rebels of our day.' The welcome 'accorded last Sunday to Larkin ... went far to wipe out the evil memories of the past.' But while there is considerable evidence that sections of the rank and file were ready to support the Dublin workers, the leadership of Britain's trade union movement were primarily concerned to crush what they saw as a developing Larkinite insurgency inside their own organisations. At the TUC Special Conference, the first ever held to discuss a particular dispute, on 9 December, the delegates ignored any rank and file pressure and instead voted overwhelmingly to censure Larkin and refused to black Dublin traffic. Larkin himself, not unreasonably, believed that the mere threat of solidarity action would have broken the employers' united front and made possible the negotiation of a satisfactory settlement, but that by ruling it out, the TUC had left the Dublin workers isolated.

The *Worker* had a remarkable scoop in its 3 January 1914 edition when it reported a speech Murphy had made to the DEF. He actually admitted his many crimes and acknowledged that to his shame he had 'never allowed any policy of Christian charity, of humane pity, even of common decency' to interfere with his pursuit of profit. He confessed that he was behind 'our latest attempt to reduce to soulless slavery the gallant workers of Dublin.' He had 'made the streets of Dublin a place of terror for every worker not prepared to sell his class.' But the workers were 'unsubduable and unconquerable'. Now, he intended to seek forgiveness for his crimes. He was going to 'cease to hold the pistol of starvation at the heads of the poor' and instead would 'beg their pardon for my crimes against their manhood.' Indeed, he had even come 'to esteem and value' Jim Larkin and was inviting him 'to dine with me on New Year's Day at the Imperial Hotel.' If only? The spoof was the work of James Connolly, who wondered, tongue-in-cheek, if the paper's reporter had made the speech up 'as Murphy's reporters have hitherto invented so many speeches attributed to Mr Larkin.' The same issue of the paper carried one of Ernest Kavanagh's most famous cartoons, featuring Murphy as Father Christmas distributing presents of starvation and disease in the slums.[29]

5. Cartoon by Ernest Kavanagh, *Irish Worker*, 3 Jan. 1914.
DCLA

Even after the disaster at the TUC Special Conference, the union still hoped that success in the Dublin Municipal elections in January 1914 might still turn the tide. 'Vote Labour and Sweep Away the Slums', the *Worker* proclaimed. As the paper pointed out, there were over 21,000 families living in one room so that 'one in every three people in Dublin has no home in any real sense of the word.' The elections proved to be yet another setback because although the labour vote went up it did not go up enough to win seats. As Larkin at last conceded, 'Labour's ranks have been broken and we have been compelled to withdraw to our base.'[30] As union members began returning to work on whatever conditions could be secured, many were turned away and blacklisted, Larkin hotly denied 'that Murphy and his clique won this fight.' In fact, they had 'been beaten to a frazzle long weeks ago', but had then been rescued by 'the foul, insidious conspiracy, based on personal vindictiveness of the alleged British Labour Leaders.' And, for the record, he told 'friend Murphy' that he had best remember that the members of the ITGWU had 'but one aim in life – the destruction of the present system and all it stands for.' The union advance had been 'repulsed', but 'we retire to our base and get our plans prepared for another advance ... we are but getting our second breath, and then we will make the pace a hot one.' This was so much wishful thinking.[31]

Connolly chronicled the depth of the defeat at Jacob's. Here the workers held out until the middle of March 1914 before returning to work on the company's terms. Connolly revealed that wage cuts had been imposed of between between two and four shillings a week and that over 500 strikers had been refused re-employment. He told of how those who applied for re-employment were publicly humiliated, paraded before the scabs, with the manager, Dawson, examining 'their clothes, their hats, skirts and blouses ... pinches their arms, and examines their physical condition and ... all through his degrading examination he keeps up a running fire of insulting remarks.'[32] Of course, while the scabs had been very useful in defeating the union, this did not mean that the employers felt that they owed them anything. Connolly reported how a scab tram conductor who had worked for Murphy for 27 years and had stood by the DUTC all through the Lockout, on his retirement was awarded. and even then only after protest. a princely pension of one penny and three farthings a week for life. As Connolly observed the scab had been 'treated scabbily'.[33]

As the Lockout came to an end, the *Worker* paid fulsome tribute to the part played by its women members in the fight. 'Shellback' eulogised them in an article that appeared on 28 February 1914:

> Beyond any doubt the working women of Dublin have surpassed all the great feats of suffering and sacrifice that history records of women in the past. They have stuck to those principles they fought for despite the coalition of money, Government and creed that was arrayed against them. They have maintained a fight for many weary months in spite of the fearful risk that hunger and despair might subject them to in the dangerous atmosphere of respectable, Catholic and virtuous Dublin.

The women, he went on, had shown 'true Spartan-like spirit'. Even now some were refusing to return to work if it meant working alongside scabs. The sentiment was somewhat compromised, however, by his comment that this steadfast militancy was all the more commendable because they were 'after all but women'.[34] It has to be said once again that the paper was a strong supporter of women's suffrage and had fought tirelessly for the rights of women workers.

'The Difference between a Priest and a Policeman'

From the time it was first established, the ITGWU met with sustained clerical hostility. How did the *Worker* respond to this? The great majority of the union's members were Catholics, including Jim Larkin himself, so this was a problem that had to be taken extremely seriously. The union strenuously tried to avoid giving offence over questions of morality or faith. In January 1912, for example, the paper spent a number of weeks denying that it had advocated the 'Malthusian doctrines' of birth control. This is not something that any other similar paper in any other country would have felt it necessary to do![35] On another occasion, Larkin himself condemned the authorities and the police for allowing the showing of a 'blasphemous' film, *The Miracle*, in the city. The film portrayed a nun breaking her vows. As Larkin piously observed, 'some creatures would barter the Cross of Calvary for money', but not 'by Socialists or Labour men, mark'.[36] None of this deflected the clerical assault. Initially, clerical hostility took the form of what can be best described as harassment. The paper reported nuns telling children to refuse to go if their parents tried to send them to buy the *Worker* and that priests were deliberately going to have their hair cut at the strike-bound hairdressers, Fergusons.[37] When the Great Lockout got underway this harassment escalated into a determined effort to help the employers crush the union.

The attacks that various priests made on the union required a response. On 20 September 1913, Larkin replied in the paper to an attack made by Fr John Condon. He wrote as a devout Catholic, outraged at the way the priests were siding with the enemies of the poor, laying bare what he saw as the cause for their betrayal:

> Reverend Father – I feel that I should be shirking a manifest duty if I allowed your insidious attack on the working class of this city to pass without comment as you were careful to explain you were not speaking as a Priest, but as an ordinary man ... May I point out to you, sir, that you forgot to explain that you were also speaking as a shareholder in a commercial undertaking, which is affected by the present deplorable dispute which you correctly describe as economic war ... (and) what of the seventy odd priests who are shareholders in the Dublin United Tramway Company and who are responsible along with that other pillar of the Church, William 'Murder' Murphy for the terrible bloodshed and tragedy of death? Have you no word of condemnation for them? ... Thank God, that there are others who dignify the high and holy calling, who instead of attacking the working class, sympathise with their efforts, and realise the great need for improvement.

Despite its ferocity, this was not an anti-clerical diatribe. Larkin was outraged as a Catholic at the conduct of the clergy, made clear his contempt for their hypocrisy and hoped to recall at least some of them to their duty towards the poor.

William Partridge continued the attack on Fr Condon the following week in an article that emphasised the Catholic character of the union and the devotion of its members:

> And may I remind him that the Union led by Larkin is the only organisation of workers in Ireland that provides a Christmas feast for the poor and homeless of our city in celebration of our Saviour's birth; that the Union led by Larkin is the

only organisation I know whose members make special provision for sending subscriptions to the Roman Catholic Church. Its members working on coal boats and others subscribe *2d* per man per boat to the City Quay or Ringsend Chapel, and that in all its club houses collecting boxes are exhibited for charitable contributions; and I have a letter of thanks from a Rev. Father praying for Larkin and the members of his Union for the generous donations made.[38]

The church's most damaging intervention was occasioned by the Children's Holiday scheme, which was condemned by William Walsh, the archbishop of Dublin as an attempt at proselytising. Priests led mobs to prevent the children leaving and the authorities lent credence to the charge by arresting the organisers for kidnapping. One of the purposes of the scheme was to highlight the suffering that the employers were inflicting on the locked-out workers' children and the priests countered that with the claim that the city's charities were relieving any genuine hardship. Connolly turned the tables on the church by sending a delegation of women and children to the archbishop's palace to ask for relief. As he reported in the *Worker*, they were told that children 'belonging to the workers engaged in the dispute were not to receive any benefit.' The children of scabs were eligible, but not those of parents fighting for the union. Indeed, only a few days earlier, Walsh had told a meeting of the St Vincent de Paul charity that they had to 'harden their hearts' against the children of the locked-out workers.[39]

The bitterness this episode occasioned led to a hardening of the tone. On 13 December 1913, the poet, James Stephens, condemned the church in the pages of the *Worker* as 'a lie' and insisted that its 'attitude ... throughout this dispute has been cynical and disgusting.' He went on: 'the difference between a priest and a policeman is too slight to talk about.'[40] This sort of ferocity was still tempered by the hope that the church would see the error of its ways. Nevertheless, the paper did become more forceful in its engagement with the clergy. On 13 June 1914, it carried a front page 'Open Letter to Cardinal Logue', entitled 'The Sin of Capitalism'. Here the idea of any shared interest between capitalist and worker was ridiculed and Logue was told, in no uncertain terms, what the ITGWU was about:

> The workers have a world to gain. And all the tinkering reform and dabbling in social science that the imagination of man can conjure up may delay, but will not prevent the march of the workers and the conquest of economic power. Your Eminence it means not reform but revolution ... Your Eminence, society and capitalism have sinned against the working classes. The working classes have sat in judgement upon the sinner, and in their good time and with their own chosen weapons shall the working classes exact the meet punishment. For the wages of sin is death.

'This Unholy War'

When war was declared on 4 August 1914, the *Worker* responded by condemning any Irish involvement in the conflict. On 8 August, the paper carried Larkin's warning that if the Irish people took the British Empire's side 'in this unholy war you are giving up your claim that Ireland is a nation.' They should have no part in Britain's 'murderous, grasping thieving work.' The same issue also carried Connolly's declaration that if a German army landed 'in Ireland tomorrow we should be perfectly justified in joining it.' This Fenian sentiment was joined in the same article by the Socialist hope that the European working class might 'proceed tomorrow to erect barricades all over Europe ... that war might be abolished.' He even hoped that a militant stand by the Irish workers might actually 'set the torch to a European conflagration.' In that same issue of the paper Seán O'Casey lamented that even good Citizen Army men were enlisting in the British Army. Confronted with the strength of popular support for the British cause, the paper retreated somewhat and instead began demanding that a price be extracted from the British for Irish support. On 5 September, an editorial, 'An Appeal in this Crisis', urged that if Ireland was a friend to Britain, then 'we want the recognition a friend should receive.' The paper urged that 'The price of our help should be not the travesty of a Home Rule Bill ... but a real measure of independence ... nothing less should be accepted, and if not granted, get ready and take it.' The same issue carried a report of Larkin's speech at a rally to commemorate the workers killed during the Lockout. Here he had argued that Ireland could win its freedom 'in a week if we told Asquith not a man shall leave Ireland unless Ireland has the rights which Canada and Australia have.' Asquith's 'bastard Home Rule' was not enough, and 'we will have the same rights as Canada.' He commented on the fact that there were men in British uniform in the crowd cheering this sentiment.

Redmond's failure to use the war as an opportunity to extract concessions from the British was regarded as both a mistake and as a betrayal. His call for Irishmen to enlist provoked a furious response. On 26 September, Larkin published an editorial, 'The Irish Judas', where he asked, 'Is there no man to provide a rope for this twentieth century Judas, who not even as clever as his predecessor, failed to receive the thirty pieces of silver.' The following week, another editorial, 'Redmond Eats his Own Vomit', reinforced the point. When the Irish Volunteers split over the war, the *Worker* enthusiastically supported the intransigent breakaway, with Connolly congratulating them on their 'Napoleon-like stroke'.[41] These were the first steps along the road to Easter Week.

October saw the Larkinite era come to an end, however. On 14 October, Larkin temporarily handed the post of ITGWU General Secretary over to Connolly and left on what was supposed to be a fund-raising tour of the United States. He was not to return until the end of April 1923. Under Connolly's editorship, the *Worker* increasingly became the voice of opposition to the war until Dublin Castle closed it down in December 1914. At the end of May 1915, the *Workers' Republic* was launched in its place, a different paper for a different time.

Conclusion

The *Worker* was the voice of the Dublin working class through a period of great conflict and bitter struggle. It subjected the movement's enemies to remorseless attack and rallied its supporters for the fight. The paper spoke for a working class that was beginning to demand its rights and even to look towards a better world, towards 'a mutual Commonwealth'. It went in fear of no one, standing up to government, politicians, police, and priests. It was a weapon in the class struggle. To a considerable extent the paper bears Jim Larkin's imprint, but it also enlisted the services of a number of other impressive individuals who contributed their talents. Nothing like it has been seen since.

Notes

1　Emmet Larkin, *James Larkin* (London, 1977), p. 69.

2　Robert Lowery, 'Seán O'Casey and the *Irish Worker*' in Robert Lowery (ed.), *O'Casey Annual No. 3* (London, 1984), pp 42-3.

3　For the rules see Francis Devine, *Organising history: a centenary of SIPTU* (Dublin, 2009), pp 888-97.

4　'OBU' featured on the standard ITGWU badge from 1918 to 1989, although for Larkinites it came to stand for 'O'Brien's Union' rather than demonstrating any syndicalist commitment.

5　Ronald James Patrick Mortished was born in London in 1891 of Irish parents. He was a graduate of the London School of Economics and in 1909 became a civil servant based in Dublin. He was an active member of the Socialist Party of Ireland and in 1912 began writing for *The Irish Worker*. When the paper was suppressed in December 1914, he was 'severely reprimanded' and denied an increment for his connection with it. He contributed to Connolly's *Workers' Republic* in 1915. In 1922, he was appointed secretary to the committee drafting the Free State constitution but resigned from the civil service later that year to become secretary to the Irish Labour Party and Trade Union Congress (ILPTUC). In 1930, he went to work for the International Labour Organisation (ILO) in Switzerland. In 1946, he was appointed the first chairman of the Labour Court in Dublin. He returned to working for the ILO in 1952, becoming ILO representative in Ireland in January 1954. He died at Killiney, Co. Dublin, on 16 August 1957. See Charles Callan, 'R. J. P. Mortished', *Saothar* 32 (2007).

6　Andrew Patrick Wilson was born in Scotland in 1886. He was an actor and moved to Ireland in 1911 to work at the Abbey Theatre. He wrote numerous articles for *The Irish Worker* and threw himself into the ITGWU's cultural activities. His dramatic satire, 'Profit', was serialised on the front page of the paper over three weeks (12, 19 and 26 October 1912). On 23 November 1912 the paper carried his 'The New Drama-Old and New', a critique of Ibsen and Shaw, on the front page, Here he argued that 'the pioneers of the newer drama have set themselves a big task in trying to revolutionise the theatre. Perhaps they would succeed better if they tried the social revolution first!' His one-act play, *Victims*, appeared on the paper's front page on 21 December 1912. He had a famous exchange, defending Socialism against the then Gaelic enthusiast, Seán O'Casey, in the paper in February and March 1913. His tenement play, *The Slough*, was staged at the Abbey in December 1914, with Wilson himself playing the Larkinite union leader. It was, without any doubt, an unacknowledged influence on O'Casey's early drama. He was for a while the general manager of the Abbey and went on to become a key figure in the Scottish theatre in the early 1920s.

7   *Irish Worker*, 24 June 1911.

8   *Irish Worker*, 16 Dec. 1911.

9   *Irish Worker*, 15 Feb. 1913.

10   *Irish Worker*, 2 Aug. 1913

11   *Irish Worker*, 15 Feb. 1913.

12   *Irish Worker*, 22 Feb. 1913.

13   James Curry, *Artist of the revolution: the cartoons of Ernest Kavanagh* (Cork, 2012), p. 27.

14   *Irish Worker*, 22 Mar. 1913.

15   *Irish Worker*, 13 Sept. 1913.

16   *Irish Worker*, 13 Jan. 1913. 'O'F' was probably Thomas O'Flaherty, who was living in the United States at this time and was actively involved in the Industrial Workers of the World (IWW). He made over 35 contributions to *The Irish Worker*.

17   For a celebration of the ITGWU's contribution to the social and cultural life of its members see Manus O'Riordan, *Next to the revolution: Liberty Hall as a cultural centre – the early years* (Dublin, 2002).

18   *Irish Worker*, 9 Aug. 1913.

19   *Irish Worker*, 11 Apr. 1912.

20   *Irish Worker*, 23 Nov. 1912.

21   *Irish Worker*, 21 June 1913.

22   *Irish Worker*, 27 July 1912.

23   *Irish Worker*, 21 Mar. 1914.

24   *Irish Worker*, 12 Aug. 1911.

25   *Irish Worker*, 14 Sept. 1912.

26   C. Desmond Greaves, *The Irish Transport and General Workers' Union: the formative years* (Dublin, 1982), p. 91.

27   *Irish Worker*, 30 Aug. 1913.

28   *Irish Worker*, 6 Sept. 1913.

29   *Irish Worker*, 3 Jan. 1914.

30   *Irish Worker*, 17 Jan. 1914.

31   *Irish Worker*, 7 Feb. 1914.

32   *Irish Worker*, 14 Mar. 1914.

33   *Irish Worker*, 9 May 1914.

34   'Shellback' was probably Joseph Foley.

35   *Irish Worker*, 6 Jan. 1912.

36   *Irish Worker*, 29 Mar. 1913.

37   *Irish Worker*, 27 Apr. 1912; 27 Aug. 1913.

38   *Irish Worker*, 27 Sept. 1913. For W. P. Partridge see Hugh Geraghty, *William Patrick Partridge and his times* (Dublin, 2003).

39   John Newsinger, *Rebel city: Larkin, Connolly and the Dublin labour movement* (Dublin, 2004), p. 74.

40   James Stephens (1882-1950) published his first of many poetry collections, *Insurrections,* in 1909 and his first novel, *The charwoman's daughter* in 1911. His most successful novel, *The crock of gold,* was published in 1912. He also wrote a number of plays and an eye-witness account of the Easter Rising, *The Insurrection in Dublin*, published in 1916. He was a friend of James Joyce.

41   *Irish Worker*, 3 Oct. 1914.

10.

'The Echo of the Battle'
Labour politics and the 1913 Lockout

....

Niamh Puirséil

Several decades after the 1913 Lockout, Jim Larkin junior, the eldest son of Big Jim Larkin, wrote of the labour movement on its eve:

> The unskilled workers had been given up as incapable of organisation by the older trade union leaders, and trade union solidarity was not considered as extending to the lower ranks of labour. Political organisations of labour had no effective existence, fragmentary efforts had all failed; a local Dublin Labour Party had dwindled away leaving behind a sorry record, while the small socialist groups had sown seed of social revolt by the harsh realities of Dublin working class existence had killed off any harvest.[1]

The picture he painted was bleak and, alas, largely accurate but just as the 'desperate, helpless unorganised workers' were becoming organised and assertive, there was also a political re-awakening of labour. Subordinate to the labour movement's industrial wing, labour politics made some significant progress in the period surrounding the Lockout, even if it was halting and unspectacular. The most notable advance, in the long run at least, was the decision made by the Irish Trade Union Congress (ITUC) in 1912 to establish an Irish Labour Party after several years of debating the question. That same year, at local level, there was also the establishment of a new Dublin Labour Party, unrelated to the ITUC, which had some success in municipal elections between 1911 and 1915. During the Lockout, then, Labour politics was nascent; in terms of elected representatives, it had no national presence and, at a local level, could boast of barely a handful of men in a Dublin Corporation of 80 members. Moreover, while the Dublin Lockout was the most political of industrial disputes, it was also one in which party politics played the most minor of roles since, beyond pronouncing on events, there was little which could be done anyway. Nevertheless, it would be a mistake to overlook the shoots of political labour which were beginning to appear around this time. It was an intrinsic part of the movement, albeit significantly weaker than the industrial side and if many of those who stood at the forefront of the locked out men did so as trade unionists, they were also endeavouring to establish a new political movement of the Irish working class. This chapter examines the development of political labour in the period leading up to the Lockout. Firstly, it looks at why at the time of the Lockout, only an embryonic national Labour Party existed in Ireland. Secondly, it looks at the development of labour politics in Dublin including the Dublin Labour Party, separate from its national namesake, which operated at municipal level.

The issue of labour representation in Ireland was merely being debated in the trade union movement at a time when it had become a real and growing entity in Britain. The Labour Representation Committee (LRC), a coalition of unions, socialist and social democratic groups, was established in 1900 and grew rapidly following the notorious Taft Vale judgement the following year which threatened the right to strike. At the 1906 general election, the Labour Party (as it became after the election), secured 29 seats which it managed to build on, winning 42 seats at the next election in 1910. Naturally, this attracted the attention of the labour movement in Ireland. Among Unionists in the labour movement, there was a desire to work closely with their British brethren, and among some Irish trade unionists, there was a desire to follow their lead, but to do so in their own right. Among many trade unionists, however, there continued to be an allegiance towards the Liberals for their support for Home Rule. And, while the Liberals supported Home Rule, the British Labour Party were mute on issues concerning Ireland. As Geoffrey Bell observed, among the various issues debated at the first ten conferences of the LRC/Labour Party, the question of Ireland was entirely absent. There was no mention of Home Rule in Labour's manifestos in the two general elections of 1910 although, as Bell notes, in a survey of 51 election addresses, 33 candidates expressed support for Home Rule, 17 made no reference to it and one was ambiguous.[2] As James Connolly noted only months before the Lockout, 'no one, and least of all the present writer, would deny the sympathy of the leaders of the British Labour movement towards the Labour and Socialist movements of Ireland, but a sympathy not based on understanding is often more harmful than a direct antagonism.'[3] Connolly explained that the Labour Party in Westminster had established:

> Home Rule in its relations with Ireland. Thus if a trades body in Ireland writes to the Labour Party asking that a certain question be raised in Parliament, if that question pertains to a district represented by a member of the Home Rule Party, the answer sent to the trades body generally is that the question has been turned over to the Irish Party, and that should that party raise it in the House, the Labour Party will support it.[4]

In effect, the British Labour Party devolved responsibility on Irish issues to the Irish Parliamentary Party (IPP). It is not surprising, then, that among the Irish in Britain, support for the Liberal Party remained strong around this time.[5]

The Irish Labour Party

1. James Connolly (1868-1916).
DCLA (BOR F01/05)

On 26 May 1912 some 150 delegates arrived at Clonmel for the annual Irish Trade Union Congress. They had been due to meet in the town's courthouse but at the last minute, were informed they were not welcome and so, on the invitation of the Mayor of Clonmel, James Meehan (a Labour councillor), they gathered in the Town Hall for proceedings.[6] The ITUC was by no means a seditious organisation and the idea that local businessmen and gentry would intervene to prevent their meeting is preposterous but their behaviour might be explained by the presence there of one delegate in particular. Big Jim Larkin's infamy had made him persona non-grata among Clonmel businessmen who determined there would be no room at the inn for the ITGWU secretary, who ended up residing at the Workmen's Boat Club house in Irishtown for the duration of congress.[7] That a sedate meeting of respectable working men could be regarded with such suspicion well illustrates the changing context of industrial relations in the country at that time as fear of the new militant trade unionism was beginning to take hold among Ireland's 'respectable classes'. The 1912 congress has gone down in Labour lore as the occasion of the party's foundation but if the truth is a little more complex, the congress remains a landmark in the politics of labour nonetheless.

There was no new party established in Clonmel that week but delegates did decide in principle that labour ought to enter the political fray in its own right. The actual motion put down by James Connolly, then an ITGWU organiser in Belfast and a first-time delegate, was as follows:

> That the independent representation of Labour upon all public boards be, and is hereby, included amongst the objects of this Congress; that one day at least be hereafter set apart at our annual gathering for the discussion of all questions pertaining thereto; that the affiliated bodies be asked to levy their members 1*s*.

per annum for the necessary expenses and that the Parliamentary Committee be instructed to take all possible action to give effect politically to this resolution.[8]

James Larkin was 'first on his feet' to support the resolution declaring that 'there was no argument against such a policy as was outlined in the resolution,' a resolution which gave them 'the lever to do their own work'. Larkin was joined in support for the motion by four other delegates, including the Dublin Trades Council secretary, William O'Brien,[9] and after a fairly lengthy debate, the motion was passed with a good majority: 49 for, 18 against, and 20 abstentions. More than a century later, it might seem perplexing how so vague and apparently innocuous a motion could represent a crucial step forward for labour politics but it was a key victory in a struggle within congress that had been on-going for some years.

The idea that the Irish trade union movement would establish its own independent Irish Labour Party had long proved controversial although opponents of the move differed profoundly in their reasons. During the 1900-10 period, there were, as Arthur Mitchell has noted, four schools of thought within congress on the subject of political activity.

> The first believed that trade unions should stay out of politics altogether. A second and more sizeable group held that the Irish Parliamentary Party (IPP) adequately served labour's interests, and that labour political action at this time might injure the home rule effort. A third group, mostly from Belfast, declared that the congress should become an affiliated or subordinate part of the advancing British political movement. A fourth, but tiny, group under separatist influence ... held that if the congress was to set up its own political machinery, it should be independent of any British connections.[10]

P. T. Daly, a senior figure in the Irish Republican Brotherhood and the Dublin Typographical Provident Society delegate to the Dublin Trades Council, was at the forefront of this last group.[11] Daly first put the idea of establishing an independent Irish Labour Party before congress in Cork in 1902. His addendum to establish 'a pledge-bound labour party, controlled by, and answerable to the Irish Trade Union Congress' passed but nothing was done to put the motion into effect.[12] Arthur Mitchell suggests that the congress executive's inertia on the issue was probably because it recognised 'that the resolution did not reflect the true feeling of the body.'[13] But if the 'true feeling of the body' was not in favour of an independent Irish Labour Party, it was deeply divided on sectarian lines. The nationalist case was well summed up by J. P. Nannetti, an IPP M.P. who had been active in the DTUC and served as Lord Mayor of Dublin when he advised the 1906 congress that a new Labour Party was unnecessary since 'the Irish

Parliamentary Party were the Labour Party ... The platform on which he was proud to stand was broad enough for any workingman. They could make the Parliamentary Party do everything they wished.'[14] The Unionist position took quite the opposite view. Less based in wishful thinking with a more explicit class analysis, its foremost proponent was William Walker.[15] Walker, a onetime Independent Labour Party councillor in Belfast, argued that the Irish trade union movement should establish its own political organisation, but that it would be subordinate to the British Labour Representation Committee. The result of this cleavage was a stalemate which maintained the status quo to the benefit of the nationalist group. As Emmet O'Connor notes, the Walker side was placated as 'Congress approved Belfast resolutions calling for "non-political" labour representation or for affiliates to set up branches of the British Labour Party. Each year the motion was passed and each year nothing happened.'[16]

As Arthur Mitchell has noted, however, before the decade was out, there were two developments which would up-end this state of affairs. In 1909, the Asquith government declared its support for Irish Home Rule. As Ireland came closer and closer to some form of self-government, opposition to an independent Irish Labour Party declined among nationalists since, if there was going to be an Irish parliament, there ought to be an Irish Labour Party in it. The second development was the founding of the ITGWU in 1909 and its affiliation to congress the following year. Considerably more militant than most affiliated unions, the ITGWU was fundamentally nationalist and strongly in favour of taking political action.[17] James Larkin and his lieutenants, most notably James Connolly, had been some of the most vocal proponents of an independent Labour Party around this time. Larkin and Connolly were trade unionists first and foremost – as Connolly had put it in 'Socialism made easy,' 'the fight for the conquest of the political state is not the battle, it is only the echo of the battle'[18] – but that did not mean that political struggle could be ignored. As Larkin observed 'I believe that the workers should use every weapon against the entrenched powers of capitalism. I am an industrialist and at the same time appreciate the fact that Labour can accomplish a great deal through the intelligent use of the ballot. Why use one arm when we have two?'[19] In 1910, it managed to secure affiliation to congress by 42 votes to 10 and the following year it provided the largest delegation.[20] Despite deep-felt antipathy towards the new union from the more established and British-based unions, the faction sympathetic to Larkin within congress began to grow in numbers and in strength.[21] That year, 1911, had seen supporters of an Irish Labour Party take up the mantle laid down by P. T. Daly some years earlier with a motion proposed by Thomas Murphy of the Carpet Planners of the City of Dublin Trade Union, seconded by William O'Brien, representing the DTUC, but after stormy debate, it was defeated while a motion supporting the Walker position scraped through by 32 votes to 29.[22] Once again nothing was done to implement the Walker proposal but the 1911 congress proved the last time that delegates engaged in this annual charade.

On 11 April 1912, the third Home Rule Bill was introduced in the House of Commons, which meant that when congress delegates met in Clonmel the following month, they did so with self-government a very imminent prospect. Connolly had asked 'when the representatives of Ireland come to meet in the old historic building in Dublin, which they had heard so much about, were the workers to be the only class that was not to be represented?'[23] This change in context was crucial to the vote, but those actively supporting an independent Irish Labour Party had grown in number. Significantly, William Walker, the staunchest opponent of the move, was not present, having accepted a post as a representative of the just established National Insurance Commissioners.[24] As Henry Patterson observed, the position of the Belfast Trades Council had already shifted towards Connolly's analysis of political action.[25] Nevertheless, to go from a 32 to 20 vote in favour of an association with British Labour to a 49 to 18 vote in favour of setting up an Irish party (albeit with 20 abstentions) was a remarkable turnaround and was indicative of the growing influence of the ITGWU within the trade union movement. The vote, vital as it was, was merely the first hurdle. Building up an actual Labour Party based on the Trade Union Congress should not have been as difficult as it proved but as they began their task, the men charged with the job – William O'Brien, James Connolly and Thomas Johnson[26] – encountered resistance from Larkin, their chairman, who having campaigned for such a thing for years, now adopted a petulant attitude towards the whole endeavour. Larkin not only refused to co-operate he was actively obstructive most notably when efforts to organise a public meeting to launch the new party in Dublin in September. Having refused to have anything to do with the meeting, he turned up and sat with a group of dockers at the back of the hall. Called on to speak from the floor, he took to the platform and denounced the whole proceedings.[27] After this fiasco, the new party effectively stalled until after the 1913 congress which reaffirmed the previous year's decision and instructed the parliamentary committee to proceed with writing a party constitution which would go before congress the following year.[28]

'Unwept, unhonoured and unsung' Dublin Labour before the Lockout

While no real progress had been made in establishing a national Labour Party, the situation at local level was more positive. Indeed the revival of local labour politics had, to some extent, grown out of the failure of congress to support a national Irish party prior to 1912. Belfast was in the vanguard of labour politics, where a Labour Electoral Association was established in 1892. It succeeded in returning six Trades Council candidates at the municipal elections in 1897.[29] There had been a short-lived Dublin Labour Party before the turn of the century, but it was regarded as something of an embarrassment among trade unionists. Its genesis lay in the Local Government

Act (LGA) of 1898, a piece of legislation which, as Eunan O'Halpin observed 'partly democratised local government without cleaning it up.'[30] Having campaigned for an extension of the franchise for several years, the Dublin Trades Council (DTC) looked favourably on the LGA, under which the electorate for the Dublin municipal elections rose from 8,000 to 38,000; some of this increase was women but the majority of new voters were working class men.[31] In light of the bill, trades councils across the country decided they should have direct political representation on the new municipal bodies and established Labour Electoral Associations (LEA) to contest local elections.[32] The LEA's first election on the revised register in 1899 had a good results. In Dublin, seven of its 11 candidates were elected, the other four missing out by small margins,[33] and the LEA enjoyed the goodwill of people as diverse politically as James Connolly and Arthur Griffith but this quickly soured. Compelled only to vote together on 'labour issues' the LEA men proved an ill-disciplined bunch who were not the reforming breath of fresh air that some had hoped, but merely fell in with the existing cliques on the Corporation which combined speechifying on national issues on which members had no power with Tammany Hall-style corruption and jobbery.[34] Even on 'labour issues', the one area on which they were supposed to follow a party line, the LEA could not act as one prompting DTC delegates to complain that they had failed to pursue a single issue in their platform at the council.[35] Their failure to represent workers was compounded by their propensity towards bribery and corruption and ultimately, as John W. Boyle summed up 'most of the labour group identified themselves with their fellow corporators and rose out of their class rather than with it.'[36]

The LEA lost most of its seats in 1900 and in 1903 the DTC officially called time. 'Unwept, unhonoured and unsung' (in Connolly's description) so ignominious was its history that few were in a hurry to return to the electoral fray[37] but as thoughts turned increasingly to establishing a national Labour Party, it seemed appropriate to return to the idea at local level. William O'Brien, one of its main proponents at congress, was also at the forefront of reviving labour representation in Dublin and when, in January 1911, the DTC voted to establish a Labour Representation Committee (LRC) once again, O'Brien was appointed its secretary.[38] Some members resisted the move because of its predecessor's dire performance, but among its supporters the LEA merely served as a lesson that this time, discipline would be key.[39] In April 1911, the new LRC adopted new rules and a constitution and became the Dublin Labour Party. It contested its first election in the summer of 1911, where it secured four Poor Law Guardians.

An important tool at its disposal was the ITGWU's new weekly *The Irish Worker,* first published on 27 May 1911 and which soon enjoyed phenomenal sales of some

20,000 copies.[40] It continually stressed the need for bona fide labour politics both nationally and locally and towards the end of November it announced that the work of drafting rules and a programme had been completed. The following month, it hailed 'with unbounded delight … the advent of a new Labour Party on the Corporation which will be composed of real, not sham, representatives; working men for working men.'[41] Seven candidates were chosen to stand with great emphasis put on their being pledge-bound, committing to resign as councillors if their conduct was called into question by the party since, as Richard O'Carroll,[42] secretary of the Brick and Stonelayers' Society and DTC reminded his comrades, 'candidates in the past had not been true to their principles.'[43] He was not alone in being wary. At least one person recorded that he had found it difficult to raise funds in part because the 'previous corruption of Labour men [means] I find it difficult to get my members to have another trial.'[44] The election took place in January 1912, with the Dublin Labour Party candidates running on a six-point programme which emphasised labour issues and housing conditions, promising a clean and healthy city under Labour where no longer would 'the children of our class [be] murdered by their unhealthy surroundings.'[45] In the end, despite a vigorous campaign of opposition from the *Irish Independent* which accused Larkin and his colleagues of various calumnies including atheism, free love and child murder, they took five of the 20 available seats on Dublin Corporation, among them Larkin himself, who took 1,190 votes compared with 464 by his opponent.[46] Further gains soon followed, with Thomas Farren elected in a by-election in Ushers Quay and the election of Peadar Macken as alderman in North Dock in June and outside Dublin, Labour representatives were elected in cities including Waterford, Clonmel, Drogheda and Sligo.[47]

Larkin's victory here was short-lived, however. A month after his election, he was sued for his seat on the grounds that he was debarred as a convicted felon, and he was prohibited from sitting on the Corporation for seven years.[48] Though it has been argued, that 'the loss of Larkin did not destroy the Labour Party [which] maintained its disciplined and independent position in the municipal councils,'[49] Larkin's removal from the Corporation had a considerable impact on him personally and on the Dublin labour movement more generally. Larkin's biographer and name-sake, Emmet Larkin, identified this as a 'crucial turning point' although the historian Arthur Mitchell down-played its importance arguing that Larkin's primary interest at the time was in the industrial struggle and that 'Dublin Corporation would hardly be likely to offer great scope for his energies.'[50] Mitchell was probably right but his abrupt expulsion from the Corporation came at a bad time not only for the Dublin Labour Party but for the new national party. Notwithstanding his mercurial character, it would help explain how one of the staunchest supporters of establishing an independent congress based party in Ireland, could then obstruct its progress at every possible turn. Moreover, while the Dublin Labour Party did survive his loss, it might have fared better had he remained. As Emmet Larkin noted of Richard O'Carroll, his successor as Dublin Labour Party leader, he was 'an able, honest and energetic man, but he was not the man Larkin was.'[51]

Larkin's involvement with the Congress Labour Party and the Dublin Labour Party is a reminder of the multiple Labour Parties which existed by the middle of 1912, all separate organisations but frequently sharing a common membership. As well as the (still largely notional) Congress Labour Party and the Dublin Labour Party, there was also the Independent Labour Party of Ireland (ILP(I)) which held its founding meeting in the Antient Concert Rooms in April.[52] An effort forged by James Connolly to establish a united socialist party in Ireland, the ILP(I) was the result of the merger of the largely Dublin-based Socialist Party of Ireland (SPI) with several branches of the Independent Labour Party which was confined to Belfast. Chaired until 1914 by Francis Sheehy-Skeffington, it was a tiny organisation which, like the SPI, was essentially propagandist and never developed into much more than 'a party of convenience for the handful of members wishing to attend lectures on Sunday evenings.'[53] Of these three Labour Parties, however, only one – the Dublin Labour Party – had any electoral presence.

Even then, its presence was not strong. In 1912 it had five seats on a Corporation of 80 and elections in New Kilmainham and North Dock in October failed to increase this number. The North Dock contest, which had come about after Larkin's earlier disqualification, was a bitter campaign characterised by disturbances, saw the Dublin Labour candidate pitched against William Richardson of the United Irish League. Richardson styled himself as a trade unionist but his bitter anti-Larkinism effectively put him on the side of the bosses with *The Irish Worker* describing him as a 'political corner boy and tool of Alfie Byrne, publican.'[54] Each managed 820 votes on the first count but after a recount found 13 spoiled ballots, Richardson was declared to have won by five votes, a result, he claimed that had 'marked the revolt of the people of Dublin against Larkin and Larkinism.'[55] The Labour campaign cried foul, listing dirty tricks during the contest and accusing their opponents of vote-rigging,[56] but there was little time for recriminations when there was another round of elections in January. *The Irish Worker* was filled with reminders to readers that they should not be hoodwinked by nationalism or bought off by porter into voting against Labour candidates:

> It is to the working class themselves the task falls to get their own men elected. If the workers fail to return workers, then it is the workers themselves that must ultimately suffer … Will a publican do as much in the interests of the workers as a carpenter or a docker? Will a race-course tout understand what the workers are striving for as well as a plasterer?[57]

The call to add 'some more men to the small but remarkably gallant band of Labourites at Cork Hill' failed to rally the troops, however. Labour fielded seven candidates, picking up two seats (William Partridge and Michael Brohoon, the two unsuccessful candidates from October) but losing one incumbent. In North Dock, the losing Nationalist candidate complained that the Labour campaign had illegally used taxi-cabs to bring voters to the polls. Rather churlishly, he noted that he would not have gone forward for election in the first place except that he 'would not allow Mr. Larkin and his crowd to have a walk-over. With time they hoped to have the opportunity of putting that party in their place.'[58] If nothing else, the Dublin Labour Party had clearly succeeded in riling the city's more reactionary politicians and disrupting the cosy cartel that operated the Corporation. By the beginning of 1913 the party had overtaken the Unionists to become the second largest group on the Corporation. Labour had ten seats, the Unionists seven, Sinn Féin four, independents four and two independent Nationalists, but they were still too few to exert any profound influence on the issues that were most important to their voters, and the Nationalist majority was so vast as to be unbreakable. The Labour councillors, including Macken, Partidge, Lawlor, Foran and O'Carroll, were capable and disciplined, were active on the Corporation and its committees (including its housing committee) and did a great deal to rescue the name of Labour politics in Dublin. Nevertheless, it is difficult to disagree with the conclusion that:

> in 1912-13 they were only in the second rank of the Dublin trade union leadership'. The 'heavyweights' of the trade union movement were not in the Corporation Labour Party. The popular leaders and speakers, Larkin and Daly, and the able organiser O'Brien, concentrated their activities on purely trade union affairs. Their formidable skills ... channelled into consolidating the progressive leadership of the trade union movement and by agitation, increasing the industrial militancy of the working class.[59]

As industrial militancy grew and the employers became determined to scotch the rise of Labour, it was inevitable that the battle between the two sides would not take place in the polling booths or on the Corporation but on the ground, in the work place. Speaking on the eve of 1913, the press reported that Larkin's assurance that 'on the question of labour that there were "stirring and strenuous times" ahead for the new year.'[60] He had rarely spoken a truer word, although it is unlikely he realised quite how strenuous it would be.

British Labour and the Lockout

Few episodes in Irish history illustrated the failure of politics as vividly as the Dublin Lockout of 1913 either at local level or beyond. Even if one took the view that there was little which could have been done in London or in City Hall to end the conflict, there was a moral failure on the part of most Irish Parliamentary Party representatives to do other than represent the interests of the employers; indeed arguably, British M.P.s showed more interest in the crisis even if ultimately their efforts bore no fruit. There was the intervention by the Liberal government in London which attempted to bring about a settlement through a public enquiry under George Askwith of the Board of Trade. The British Labour Party also became active. Its involvement, along with that of the British TUC, proved difficult, achieved nothing and ended badly. Even before the Lockout there was bad blood between Larkin and several of the British trade union leaders, a number of whom were M.P.s. Unlike the situation in Ireland at the time, the British TUC and the British Labour Party were separate organisations although they shared some of the same personnel. The British trade union leadership did not support Larkin's militancy and they were concerned that any of their own members might emulate it but after Bloody Sunday on 31 August which left two men dead and hundreds injured, the mood shifted. The TUC was in the middle of its annual congress when word reached them of the scenes in Dublin. The following day, standing orders were suspended and delegates voted to demand an enquiry, as Emmet O'Connor notes, 'subsequently, the TUC and the [British] Labour Party were to be integral to the search for a settlement.'[61] James Larkin had invited the former Labour leader Keir Hardie to Dublin to lend his moral support and he arrived on Tuesday morning for the funeral of James Nolan, one of the two killed on Bloody Sunday.[62] During a short visit, Hardie attended Nolan's funeral, spoke at a public meeting at Beresford Place, went to a private meeting of the DTC and visited Larkin and Connolly in prison before travelling to Belfast to seek support from its trades council.[63] At the TUC, further discussion about the situation on Tuesday led to a deputation including Arthur Henderson M.P., the secretary of the British Labour Party,[64] leaving for Dublin the next day. The TUC deputation did little to make themselves popular with their hosts by refusing to address a public meeting when they arrived on Wednesday night. Then, on Thursday morning they had a meeting with the Under-Secretary in Dublin Castle. William O'Brien recalled, when they returned 'they were very changed men. Apparently they had got a bad opinion of us from the Castle authorities.'[65] They saw themselves as intermediaries in the dispute but the strikers wanted allies and Councillor William Partridge publicly warned of attempts to settle the dispute 'behind the back' of Larkin.[66] Ultimately the British delegation agreed to send financial support, although at William O'Brien's suggestion, it was decided to send it in kind.[67]

The problem was that Larkin (and others) did not want charity, they wanted solidarity. Larkin wanted a sympathetic strike and the British Labour leaders had no intention of letting him have one and neither were they supportive of blacking goods to Ireland. Larkin, who had been arrested on Bloody Sunday was finally released and travelled to England on 12 September. Once there, diplomatic as ever, he denounced the British trade union movement as 'absolutely rotten' to a public meeting in Manchester, adding that the British Labour leaders were 'damnable hypocrites'.[68] He damned them collectively and then lambasted them by name. Connolly, for his part, called them 'old fossils … willing to sell the pass any time.'[69] The hostility from the Irish leaders met with a more measured response from their British counterparts (in public at least) but it was clear that they believed the Dublin unions were 'undisciplined and dangerous' (Snowden) and that Larkin's syndicalism was 'poor fighting' and '15 years out of date'.[70] The British

TUC decided to wait until December to hold a conference to try to resolve the dispute but the level of mutual suspicion mitigated against a settlement. The final TUC peace initiative, headed by the British Labour leader Arthur Henderson, took place in Dublin on 18 December but ended in a shambles amidst mutual recrimination.[71] There was not only no deal, but the British side had lost patience and the monetary support which had been so crucial in keeping the strike going, largely dried up thereafter.

City Council Elections, January, 1914.

VOTE FOR LABOUR
AND
SAVE YOUR CHILDREN'S LIVES.

The Massacre of the Innocents.

Every year about 2,600 babies under 5 years of age die in Dublin ; 9 out of every 10 of them belong to the working class. In proportion to the population, for every baby that dies in an upper-class home, and for every three babies that die in middle-class homes, no less than fourteen die in the homes of labourers. That is the case for children up to 5 years of age. But out of every 4 children born only 3 ever reach the age of 5. Think of the babies less than a year old. For every 1,000 births there are 140 or more deaths of babies under one year. In 1909 the figure was 141 per 1,000 in Dublin, as compared with 139 in Belfast, 126 in Cork, 122 in Edinburgh (in 1908) and 108 in London

Think of seven of your fellow-workers to whom a baby has just been born. Before the year is out, at least one of those babies will be dead.

Why do Your Babies Die ?

THEY DIE BECAUSE THEIR PARENTS ARE POOR. The children of the well-to-do stand a more than tenfold better chance of living than do your children Sir Charles Cameron, the Medical Officer of Health to the Corporation, says that the chief causes of these deaths are : —

"Exposure to cold, want of cleanliness, neglect of medical advice and proper treatment in illness, and especially the want of proper and sufficient food."

How You Can Save the Children's Lives.

Compel the Corporation to begin at once to provide : -

1. HOUSING AND SANITARY REFORM, so that the children can get plenty of pure air and water.
2. MUNICIPAL MILK, so that mother and baby can have pure, good and cheap food.
3. A proper staff of HEALTH VISITORS, so that mothers can be sure of kindly advice and skilled help when they most need it.
4. BABY AND SCHOOL CLINICS, so that children may get proper medical attention.
5. MEDICAL INSPECTION OF SCHOOL CHILDREN, so that disease may be nipped in the bud.
6. MEALS FOR SCHOOL CHILDREN, so that the children of poverty-stricken parents shall not starve and their education shall not be wasted.
7. HIGHER WAGES AND SHORTER HOURS FOR WORKERS as far as the Corporation's influence can secure them; so that the workers may have means and leisure to rear their children as good, stalwart citizens of Dublin.

All the Labour Candidates will do their best to secure these Reforms.

Vote for the Labour Candidates
BECAUSE
THEY VALUE THE LIVES OF YOUR CHILDREN.

[We would be glad if any woman or man interested in the question of social betterment in any or all its phases would write us on the subject.—ED.

2. *Irish Worker*, 2 Jan. 1914.
DCLA

Irish politics and the Lockout

Among the representatives on Dublin Corporation, the police's behaviour on Bloody Sunday was trenchantly criticised by the vast majority of councillors regardless of their party. The brutality of the police on this occasion and its indiscriminate nature, not to mention the vast number of witnesses to the violence, meant that the sympathy of the council was with the strikers on this occasion and as Yeates pointed out, even anti-Larkinites were put in a quandary of not wanting to defend the British-controlled police force.[72] There were exceptions, one being Larkin's old foe, William Richardson, who accused the strikers that day of 'terrorism' a view which was echoed by a handful of businessmen councillors,[73] but though the vote came close, the Corporation decided against a motion calling for the removal of the police from Dublin's streets. It mattered little since it was not within their power to do so anyway although the Corporation did decide to hold an inquiry.

The call for an inquiry into the police was echoed in a letter to the Lord Lieutenant signed by four of the six Home Rule M.P.s for Dublin including William Field and J. P. Nannetti, both of whom had been conduits between the Home Rule party and the trade union movement.[74] By now, however, they were long out of touch with their colleagues in the craft unions and had no relationship whatever with the new unionism which, in their eyes, was too militant by far. Furthermore, on a personal level Nannetti had suffered a series of strokes and by 1913 was terminally ill.[75] But while the Dublin M.P.s expressed regret at the 'deplorable crisis' and offered their assistance in finding a resolution their colleagues outside of the capital were less helpful. Prior to the Lockout, where Home Rule M.P.s expressed an opinion on industrial relations, they sang from a hymn sheet that could have been composed by William Martin Murphy himself. James McConnel noted the words of the Tipperary East Home Rule M.P. (and former Fenian), Tom Condon, during the rail strike in 1911: 'In a fair fight for better terms the workers would always have the warm support of the people, but no such question arose in this case' since the strike had been 'forced upon them by the action of a few outsiders from England.' As McConnel observed:

> Subsequent pronouncements by nationalist M.P.s closely followed this line: in principle the party supported the right of Irish trade unions to strike when they had 'legitimate' grievances, but that the sympathetic strike was not only an illegitimate means of protest, but one foisted on Irish workers by 'foreign' interests.[76]

The Lockout, initially, seemed to find the Home Rule M.P.s without a voice, but several weeks in, David Sheehy broke the silence, declaring that the good relations between employer and worker in Dublin had been subverted by the 'hideous monster' Jim Larkin. With this, Sheehy started a steady stream of abuse aimed directly at Larkin who was described as an autocrat and 'wild egotistical fanatic', a socialist, an Englishman and an opponent of the church.[77] Of those publicly lending support to Larkin, there were almost none. The progressive Galway M.P., Stephen Gwynn, was a notable exception, although he remained silent until November and others gave their full sympathies to the workers but only in private.[78] The extent to which there was hidden support for the workers in the IPP is something of a moot point however since the locked-out members needed more than silent goodwill, they needed moral and practical support which was not forthcoming. More telling was the determination of the senior Home Ruler, John Dillon, to enforce silence among those who might sympathise with the Larkinites. There was no love lost between Dillon and William Martin Murphy whose personal and political antipathy went back decades. Murphy was a key patron of Dillon's bitter IPP rival the anti-Parnellite T. P. Healy (who would subsequently appear for Murphy at the Askwith enquiry) and Dillon cherished a victory when his candidate defeated Murphy in a by-election in South Kerry in September 1895. As Dillon wrote to a colleague in October, 'Murphy is a desperate character, Larkin as bad. It would be a blessing to Ireland if they exterminated each other.'[79] But Dillon was being disingenuous for if he hated Murphy personally, his antipathy towards Larkin and his politics was far greater. As a middle class, property owning member of the political elite, he abhorred the socialism and militancy espoused by Larkin and as his biographer has noted his enmity towards Larkin 'was instinctive and went deeper, perhaps, than he wanted to admit even to himself.'[80] Quite apart from this, Dillon was perceptive enough to see Larkinism as a 'very dangerous enemy to Home Rule, the government and the Nationalist Party'[81] and he was not alone in this view.

This very real fear that Labour threatened the Nationalist party's hegemony was clearly evident at the municipal elections in January 1914 which was deemed sufficiently dangerous that in some wards, other candidates withdrew so as not to split the vote and give the Nationalists a better chance against Labour.[82] Naturally, those involved in the conflict regarded the contest as an important opportunity to secure public support. Coming almost five months after the Lockout began, a strong result for Labour would have represented a display of solidarity when it needed it most. There was a problem however; though the Labour side recognised that they needed to do well in the contest, they were slow to organise. As Yeates noted, discussions on the elections had begun two months before the polls but the full list of DTC candidates was not ratified until 13 January, three days before polling and six days after nominations had closed.[83] Initially intending to field candidates in all 20 wards,[84] half that many were endorsed along with the socialist Walter Carpenter who stood as Independent Labour.[85] Despite the fact that he was not a candidate in the election, the character of Larkin overshadowed the whole of the Dublin Labour Party. Perhaps this is unsurprising, but it is significant that even *The Irish Times* which though not sympathetic to the workers was somewhat less partisan than the *Independent*, labelled the DLP candidates as 'Larkinite' rather than Labour.[86] The *Independent* even suggested that Dubliners had 'been wondering why it is that of late Mr Larkin has been apparently devoting no attention to the strike and all his energies to municipal electioneering.'[87] It was part of a narrative which suggested that, along with reasonable people, the *Irish Independent* had no problem with 'Labour' as such, but that the kind of militant radicalism prescribed by Larkin had to be stopped. In fact, of ten candidates, six were actually from craft unions and there was a distinct failure on the part of the leaders of the strike to actually run themselves.[88] Ultimately, while the Labour men who stood for the Corporation in 1914 were in solidarity with those who had been locked out, they were not at the forefront of the dispute. Not that this could get in the way of the anti-Labour propaganda as the *Independent* contrasted the old-style trade unionism of earlier years, practiced 'by men who had some sense of their responsibilities not only to their class but to the community of which they were a part' with the ITGWU's policy 'of organised revolt against society, of pure destructiveness. Constructive programme they have none.'[89]

Of course, this was scare-mongering hyperbole but it was also incorrect to suggest that Labour had no constructive programme. The opposite was the case. Industrial issues generally, or the Lockout specifically, did not feature at the front of Labour's campaign. Instead, Labour decried the corruption on the Corporation and the disregard which councillors showed towards their voters. In common with previous years, the key part of the platform was the obscene housing conditions in the city. Calling on voters to 'vote Labour and sweep away the slums,' the party's case was bolstered by the public hearings of the Dublin housing inquiry which shone a light on the unsanitary and degrading circumstances in which tens of thousands of people lived in the city, many of them in slum buildings owned by Nationalist members of the Corporation. It should have been manna to the Labour campaign but, as Yeates points out, the impact was lessened to a degree by the intervention of the Christmas holidays which allowed 'the damaging newspaper reports to recede from public memory before polling day.'[90]

The campaign itself then, was short but predictably acrimonious. Nationalist candidates and the press at large rounded on the Labour candidates as godless syndicalists and were assisted enthusiastically by the city's clergy leaving the Labour candidates to defend themselves against attack. The Nationalists and their allies used every tool at their disposal to smear the Labour candidates, which included the distribution of blasphemous pamphlets purportedly published by the 'American Labour Party'.[91] Labour's campaign was energetic with open air meetings, demonstrations and parades featuring bands and the Citizen Army.[92] The special election edition of *The Irish Worker* declared Labour's call to arms, declaring 'every vote given against the Labour candidates tomorrow is a stab at the heart of Labour and the workers ... We work together, live together, and tramp together, we strike together, are locked-out together and are shot together. The time has come when we must learn to *vote together*.'[93] The campaign was successful in increasing the Labour vote but not by enough. Though reasonably close run, the Nationalists won practically every seat in the city with Labour taking only a single seat, that of Henry Donnelly, a coach maker who worked at the Tramway Company's workshop in Inchicore, who topped the poll in New Kilmainham and joined William Partridge as a Labour representative for that ward. Some solace could be found in several narrow results: in four seats, it had lost out by some 150 votes, in another by a baker's dozen,[94] but that was not going to stop the Murphyites from claiming that the contest had seen Labour properly routed and that the result was 'a final blow to Larkin'.[95] Farcically, the *Irish Independent* painted a picture in which the Nationalist Davids had fought against the Goliath that was the ranks of organised labour which had been swollen by those who had been locked out:

> It has to be borne in mind that the Larkinites chose their ground and they brought up their full strength. Their defeat is all the more significant on that account. They had no reserves to draw upon. With so many men disemployed in consequence of hearkening to the dictates of Liberty Hall, there was no lack of canvassers, and organised intimidation was rife.[96]

Labour suffered defeats in local elections outside Dublin too, in Cork, Wexford and Castlebar. Only in Sligo, where John Lynch, a Transport Union man, was elected mayor, was there anything that could be chalked up as a success.[97] It was a bad result, made all the worse because it was unexpected. Even Larkin was circumspect afterwards, his editorial in the next *Irish Worker* taking a less trenchant tone than would have usually been the case: 'the noise and turmoil has ceased for a time. Labour's ranks have been broken and we have been compelled to withdraw to our base,' but if he acknowledged that they had lost he tried to sound a defiant note proclaiming 'they beat Larkinism by votes; but they can never beat Larkinism by reason, by fact, by principles. They may delay the advent of the coming time, but delay is not always dangerous to the newer ideas.'[98] Though accusing the Nationalist candidates of using Corporation workers to canvass for them and decrying their smear campaign against the Labour candidates, Larkin suggested that timing had been the deciding factor, claiming that had the election taken place two months earlier, they could have claimed eight victories. Perhaps that could have happened; it is impossible to know but if the figure of 'eight victories' is somewhat arbitrary, it does suggest that Larkin himself knew that antipathy towards him personally had grown stronger in the city as the dispute went on. Arthur Mitchell has argued that 'the failure of Labour in the Dublin elections was crucial in ending the lock-out. The lack of support for the party made it clear that a majority of Dubliners accepted the image of Larkin, Connolly and the other leaders as anti-clerical socialist revolutionaries – the picture painted by the nationalist politicians, the press and the church.'[99] That might somewhat over-state its importance – other factors were coming to a head at this point, including the return to work by canal workers and by members of the NUR on the direction of their London-based leadership[100] and only two days after the poll, there was a meeting at Croydon Park to discuss a return to work, as strike pay grew perilously low.[101] There was a sense among the strike leadership that the time had come to bring it to an end, a position rejected by Larkin who, according to William

O'Brien, denied they were defeated and declared they could fight 'for another twelve months and another twelve months on top of that' but no one was convinced and his remarks were met by silence.[102] As Francis Devine notes: 'two hours later the press were informed. The dispute was effectively over.'[103]

Some months later, at a meeting of Dublin Corporation held on 20 April, the Labour councillors tabled a motion asking that the Irish Trade Union Congress (ITUC) be allowed to use City Hall for its annual meeting in June. Councillor John Saturnus Kelly,[104] a renegade trade unionist, vehement anti-Larkinite and (until its collapse in October 1913) leader of Murphy's yellow union, the Irish Railway Workers' Trade Union, spoke trenchantly against the idea saying he objected to 'the national flag being pulled down from the City Hall in Whit week and having it replaced by the red flag of syndicalism and socialism,' but he was very much in the minority on the council as the motion was carried on a division by a large majority.[105] Coming so shortly after the Lockout had ended, it is significant that Irish Labour would be allowed to use Dublin's municipal buildings for its annual gathering, not forgetting it had been barred from so doing in Clonmel two years earlier. Perhaps councillors felt safe because they believed Larkin had been vanquished. More likely, however, is that while the majority of Nationalist councillors regarded Labour as a very real political threat to their position, they did not regard the labour movement as socially dangerous and their campaign of vilification against Labour at the elections in January was nothing more than burlesque. In any case, it was in City Hall that delegates to the twenty-first annual congress met on the morning of 1 June when, on the motion of William O'Brien (as DTC secretary), Jim Larkin was unanimously elected President of Congress. Larkin's address to congress was informed by two main events of the past year, the Dublin Lockout and the new Home Rule Bill which proposed to exclude Ulster. The lesson he took from both was that for the first time in history, 'the Labour movement in Ireland could have a party of its own and that Labour party would be born and got upon its feet that week.'[106] And, unlike previous occasions, this time it was with one of the first items of business being the adoption of a draft constitution for what would be, from that point, the Irish Trade Union Congress and Labour Party (ITUC&LP).[107] Of course, Larkin had spoken of the pressing need for an Irish Labour Party many times before only to wreck its progress just as it was starting out two years previously, but this time was different. The Lockout had demonstrated most clearly that industrial action on its own was not enough. As Mitchell observed, both Larkin and Connolly recognised that 'Labour's lack of political power weakened the cause of the industrial struggle in 1913-14.'[108] Neither had reached the point, however, where they would place the same weight on political action as industrial. As Connolly told congress: 'Political power must wait upon economic or industrial power; you must be strong on the dock, ship, railway or workshop before you can be strong in the halls of legislation. But if political *power* will only come as the ripened fruit of economic power *agitation* need not wait. Nor yet need wait political organisation. Let them march abreast – the army of organised Labour the director of the campaign on both fields.'[109]

The adoption of a new name and a new constitution can be said to mark the beginning of the Labour Party proper although the party remained something of a 'head without a body' for several years, being virtually indistinguishable from the old congress parliamentary committee. Unlike the situation in 1912, however, where Larkin had hindered the party's development at its earliest stages, this time it was the result of external factors, most important being the outbreak of the First World War in August 1914 which turned the political context on its head and led Connolly away from constitutional politics towards a more militant separatist strategy. Labour stood aside at what would have been its first general election in 1918 and again in 1921, standing for the first time at the election of 1922 but in the meantime it contested the local elections in 1920 and secured at least 329 seats.[110] The decision to draft a new constitution for congress with a view to establishing the new Labour Party had been made at the annual congress in 1913 and was merely ratified in 1914 so it would be wrong to suggest that the Lockout played a fundamental role in the party's development. It was, however, an important and timely reminder of just how necessary a political wing of the movement really was.

At a national level, the strikers had been wholly isolated. They had received almost no support from the IPP and the behaviour of the British Labour Party had shown that their sister party could not be relied on either. If the relationship between the Irish and British Labour Parties had been not good prior to the Lockout, it was positively poisonous afterwards. Fraternal relations were so bad that in 1914, a request by the ITUC&LP that it keep a proportion of the political levy collected by British trade unions organising in Ireland, rather than go in its entirety to the British Labour Party, was rejected outright by Ramsay MacDonald and Arthur Henderson.[111] They had no allies beyond themselves and the only answer was to establish a strong, independent Irish Labour Party.

Politically, as well as industrially, however, the Lockout ended with no winners. The IPP had staved off the threat from Labour in the short term but at what cost? Observing events from exile, V. I. Lenin wrote:

> The Dublin events mark a turning point in the history of the labour movement and of socialism in Ireland. Murphy has threatened to destroy the Irish trade unions. He has succeeded only in destroying the last remnants of the influence of the Irish nationalist bourgeoisie over the Irish proletariat.[112]

Lenin was looking for victories and could be said to be over-stating the case here, but it is difficult to gauge. Too much happened in the years immediately after 1913 to treat it in isolation but it is likely that the IPP's indifference to the labour issue helped turn some voters towards political alternatives after 1916, even if the main beneficiary was not Labour but Sinn Féin. It didn't happen overnight: when J. P. Nannetti died in April 1915, he was denounced by a Labour councillor (Peadar Macken) who called him 'an example of what a labour man ought not to be. He had been tied up with a party which was inimical to Labour' but when the Dublin Labour Party forced a by-election, its candidate was beaten. It was beaten by a respectable margin though with 2,445 votes to 1,816,[113] a result which would have been unlikely only two years earlier. If politics had little impact on the Lockout, the Lockout had an impression on politics.

The Lockout provided the labour movement with a vivid example of the need to be represented politically, and to voters it illustrated how detached its Nationalist representatives had become. Connolly told delegates to the 1914 congress, they could not wait to organise politically: 'Let them march abreast – the army of organised Labour the director of the campaign on both fields.'[114] It was the 'echo of the battle' no more.

Notes

1   Jim Larkin junior witness statement (MAI, BMH, p. 8).

2   Geoffrey Bell, *Troublesome business: the Labour Party and the Irish question* (London, 1982), pp 21-3.

3   James Connolly, 'The United Irish League and the Labour Party' in *Forward* (3 May 1913), in Donal Nevin (ed.), *James Connolly: political writings 1893-1916* (Dublin, 2011), p. 357.

4   Ibid., p. 358.

5   See Steven Fielding, *Class and ethnicity. Irish Catholics in England 1880-1939* (Buckingham, 1993).

6   Patrick C. Power, 'The Irish Labour Party: foundation in Clonmel in 1912' in *Tipperary county: people and places* (Dublin, 1993), pp 151-2.

7   Power, 'The Irish Labour Party: foundation in Clonmel'.

8   Quoted in Emmet Larkin, *James Larkin* (London, 1965), p. 91.

9   William O'Brien (1881-1968) was born in Cork but moved to Dublin in 1896. Soon after, he became active in the Irish Socialist Republican Party, of which he became secretary and financial secretary, and subsequently became active in the Socialist Party of Ireland. A member of the Amalgamated Society of Tailors, he became active in the Dublin Trades Council. He joined the ITGWU in 1917 and was a key figure in its revival at that time but clashed with Larkin on his return from the USA in 1923. Larkin was expelled from the union in 1924 and their mutual enmity proved hugely divisive to the Irish labour movement over the decades which followed. As Emmet O'Connor notes, 'one of the most powerful union leaders from 1917 to his retirement [as ITGWU general secretary] in 1946; his cold, dictatorial, managerial style and bitterness towards Larkin from 1923 made him the most vilified Labour leader of the twentieth century' Emmet O'Connor, *A labour history of Ireland 1824-2000* (Dublin, 2011), p. 86.

10   Arthur Mitchell, *Labour in Irish politics 1890-1930* (New York, 1974), p. 22.

11   See Seamus Cody 'The remarkable Patrick Daly' in *Obair,* no. 2 (January 1985); Desmond McCabe and Owen McGee 'Patrick Thomas Daly' in *Dictionary of Irish biography* (Cambridge, 2009).

12   See J. D. Clarkson, *Labour and Nationalism in Ireland* (New York, 1926), p. 207.

13   Mitchell, *Labour in Irish politics*, p. 22.

14   Quoted in Clarkson, *Labour and nationalism*, p. 252.

15   William Walker (1870-1918) was born in Belfast where his father worked in the Harland and Wolff shipyard and was a trade union official. Walker became an apprentice joiner and later became an officer of the Amalgamated Society of Carpenters and Joiners. He became a prominent activist in the Independent Labour Party in Belfast, was an active member of Belfast Trades Council and, from 1901, was a delegate to the British TUC where he represented Belfast joiners. Elected to Belfast Corporation in 1904, he was the best-known labour leader of his day, before Jim Larkin, but as John W. Boyle noted Walker was 'probably the least well-known of Irish labour leaders', best known for his newspaper controversy with James Connolly over the issue of setting up an Irish Labour Party. For more on Walker see J. W. Boyle 'William Walker' in J. W. Boyle (ed.), *Leaders and workers* (Dublin, 1966) and Henry Patterson, 'William Walker, Labour, sectarianism and the union, 1894-1912' in Fintan Lane and Donal Ó Drisceoil (eds), *Politics and the Irish working class, 1830-1945* (Basingstoke, 2005).

16   O'Connor, *A labour history of Ireland*, p. 66.

17   Mitchell, *Labour in Irish politics*, p. 24.

18   Donal Nevin (ed.), *Writings of James Connolly: collected works* (Dublin, 2011), p. 115.

19   Larkin, *James Larkin*, p. 88.

20   Francis Devine, *Organising history: a centenary of SIPTU* (Dublin, 2009), p. 32; O'Connor, *Larkin*, p. 29.

21   See Thomas J. Morrissey, *William O'Brien 1881-1968* (Dublin, 2007), pp 54-5.

22   Mitchell, *Labour in Irish politics*, p. 33.

23   J. A. Gaughan, *Thomas Johnson* (Dublin, 1980), p. 25.

24   Boyle, 'William Walker', p. 63.

25   Patterson, 'William Walker, Labour, sectarianism and the union', p. 167.

26   Thomas (Tom) Johnson (1875-1963) was born in Liverpool where he joined the Independent Labour Party in 1893. After moving to Belfast in 1903, he joined the National Union of Shop Assistants and Clerks and in 1905 was elected to the executive of the Belfast Trades Council. He represented his union at congress in 1911 when he spoke in favour of setting up an Irish Labour Party. Elected to Dáil Éireann in 1922, he became the first leader of the parliamentary Labour Party until he lost his seat in the general election of September 1927. See Gaughan, *Thomas Johnson*.

27   Larkin, *Larkin*, p. 93; William O'Brien, *Forth the banners go* (Dublin, 1969), p. 48; Donal Nevin, *Connolly: a full life* (Dublin, 2006), pp 427-8. Subsequently, Larkin was prosecuted for allegedly assaulting James O'Farrell (who happened to be sitting beside Bill Richardson at the time) when he tried to throw him out of the meeting. *Irish Times,* 4 Oct. 1912.

28   See Mitchell, *Labour in Irish politics*, pp 36-7; Larkin, *Larkin,* p. 93; Nevin, *Connolly: a full life*, p. 428.

29   Patterson, 'William Walker, Labour, sectarianism and the union' p. 159.

30   Quoted in Diarmaid Ferriter, *A century of challenge* (Dublin, 2001), p. 11.

31   Mary E. Daly, *Dublin: the deposed capital* (Dublin, 1984), p. 215.

32   Seamus Cody, John O'Dowd and Peter Rigney, *The parliament of Labour* (Dublin, 1986), p. 36.

33   Ibid., pp 40-1.

34   See Daly, *Dublin*, p. 15.

35   John W. Boyle, *The Irish Labor movement in the nineteenth century* (Washington D.C., 1988), p. 253.

36   Boyle, *The Irish Labor movement*, p. 255. See James Connolly 'Labour politics in Ireland', *The Harp* (April 1910) in Nevin, *James Connolly: political writings*, pp 299-302.

37   Boyle, *The Irish labor movement*, p. 259.

38   O'Brien, *Forth the banners go*, p. 39.

39   Mitchell, *Labour in Irish politics*, p. 27.

40   O'Connor, *Larkin*, p. 31.

41   *Irish Worker,* 25 Nov. 1911; 2 Dec. 1911.

42   Richard O'Carroll served on the executive of the ITUC, 1911-14. A former member of Sinn Féin, he joined the Irish Volunteers, and fought in the 1916 Rising. On 26 April, he was captured after an engagement near Jacob's factory. Captain J. C. Bowen-Colthurst marched him into a backyard on Camden Street and shot him through the lung. O'Carroll was taken to the Military Hospital at Portobello Barracks but died of his wounds nine days later on 5 May. Bowen-Colthurst was also responsible for shooting the journalist Francis Sheehy-Skeffington who was, among other things, the secretary of the Independent Labour Party of Ireland.

43   Minutes of the LRC and Dublin Labour Party, 1911-15 (NLI, MS 16271, 4 Sept. 1911). O'Carroll had previously urged the necessity of a pledge in April.

44   Minutes of the LRC and Dublin Labour Party, 1911-15 (NLI, MS 16271, 21 Dec. 1911).

45   *Irish Worker,* 13 Jan. 1912.

46   See O'Connor, *Larkin*, p. 35; Larkin, *Larkin*, pp 89-90. Elections to the Corporation were rather labyrinthine with different terms. There were 80 seats on the Corporation, of which a certain proportion were contested each year. The contest in which Larkin stood was delayed by three weeks. The other four successful candidates were Richard O'Carroll, Tommy Lawlor, John Bohan and William Hopkins.

47   Cody et al, *Parliament of Labour*, p. 89.

48   Larkin, *Larkin*, pp 91-2; Cody et al, *Parliament of Labour*, pp 89-90.

49   Cody et al, *Parliament of Labour*, p. 90.

50   Larkin, *Larkin*, p. 92; Mitchell, *Labour in Irish politics*, p. 29.

51   Larkin, *Larkin*, p. 93.

52   To add further to confusion the (congress) Irish Labour Party also held its inaugural meeting in the Antient Concert Rooms in Dublin, a few months later, in September. Then the chair, Thomas McPartlin, took the opportunity to point out that they had 'absolutely nothing to do with the present Independent Labour Party which existed in Dublin' prompting one of those there to lament 'more's the pity' nor had it any connection with the Dublin Labour Party. *Irish Worker,* 21 Sept. 1912.

53   Nevin, *Connolly: a full life*, p. 429.

54   *Irish Worker,* 11 Jan. 1913.

55   *Irish Times,* 2 Oct. 1912.

56   *Irish Worker,* 5 Oct. 1912; 12 Oct. 1912; 9 Nov. 1912.

57   *Irish Worker,* 11 Jan. 1913.

58   *Irish Times,* 16 Jan. 1913.

59   Cody et al, *Parliament of Labour*, p. 90.

60   *Irish Times,* 10 Dec. 1912.

61   O'Connor, *Larkin*, p. 45.

62   O'Brien, *Forth the banners go*, p. 94; Yeates, *Lockout*, p. 118.

63   Ibid.

64   Harry Gosling, John Ward M.P. (Lib-Lab), Arthur Henderson (Lab), James Seddon (Chairman of TUC parliamentary committee and leader National Union of Shop Assistants), William Brace M.P. (Lib), George Barnes M.P. (Co-Operative Party), George Roberts M.P. (Typographical Association), Jack Jones (Gasworkers' and General Labourers' Union).

65   O'Brien, *Forth the banners go*, p. 95.

66   Yeates, *Lockout*, p. 121.

67   O'Connor, *Larkin*, p. 45.

68   Ibid.

69   Bell, *Troublesome business*, p. 26.

70   Ibid.

71   See O'Brien, *Forth the banners go*, p. 98; O'Connor, *Larkin*, pp 47-8.

72   Yeates, *Lockout*, p. 90.

73   Ibid., pp 87-91.

74   Ibid., p. 102.

75   James McConnel, 'The Irish parliamentary party, industrial relations and the 1913 Dublin Lockout', *Saothar* 28 (2003), p. 26. He died on 26 April 1915. See Marie Coleman, 'Joseph Patrick Nannetti' in *Dictionary of Irish biography* .

76   McConnel, 'The Irish parliamentary party', p. 29.

77   Ibid., p. 31.

78   Ibid., pp 32-3.

79   Yeates, *Lockout*, p. 240.

80   F. S. L. Lyons quoted in Mitchell, *Labour in Irish politics*, p. 48.

81   McConnel, 'Irish parliamentary party', p. 33.

82   Mitchell, *Labour in Irish politics*, p. 51.

83   Yeates, *Lockout*, p. 500.

84   There were 20 council seats and ten alderman seats vacant on this occasion. *Irish Independent*, 6 Jan. 1914; Mitchell, *Labour in Irish politics*, p. 51.

85   The candidates were: Thomas MacPartlin (alderman seat, North Dock), P. T. Daly (councillor seat, North Dock), Andrew Breslan (Merchant's Quay), Thomas Foran (South Dock), Joseph Farrell (Inns Quay), Edward Hart (North City), Henry Donnelly (New Kilmainham), Thomas Irwin (Wood Quay), Arthur Murphy (alderman seat, Mountjoy) and James Campbell (councillor seat, Mountjoy). *Irish Worker,* 14 Jan. 1914.

86   *Irish Times,* 7 Jan. 1914.

87   *Irish Independent,* 13 Jan. 1914 quoting a report in the *Morning Post.*

88   Yeates, *Lockout*, pp 504, 510.

89   *Irish Independent,* 7 and 13 Jan. 1914 quoted in Mitchell *Labour in Irish politics*, pp 51-2.

90   Yeates, *Lockout*, pp 500-2.

91   Mitchell, *Labour in Irish politics*, p. 52.

92   Ibid.

93   *Irish Worker,* 14 Jan. 1914.

94   Yeates, *Lockout*, p. 511.

95   *Irish Independent,* 17 Jan. 1914.

96   Ibid.

97   Mitchell, *Labour in Irish politics*, p. 53.

98   *Irish Worker,* 17 Jan. 1914.

99   Mitchell, *Labour in Irish politics*, p. 54.

100   Morrissey, *O'Brien*, p. 84.

101   O'Connor, *Larkin*, pp 48-9; Morrissey, *O'Brien*, p. 84.

102   O'Brien, *Forth the banners go*, p. 101.

103   Devine, *Organising history*, p. 61.

104   Kelly was one of a group of labour mavericks at this time, among them William Richardson, E. W. Stewart and P. J. McIntyre of the anti-Larkin paper *The Toiler*. See Yeates, *Lockout*, pp 10-12.

105   *Irish Times,* 21 Apr. 1914.

106   *Irish Times,* 2 June 1914; *Irish Worker,* 20 June 1914.

107   An amendment to call the organisation simply 'the Irish Labour Party' was defeated.

108   Mitchell, *Labour in Irish politics*, p. 54.

109   See Nevin, *James Connolly: political writings*, p. 457.

110   Conor McCabe, 'The Irish Labour Party and the 1920 election', *Saothar* 35 (2010), p. 7.

111   Bell, *Troublesome business*, pp 25-6.

112   *Severana Pravda* (29 Aug. 1913), quoted in Mitchell, *Labour in Irish politics*, p. 50.

113   Cody et al, *Parliament of Labour*, pp 111-13.

114   Nevin, *James Connolly: political writings*, p. 456.

11.
Poverty paraded in the streets, 1913: the mothers and children

....

Ann Matthews

The Lockout is deemed a significant chapter in the story of Irish labour in the last century. However, it is largely considered by Irish academic historians as an episode of political awakening of the working-classes in Dublin a mere three years before the Easter Rebellion of 1916. The Lockout has had very little analysis and Emmet O'Connor, in his work *A labour history of Ireland 1824-2000*, made a very forceful point when he said that, 'the first book on Labour by an Irish based academic appeared in 1920. The second appeared in 1977. That says a lot about Irish academics.'[1] The same could be said for Irish social history. Until such time that a meaningful body of work exists on the lives of urban and rural workers in the 20th century those who were affected by the Lockout will remain invisible.

Pádraig Yeates, in his comprehensive work *Lockout*, has written an excellent exploration of all aspects of the turmoil. He examined the provision of food for women and children within the political and religious proselytism that existed in Dublin at that time. The politics of religious proselytism existed since the early 19th century and Jacinta Prunty explores this in detail in her work *Dublin slums 1800-1925*, and her analysis of the conditions of life in the slums of Dublin is unsurpassed.

The purpose of this chapter is to start a dialogue on the story of the aid given to the workers and their families during the Lockout, within the ethos of humanitarianism and show that provision came from across the religious and political divide. This will involve looking at the charities that existed in the city who were providing food to the poor before August 1913. It will also examine the provision of food aid during the conflict, by the British Trades Union Congress (TUC), the two food kitchens at Liberty Hall, under Larkin and Connolly, the Ladies' Relief Committee formed by Catherine Sherlock, the Lady Mayoress of Dublin, and the Dublin Children's Distress Fund founded by the Archbishop of Dublin, Dr William Walsh. The latter operated as an umbrella organisation for the innumerable associations and charities already providing aid to the poor.

The Lockout began with the strike on the 27 August 1913 and almost immediately many families were feeling the economic strain as wages disappeared overnight. When the primary schools re-opened after the summer holidays, the teachers discovered that many children were already hungry. Unlike the situation in Britain there were no school dinners supplied in Dublin under the School Meals Act, 1906, because the act was not extended to Ireland. This act empowered local authorities to strike a rate of a halfpenny in the pound for this purpose, and it was extended to Scotland and Wales, but not to Ireland. Consequently, in Britain, during labour disputes the children of strikers had access to a dinner each day through the municipal authority, and this was supplemented by fundraising of the labour movement, and existing charities. The Irish Party refused to campaign to have it extended to Ireland and, in particular Dublin Corporation declined to do so, in order not to alienate the rate payers of the city by increasing taxes.

Penny Dinners

In Ireland and particularly in the cities of Dublin, Cork, Galway and Limerick, the poorest of families were dependent on the charity of various bodies. During the middle to late 19th century, many charitable bodies were established to provide aid to the poor in

1. Penny Dinner Hall, St Laurence O'Toole's, Seville Place, Dublin.
Courtesy of the Sisters of Charity, Seville Place

the form of a daily breakfast or dinner and, they supplied clothing. Dinner was the most common form of food aid for which the recipient paid one penny and it became known universally as the 'penny dinners'.[2] There were many charities in Dublin supplying these dinners like the Saint Anthony's Penny Dinners in Seville Place that was run by the Sisters of Charity and the non-denominational Penny Dinners at Denzille Lane in operation since 1887, that 'in 1912 provided 27,613 meals'.[3] At Lower Abbey Street, the Evangelical Christian Union Buildings provided food, and, in Meath Street there was the Communal Food Kitchen. Several schools, in particular those run by religious orders, provided school dinners, for example the 'Sisters of the Holy Faith at the Coombe, the Sisters of Charity at North William Street, St Saviours' Denmark Street, Our Lady Mount Harold's Cross.'[4]

In November 1910, the Ladies' School Dinner Committee was formed to campaign for the extension of the School Meals 1906 Act to Dublin. This committee was formed by a number of women who had founded Inghinidhe na hÉireann in 1900. They were Maud Gonne, Helen Laird (secretary), Mrs Molloy, Mrs McCall, Miss O'Connor, Mrs Quinn and Mrs Tuohy (treasurer).[5] By November 1911, this committee was providing 450 dinners to children in the parish schools of St Audoen's and nearby John's Lane. These schools were Catholic parish schools but were not run by a religious community and did not have the facilities to provide school dinners. The food was cooked at the Communal Food Kitchen in Meath Street and Maud Gonne, in her witness statement to the Bureau of Military History (BMH) said, that they 'hired donkeys and carts to bring the hot Irish stew to the various schools from the central kitchen' for which the children paid one penny.[6]

One of the most interesting aspects of the stories/myths of the Lockout is the tendency to concentrate on the experience of the population within the small geographic areas of the south and north city. This has created the impression that the labour conflict was confined solely to these areas of Dublin city, but from 22 September 1913, 'more than 20,000 workers were locked out in city and county.'[7] It is estimated the dependents of these workers numbered approximately '80,000' and, they came from the Dublin rural labouring classes, mill workers, as well as the city workers.[8] The tendency to concentrate the story within the boundaries of a narrow geographic area has led to the misconception that the working-class was a homogenous group, confined to the slum areas of the city.

However, like the middle class it too comprised a very stratified structure. The working-class women who were reduced to extreme poverty by the Lockout were not a one-dimensional group of shawl wearing derelicts. They came from across a developed working-class structure that had its own multiple forms of well-defined and distinctive norms of implicit rules and petty snobbery. In 1911 when the fledging Irish Women

Workers' Union (IWWU) was trying to convince working-class women to embrace each other in solidarity, an appeal was published in *The Irish Worker* that explains the difficulties of bringing working-class women together:

> The existence of class distinction among the women workers of Dublin is deplorable. Each different section of workers keep entirely to themselves ... You find the girl who earns her living as a typist stands icily aloof from the girl who works in the shop and the trades' girl: they in their turn look down haughtily on the factory hand and again you do not find the factory girl associating with the girls who hawk their goods in the streets.[9]

Nora Connolly, James Connolly's daughter, was a factory worker in Belfast and she addressed this issue when she explained the difference between a woman who worked in a wareroom/workroom (dressmaking emporium) and a factory, she said:

> Factory workers were weavers, rope workers, and tobacco workers. A wareroom was ever so much higher in the social scale than a factory, and the wages were much higher. Isn't it ridiculous ... the caste system of such a thing?[10]

Food ships

On 23 September 1913, the TUC convened in Manchester and, in discussing the situation in Dublin, decided to send aid to Dublin. They pledged £5,000 immediately and made an appeal to the British unions for funds 'in order to supply provisions to the men, their wives and families for as long as necessary.'[11] Within five days the *SS Hare* arrived in Dublin carrying an estimated 60,000 food parcels for the members of the ITGWU and the other eight unions whose members were on strike. Almost immediately across Britain subscriptions rolled in, and it was known as the TUC Dublin Food Fund.[12] The money was paid through the TUC parliamentary committee and the *Daily Citizen*. The latter was a newspaper launched in October 1912, as the official paper of the British Labour Party and it was supported by the TUC.

The *Hare* was greeted in Dublin with much fanfare, speeches and liberal amounts of bunting. There was criticism that the money was not being spent in Dublin but, James Larkin said that if the £5,000 had been 'sent in hard cash and distributed in five shilling pieces or even half sovereigns it would not have been so powerful a factor as the food ship.'[13] Harry Gosling president of the National Transport Workers' Federation explained that the funds were used to send food in order to avoid the risk of 'any money being spent on drink or paid away for rent.'[14] The *Hare* docked on the South Quay and

The Freeman's Journal reported that the City of Dublin Steam Packet Company 'placed sidings at the disposal of the (Dublin) Relief Committee' and Cadburys 'offered to send a large consignment of cocoa as part of the relief supplies.'[15]

THE DUBLIN LABOUR WAR.

COURT OF INQUIRY TO-DAY.

FOOD SHIP ARRIVES.

BRITISH DELEGATES' SPEECHES

FUNDS FROM ABROAD.

GRAND CANAL STRIKE.

THE BOARD OF TRADE COURT OF INQUIRY INTO THE LABOUR TROUBLES IN DUBLIN WILL BE OPENED AT DUBLIN CASTLE AT ELEVEN O'CLOCK THIS MORNING. THE COURT CONSISTS OF SIR GEORGE ASKWITH, CHAIRMAN; SIR THOMAS R. RATCLIFFE ELLIS AND MR. J. R. CLYNES, M.P.

AT THE INVITATION OF SIR GEORGE ASKWITH, MR. HARRY GOSLING AND MR. ROBERT WILLIAMS, CHAIRMAN AND SECRETARY OF THE TRANSPORT FEDERATION, HAVE COME TO DUBLIN TO USE THEIR INFLUENCE IN SETTLING THE DISPUTE. THEY WILL GIVE EVIDENCE AT THE INQUIRY TO-DAY.

THE STEAMSHIP HARE, CHARTERED BY THE BRITISH TRADES CONGRESS TO BRING PROVISIONS TO THE WORKERS IN DUBLIN, ARRIVED IN THE PORT ON SATURDAY AFTERNOON AND THE CARGO WAS UNLOADED AND DISTRIBUTED DURING THE EVENING.

IT IS ANNOUNCED THAT SUPPLIES WILL CONTINUE TO BE SENT WHILE THE DISPUTE LASTS.

THE REFUSAL OF SOME OF THE MEN EMPLOYED BY THE GRAND CANAL COMPANY TO HANDLE "TAINTED" GOODS LED TO THE HOLDING UP OF A NUMBER OF BOATS ON SATURDAY.

THE BRITISH DELEGATES—MESSRS. SEDDON, GOSLING AND WILLIAMS—YESTERDAY ADDRESSED A BIG MEETING IN BERESFORD PLACE, WHEN IT WAS ANNOUNCED THAT SUPPORT WAS COMING FROM ABROAD TO HELP THE MEN IN DUBLIN.

THE EMPLOYERS HAVE ISSUED A REPLY TO THE TRADES CONGRESS DELEGATES' REPORT. AND THEY REPUDIATE ANY INTENTION TO ATTACK PROPERLY CONDUCTED TRADES UNIONISM

a bad settlement we shall reach in consequence a bad settlement in our own country. Therefore we want just arrangements here, so that we can point to the Dublin settlement as the kind of thing we want in our dispute."

Help from Abroad.

Mr. Gosling went on to explain that he had practically a million men behind him in the movement he represented, while Mr. Seddon represented as President of the Trades Union Congress two-and-a-half millions of workers. These men believed that the Dublin fight was their fight. There was only a little drop of water between them which joined and did not separate them as regarded the Labour movement. Alluding to the Congress of Transport Workers in London, he said that the delegates from all over the world were inquiring what was going on in Dublin. He believed help was coming to the Dublin workers from France and Germany, as well as Scandinavia. He asked for a united force behind them. In a great army two or three things were necessary. Those who were fighting could do nothing else but fight, but there was a big army of reserves behind, and they could keep bringing up the "grub" so long as the fighting lasted. So far as the Labour movement was concerned they had no talk about Ireland for the Irish or England for the English, but the world for all of them (cheers).

MR. SEDDON'S SPEECH.

Mr. Seddon said they had entered into a historic struggle. It was no ordinary trade union dispute. In the despatch of the Hare they had demonstrated the power of organised labour and of the co-operative movement. Discussing the question of importing the foodstuffs from England, he said that they recognised that in Dublin prices were at famine height, and, moreover, they knew that when they invested £5,000 in one firm they would get the food at wholesale prices. If the shopkeepers of Dublin wanted the money spent in Dublin let them show in a practical way that they were supporting the workers.

Foreign Appeal if Necessary.

Continuing, Mr. Seddon referred to the project of raising an employers' defence fund of fifty million pounds. "That is not syndicalism," he added ironically. "That is different medicine for a different dog." If the employers thought that they were only dealing with the British trade union movement they were making a huge blunder. If there was no settlement arrived at, if the reserves became attenuated they would not hesitate to send an appeal across the sea, and he was convinced that that appeal would be nobly re-

2. Food ship arrives, *Freeman's Journal*, 8 Sept. 1913.
DCLA

The paper also reported that the *Hare* carried 60,000 food parcels with 22,000 for the union members. In August 1913 the membership of the ITGWU was 24,000, with 'half of them in Dublin, so membership in the capital was c.12,000'.[16] This level of aid from the TUC was a very generous gesture of support for the unions in Dublin.

The parcels were brought to the old Manchester Company sheds on Sir John Rogerson's Quay where Patrick Kenny was in charge. Kenny was a locked-out worker who was appointed by the Dublin Food Fund Committee 'to take sole charge of the food depot.'[17] No food parcels were distributed from Liberty Hall and the Manchester Company sheds on the quays remained the location of the food depot.

Each food parcel contained 20 pounds weight of food for five people, and included a bag of potatoes, a parcel of butter, sugar, tea, jam and fish. From early Saturday morning on 28 September men, women and children began to queue on the quayside. As the numbers grew 'William Partridge (who was a full time paid organiser for the ITGWU), 'arrived leading a couple of hundred Transport Workers, wearing badges and carrying sticks and they marched down the quay and set about their function of maintaining order.'[18]

The Irish Times, *The Freeman's Journal* and the *Irish Independent* gave the event good coverage. *The Irish Times* gave the most extensive account and there is a strong sense that the reporter (who is unnamed) had never seen a significant group of working-class people gathered in one place, especially women, and the tone of the article is perceptive, compassionate, and consequently very moving.

The writer described the clothes worn by the women and in doing so gave readers of the newspaper a sense of the wide spectrum of the class awareness among the families of the Dublin workers. A carter was superior in terms of wages and status to a labourer and their home address, and the apparel of their wives and children reflected this. The reporter described the degrees of poverty as manifested by the women's clothing:

> Here were seen the wan dweller of some noisome tenement wrapped in a shawl and huddling a baby to her breast; the carters wife who had a bonnet as well as a shawl; a decently attired housewife with gloves and ribbons evidently ill at ease on such an errand.[19]

For women in general, regardless of their class, clothes were an external manifestation of their sense of place in the class structure and working-class women were no different. The importance of wearing a hat or bonnet was an indicator of status, and 'was a badge of respectability'.[20] At the lower end of the working-class structure, this was very important because wearing a shawl indicated that the wearer's family was the poorest of the poor.

Now here on the South Quays they all stood together in the solidarity of desolation and extreme want. For many women, in particular those who aspired to respectability, queuing for food in such a public manner would have been torturous, and engendered a deep sense of degradation that their poverty was the focus of such public attention. James Larkin and many of the men of the union would not have understood this aspect of women's lives. They had no understanding of the female sensitivity to the infinitesimal issues of rank (which still exist) and that having to queue for hours in such a public way for food could be degrading. It is always assumed that the poor have no feeling in these situations, but the need to feed their children made the women overcome any embarrassment they might have felt at having to queue in such a public way for basic food.

In addition to the food parcels, there were 12,500 loaves stored in the sheds, paid for by the TUC fund and supplied by the co-operative societies in Dublin and Belfast.[21] 'Distribution of the parcels began at 4 p.m., with a large number of girls who were locked out helping supported by a large representation of the Irish Drapers' Assistants' Association, and within two hours, they 'handed out an estimated 8,000 parcels'. [22] *The Irish Times* reporter observed:

> Outside the spectator saw the long queue go in orderly and patient - at one door, and also the stream of the supplied emerging from a side street … The poorest woman dislikes to carry a loaf uncovered, to do so is to proclaim her poverty to the world. But here were respectably-attired women who were thus humiliated before the curious crowd of onlookers; for many had not thought of bringing baskets to carry the provisions. Fortunately, there was room at the top of the potato bag for some more.[23]

The *Irish Independent* newspaper, which was owned by William Martin Murphy the leader of the employers, was biased against the workers, but its report is nonetheless relevant and it stated:

> Many respectable Irish workers and their families had the humiliating experience on Saturday of having to trudge along the quays to obtain a package of food from a British relief Ship … It was a pitiable spectacle … Mothers with babies in their arms endeavoured to push their way through the serried masses of dock labourers … Many of the women were respectably attired, and were weeping bitterly.[24]

The *Irish Times* reporter observed those leaving the building with their parcels:

> When at a distance from the centre of distribution a number of the humblest recipients stopped to examine the contents of the grocery boxes. One tattered woman appeared to be dividing her tea with a friend who was not so lucky herself. Indeed, those of the

poor who were about but, were unentitled to have a portion of the food must have been envious. Not far from the door of the shed sat a pallid woman and her daughter, utterly forlorn looking wonderingly upon the bustle around.[25]

Many working-class men supported mothers, and female siblings, and the Sick and Indigent Roomkeepers' Society expressed concern for these women, saying that:

> Many workers supported poorer relatives like a widowed sister or sister in law who usually received a few shillings a week from their friends the workers "for" the poor are very good to the poor and when men are not working this help is not available.[26]

By eight o'clock on Saturday night, the food parcels had all been landed and it is estimated that about 9,000 people had received food relief, and parcels were sent to union members in county Dublin at Kingstown, Clondalkin, and Swords. This was the first of eleven food ships that arrived in Dublin during the Lockout. Between 28 September 1913 and February 1914, a total of £93,518 13s 3½d. was raised by the TUC and the *Daily Citizen* appeals. Of this £62,898 6s 6d, was used to fund the food ships, while the Dublin Trades Council was allocated £28,975 16s to dispense as strike pay with the ITGWU receiving £23,456, while the remainder was divided between the 'eight other unions involved in the conflict'.[27]

Liberty Hall food kitchen

With rare exceptions, most working-class women cooked for their families on an open fire, and now they had difficulty cooking any form of hot food, because the coal distribution in the city was affected by the Lockout. With men receiving between four and five shillings a week strike pay and women receiving two shillings and sixpence, coal now became an unattainable and unaffordable commodity. Cooked food was being distributed from Liberty Hall from about 28 September and the *Evening Telegraph* recorded that:

> A cooking apparatus has been installed in Liberty Hall and during the day, a large number of people were supplied with bread, stew and soup. Children were also provided with teas. The recipients were admitted by ticket, and everything was orderly.[28]

Seán O'Casey identified this apparatus as a Dagdan Cauldron.[29] The TUC had given a grant of £300 to Countess de Markievicz for this work.[30] Using James Connolly's calculation that 'ten shillings would feed one child for three weeks,' so this sum could feed 600 children for three weeks.[31]

3. The Food Committee outside Liberty Hall (Keogh Collection). Delia Larkin is seated front row centre.
Courtesy of the National Library of Ireland

At Liberty Hall de Markievicz was helped by the members of the IWWU who prepared the food for cooking. Within a week of the opening of the kitchen, a report on the operation of the scheme appeared in *The Irish Citizen*. This paper was launched in 1912 by the Irish Women's Franchise League (IWFL) as Ireland's suffrage paper. The IWFL was founded in 1908 by Hanna Sheehy-Skeffington and Margaret Cousins, and their respective husbands Francis Sheehy-Skeffington and James Cousins were the editors of the paper. The report is written in the third person by someone who used the initial E and it is simultaneously factual and detached. The headline on the piece reads, '*Sunt Lacrimae Rerum*' (There are tears shed for things).[32] It begins:

> Outside Liberty Hall. Crowds of waiting women press close to the railing waiting, watching with the intense concentrated gaze of the hungry. Numbers of children, all ages, all sizes whose grimy little hands clutch vessels of every known shape - waiting. One passes by through the patient group with a lump in one's throat.[33]

The reporter then went on to describe the scene inside Liberty Hall and said that as she entered the building she was met with an atmosphere laden with 'an appetising smell of good food'.[34] The article described the kitchen:

> Under the capable supervision of Madame de Markievicz ... A score of girls are at work peeling potatoes and cutting up meat. They are all intelligent, they are all keen, they are all tidy, and they are all 'locked out'. Some half a dozen men are also busy - stoking the fire under the boiler – fetching water and bringing from the storeroom great stacks of bread. [35]

This account tallies with Nora Connolly's account when she observed:

> Here the Countess reigned supreme ... all meals were prepared under her direction. There were big tubs on the floor and around these were about a half dozen girls peeling potatoes and other vegetables. There were more girls cutting up meat. The Countess kept up a steady march around the boilers as she supervised the cooking ... some of the striking girls were there to act as waitresses.[36]

The Irish Citizen described how the food was distributed:

> Now comes the great moment. The doors are thrown open and in stream the waiting women and children; each one presents a ticket, and is given in exchange a loaf of bread and about a quart of stew, (two pints).[37]

Each person as they entered the building handed up their ticket and container. The container was then taken away and filled with stew and each recipient was given a loaf of bread. Seán O'Casey in his autobiography recalled that people brought 'jugs, saucepans and kettles to collect their ration of stew.'[38] *The Irish Citizen* report ended with the writer recording,

> The Big Cauldron is empty at last, and about 200 people have been fed. Two more meals will be given before nightfall, and perhaps the last child in that patient queue will have been fed -perhaps; but the queue is long.[39]

The food kitchen had many significant visitors including members of the IWFL who helped to collect the tickets and dole out the food. Seán O'Casey described how the painter William Orpen regularly visited the kitchen to 'sketch the tired and hungry faces surrounding the pale hardy, handsome face of their leader Jim.'[40] He also said he never saw the countess do anything 'one would call a spot of work' and he backed this with the observation that 'Orpen's sketch of the exkitchen (sic) doesn't show sign or light of the Countess.'[41] Peadar Kearney recalled that 'the Countess was a prominent figure at the kitchen, dressed in trousers and smoking cigarettes, both of which were regarded as astonishing things for women to do in those days.'[42] The constant stream of visitors to the food hall who came to see the poor receiving their food was not controlled and coupled with a lack of efficient organisation problems ensued. Dora Montefiore recorded that on 18 October 'a special correspondent to the *Daily Herald* from Dublin wrote, "I have just left Liberty Hall, where I have seen women and children fighting — actually tearing at one another — to get a jug of soup and a loaf of bread."'[43] Aside from the food kitchen, a committee was formed to raise funds to provide clothes and boots for the women and children of locked out workers.[44] The secretary of this committee was Patrick Lennon who was a member of the ITGWU and he used his home at Irvine Crescent in East Wall as his office.[45]

The second food ship *Fraternity* arrived in Dublin on 4 October and carried 20,000 packages of groceries, and 20,000 packages of potatoes. It also carried half a ton of peas, half a ton of salted ribs and 10,000 packages of haricot beans. The third ship also carried a similar load. A significant portion of the peas, salted ribs, and haricot beans, were 'specially destined for Liberty Hall to be cooked.'[46] Those in receipt of this food had to produce a food ticket, and no one was allowed inside the building without one. These tickets were allocated to the members of the ITGWU and the eight other unions involved in the conflict. They were also allocated food vouchers for the food ships.

Ladies' Relief Committee

There were many workers who were not members of a union when they were locked out, and they had to seek help elsewhere. It is within this situation that the Ladies' Relief Committee was founded by Catherine Sherlock, the Lady Mayoress of Dublin. It was formed on 25 September 1913, its purpose was outlined in the motion proposed by Mrs Noel Guinness and seconded by Mrs Rowlette, and it stated in part:

> That having regard to the great distress at present in Dublin, and the urgent need to provide for the necessities of life for a very large number of women and children, who had been rendered temporarily destitute owing to the labour crisis … The Lady Mayoress resolved to make an urgent appeal to the better instincts of humanity in the city with the object of providing immediately for the urgent needs of the families of workers at present deprived of their earnings.[47]

Louie Bennett who joined the committee was a regular contributor to *The Irish Citizen*. Bennett was a suffragist, and a pacifist and she founded the Irish Women's

Reform League in 1911 as 'a non-militant suffrage organisation whose remit was to focus attention on the social and economic position of women workers.'[48] In a letter on behalf of the Ladies' Relief Fund Bennett appealed to its readers of *The Irish Citizen* for help. She wrote:

> We all know that this distress is very great, and is daily increasing ... we cannot stand aside ... When children are hungry we cannot refuse to give them food because of their father's actions. Every Suffragist will surely respond to the appeal made by the Lady Mayoress for funds to provide food ... We want a response to this appeal to come from the rich and poor alike, to come in small sums as well as in great. A widespread expression of fellow feeling amongst women such as this would do much to soften the bitterness of spirit aroused in our working-classes.[49]

The editorial response was immediate and robust, and it said in part:

> It is natural and fitting that the lead in this direction should be taken by the public spirited women who are also foremost in the fight for Woman Suffrage ... But we must again express the hope that this task will not be left to active suffragists alone. There is too great a tendency to suggest work in various directions for suffragists ... as if it was in some special manner their business. If it is their business to lead, it is the business of other women to follow.[50]

It continued:

> We trust the suffragists who are taking the initiative in this movement will above all exert themselves to secure the co-operation of women not ordinarily interested in suffragist or public work.[51]

Bennett replied, saying that without the aid given by the fund 'many children would have to remain hungry', and 'this is an unpleasant reflection for those who need never know hunger!'[52] She also informed the readers that the Ladies' Relief Committee comprised seven women of whom five were members of the Irish Women's Reform League.[53]

The remit of the Ladies' Relief Committee was to collect money and then distribute it in the form of weekly grants to those schools and charities already providing cooked food, so they could cope with the increasing numbers. In early October, the archbishop of Dublin, Dr Walsh, gave the committee £100. The Dublin Bread Company gave the committee 100 pints of soup each day and this was distributed to the city schools in Strand Street, The Coombe, North William Street and Seville Place while the timber merchants, T. & C. Martin, 'gave a cheque for £10 to provide breakfast for the children of the strikers in the North Docks area'.[54] The committee also gave aid to other charitable associations.

Table 1. The 19 schools already providing food aid, who received weekly grants from the Ladies' Relief Committee.

Schools receiving aid	Amount granted weekly
Fr Early Westland Row for South Gloucester Street Schools	£5
Fr Hatton Westland Row to supply Saturday meals only	£5
Fr Flavin's Schools Rutland Street	£10
Francis Street Schools	£3
John's Lane	£5
Meath Street Schools	£5
Michael & John's School, Exchange Street	£4
Upper Sandwith Street	£5
Sisters of Charity, Harold's Cross	£5
Sisters of Charity, Milltown	£5
Sisters of Charity, North William Street	£10
Sisters of Charity, Seville Place	£10
Sisters of the Holy Faith, Clarendon Street	£5
Sisters of the Holy Faith, Coombe	£10
Sisters of the Holy Faith, Glasnevin	£5
St Audoen's High Street	£5
St Peters Whitefriar Street	£5
St Saviour's Schools Denmark Street	£5

Source: Catherine Sherlock letter to Archbishop Walsh, October 1913 (DDA)

Table 2. Associations that received aid from the Ladies' Relief Committee

Associations and Charities	
Archdeacon Fricker £12.10s to be distributed between Crèche and the Ladies' Association of Charity to deal with special cases	£12.10.0
Dublin Society for the Prevention of Infant Mortality to enable the society supply milk to infants	£10
Jubilee Nurses	occasional grant
Sisters of Assumption Camden Street to deal with the poor in their neighbourhood	occasional grant
St Vincent de Paul Society for providing breakfasts on Sunday morning	Not stated

Source: Catherine Sherlock letter to Archbishop Walsh October 1913. (DDA)

The St Vincent de Paul Society had been providing breakfast since late 1911 in the back parlour of 8 Gardiner Street that was loaned to them by the local Penny Dinner committee.

Dora Montefiore's scheme

In mid-October, a new development took place when the ITGWU became involved in a plan to help members of the union to send their children to homes in England. This idea was suggested to James Larkin by Dora Montefiore who was an English socialist and suffragist. She suggested that the children of the locked out workers could be brought to Britain and placed with families until the conflict was over. He assented and Dora Montefiore and a committee mostly of women from the *Daily Herald* League began fundraising for the venture.[55] The background to the league lies in the dockers' dispute in London in 1912. Ben Tillett the dockers' leader, along with other radical trade unionists raised funds to create a daily paper and they adopted the name of the defunct newssheet *Daily Herald*. In May 1913 it was taken over by a new committee whose ethos was syndicalist. This committee formed the *Daily Herald* Company and the paper's readers and supporters created the *Daily Herald* League with branches operating at local level all over the country. The *Daily Herald* League operated as a vehicle whereby its members could become involved in various causes. During the dockers' strike in London in 1912, a committee of women under the auspices of the league successfully organised the boarding out of hundreds of children throughout England and now Dora Montefiore sought to do the same again in Dublin.[56]

Montefiore arrived in Dublin on 15 October 1913 with Mrs Lucille Rand, an American, and Grace Neal, secretary of the Domestic Workers' Union of Great Britain. However, Montefiore had never been in Ireland and had no knowledge of the intensity of the arguments around the issue of proselytism as it was manifested in Dublin city. Proselytism existed in Britain but it was dispersed through a significantly larger population over a wider geographic area, so it appeared less passionate, whereas in Ireland and in particular Dublin with a smaller population concentrated in a smaller geographic area it was acutely intense. Montefiore appeared to believe that Dublin was the same as any British city, and consequently, she innocently walked into a virulent hotbed of religious and political proselytism. When she arrived in Dublin in mid-October to organise the removal of children to England the protests rose to a frenzy and amidst accusation of kidnapping and socialist proselytism, she left Ireland within weeks.

Meanwhile, on 27 October 1913, the Dublin Children's Distress Fund had been launched by Dr Walsh, the archbishop of Dublin. The inaugural meeting was held at the offices of St Vincent de Paul in Upper Sackville (O'Connell) Street. In his address, he said that 'in the wake of the publicity given to the protests against the deportation of children' he had received many letters enquiring:

> Why he did not get the priests and the nuns of Dublin to provide the school children' with some sort of meal each day. He continued ... one would think that the clergy and the nuns were the relieving officers of the city! Many thought that was what they really were.[57]

He then went on to defend his administration and said that 'in the year before the Lockout the three parish schools (unnamed) served by his administrators, had provided 1,280 breakfasts and 690 dinners each day and that this number had increased to 2,450 since the Lockout began and that the number of people needing help had nearly doubled.[58]

Walsh's public statement offended Catherine Sherlock and, in a letter of protest, she told him he had created the impression that 'up to this nothing has been done to relieve distress amongst the children of the city.'[59] She was concerned that people who subscribed to her committee might 'come to the conclusion that the money received had not been applied in the proper direction.'[60] She also enclosed a detailed account of the charities that the Ladies' Relief Committee was helping (see Table 1).

On 28 October, when James Larkin was imprisoned in England, James Connolly acted in his place. Connolly took charge and he made some changes at Liberty Hall. He altered the system whereby the food vouchers were allocated. Heretofore the men and women collected them at Liberty Hall but the new scheme required them to collect the tickets from their 'respective committeemen, delegate, or shop stewards to whom they were required to report every morning.'[61] The dinner scheme was also cancelled. This significantly reduced the daily congestion at Liberty Hall. Seizing its chance to criticise Connolly the *Irish Independent* stoked tensions by quoting the *Daily Herald* and reported:

> Connolly stopped the dinners at Liberty Hall under the supervision of Countess Markievicz, for about 600 families. 'Go to the Archbishops and the priests' said Connolly. 'They are loud in their professions; put them to the test'. [62]

However, Dora Montefiore gave another perspective on this issue in her biography and she recorded that:

> That authorities at Liberty Hall relying on the publicity given to the statements by the Archbishop that the Dublin clergy were ready to deal with all cases of

distress in the city, decided to discontinue the free dinners, which have been the feature at Liberty Hall for some weeks; and, in order to prevent the possibility of overlapping, the women and the children who had thus been hitherto fed, were told to present themselves at the Archbishop's Palace or the presbyteries of the various chapels in the city.[63]

Women and Children's Fund

After the collapse of the 'deportation' scheme Dora Montefiore, Grace Neal and Mrs Rand sought advice from the *Daily Herald* League in London on how to use the funds they had raised for the scheme and Montefiore said a decision was taken that, 'the money should be spent in Dublin for the benefit of the children.'[64] It was decided to use the money to open a new breakfast kitchen at Liberty Hall for children. The existing committee under the stewardship of Patrick Lennon called officially 'Women and Children's (of Locked-out Workers) Relief Fund' now became the official committee that provided food as well as clothes for the children at Liberty Hall.[65] Seán O'Casey, at this time using the Irish form Seaghán Ó Cathasaigh, was appointed assistant secretary.

The 1911 census shows that Lennon was a carter and insurance agent, aged 53, with five children. His eldest daughter was a schoolteacher, his second daughter a seamstress and, his eldest son was a clerk with an oil company. His home was a five-room house in Irvine Crescent in East Wall and he kept two lodgers. The two men were skilled workers, one George Townsend was a fitter in an iron works and Charles Browne was a riveter. Both men were English; the former was a Presbyterian while the latter was Wesleyan. The assistant secretary, Seán O'Casey, was also a resident of East Wall. He is recorded under the name Seaghán Ó Cathasaigh and he lived in 18 Abercorn Road in a cramped four-room cottage with his mother and brother. They occupied two rooms and the other rooms were occupied by a widow, Mrs. Elizabeth Duffy, and her four children who ranged in age from 26 to 13 years of age. O'Casey is one of the many workers who supported their widowed mothers because at this time, the widow's pension did not exist and without the support of family, these women lived very precarious lives.[66]

The Women and Children's (of Locked-out Workers) Relief Fund was now allocated an office at Liberty Hall and Grace Neal stayed in Dublin to oversee the scheme. With Delia Larkin, she formed the Ladies' Committee and both women took charge of organising the necessary staff for the new scheme. The new food kitchen was opened on 12 November 1913 with a new breakfast-room, and a clothing room for the children of the workers. Neal said that initially they 'provided meals for 500, but the lane outside (Old Abbey Street) was crowded and we had to empty the room and refill it again, having enough bread and jam and cocoa for more.'[67] The work of cooking was organised by:

Paddy Murtagh, 'of hornpipe fame' ably supported by a number of locked-out women and girls, as well as by the daughters of locked out workers who performed the cleaning and, serving of food.[68]

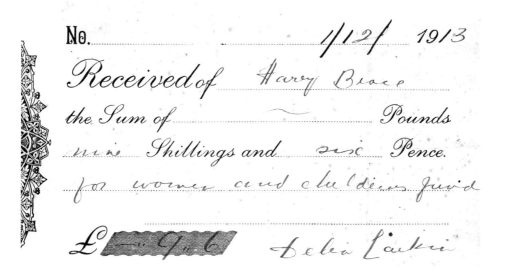

4. Receipt for 9s.6d. for the Women and Children's Fund, signed by Delia Larkin. DCLA (BOR F33/11)

The dinner scheme was scrapped completely, the kitchen now only prepared and cooked breakfast for the children, and in December, the committee began providing dinner every day for 'seventy-five nursing mothers and their babies and these dinners were looked after by John O'Brien who was a locked out tramwayman.'[69] This committee also welcomed visitors/volunteers but it was controlled by Grace Neal and unlike the earlier food kitchen, they were not allowed to become involved in any aspect of the work inside the building. This kitchen was well organised and the children and women were seated at tables and served their food in a dignified manner.

Grace Neal gave the visitors the task of visiting families in their homes, to allocate the food and clothing vouchers, where she recorded that they 'saw the horrors of the tenement houses' and she said 'it was the hardest job to keep filled.'[70] When they were short of volunteer visitors, the women and girls working in the kitchen did this work. By late November, the kitchen was providing 1,000 breakfasts every day and by January 1914, the number receiving breakfast increased to between 2,500 and 3,000.[71] This food kitchen did not receive any aid from the TUC and its funding came solely from the *Daily Herald* League's Dublin branch, and various fundraising events in Dublin.

Dublin Children's Distress Fund

Meanwhile, under the auspices of the Dublin Children's Distress Fund the St Vincent de Paul Society had organised parish committees based on the work of the Ladies' Relief Committee. Mr W. A. Ryan who was a barrister and a member of the St Vincent de Paul Society agreed to act as treasurer of the fund and all monies were channelled through this office. The charity established a central committee and this committee then created 16 parish committees across the city and county. Each parish committee comprised the parish priest and members of the St Vincent de Paul Society.

Within two weeks, the parish committees were providing a meal or two meals every day to 10,000 children, with 'the sisters in the convent schools' and, 'the teachers in the parish national schools' doing 'the actual work of feeding and clothing the poor children under their care.'[72] The work of the parish committee of St John's in Dolphin's Barn provides an insight into how the committees operated. This committee fed an average of 35 children each week and this involved an outlay of 'something like £2.5s a week while 'the local tradesman gave food stuff very cheap, and the coal was given free to us by a parishioner.'[73] The committee also reported that:

> No child is supplied with food unless he or she is actually attending school here, and that this is certified by the teacher upon the meal order issued by the St Vincent de Paul Society for that purpose.[74]

Many mothers were unable to cope with their poverty, and they refused to queue openly for food. The committee devised a strategy to help them by channelling aid to the various religious orders, and the sisters on their parish visitations discreetly found these families and provided aid.[75]

One of the district visitors for St Vincent de Paul whose role was to seek out these families recorded a sad case in November 1913. This family comprised a husband, wife and six children less than nine years of age from the Gardiner Street area who were reduced to absolute penury. The husband had worked for 18 years in a soap factory. The visitor's report said that the family 'formerly occupied the best room in one of the large tenement houses' but now unable to pay the rent they were moved 'by their landlord to the basement because the rent was smaller.'[76] At this point they had 'practically no furniture, most of the contents of a fairly comfortable room having been pawned to buy food and pay rent' and 'they were short of food, clothing and fire and the outlook is hopeless.'[77] The visitor observed that this family's situation represented:

The plight of struggling people who bear their privations bravely and patiently and do not readily seek aid from charitable or philanthropic agencies ... The suffering of the respectable poor, mental and physical, is in fact much more acute ...[78]

On 10 December, the Dublin Children's Distress Fund reported that:

The numbers of poor children supplied with meals have been in some localities, on the increase, while in a few schools it is understood that the demand for meals has slightly diminished. Taking the city as a whole it may be stated that the work of providing the schoolchildren with daily meals continues to be one of enormous magnitude.[79]

By this time Catherine Sherlock's Ladies' Relief Committee and, the Ladies' School Dinner Committees were having difficulty raising money and they placed their organisation under the umbrella of the Dublin Children's Distress Fund, so they could have access to its funds. Apparently, subscriptions were dwindling as most were given to either the Dublin Children's Distress Fund, or the Women and Children's (of Locked-out Workers) Relief Fund. On Christmas Eve 1913, the Denzille Lane Penny Dinners recorded that 'in 1913 the number of meals they distributed was 50,850 almost double the number provided in 1912.'[80]

Providing clothing for children was another major part of the aid given to the poor. At Liberty Hall, Delia Larkin and Grace Neal provided clothes for the children. They had 'received large cases of new and second hand clothing from Glasgow, Plymouth and London, as well as rolls of cloth and flannelette.'[81] On 24 November, they opened a sewing room, with three machines donated by the women workers, who made clothes and altered the second hand clothing. This workroom provided clothing for 2,907 children, maternity wear for 150 women, and the women and girls who were locked out were given 'a few articles of clothing'.[82]

The Dublin Children's Distress Fund also provided clothing. In his final report Dr Walsh said the fund had provided 809 boys and girls with boots and stockings. It also distributed boys' clothing that included 1,434 boy's suits, and 1,416 pairs of knickers, while clothing for girls included 2,840 dresses and '4,994 other articles of clothing'.[83]

In some areas, the committee gave grants of material to be made up into articles of clothing by local agencies. Several convents opened up workrooms and women who were locked out were given work making and altering clothes for women and children. For example, the Sisters of Charity organised St Brigid's Workroom at Belvedere Place, and another workroom in Mountjoy Square, while in Seville Place a workroom provided work for the women and clothes for the strikers.

Conclusion

On the 18 January, the ITGWU informed the press that 'the dispute was effectively over.'[84] The last food ship landed its cargo on 28 January 1914 and the Lockout ended. By '15 February there were 4,000 men and more than 1,000 women still locked out.'[85] On 28 February 1914, due to lack of funds, the provision of daily meals for 3,000 children and the 75 dinners were stopped at Liberty Hall. Likewise the Dublin Children's Distress Fund, which had provided food for between 9,000 and 10,000 children daily was closed in the middle of February 1914 and its 'clothes depot was also closed.'[86]

In the immediate aftermath of the Lockout, many working-class families were rendered helpless in the face of extreme poverty. Thousands of children were still hungry as many men failed to get their jobs back. They were now dependent on the long established charities in the city and for thousands of women and children in Dublin life had become a nightmare of unimagined proportions. Within weeks, the stories of the Lockout and the suffering of women and children disappeared from the newspapers. By August 1914, the heroic respectable poor had become the ghosts of a failed enterprise as many of the men joined the British Army, and the women with their children were left to pick up the pieces of their shattered lives whatever way they could.

Notes

1   Emmet O'Connor, *A labour history of Ireland* 1824-2000 (Dublin, 2011), p. xi.

2   Jacinta Prunty, *Dublin slums 1800-1925: a study in urban geography* (Dublin, 1998).

3   *Irish Times,* 24 Dec. 1913.

4   Ibid., 4 Oct. 1913

5   Ann Matthews, *Renegades: women in Irish Republican politics 1900-1922* (Cork, 2010), pp 77-8.

6   Maud Gonne, witness statement (MAI, BMH WS 317, p. 3).

7   Francis Devine, *Organising history: a centenary of SIPTU 1909-2009* (Dublin, 2009), p. 56.

8   Emmet Larkin, *James Larkin: Irish labour leader 1876-1947* (London, 1989).

9   *Irish Worker,* 2 Sept. 1911

10   Nora Connolly O'Brien, *Portrait of a rebel father* (Dublin, 1935), pp 124-5.

11   Jimmy Sweeney, ' Document Study The Dublin Lockout, 1913: the response of British labour', *Saothar* 6 (1980), pp 104-8.

12   'Dublin Food Fund' statement of accounts; 'Trade Union Congress Parliamentary Committee', final report 1914 (Irish Labour History Archives).

13   *Weekly Irish Times,* 4 Oct. 1913, p. 1.

14   *Freeman's Journal*, 11 Oct. 1913.

15   Ibid., 27 Sept. 1913.

16   Devine, *Organising history,* p. 57.

17   'Dublin Food Fund' final report 1914, p. 5 (Irish Labour History Archives).

18   *Freeman's Journal*, 27 Sept. 1913.

19   *Weekly Irish Times*, 4 Oct. 1913, p. 1.

20   Jill Liddington and Jill Norris, *One hand tied behind us: the rise of the women's suffrage movement* (London, 2000), p. 13; Matthews, *Renegades,* p. 127.

21   Pádraig Yeates, *Lockout: Dublin 1913* (Dublin, 2000), p. 183.

22   *Freeman's Journal*, 29 Sept. 1913.

23   *Weekly Irish Times*, 4 Oct. 1913, p. 1.

24   *Irish Independent*, 29 Sept. 1913.

25   *Irish Times*, 4 Oct. 1913.

26   *Irish Times*, 9 Oct. 1913.

27   'Dublin Food Fund' statement of accounts, p. 4 (Irish Labour History Archives); Devine, *Organising history*, p. 57.

28   *Evening Telegraph*, 29 Sept. 1913.

29   Seán O'Casey, *Autobiographies 1* (London, 1992), p. 595.

30   Although commonly referred to as Countess Markievicz, she always signed her name de Markievicz, it is on her marriage certificate, her daughter Maeve is de Markievicz, she signed the Fianna minutes de Markievicz, her will and probate are in the name de Markievicz.

31   *Irish Independent,* 29 Oct. 1913.

32   With thanks to Mícheál Mac Aonghusa for the translation.

33   *Irish Citizen,* 4 Oct. 1913.

34   Ibid.

35   Ibid.

36   Nora Connolly, *The unbroken tradition* (Michigan, 1918), pp 3-4.

37   *Irish Citizen*, 4 Oct. 1913.

38   O'Casey, *Autobiographies 1,* p. 595.

39   *Irish Citizen,* 4 Oct. 1913

40   O'Casey, *Autobiographies 1,* p. 595.

41   Ibid.

42   Peadar Kearney, witness statement (MAI, BMH WS 868, p. 4). Peadar Kearney was active in the Irish Cultural Nationalist Movement. He is the author of the Irish National Anthem.

43   Dora Montefiore, *From a Victorian to a modern*, (London, 1927), (www.marxists.org/archive/montefiore/1915/autiobiography/13/htm).

44   O'Casey, *Autobiographies 1,* p. 594.

45   *Irish Worker*, 1 Nov. 1913.

46   *Freeman's Journal*, 13 Oct. 1913.

47   *Freeman's Journal*, 25 Sept. 1913.

48   Mary Muldowney (www.redbannermagazine.com/IWFL.pdf). In 1918, Louie Bennett became the president of the Irish Women Workers' Union.

49   *Irish Citizen,* 27 Sept. 1913.

50   Ibid.

51   Ibid.

52   *Irish Citizen*, 4 Oct. 1913

53   Ibid.

54   'Annals of the Sister of Charity' (Sisters of Charity Convent, Seville Place).

55   George Lansbury, *The miracle of Fleet Street: the story of the Daily Herald* (London, 1925), pp 49-50.

56   Ibid.

57   *Irish Independent*, 28 Oct. 1913.

58   Ibid.

59   Lady Mayoress Catherine Sherlock to Archbishop Walsh, 27 Oct. 1913 (DDA, Archbishop Walsh Papers, Box 293, Laity Folder, Oct. 1913).

60   Ibid.

61   *Irish Worker*, 8 Nov. 1913.

62   *Irish Independent*, 5 Nov. 1913.

63   Montefiore, *From a Victorian to a modern*.

64   *Irish Worker*, 7 Feb. 1914.

65   Ibid., 22 Nov. 1913.

66   1911 census (www.nationalarchives.ie).

67   *Irish Worker*, 22 Nov. 1913.

68   Ibid., 22 Nov. 1913.

69   Ibid., 10 Jan. 1914.

70   Ibid., 7 Mar. 1913.

71   Ibid., 6 Jan. 1914

72   *Irish Times*, 24 Nov. 1913; see also *Irish Independent* and *Freeman's Journal*.

73   Letter from St John's Parish committee to Archbishop Walsh, 7 Dec. 1913 (DDA, Archbishop Walsh Papers, Box 293, Laity Folder, 1913).

74   Lady Mayoress Catherine Sherlock to Archbishop Walsh, 27 Oct. 1913 (DDA, Archbishop Walsh Papers, Box 293, Laity Folder).

75   'Annals of the Sisters of Charity 1913' (Sisters of Charity Convent, Seville Place).

76   *Irish Times*, 12 Nov. 1912.

77   Ibid.

78   Ibid.

79   Ibid., 10 Dec. 1913.

80   Ibid., 24 Dec. 1913.

81   *Irish Worker,* 3 Feb. 1914.

82   Ibid.

83   *Irish Times*, 24 Nov. 1913; *Freeman's Journal*, 24 Nov. 1913.

84   Devine, *Organising history*, p. 61.

85   Ibid.

86   (DDA, Archbishop Walsh Papers, Box 293, Laity Folder, Oct. 1913).

12.

A bridge to the future: Hugh Lane's Municipal Gallery of Modern Art, 1913

....

Ciarán Wallace

Introduction

For much of 1913 Dublin's Municipal Council and the city's newspapers, supported by citizens' associations and the Chamber of Commerce, were engaged in a bitter dispute about modern art. The Council, or Corporation as it was then, held a series of Special Meetings on the subject but failed to resolve the matter, rival newspapers championed opposing sides and their letters pages made claim and counter claim about the personalities involved. Strictly speaking, the dispute was about spending public money on a new art gallery spanning the Liffey, but the argument revealed deeper divisions. At a time of radical transformation in Irish social and political life the bridge gallery dispute pointed to two very different visions for Ireland's future. On one side was Hugh Lane, committed promoter of Irish art, and his eclectic group of supporters which included Gaelic revivalists, labour organisers, women's suffragists and Sinn Féin councillors. Their ambition, inspired by developments in European painting, was to build a world-class gallery in Dublin which would encourage the development of a distinctly Irish school of modern art. Both the physical building, and its artistic influence, would be valuable additions to the capital of the new Home Rule Ireland. On the opposing side was William Martin Murphy, newspaper proprietor and business magnate, supported by the Dublin Chamber of Commerce and a group of major ratepayers. Commerce and industry were central to their vision for Ireland's future. Murphy was living proof that all Irishmen, not just Ulster Protestant Irishmen, could prosper in the international business world. Instead of an extravagant gallery with a pedestrian walkway, they insisted that Dublin needed a major new highway with a wide traffic bridge across the Liffey. While Unionist city councillors and ratepayers played an important part in the debate, the great majority on both sides of the argument were conventional Nationalists seeking Irish independence within the British Empire. The bridge gallery dispute, however, shows how wide the spectrum of Home Rule Nationalism actually was, suggesting the range of possible futures that might have been. Two bridges came to symbolise the divide, one an elegant edifice dedicated to art, the other an artery for business and development. A point on which both sides were agreed, however, was that the old Metal Bridge, as the Ha'penny Bridge was called, should be removed as soon as possible.

Proposed Municipal Art Gallery for Dublin

In February 1903 a deputation from the Royal Hibernian Academy (RHA) attended a meeting of Dublin's Municipal Council. The RHA promoted public appreciation of the visual arts, primarily through an annual exhibition, and it sought the support of the Corporation in obtaining additional funding and larger premises which would include a municipal art gallery. Other cities across the United Kingdom enjoyed the benefits of larger arts funding, they claimed, and Dublin was being left behind. Sir Thomas Drew of the RHA explained their plan to reinvigorate the Independent Chartered National Guild of Artists to encourage interest in modern and contemporary art. He claimed that the time was ripe for such a move since Hugh Lane's recent exhibition of Old Masters, borrowed from mansions around the city and country, had been a spectacular success, demonstrating the public appetite for art. As government plans were under way for a major new building on Merrion Street to house institutes for science and art, surely, Drew argued, space could be found for the National Guild and the new gallery. In the event, there was no room in Merrion Street, but the idea of a city gallery began to take root.

1. Watercolour drawing of Edwin Lutyens' proposed new art gallery on the River Liffey by R. Walcot.
Collection: Dublin City Gallery The Hugh Lane

At this period cities in Britain and Ireland were expanding their services to include the provision of parks for recreation and libraries and technical colleges for education, and many had built art galleries for the pleasure and moral improvement of the public. The Corporation were happy to support the RHA's campaign, particularly as they were not required to contribute any money but merely to attend as part of a delegation to the Lord Lieutenant. Expanding municipal activity, growing public interest in art and a vague sense that Dublin had been treated unfairly combined to produce agreement; the inclusion of Hugh Lane, and the absence of any discussion of finances, helped ensure consensus.

Hugh Lane

Hugh Lane was a self-taught art critic with social and family connections to luminaries in the artistic and literary world including Edward Martyn, Douglas Hyde and the brothers William B. and Jack B. Yeats. Lane's father, the Rev. James W. Lane, was the rector of Ballybrack in Co. Cork and his mother was Adelaide Persse of Co. Galway, elder sister of Lady Augusta Gregory. Aunt Augusta and her nephew enjoyed a close connection throughout his life, and she would continue to champion his plans and reputation after his death. The rectory at Ballybrack was not a happy home, the rector and his wife were not well suited and eventually separated when Hugh was 18. He was described as a 'handsome but delicate boy caring nothing for sport, interested instead in pictures and ornaments.'[1] Lane's keen interest in art led him to work as an apprentice to Martin Colnaghi, a renowned London art dealer and major beneficiary of the National Gallery in London.[2] The two did not get along and the apprenticeship lasted less than a year, but the young trainee was a quick learner and within a few years he had his own dealership on Pall Mall Place. It was probably under Colnaghi that Lane learnt the value and pleasure of donating important artworks to a gallery; by 1900 he was a successful and prosperous art dealer with the reputation and resources to become a major philanthropist. His successful gallery in London specialised in Old Masters but an interest in Irish art emerged following his visit to an exhibition in St Stephen's Green, Dublin, in 1901.[3] Public enthusiasm for Lane's 1902 exhibition of Old Masters at the RHA's Lower Abbey Street premises, contributed to his appointment as a board member of the National Gallery of Ireland. Lane felt strongly that Irish artists were not recognised at home or abroad and for the rest of his life he promoted their reputation, he also brought important works of modern art to Ireland, hoping to encourage the development of a distinct 'Irish school'. His efforts to create a separate gallery of Irish art at the 1904 World's Fair in St Louis, Missouri, failed due to high insurance costs. Never one to give up easily, Lane showed the collection at the Guildhall in London where it was very well received.[4] The show opened with 465 Irish works by artists, some of whom 'had never claimed, nor even adverted to, their Irish nationality', however, as Lane defined Irishness as 'men who belong to us by birth or by blood' exhibitors were included under the art equivalent of soccer's 'grandmother rule' whereby having an Irish grandparent qualified you to represent Ireland.[5] The exhibition was a revelation to the critics who had presumed no place for Ireland in the art world and 80,000 visitors paid for admission.

His ambitions for a distinctive school of Irish art resonated with wider cultural movements such as the Gaelic League's revitalisation of the Irish language and parallel literary and theatrical developments in Ireland. Attracted by Lane's reputation, and his ability to elicit works on loan from leading artists and collectors, supporters of art in Belfast asked him to stage an exhibition there. With his usual enthusiasm he enrolled William Orpen in a trip to the Manet exhibition in Paris where they procured several French paintings and gave Belfast a most successful show in April 1906.[6] In 1910 Lane would establish the Johannesburg Art Gallery in South Africa, demonstrating both his energy and commitment to the international world of art.[7]

The success of Lane's RHA exhibition in 1902 meant that many of Dublin's City Council members would have recognised his name when Sir Thomas Drew mentioned it in February 1903, but within a few years every member, along with the vast majority of Dubliners, would be familiar with the name of Hugh Lane, and many would have strong opinions of the merits or otherwise of modern art. The Corporation had been generally supportive of the RHA's idea of a Municipal Gallery but in the winter of 1904/05 Lane made a startling offer to Dublin Corporation which called for a real decision; he would donate a valuable collection of artworks, including over 30 important Impressionist pieces, to the city – on condition that the Corporation would provide a permanent gallery to house them. His motives were to promote an awareness of international developments in modern art in Ireland, to educate emerging Irish artists and to allow Dublin to take her place among the capitals of Europe. At a time of widespread cultural revival and interest in all things Irish, and in a period of growing anticipation of a future Home Rule parliament in Dublin, this was a most attractive proposition.

Dublin Corporation

The Corporation voted £500 as an annual allowance to the proposed Municipal Gallery of Modern Art and the project was eagerly supported by Alderman Thomas Kelly, chairman of the Public Libraries' Committee which took responsibility for it.[8] The inner workings of municipal councils, their members and committees, may not spring to mind as an arena for dramatic social and artistic dispute, but the particular combination of personalities and interests that would collide over the new gallery gives a fascinating insight into Dublin's rapidly changing public scene. Tom Kelly had been elected as a councillor for the city's Mansion House Ward in the reformed elections of January 1899 when a greatly expanded electorate could choose from a much more diverse range of candidates than previously. As a nominee of the Total Abstinence and Workmen's Club on York Street, Kelly combined the credentials of a working-class activist and a committed Nationalist.[9] He headed the poll in 1903 becoming an alderman and in 1905 was among the first candidates to stand for Sinn Féin, Arthur Griffith's 'Irish Ireland' movement, as it added electoral politics to its existing economic and intellectual platform. Aside from their pronounced Nationalist and separatist agenda, Sinn Féin members were a local manifestation of the urban reformers who had appeared in cities across the United Kingdom and much of the United States in the preceding decades.[10] They refused to accept paid employment from the Corporation for themselves or their family members, and they undertook to expose jobbery and corruption in council activities.[11] It might seem unlikely that a workers' representative with radical political ambitions should choose to support the establishment of a gallery of modern art, but Kelly's commitment was sincere and his involvement was vital to the project's initial success. Providing free access to art for all Dubliners, and enhancing Ireland's artistic reputation internationally, appealed to the alderman's politics. At a time when corruption was almost expected and all municipal finances were regarded with grave suspicion, Kelly's reputation as an upright public representative, and his position as chairman of the committee in charge of the gallery, initially made the project unassailable on financial grounds. His membership of Sinn Féin and his working-class profile shielded the gallery from accusations of social elitism – had he been among the Unionist councillors or an Irish Parliamentary Party (IPP) councillor in the professions things might have worked out quite differently.

To support the Corporation in its unfamiliar role as patron of the arts a public committee was established to gather money, and maintain momentum. Its membership was an interesting mixture of cultural and political strands in Irish life including writers and commentators such as George Russell ('Æ'), Edith Somerville, W. B. Yeats, Douglas Hyde and Lady Gregory. Nationalists, Unionists, artists and scientists found common ground in the neutral space provided by the Municipal Gallery project; Count Markievicz, artist and husband of the future revolutionary Constance Markievicz, rubbed shoulders with Lord Iveagh of the Unionist Guinness family, and Sir Charles Cameron, Dublin's renowned Chief Medical Officer for Health.[12] The committee secretary was the artist Sarah Cecilia Harrison who would become Dublin's first female councillor in 1912, and whose involvement in the gallery would continue and intensify beyond the death of both the project and its promoter.[13]

Just as Kelly might appear an unlikely champion of modern art, so Sarah Cecilia Harrison's early background does not suggest the strong collaboration which she and Kelly would create over the gallery. An Ulster woman of liberal Nationalist stock, her brother Henry was an M.P. in the Irish Parliamentary Party. Sarah spent her youth in London where her skill as an artist was recognised. Perfecting her craft by studying in France, Italy and Holland she exhibited at the Belfast Art Exhibition in 1895 and 1906, finally settling in Dublin in 1889 where she worked as a portraitist and gave private lessons to students. Harrison was an inveterate activist and it was in Dublin that her commitment to social equality for women, workers and the poor came to the fore. She worked as secretary to the Dublin City Labour Yard, a volunteer-run employment agency for unemployed men who did not qualify for relief from the City Council, and she wrote for the Irish Women's Franchise League publication *The Irish Citizen*.[14] Her successful 1912 campaign to be elected as Dublin's first female city councillor demonstrated her commitment to the cause of women's suffrage, but her standing as an independent was equally telling. Harrison's contributions in council debates show a fresh and acute sense of political mission, her assertiveness and her gender disturbed the 'old boys' club' atmosphere and she enthusiastically added her voice to those of Labour and Sinn Féin, the Corporation's other radical reformers.[15] It was this combination of firm Nationalism, practical concern for Dublin's working class and a career in art which placed her alongside Thomas Kelly at the centre of the gallery dispute.

This illustration is reproduced from the photograph and scale-drawing of the proposed Dublin Art Gallery on the Metal Bridge site, on view at the Health Exhibition in the Rotunda Rink. It gives an idea of the effect of such a building in blotting out the fine view westwards from O'Connell Bridge, and how much out of harmony it would be with its surroundings.

2. *Irish Independent*, 10 Apr. 1913.

Lane's offer of an art collection was not taken up immediately by the city. Occasional prompting was required from Richard Caulfield Orpen, George Russell and others on the public committee, who felt it would 'reflect grave discredit on the capital of Ireland if such a generous gift were ... allowed to lapse through mere lack of wall space.' Astutely playing on tribal and municipal rivalry they expressed the fear 'that the pictures may pass from Dublin to Belfast, where the project of starting a Municipal Gallery has been taken up with great energy.'[16] By 1908 the Corporation and the gallery's supporters had secured temporary premises at Clonmell House, an 18th-century townhouse at 17 Harcourt Street.[17] At the opening ceremony on 20 January the great and the good of the city gathered to launch a most promising endeavour, one which had attracted support and approval from all shades of opinion at home and abroad. Among the guests to receive invitations (printed in both Irish and English) were the Anglican and Roman Catholic archbishops of Dublin, the journalist and economic Nationalist Arthur Griffith and Trinity College polymath the Rev. Dr Mahaffy, along with councillors from all sides.[18] It was satisfying to read that London's art world watched with envy, and Dublin Corporation was pleased with the praise of D. S. McColl, director of the Tate Gallery, who marvelled that 'An artistic project has actually been carried through without being smothered in compromise, with hardly a trace of the official sterilising which is useful, applied to sewage, but not to art.'[19] In his speech at this happy event the Lord Mayor, Joseph Nannetti, emphasised the financial risk which the council had undertaken in funding the gallery.[20] Warning that its continued operation would require additional local taxes, he expressed confidence that 'in the future the citizens would be behind the Corporation in this matter.'[21] This confidence in the city's taxpayers would prove to be misplaced.

The following month two Sinn Féin councillors proposed 'That in recognition of the valued service rendered to the City of Dublin and to Ireland by Mr Hugh P. Lane, in his successful efforts to establish a Municipal Art Gallery in our metropolis, he is, hereby constituted an Honorary Freeman of the City of Dublin.'[22] The proposal led to some dispute, not over the worthiness of the recipient but because of the source of the nomination. Some IPP councillors were unhappy with Sinn Féin's control of the committee overseeing the gallery, and the glory which this reflected on the new party. The immediate objection to Lane's nomination was on the technical grounds that notice of the motion had not been given, but the proposal was carried and Lane received the only honour that Dublin could bestow. Unfortunately, for a man who enjoyed pageantry, there was no public conferring ceremony and he does not appear to have received the customary illuminated scroll marking his new dignity. Lane would get his day out in 1909, however, when, at the relatively young age of 34, the Sinn Féin favourite was knighted for his services to Irish art.[23]

Over the following years the Harcourt Street gallery was regarded as a popular success, but it created two problems for the Corporation. First, its short term funding was uncertain. In a split vote on whether to continue spending Libraries Committee money on the gallery, Sinn Féin and the Unionists were in favour while most IPP councillors were against it. Opponents argued that library services were suffering to pay for less essential, and less popular, services for art-lovers. Second, Harcourt Street was not the permanent home stipulated in Hugh Lane's gift. The solution was to expand the Public Libraries Committee, giving it a large subcommittee, including additional councillors and external experts from the art world dedicated to managing the new gallery. Sinn Féin were far from happy with this plan which removed their control of a high profile project, but the IPP strongly endorsed the new scheme, as did most Unionists.[24] The IPP may have welcomed a chance to undermine their Nationalist competitor while the Unionists were growing uneasy with the gallery's continuing drain on public funds.

This larger committee, with so many members from beyond City Hall, worried some councillors. The prospect of finding or building a permanent gallery did not sit comfortably as an economic downturn put the Corporation under increased financial pressure. In January 1912 councillors voted to return full control of the gallery to the Public Libraries Committee, and a month later they ordered a valuation of the gallery's paintings.[25] These steps appear to have calmed the nerves of doubters and, with decisions firmly under council control, the city borrowed £3,000 to repay the money already raised and spent by the public committee, now called the Modern Art Gallery [Citizens'] Committee.[26] In December 1912 this demonstration of commitment produced a letter from Sir Hugh Lane formally handing over the 'Lane Gift' to the Corporation of Dublin and in early 1913 Lord Mayor Lorcan Sherlock (IPP) steered a motion through the council that as 'the overwhelming majority of the citizens is in favour' of building a permanent gallery the city will borrow £22,000 - provided that the Citizens' Committee present a site free of cost and an additional £3,000. Sherlock's reference to the 'overwhelming majority' implicitly acknowledged the existence of a small but growing body of opposition to the additional burden on the city's ratepayers. The gallery's supporters had shown their ability to raise substantial sums of money, however, it would be a challenge to raise enough to buy a prominent city centre site large enough to house the Municipal Gallery.

Bridge Gallery proposal

In an effort to move events along Lane had commissioned the renowned architect Edwin Lutyens to make preliminary drawings for a gallery, thus placing his preferred scale and style at the heart of the debate – the location remained a problem.[27] St Stephen's Green and Merrion Square were both ruled out after initial approaches. At about this time a clever suggestion came from Francis B. Craig, a 30-year-old architect from Rathmines.[28] Craig, a member of the Arts Club along with Lane and many of the leading gallery supporters, wrote to *The Freeman's Journal* with 'a suggestion which appears … at least worthy of consideration. It is that the gallery should be built over the river on the lower or eastern side of O'Connell Bridge between Burgh Quay and Eden Quay.' Citing Florence as an example of a leading city with a gallery spanning its river, he dealt briefly with the construction methods and dimensions of his proposed building.[29] The fact that a location spanning the River Liffey involved no site costs, and that the view downstream to the Custom House had already been destroyed by the elevated Loop Line railway bridge (completed 1891), added to the appeal of this novel proposal. The bridge idea began to take hold and as 1913 arrived Dubliners, native, honorary and adoptive, debated its merits.

Opponents of the gallery project were probably in the minority at the start of the new year, but they had a very significant ally. Leading commercial figure and ratepayer William Martin Murphy did not relish the thought of paying higher municipal rates to build something as impractical as an art gallery, let alone one which was dedicated to unconventional modern art. Murphy was a phenomenally successful businessman in his mid-sixties. The son of a builder from Co. Cork, through hard work and determination he created an impressive portfolio of commercial enterprises. Experience in building and operating railways, in both Ireland and the African Gold Coast (present day Ghana), helped him to consolidate Dublin's competing tram companies into the Dublin United Tramway Company (DUTC). Under his direction, in 1901 Dublin became the first city in the United Kingdom to have a fully electrified network. He went on to construct tramways in Cork, Belfast and Buenos Aires. Murphy's other business interests included the Imperial Hotel and Clery's department store in the centre of Dublin and, most significantly for the modern art gallery, he owned the *Irish Independent* newspaper, a modern halfpenny daily title with a large circulation.[30] Politically Murphy was a Nationalist and had been an M.P. in Parnell's Irish Party, however his strong Catholic beliefs and an inherent dislike of social superiority meant that he was among the majority of M.P.s who abandoned the autocratic Parnell when his scandalous relationship with Mrs Katherine O'Shea became public. His twin passions of religion and business led one commentator to describe Murphy as going through life 'with the *Imitation of Christ* in one hand and the Companies Act in the other.'[31] In the bitter days of 'the split' Dublin Corporation was a bastion of Parnellite support. The city opposed Murphy's ambitions to electrify the trams, preferring to take them over as a municipal enterprise, but this was not to be. The mutual dislike between Murphy and the Corporation was sealed when he became vice-president, and then in 1912-13 president, of the Dublin Chamber of Commerce. In a city dominated by the IPP the Chamber of Commerce acted as a *de facto* opposition, its members declined to stand for election thus denying the City Council their commercial experience. Criticising from the outside, the chamber campaigned against the Corporation's wasteful or inefficient practices, and it highlighted failings in bookkeeping and service provision. The fact that the Dublin Chamber was predominantly Unionist, and its membership mainly Protestant, only deepened the divide between it and the city's elected representatives.

In January 1913 William Martin Murphy wrote the first in a long series of letters to the *Irish Independent*, in which he denigrated the value of the 'Lane Gift', questioned the need for a gallery and ridiculed the Corporation's abilities to handle the whole affair. From the start he personalised his attack, presenting Hugh Lane as self-serving and describing the gallery as nothing more than a monument to his vanity, 'generally speaking, benefactors have to depend on posterity for the erection of public monuments to their memory.'[32] As a major ratepayer himself, and as representative of the city's largest ratepayers, Murphy objected to the expense of the project but he claimed that it was not simple parsimony which drove him, he was keen to avoid appearing as a philistine incapable of appreciating art. Dublin's slums were notorious at this time so, while Murphy explained that he admired good pictures and could appreciate them, he 'would rather see in the city ... one block of sanitary houses at low rents replacing a reeking slum, than all the pictures Corot[33] and Degas ever painted.'[34] This public declaration against the gallery by a leading citizen opened the door for other doubters to voice their opposition. Councillor Dr J. C. McWalter (IPP), a long-time advocate on behalf of the poor, questioned how the Corporation could afford to spend £22,000 on a gallery when decaying tenements were crowded with cases of tuberculosis.[35] To make matters worse, McWalter continued, the Collier Memorial Dispensary, a free clinic for the poor, faced closure due to lack of funds, and why? 'Because a few plutocrats from Pembroke [Ballsbridge & Donnybrook], a few artists from Rathmines, a stray stockbroker, a curio-hunter, an occasional old lady from Bray, an odd bounder from Blackrock, would like to give their friends a cheap treat by showing them specimens of Corot and other modern French mediocrities in the Dublin Picture Gallery.'[36] McWalter's wit touched on a sensitive point, all the locations he mentioned were self-governing suburban districts whose middle-class ratepayers enjoyed the benefit of the city's gallery without contributing to its upkeep. Meanwhile, the city had the responsibility of caring for the poorest, and consequently the sickest, portion of the population. In his letter McWalter also referred to the gallery site being near Grattan Bridge at Capel Street, the position of the proposed gallery was moving away from O'Connell Bridge. In March 1913 a report to the Corporation set out the benefits of a bridge site, and councillors voted overwhelmingly to adopt the location where the Ha'penny Bridge now stands.[37]

Officially named the Wellington Bridge, then the Metal Bridge and subsequently the Ha'penny Bridge, the single iron span across the Liffey was opened in May 1816 when the *Dublin Evening Post* described it as both ornamental and eminently useful to the city's inhabitants. The editor praised it as 'one of the most beautiful in Europe, the excellence of its composition, the architectural correctness of its form, the taste with which it has been executed, and the general airiness of its appearance, renders it an object of unmixed admiration.'[38] A commercial lease, effective until 1919, allowed the

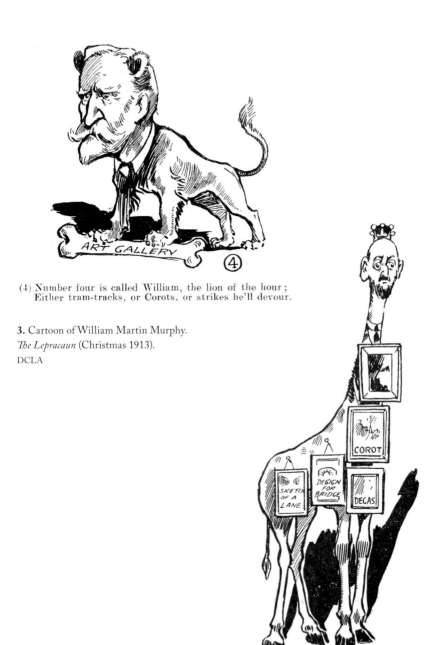

(4) Number four is called William, the lion of the hour;
Either tram-tracks, or Corots, or strikes he'll devour.

3. Cartoon of William Martin Murphy.
The Lepracaun (Christmas 1913).
DCLA

4. Cartoon of Hugh Lane.
The Lepracaun (Christmas 1913).
DCLA

(19) Here's Hugh the giraffe, who went for a "trek,"
When he heard someone say "he'd a hell of a neck."

bridge's operators to charge a toll for pedestrians using it. Over time the toll became a source of public irritation as low-paid workers were forced to make a longer journey between work and home. In 1906 the Corporation investigated the possibility of buying out the remaining lease to make the bridge toll-free but this proved impossible.[39] Four years later a joint Sinn Féin-IPP motion called, unsuccessfully, for the owners of the Metal Bridge to suspend the toll between 1 pm and 2 pm 'to allow working people to cross over and back at dinner hour.'[40] The toll was unpopular but the bridge itself was considered unsightly. Advertising hoardings along the railings created a prominent eyesore which blocked the view upriver towards the distant spire of John's Lane church and the setting sun, one commentator remarked that 'everyone in Dublin was now ashamed of that structure.'[41] For most of 1913 Dublin's newspapers were filled with letters and articles for and against the art gallery; one opinion shared by all sides, however, was the need to remove the ugly metal bridge.

The rival campaigns concentrated on a number of central arguments; the cost, the slum question, the view upriver and the quality of the art. Behind these questions lay political wrangles in City Hall, personal rancour over past slights, issues of class and starkly different visions of Ireland's future. The first two arguments, the cost of the gallery and the need to tackle the slum question, were linked. How could the city afford such an extravagant folly while thousands of families lived in wretched tenements? Dr McWalter was a little disingenuous when he presented the argument as one of an art gallery versus a TB clinic. As a councillor of long experience he knew that every area of Corporation activity was funded through separate income streams, each of which was dedicated to its specific purpose. So rates raised for a mains drainage project could not be diverted to a public lighting scheme, and funds raised for libraries and an art gallery could not be spent on housing, the Local Government Board for Ireland conducted rigorous annual audits and charged councillors personally for any unapproved expenditure. William Martin Murphy also argued that sanitary housing was more essential than an art gallery, however, despite his involvement with the Society of St Vincent de Paul he did not enjoy a reputation as a friend to Dublin's poor and was not known as a campaigner for affordable housing. In the gallery supporters' camp, Alderman Kelly had a track record as a labour activist and an advocate for improved housing, and he found no difficulty in supporting the gallery project on educational, aesthetic and class grounds. Kelly maintained that workers were just as capable of enjoying, and benefiting from, art as any other section of society.

Many commentators referred to the loss of the view westwards up the River Liffey. A deputation from the Housing and Town Planning Association of Ireland to the Mansion House described the proposed building as a 'screen across the river …

It would be a blot on the landscape.' In an example of the emotive language which the dispute produced the report on the deputation carried the subheading 'Taking the city by the throat.'[42] Murphy's *Irish Independent*, which always had space for opposition to the gallery, reproduced an artist's impression of how a bridge location might look. The caption beneath the image of a heavy blockish building sitting on three squat arches, explained how it gave 'an idea of the effect of such a building in blotting out the fine views westwards from O'Connell Bridge, and how out of harmony it would be with its surroundings.'[43] A further, rather spurious, objection was that the gallery would block the movement of fresh air down the river, exacerbating the high levels of disease in the tenements along its banks. Perhaps in response to both these points, in late June *The Freeman's Journal* printed three artist's impressions based on Lutyens' own plans. These show a light central structure of open pillars linking elegant pavilions on either side of a bridge which sits primarily on a broad single span.[44] *The Weekly Irish Times* ridiculed the argument that the bridge would lead to disease.[45] An anonymous architect wrote to *The Irish Times* in favour of Lutyens' design for the bridge site, claiming that objectors exaggerated the degree of visual obstruction involved and that the building would bring dignity to the city centre.[46]

Murphy continued his letter writing campaign, undermining the merit and popular appeal of Lane's paintings. 'I assert', he wrote, 'that outside of a very small number of people who see, or pretend to see, transcendent beauties in an eccentric school of French painting, the mass of people in Dublin don't care a thraneen whether Sir Hugh Lane's conditional pictures are left here.'[47] Having presented the paintings as eccentric and foreign, and identified himself as one of the common people through the use of the Irish 'thraneen' to mean a trifle or a worthless amount, he then took careful aim at the class identity of his opponents. He sarcastically congratulated the 'handful of dilettanti on capturing such a handsome subsidy',[48] and portrayed those city councillors who supported the project as aristocrats disguising themselves as men of the people, before alleging that poor schoolchildren were going hungry as a result of the Corporation's obsession with the gallery.[49] The owner of the *Irish Independent* wrote as a disgruntled individual ratepayer and man of common sense, initially rejecting claims that he was part of an organised opposition and denying that there was any personal enmity in his stance.[50] By July 1913, however, he was clearly an organising force against the Corporation's plan and an unpleasant personal aspect had entered the debate. On two occasions in July Murphy called on opponents of the Corporation to write to him, with the intention of holding 'a public meeting … to take every possible step to defeat the present proposals.'[51] To Murphy's embarrassment, Sarah Harrison accosted him near his office on Dame Street. In a letter to the *Independent* he responded by describing the proposed bridge gallery as a 'blatant advertisement' to Miss Harrison's 'idol' Sir Hugh Lane. This rancour became a regular feature of Murphy's correspondence, as he continued to attack Lane's alleged vanity and arrogance in insisting on the bridge site. Others followed Murphy's lead, accusing Lane of using the entire gallery project as a scheme to promote his own business as an art dealer. This eventually produced a defence of Lane's character and motives from Colonel Hutcheson Poe, a board member of the National Gallery of Ireland and a supporter of the Municipal Gallery. In most polite terms he lamented the 'spirit of personal antagonism and bias' which lay beneath William Martin Murphy's comments on Sir Hugh Lane. In reply to insinuations appearing elsewhere, Hutcheson Poe wrote of Lane's 'extraordinary genius … his singularly unselfish nature … his simplicity of character … and above all by his entire freedom from anything approaching affectation or conceit.'[52]

How was it that a practical businessman like Murphy, with a lifetime of dealing with all sorts of people, felt such apparent acrimony for a self-made art dealer half his age? Murphy stated that he had only met Lane on one occasion, in a small social and commercial city like Dublin such an encounter was unremarkable, unfortunately no record exists of the circumstances of their meeting or what transpired between them. In a biography of Murphy the author defends him against charges of philistinism stating that his awareness of the philistine reputation of business led him to read widely, including works of history, some literature, engineering and law. He was also involved in the committee that erected the statue to Henry Grattan on College Green.[53] Set against this, however, are Murphy's own words when he wrote 'there are no greater humbugs in the world than art critics and so-called experts, and no subject concerning which there is more affectation than that of pictures.'[54] To a practical commercial mind such as Murphy's, Lane's character must have seemed at best an oddity, and at worst an affront. Following Lane's death in 1915 a number of his associates wrote character sketches of him, these reveal 'a pale, slender, dark-eyed knight, with his trim black beard, his slim hands and his poised, nervous, elusive manner.'[55] In another account the unidentified author recalled how Lane had initially 'impressed me as a very feminine person, rather ineffective, but quite amiable', echoing the earlier depiction of 'his delicate, nervous hands & his voice also had a kind of thrill in it – it seemed almost as if his spirit was outside his body.'[56] Such an apparently nervous and ineffective personality could easily create a false first impression, and this is possibly what William Martin Murphy based his judgment upon - but he may have been misled. The anonymous writer continued 'gradually I became more and more convinced that that feminine manner & the restless eyes had behind them an intense force', and ended his piece stating that he had 'never before or since met anyone who gave me the same sense of will power.' Indeed Lane and Murphy may have had more in common than they realised as both men were absolutely convinced of the correctness of their opinions, both were noted for their courtesy and personal amiability, and neither had an extravagant appetite for food or drink. Murphy supported the Society of St Vincent de Paul throughout his career,[57] leaving £2,700 to various charities in his will.[58] One of Lane's friends recalled how he would pay £70 for a box at a charity ball, but eat at a simple coffee stall on the way.[59] A further characteristic shared by the two Corkmen was a habit of giving frank and honest opinions, an inconvenient trait in two men with such high personal and professional standards.

Lane enjoyed the support of both the cultural intelligentsia and the representatives of labour. He attracted deep personal loyalty with a skill for attentive friendship and great generosity. Murphy appealed to a less romantic, but equally passionate, side of human nature, drawing business owners and major ratepayers to his cause with a powerful financial argument, and some 'common sense' jibes at the effete arty set. Among the groups backing Murphy's campaign was the Central Highway Committee, a gathering of commercial interests who wanted a new highway from Parnell Street to Dame Street, crossing the river at the site of the proposed bridge gallery. This body of men had members in common with the Dublin Chamber of Commerce, of which Murphy was president, and they complained that the bridge gallery with its pedestrian walkway would be a wasted opportunity to build a modern traffic bridge. Dublin, they argued, badly needed a major new thoroughfare along the lines of Belfast's impressive new Royal Avenue, to stimulate growth in the city centre.[60] While this group may not have been formally connected to Murphy a second organisation, the Liffey Protection Association, appeared in August 1913 with a postal address in Murphy's offices at 39 Dame Street.[61] With an increasing number of commercial interests against the plan and a major daily newspaper dedicated to defeating it, the gallery's supporters faced a serious challenge. It was not the blunt force of Murphy's protest, however, that ultimately defeated the bridge gallery, it was a combination of personalities, politics and poverty.

By 1913 Sir Hugh Lane had grown increasingly impatient with the delay in meeting the terms of his original offer made a decade earlier. He threatened to withdraw an unspecified number of artworks from the collection if a decision was not reached on a permanent gallery. Just as Lane was sure of his judgement in art, so he was convinced that Lutyens was the only man to design the new premises. In a way Lutyens' involvement became part of the collection, and Lane would never allow any interference in his selection of works, so Lutyens' appointment became non-negotiable. The same steely determination that had propelled Lane to the top of his profession, and brought a world-leading Municipal Gallery within reach, would play a major part in ruining the entire project.

In a year of widespread industrial unrest it may well have suited Labour members on Dublin Corporation to support the gallery against the wishes of William Martin Murphy, owner of the DUTC and representative of the city's main employers.

Hugh Lane's ambition of stimulating an Irish school of modern art, and his links to the Gaelic movement, made him a favourite with Sinn Féin councillors and the more 'advanced' Nationalists. Both these strengths were undermined as the gallery dispute progressed. Lane had chosen Edwin Lutyens as the architect and was prepared to pay his fees from his own funds, but part of Sinn Féin's reformist agenda was the requirement that all public contracts be filled by open competition in which Irish candidates had an equal chance.[62] They pursued this policy for appointments within the Corporation and they criticised the unfair hiring practices of major companies commonly regarded as Unionist, such as the Bank of Ireland, the Guinness brewery and the major railways. Lane's appointment of a non-Irish architect, regardless of his international prestige, placed Sinn Féin in a very awkward position, in the party's judgment Lutyens' Irish mother did not qualify him as Irish.[63] It was, technically, a private contract as Lane was paying for the design but the construction and operation of the gallery were to come from public funds. The protracted press and public attention caused councillors to grow nervous and many began avoiding council meetings when votes on the gallery question were scheduled. In these circumstances the defection of the small Sinn Féin group to the other side would bring the whole project to an end. The IPP members in City Hall had envied Sinn Féin's initial success with the gallery but, as the public debate grew in ferocity, more and more IPP gallery supporters joined their colleagues in opposing the scheme. The Unionists had begun by supporting the gallery, flattered by Lane's generous offer and glad of the prestige which the gallery would bring to the city. Ever watchful of public expenditure, however, and sensitive to the opinions of commercial ratepayers, most Unionist councillors switched to the opposition. As a series of special meetings of the council failed to resolve the issue tensions increased and former allies were forced into opposing corners. At a council session in August 1913 Alderman Kelly, long time stalwart of the gallery and the bridge site, advised his colleagues to reject Lane's offer of the pictures. 'The principle of the Art Gallery', he said, 'was that it would be of educational value. Yet the very first thing that was done was to say to the architects "No Irish need apply".' In a final sting he echoed Murphy's attack on Lane, and included Lutyens in his criticism asking 'Was the bridge site to be adopted and a gallery erected just as an advertisement for two men?'[64]

On top of these political developments, the theoretical discussion of the slum crisis, which had been going on for over a generation, was finally overtaken by events. The city contained hundreds of overcrowded tenements inhabited by the poorest families, owned and sublet in a complex web of leases which made enforcement of building regulations impossible. These ancient buildings had been neglected by their owners and occupiers for years, poverty had forced tenants to remove wooden door frames, floor boards and banisters for fuel. On 2 September 1913 two houses on Church Street in the north inner city collapsed from the architectural equivalent of exhaustion. Six people were killed, and more were seriously injured. This human tragedy would eventually produce a major parliamentary report into Dublin's chronic housing problems, but in the immediate aftermath the prospect of spending thousands on an art gallery became untenable. Among the many donations sent to *The Freeman's Journal* Disaster Relief Fund one contributor spoke for many, 'Please find enclosed Postal Order 4s. being a small donation towards the Relief Fund … Let us fervently hope that the civic authorities will turn their attention to the proper housing of the poor instead of wasting time and money on and Art Gallery. "A Ratepayer"'.[65]

On 19 September the bridge gallery project was abandoned. Thirty-two councillors supported a joint Unionist-Sinn Féin motion to reject Hugh Lane's conditions regarding the site and the architect, while 25 continued to support the plan. All the Unionist and Sinn Féin councillors voted against the gallery, two Labour members supported it and two did not.[66] The *Sunday Independent* was jubilant, its coverage of the meeting was headed 'Scotched! End of the Bridge Art Gallery.'[67] As Lucy MacDiarmid observed in her essay on the controversy, the conflict was also about two very different visions of Ireland under Home Rule.[68] Lane, with supporters such as W. B. Yeats, Lady Gregory and George Russell, represented an aesthetic and an elite, both of which Murphy found distasteful and even threatening. Murphy, who saw Ireland's future as a self-governing industrial and commercial entity within the British Empire, represented all that the Celtic Twilight and the Gaelic Revival despised. As with so many of Home Rule's potential futures, neither of the proposed new bridges was ever realised. Unexpectedly, it was the Ha'penny Bridge which, despite losing the 'unmixed admiration' of its early days, regained a place in the affections of Dubliners and visitors alike.

Epilogue

Hugh Lane's untimely death aboard the *Lusitania* in May 1915, as it sank in a German submarine attack, seems out of step with his life. In 1919 William Martin Murphy died of a heart attack, a businessman's death. The two men's legacies could hardly have been more different. Lane tinkered with his will over the years, his unwitnessed (and hence invalid) codicil leaving his collection to Dublin caused years of legal wrangling.[69] Murphy's will, in eight neatly typed pages, naming four executors, and providing against every possible legal eventuality or confusion, is a model of business-like efficiency.[70] Their reputational legacies speak for themselves, with Lane remembered in the Dublin City Gallery and Murphy (perhaps unfairly) remembered only as the 'villain of the Lockout'. Murphy, who berated Lane for attempting to erect a monument to himself during his own lifetime, lies beneath a handsome mortuary chapel in the prestigious O'Connell

Circle in Dublin's Glasnevin Cemetery. But Lane eventually got his Lutyens' memorial. On the upper gallery of St Anne's Church on Dawson Street in Dublin is a simple white marble slab, commissioned from Edwin Lutyens by Sarah Harrison. It commemorates 'Hugh Percy Lane, Knight', who 'dedicated his gifts to the service of art and his fortune to spreading a knowledge of it in his own country. The memory of his self-forgetful life, inspired by a devout and humble faith is the precious possession of his friends.'

Notes

1   Lennox Robinson, *Lady Gregory's journals 1916-1930* (London, 1946), p. 283.

2   John Callcott Horsley, Notes on *portrait of Martin Colnaghi* (1889) (www.nationalgallery.org.uk).

3   This exhibition, at 6 St Stephens Green, was organised by Sarah Purser to show works by living Irish artists. Lane bought a number of paintings by Nathaniel Hone and John Butler Yeats, and went on to patronise many other Irish painters including William Orpen, Augustus John, and Gerald Kelly. Margarita Cappock. 'Lane, Sir Hugh Percy'. James McGuire and James Quinn (eds), *Dictionary of Irish biography* (Cambridge, 2009). (http://dib.cambridge.org/quicksearch.do;jsessionid=4B92D5D43312C47A60CAF957067E9BA8#).

4   Cappock, 'Lane, Sir Hugh Percy', *Dictionary of Irish biography*.

5   Thomas Bodkin, *Hugh Lane and his pictures* (Dublin, 1956), p. 8.

6   Alderman Thomas Kelly, T.D. 'Pallace Row' in *Dublin Historical Record,* IV no.1 (Sept.-Nov. 1941), pp 1-13.

7   Cappock, 'Lane, Sir Hugh Percy', *Dictionary of Irish biography*.

8   Kelly, 'Pallace Row', p. 6.

9   Sheila Carden, *The alderman: Alderman Tom Kelly (1868-1942) and Dublin Corporation* (Dublin, 2007). Kelly was also invited to write for the socialist *Irish Worker* newspaper.

10   Ciarán Wallace, 'Local politics and government in Dublin city and suburbs: 1899-1914' (Unpublished PhD thesis, Trinity College, Dublin, 2010).

11   Carden, *The alderman*, p. 29.

12   *Irish Times*, 19 Aug. 1905, p. 7.

13   Carden, *The alderman*, p. 47.

14   Diarmaid Ferriter, 'Harrison, Sarah Cecilia ('Celia')', *Dictionary of Irish biography*. Louise Ryan, 'The Irish Citizen, 1912-1920', *Saothar* 17 (1992), pp 105-11.

15   Wallace, 'Local politics and government in Dublin city and suburbs'.

16   *Minutes of the Municipal Council of Dublin* (hereafter *Minutes*), 5 June 1907.

17   The motion to sign the lease for 17 Harcourt Street was proposed by a Sinn Féin councillor and seconded by a Unionist. *Minutes*, 6 Sept. 1907, Item 542.

18   *Freeman's Journal*, 21 Jan. 1908, p. 5.

19   *Saturday Review*, 25 Jan. 1908 quoted in *The Irish Times*, 10 Feb. 1908, p. 5.

20   Nannetti was elected as Dublin's first Labour Lord Mayor (1906-1908) but ended his career as an IPP M.P. in Westminster.

21   *Irish Independent*, 21 Jan. 1908, p. 5.

22   *Minutes*, 10 Feb. 1908, Item 137, p 101.

23   *London Gazette*, 30 July 1909, p. 1.

24   There were to be ten councillors and nine art representatives on the new subcommittee. *Minutes*, 5 July 1909, Item 465.

25   *Minutes*, 22 Jan. 1912, Item 87; 12 Feb. 1912, Item 213.

26   *Minutes*, 4 Mar. 1912, Item 253; 12 Aug. 1912, Item 669.

27   Lutyens worked with Lane on the new Johannesburg Gallery and other contracts brought him to Dublin at this time. Mary Lutyens, *Edwin Lutyens, by his daughter* (Reading, 1991), pp 81-2.

28   Maurice Craig, 'Francis Brownrigg' (http://www.dia.ie/architects/view/1286/CRAIG-FRANCISBROWNRIGG). Census of Ireland 1911 (www.nationalarchives.ie).

29   *Freeman's Journal*, 29 Nov. 1912, p. 9.

30   Patrick Maume, 'Murphy, William Martin', *Dictionary of Irish biography*.

31   Frank Callnan, *T. M. Healy*, p. 711 n. 31, as cited in Thomas J. Morrissey, *William Martin Murphy* (Dundalk, 1997), p. 32.

32   *Irish Independent*, 18 Jan. 1913, p. 5.

33   Jean-Baptiste-Camille Corot, (1796-1875), a French artist popular from the mid-19th century, his work was an important influence on the Impressionists. (http://www.nationalgallery.org.uk/artists/jean-baptiste-camille-corot).

34   *Irish Independent*, 18 Jan. 1913, p. 5.

35   James McWalter was a leading light in the United Irish League (UIL), effectively the Irish Parliamentary Party's constituency organisation, and a member of the Dublin Catholic Association. His efforts to help the city's slum-dwellers, to improve health services and to uncover municipal corruption, won him the respect of the trade union movement. James Curry and Francis Devine, '"Merry May Your Xmas Be and 1913 Free From Care": *The Irish Worker Christmas Number, 1912*' (Dublin, 2012).

36   *Irish Independent*, 23 Jan. 1913, p. 5.

37   *Minutes*, 19 Mar. 1913, Item 261.

38   *Dublin Evening Post* as quoted in *The Freeman's Journal*, 20 May 1816, p. 2.

39   *Minutes*, 8 Oct. 1906, Item 550; 7 Nov. 190, Item 596; 17 Dec. 1906, Item 651.

40   *Minutes*, 13 June 1910, Item 439. In 1909 the council had voted to take control of the Metal Bridge when the lease expired, *Minutes*, 11 Oct. 1909, Item 606.

41   J. C. Irwin, chairing a meeting opposed to the Bridge Gallery, *Freeman's Journal*, 1 Apr. 1913, p. 8.

42   *Sunday Independent*, 6 Apr. 1913, p. 1.

43   *Irish Independent*, 10 Apr. 1913, p. 3.

44   *Freeman's Journal*, 19 June 1913, p. 5. The *Irish Independent* carried one of these images on 21 June 1913.

45   *Weekly Irish Times*, 26 June 1913, p. 4.

46   *Irish Times*, 18 July 1913, p. 10. Lutyens, who was involved at this time in designing the new imperial capital of India at New Delhi on a 25 square mile site and at a cost of £12,000,000, must have been bemused by the strength of opposition over Dublin's comparatively tiny project. Lutyens, *Edwin Lutyens*, p. 117.

47   *Irish Independent,* 14 July 1913, p. 7.

48   *Irish Independent*, 22 Jan. 1913, p. 7.

49   *Irish Independent*, 14 July 1913, p. 7. Murphy subsequently withdrew this allegation when the Corporation explained how its funding and expenditure mechanisms worked.

50   *Irish Independent*, 30 June 1913, p. 7.

51   *Irish Independent*, 7 July 1913, p. 5. He also called for a meeting in a letter on 12 July 1913, p. 3.

52   *Irish Times*, 21 July 1913, p. 8.

53   Morrissey, *William Martin Murphy*, p. 38.

54   *Irish Independent*, 18 Mar. 1913, p.6.

55   J. M. Solomon, 'Sir Hugh Lane, a memoir', *Country Life in South Africa*, 1, no. 3 (June 1915), pp 11-12.

56   Anonymous handwritten character study of Hugh Lane (NLI, MS 35,826/1(5)).

57   Morrissey, *William Martin Murphy*, p. 8.

58   This represented almost 8% of his total estate valued at £35,185. It is typical of the man that his accountant was the first of a number of personal and domestic staff to receive bequests, Murphy left him one year's salary after tax. Will of William Martin Murphy (NAI, Will Ref No: 28-7-1919 Pr).

59   Henry Tonks, 'Obituary for Sir Hugh Lane', *A Monthly Chronicle* [n.d.] p. 128 (NLI, MS 35,826/1(5)).

60   *Freeman's Journal*, 1 Apr. 1913, p. 8; 12 Aug. 1913, p. 8; *Irish Independent,* 1 Apr. 1913, p. 5.

61   *Freeman's Journal*, 22 Aug. 1913, p. 8.

62   Lane paid Lutyens in paintings, which the architect's daughter and biographer recalled hanging in the family home. Lane's taste was evidently good as Lutyens' was very particular about his surroundings. Lutyens, *Edwin Lutyens*, p. 159.

63   Murphy also queried Lutyens' nationality, describing him as 'a London architect, with a Dutch name, who, we are told, is of Irish descent on his mother's side.' *Irish Independent*, 23 June 1913, p. 5. As a convert from Catholicism to Evangelical Protestantism Lutyen's mother, Mary Gallwey, may have been unconventional but she was undeniably Irish. Lutyens, *Edwin Lutyens,* pp 14-15.

64   *Irish Independent*, 23 Aug. 1913, p. 6.

65   *Freeman's Journal*, 9 Sept. 1913, p. 9.

66   Labour members J. P. Delany and William Richardson voted against the gallery while their party colleagues William Partridge and Michael Brohoon were in favour. Interestingly, Dr McWalter of the IPP voted for the gallery. *Minutes*, 19 Sept. 1913, Item 723.

67   *Sunday Independent*, 21 Sept. 1913, p. 9.

68   Lucy MacDiarmid, 'Hugh Lane and the decoration of Dublin' in *The Irish art of controversy* (Dublin, 2005) pp 10-34.

69   His papers in the National Library of Ireland contain an earlier handwritten will from 1898, with a codicil in 1905 and a further amendment in pencil in 1909, neither is witnessed (NLI, MS NLI 35,826/1 (5)).

70   Will, William Martin Murphy (NAI, Will Ref No: 28-7-1919 Pr).

13.

A spent force? *An Claidheamh Soluis* and the Gaelic League in Dublin 1893-1913

....

Séamas Ó Maitiú

On 8 November 1913, in a famous article in *An Claidheamh Soluis*, the organ of the Gaelic League, Patrick Pearse announced:

> I have come to the conclusion that the Gaelic League, as the Gaelic League, is a spent force; and I am glad of it. I do not mean that no work remains for the Gaelic League, or that the Gaelic League is no longer equal to [the] work; I mean that the vital work to be done in the new Ireland will be done not so much by the Gaelic League itself as by men and movements that have sprung from the Gaelic League or have received from the Gaelic League a new baptism and a new life of grace.

He went on to announce the coming revolution, claiming that there were many things more horrible than bloodshed. The year 1913 was a critical one for the Gaelic League. In the issue of *An Claidheamh Soluis* on 1 November, a week previous to Pearse's dramatic pronouncement, Eoin MacNeill had penned the article 'The North began' which would lead to the founding of the Irish Volunteers, with momentous consequences.

In June of the same year, Douglas Hyde, the president of the league and one of its founders, made a dramatic appeal to all its members. He sought their support in an internal struggle which was threatening to tear the movement apart. This would be the first public salvo in a struggle which would lead to his resignation two years later. Also in 1913 for the first time since it was established in 1896, the cultural festival, An tOireachtas, the highlight of the language movement's calendar, moved out of Dublin and was held in Galway. The league's annual conference, the Ardfheis, held during Oireachtas week, also moved.

This chapter examines to what extent the Gaelic League appeared a spent force in 1913 in Dublin, the city of its birth, after 20 years of its existence. It looks at its impact, great or small, on the life of the city, its activities, aims and aspirations and the work of its branches. While the class structure of the league, in the city and elsewhere, has been already very masterfully examined,[1] this essay will make some further observations on the topic, and examine the organisation's attitude to the labour movement in the tumultuous year of 1913. The detailed chronicling of the fortunes of the league in the pages of *An Claidheamh Soluis* at the beginning of the 20th century allows the world of the Dublin Irish Irelander of the period to stand revealed. To a greater or lesser degree the philosophy and political history of the league and its impact on national life has been examined by historians and these can be read to contextualise the essentially local study presented here.[2]

A dilemma for the league was that if its aim was the preservation and extension of Irish as a living community language, the centre of its operations should have been in the Gaeltacht, or, as that term was not widely known, the 'Irish speaking districts'; however the nerve-centre of the league's activities remained Dublin. For many, friends and foes alike, the league entered a new phase of its existence in 1913. In that year there were ten active branches of the Gaelic League in Dublin. In the 20 years under consideration, a period of slow progress can be discerned, then one of rapid growth, followed by a period of consolidation and then one of decline.

The origins of *An Claidheamh Soluis* lie in the league's coiste gnótha (executive committee) backing of a newspaper called *Fáinne an Lae* established by a language enthusiast, Bernard Doyle. However a falling-out ensued and the organisation withdrew support from Doyle and founded its own paper the following year. This was *An Claidheamh Soluis*, the first number of which appeared on St Patrick's Day 1899. Eoin MacNeill, a prime mover in the establishment of the league, became the first editor of *An Claidheamh Soluis*. He was succeeded in October 1901 by the writer, Eoghan Ó Neachtain. By the beginning of 1903, the coiste gnótha was growing unhappy with Ó Neachtain's journalistic standards and some of his editorial stances, and he resigned in February of that year. The position was then hotly contested, particularly by two factions emerging in the movement at the time: those largely associated with the coiste gnótha and espousing Connacht Irish on the one hand, and the members of the Keating branch who championed the Munster dialect on the other. Patrick Pearse, promoted by the coiste gnótha, was appointed.

Pearse was a dynamic editor who transformed the paper from a fairly staid, somewhat literary journal to an attractive, campaigning organ which the burgeoning movement needed. Circulation rose modestly from 2,700 copies per week in 1900 to 3,200 by April of the following year: it appears to have peaked at about 3,350 in 1904, when Pearse was forced to cut back the scope of the paper due to lack of funding from the league. By 1912 circulation had fallen to a little over 2,000 copies. From 1903 until he gave up the editorship in 1909 *An Claidheamh Soluis* very much reflected Pearse's view of the movement. As Regina Uí Chollatáin points out in *An Claidheamh Soluis agus Fáinne an Lae, 1899-1932* (2004) 'is é guth an Phiarsaigh féin atá ann agus is é meon an Phiarsaigh a léirítear ann' (it is Pearse's voice that is found in it and it is Pearse's thinking that is shown). After he established St Enda's School in 1909, Pearse resigned the editorship due to lack of time. Seán Mac Giollarnáith was then appointed editor, the last in the period under review, and remained in the post until 1917. Although not appointed editor, but manager, The O'Rahilly (Mícheál Seosamh Ó Rathaile) was instrumental in creating a new-look illustrated *An Claidheamh Soluis* from September 1913.

[AN CLAIDHEAMH SOLUIS.]
aᵹus ꝼáinne an Lae.

Leaḃaꝛ XV.   Uiṁiꝛ 26.   baile áṫa cliaṫ, meaḋón ꝼóᵹṁaiꝛ 6, 1913.   Pinginn.
Vol. XV.   No. 26   [*Registered as a Newspaper.*]   DUBLIN, SEPTEMBER 6, 1913.   ONE PENNY.

1. Masthead of *An Claidheamh Soluis.*
DCLA

In 1913, the 'ten flourishing branches' reported by *An Claidheamh Soluis* were four less than documented in 1910. A detailed account of this year informs us as to how the league was organised on the ground in the years 1910-13. This description is based on a plan published in *An Claidheamh Soluis* (17 Sept. 1910) of the districts allotted to them for the language collection of September 1910. A number of the large city branches were not local as such, but drew their membership from many parts of the city and suburbs.

The Ardchraobh (central branch), Craobh an Chéitinnigh and MacHale branches shared the north inner city area centred around Rutland Square where they had their headquarters. The Glasnevin branch took in the Glasnevin and Phibsborough areas. The Fr Anderson branch covered the Westland Row area, and was bound on its west by the Cúig Cúigí branch which covered the St Stephen's Green area. Moving further west, the Old City branch covered the area between St Stephen's Green and the old medieval city around Christ Church Cathedral. The impoverished Liberties area was served by the Cleaver branch. The Dolphin's Barn branch took in that area and much of the adjacent South Circular Road. The St Kevin's branch covered the Whitefriars' Street and Aungier Street area; its southern suburban neighbourhood was covered by the Rathmines and Mount Argus branches.

Foundation and growth of the league in Dublin

This was the situation on the ground at the close of the period under review. However, the Gaelic League or Conradh na Gaeilge, had been founded some 20 years previously with a meeting of ten men called by Eoin MacNeill and held at 9 Lower Sackville (O'Connell) Street, Dublin, on 31 July 1893. Early meetings of the league were held in the rooms of the National Literary Society at 4 College Green, and in the Café Royal in Sackville Place. The less militant Society for the Preservation of the Irish Language, founded in 1876, continued to meet in the city under the aristocratic leadership of The O'Conor Don.[3]

The league was slow to grow at first but the quickening of Nationalist enthusiasm brought about by the centenary commemoration of the 1798 rebellion and the outbreak of the Boer War in 1899 changed this. The ready-made vehicle of the league provided common ground for an expression of Irish Nationalism by all, free from the venalities of inter-party strife common at the time. Idealistic crusades thrive on opposition. When, also in 1899, John Pentland Mahaffy, provost of Trinity College, Dublin, proposed that Irish be removed from the Intermediate School syllabus, the campaign waged against this by the league garnered it much publicity and wide support.

'As its title implies, the Gaelic League will not be a one-branch society', so wrote MacNeill within a few weeks of its foundation, and within the first year there were branches in Cork, Galway, Derry and New Ross.[4] By 1899 the league had an estimated 80 branches nationwide. It then took off, and by 1902 this number had quadrupled. It continued to grow from then until 1908 but at a much reduced rate and from then on contracted for the rest of the period under consideration.[5]

For a number of years only the parent body existed in the city of Dublin (then the area largely between the canals). An upsurge in the fortunes of the league at the turn of the new century saw the establishment of the first Dublin city branch. In April 1899, *An Claidheamh Soluis* reported:

> We hail the establishment of the first Dublin city branch (other than the parent body) as a further proof of the fact that the youth of the city is rallying to the language. Already branch after branch has been formed in Belfast, until there are now in the northern capital seven young, strong vigorous camps of missionaries.[6]

The Dublin branch was formed by members of the literary society of the staff of the Dublin Telegraph Office based in the G.P.O. Written Irish was then so unfamiliar, the inaugural notice caused some confusion:

The new Dublin branch has already attracted attention. A notice of the first meeting was posted up in Irish in the GPO and several persons thought the writing was in Greek. The infant branch is named after Óisín, and meets at 8 o'clock on Saturdays at the Gaelic League Rooms. We hope to see the branch a brigade ready for active service in 'camp, garrison, or guardhouse'.[7]

The militant language was to become routine in the league and distinguished it from Irish language societies which went before it.

The Óisín branch was not quite the first branch in the greater Dublin area. About three months before, at the beginning of 1899, branches had been formed at Blackrock and 'Dunleary' (then officially called Kingstown), two Dublin townships. A rapid expansion followed in the city, townships and county with new branches reported in Rathmines and The Naul in October 1899. These were followed by two more in November, the O'Growney branch in Eustace Street, formed within the Dublin Vintners' Assistants' Association which had been established in 1896, and one in Donnybrook. In December the St Brendan branch was reported as having been set up in Johnson's Court, off Grafton Street.

Individual branches experienced steady growth in membership. The Dublin central branch, An Ardchraobh, had 444 members in the summer of 1899. In the seven months from November 1898 to June 1899, 68 new members joined. A house to house canvas to support Irish had been carried out on a tentative scale with good results. By February 1900 the league had 130 branches nationwide.[8] The upsurge of 1899 was a prelude compared to 1900. In January 1901, *An Claidheamh Soluis* reported that during the previous twelve months the movement had spread like wildfire (see Table 1), with thousands joining and scores of new branches.[9]

Table 1. Dublin branches of the Gaelic League formed in 1900

(**Source:** *An Claidheamh Soluis*)

Feb.	Post Office Officials; Talbot St (Fr O'Leary branch)
Mar.	St Kevin's Clanbrassil Street
	Drumcondra
	John Street (Cleaver branch)
June	Phibsborough (Brian Bóroimhe branch)
	Smithfield (St Columba's)

	York Street (Michael Dwyer branch)
Sept.	Brunswick Street (St Andrew's)
Nov.	Inchicore
	Milltown/Donnybrook
Dec.	Dundrum
	Sandymount
	Howth
	Clontarf
	St Brendan's (Johnston's Court)

Further branches established in 1901 were in Rathfarnham and Terenure [Macartan branch].

It was in 1900 that the slogan 'Sinn Féin, Sinn Féin amháin' was adopted as the motto of the organisation and was included in the letter heading of the correspondence of the Ardchraobh (five years before the founding of the political party of that name).[10] Wildly divergent figures are given about the number of branches of the league in existence in Dublin at the height of its popularity about 1903, with Seán T. Ó Ceallaigh claiming up to 100, almost certainly an exaggeration.[11] In that year 54 branches are listed in *An Claidheamh Soluis* in the city and suburbs. This seems to be the high water mark.

What kind of people were flocking to the movement in such numbers? Timothy MacMahon has identified a high representation of the skilled artisan and lower middle class, such as clerks, minor civil servants, teachers etc., in the movement (over 50%), followed by categories covering professionals, clergy, employers and managers. Unskilled and semi-skilled workers were under-represented, indeed MacMahon states that, with a few exceptions, 'they simply did not join the league'.[12]

One exception was Seán O'Casey. He was a member of the Lámh Dhearg branch of the league in Drumcondra in the early 20th century, while working as a bricklayer's assistant in the Great Northern Railway.[13] Feeling something of an outsider, O'Casey writes of the 'respectable, white-collared, trim-suited Gaelic Leaguers, snug in their selected branches, living rosily in Whitehall, Drumcondra, Rathgar, Donnybrook, and all the other nicer habitations of the city.'[14]

However, like the Post Office Officials' branch, many branches of the league were established on vocational lines. As we have seen, a branch for grocers' and vintners' assistants was formed in 1899;[15] a drapers' assistants branch, Craobh na nÉadaitheóirí, followed. In October 1905 it was reported that the Irish Typographical Union had formed itself into a branch when Pearse spoke at it and this is most likely the Clódóirí branch mentioned in later reports.[16]

While these could be regarded as skilled and craft workers, there is some evidence that unskilled workers and labourers were attracted to the league. The York Street Workingmen's Club asked that Irish speakers be sent to a public meeting they were organising with the intention of starting Irish classes. Dr Hyde promised to attend. Also a branch was formed by the Inchicore Workingmen's Club. The housepainters on the border between skilled and unskilled established a branch in their hall in Aungier Street in 1901.

Many other branches were established in working class areas, such as Francis Street, Clanbrassil Street and in the St Laurence O'Toole premises in the North Dock Ward. This working-class presence, gives the impression that O'Casey, speaking of his 'selected' branches, was himself somewhat selective.

The activist, Agnes O'Farrelly, writing in *An Claidheamh Soluis* saw 'signs and portents' of the imminent Gaelicisation of the city everywhere from the fashionable Grafton Street where she heard university students discussing the finer point of Irish grammar to the mean streets of the slum areas of the north side. It was among the poor that she saw the Gaelic future of the city:

> But it is in the smaller streets, especially on the north side, in the less pretentious quarters teeming with young life, that one comes across the most inspiriting signs of the movement. Most inspiriting and most inspiring; for a movement of this kind which does not touch the mass of the people cannot appeal to us any more than a winter exotic, born only to live under abnormal conditions here in the bye-ways and side streets, where the children laugh and rollick about all day long, and the mothers, in the intervals of washing and house-work run out to the neighbouring threshold to snatch a refreshing gossip; here it is you see the very pulse of the movement. The children of a school-going age keep up a desultory conversation in broken Irish, or gather in groups to help others in the battle with O'Growney.[17]

She goes on to recount a conversation she conducted in simple Irish in the gloom and poverty with 'the prophet of the newer Dublin' in the form of a 'little bare-footed gossoon.'

Apart from vocational groups a number of educational bodies and voluntary groups formed branches. In June 1900 a meeting was held in John Street school to establish a new branch, to be known as the Cleaver branch (after Eusebius Cleaver, an early benefactor of the movement) with an active priest in the movement, Fr Anderson, presiding. Up to 80 children were enrolled in this branch which specialised in activity for children.

The Baggot Street Catholic Training College for Female Teachers began an Irish class in September 1900. In 1905 a Gaelic Society was active in the Metropolitan School of Art. Three years later a Gaelic Society was established in Trinity College. At its inaugural meeting J. P. Mahaffy, a bête noir of the language activists, spoke, and it was claimed that he had now changed his mind about Irish.[18]

The craze was not confined to educational groups. The Oliver Bond '98 Club began Irish language classes in Rutland Square, which were open to the public, as did St Teresa's Total Abstinence Society. Other groups formed themselves into branches or held classes. In July the Dublin Press Club reported in its half-yearly report that its 'Irish section' held Irish entertainments and that classes were being taught by Tadgh O'Donoghue, and that Willy Rooney and other members of the Celtic Literary Society were helping.[19]

A feature of the branches was the involvement of the Catholic clergy in their establishment and administration, as in the case of the Cleaver branch above. A local priest often presided at the branches, especially at their inaugural meetings. While they may have been active in the founding of the branches many more may have been invited to preside as a matter of courtesy. In October 1900, a crowded meeting of grocers' and vintners' assistants, already mentioned, met in Eustace Street to form what would be called the O'Growney branch, with a Fr Byrne presiding. At the same time a branch was formed in St Andrew's parish with a Fr McEnereney presiding. The following year the Rev. P. Gosson P.P. presided at a meeting to establish a branch in Rathfarnham and a local priest was presiding at the committee meetings of the Howth branch.[20]

A key element in the philosophy of the league was that it be non-sectarian. League literature constantly highlighted this. *An Claidheamh Soluis* pointed out that leaguers could be Orangemen or 'Mohomadans' if they wished. However, it was the association of the Catholic clergy with the league, perhaps, which lead some language enthusiasts in the city to form a branch which would have a Protestant complexion.[21] This was Craobh na gCúig Cúigí (Five Provinces branch, re-instating the ancient province of Meath) – sometimes humorously called Craobh na gCúig Phrotastúnach

(The branch of the Five Protestants). It met at 5 St Stephen's Green and the literary figure, T. W. Rolleston, and Douglas Hyde acted as president of the branch at various times; other prominent members included Seán O'Casey and Ernest Blythe.[22] When the Cúig Cúigí was labeled a 'Protestant branch' Rolleston was moved to respond that this was a misunderstanding and that it was not their intention to 'ring fence' themselves from other Gaelic Leaguers.[23]

The Ardchraobh itself took up the question of the promotion of the language among Protestants and in May 1907 a meeting of Protestant members of that branch was held to consider how to 'bring the principles of the league prominently under the Protestants and inducing them to take their place in the movement.'[24] The meeting also resolved to set up a group to pressurise St Patrick's Cathedral to have a monthly service in Irish there and looked to holding lectures in the parochial halls in the city and to investigate the status of Irish in Protestant schools. The group gave itself the unwieldy title The Committee of Gaelic Leaguers for Propagation of Gaelic League Principles among Protestants.[25] O'Casey and Blythe were regarded as radical members of the Cúig Cúigí branch. When O'Casey was hauled before its committee to answer for behaviour not officially approved, he deliberately turned up in a muffler, a working-class item of clothing, to annoy them.[26]

The question of mixed sex branches and language classes was to cause controversy in Portarlington in 1905, but as early as 1899 the Blackrock branch started separate classes for ladies and about 60 attended. In Kingstown a further step was taken with the establishment of a ladies' branch, called the Fionnghuala Branch.

In 1901 a proposal was made that a Dublin district committee of the league be established. This idea was particularly espoused by the Keating branch (a particularly energetic branch discussed in more detail below). This was acted on, and the first meeting of the Dublin committee, known as Coiste Chathair Bhaile Átha Cliath, met on 12 October 1901. It subsequently held monthly meetings on Saturdays. It was also reported that district committees were being established in Cork and Wexford.[27]

Having established the local committees, the Keating branch pressed for more power to be granted to them over the activities of the branches. In a motion they proposed for the Ardfheis of 1902 they advocated, under the chairmanship of W. R. Colbert, a new constitution for the league giving 'full power' to the local committees over the branches and a need to put the committees on a surer footing.[28] It was also hoped that the coiste cathrach would attempt to co-ordinate the events taking place in an increasing Irish-Ireland calendar in the city.[29] By the end of 1903 a sub-committee was also set up to cover branches in the south Dublin area, Rathmines, Terenure, Dundrum and Milltown.[30]

On a visit to Dublin in May 1903, William Bulfin, a keen Irish Irelander based in Argentina, attempted to portray the bustle of the language movement at its height in the city for the readers of the *Southern Cross* newspaper. He paid a visit to the league's headquarters in Upper O'Connell Street and was much impressed: 'it is a house which takes Irish Ireland for granted. The large gilt letters on the façade are the handsomest in all Dublin of their kind. They are Irish. They stand out bravely on the red brick wall, and you can see them from the General Post Office and the Rotunda – "Conradh na Gaeilge"'.[31]

Coming up to St Patrick's week of that year, the Sackville (O'Connell) Street nerve centre had seen a fever of activity. The mood was captured in the section in *An Claidheamh Soluis* headed 'Gleo na gCath' which could be translated as 'The Heat of Battle'.

> Life in Irish Dublin is heartening just now. Work is in the air. Committees are constantly sitting - some at the Central Offices, some at the Keating branch rooms, some at the Grocers' Assistants Hall, some at the Trades Hall. Messengers are passing backward and forward between the various Committee Rooms and the newspaper offices. Deputations are tramping the streets on their rounds to the leading traders. The League Offices at O'Connell Street present the appearance of some great national bureau. Committees are meeting upstairs and downstairs. Bales of literature – collection sheets, collecting cards, posters, window cards, and what not - are arriving hourly from the printers. Decoration and Tableaux Sub-Committees are holding furtive meetings on the staircases and in back kitchens. Where Leaguer meets Leaguer nothing is talked about but the coming Demonstration and the National Holiday. In tramcars and tearooms – we cannot speak for public houses – these are also the prevailing topics of conversation.[32]

By 1908 the league had outgrown its headquarters at 24 Upper Sackville Street and moved to 25 Rutland Square. Activity transferred included meetings of the various committees and of the Ardchraobh and classes of the league's advanced language school, Cóláiste Laighean. The league's publishing activity also moved. The new premises had a hall with a capacity of 400 and it accommodated a library built up around a nucleus of books presented by R. J. Mulrenin, a prominent supporter.[33] By 1908 a 'young Gaelic League' had been established and many Dublin branches, including the Ardchraobh and St Kevin's, had it associated with them under the name Éire Óg Clubs. The Ardchraobh youth group had up to 100 children learning the language. By 1912 the youth organisation had its own badge.

'The Gael in the Pale': branch activities

What did the branches of the Gaelic League in Dublin actually do? The activities of the branches mainly consisted of language classes; secondary to this was the singing of Irish songs and dancing. Lectures on aspects of the language, Irish history and culture were also a feature, especially of the large centre-city Dublin branches. So rapidly did the league expand in the city that the lack of competent teachers of Irish became a problem as early as 1900. *An Claidheamh Soluis* complained that not a single branch around Dublin was properly equipped to teach the language for lack of suitable teachers.[34] The short-lived Terenure branch put out an appeal for co-operation of native speakers in the area and by the end of 1900 a panel of teachers for the city and suburbs was being created.

By May 1904 the Céitinnigh were proudly proclaiming themselves a fully Irish-speaking branch. Results elsewhere were disappointing. Also in 1904, *An Claidheamh Soluis* pointed out that after years of the branches teaching the language to little effect, some plan was needed. It also commented that 'the Craobh whose members, after two or three years work, are still mere Béarloirí (English speakers) is practically a dead limb of the organization.' The Rathmines Branch did attempt to bring science into its language teaching by adopting the Gouin system, popular at the time.

A number of newly-invented social occasions were promoted in the branches. Céilithe, figure dances on the Scottish model, were popular, as were scoraíochtaí, social evenings including a varied musical programme. Outdoor events included feiseanna, competitive events, and aeríochtaí, concerts in the open air. The scoraíocht of the Ardchraobh held in December 1901 in the Gresham Hotel was so popular that it spilled out into the garden. The following year the same branch held its first annual aeríocht in the Hollow in the Phoenix Park. It was claimed that tens of thousands attended.[35]

The first suburban feis was held in Dalkey in 1902 and was limited to participants from Dalkey, Sandymount, Blackrock, Kingstown, Dalkey, Bray, Cabinteely, Milltown and Dundrum.[36] Outdoor entertainment became so popular that *An Claidheamh Soluis* published a template in plan form for a model aeríocht.[37] Two further developments were the setting up of a Gaelic orchestra and an Irish-Ireland artistes bureau to provide singers and other performers for events, especially in country areas.[38] Many prominent personalities of the day lectured to the branches of the league, including Hyde, Eoin MacNeill, Patrick Pearse and W. B. Yeats. In October 1900 Yeats presided at a scoraíocht of the Ardchraobh and delivered a speech. In February 1902 Eoin MacNeill gave a lecture to the St Kevin's branch on, tellingly, 'How to be Irish'.[39]

The Céitinnigh and Ardchraobh were particularly active in organising lectures. Indeed so extensive was the series of lectures held at the Ardchraobh that it was compared to a university. In 1907 and 1908, Cathal Brugha and Piaras Béaslaí spoke at these branches. In November 1910, Éamon de Valera spoke to the Ardchraobh on the study of early Irish history. However, the Blackrock branch broke new ground when its vice-president, Dr Heron, gave what was heralded as the first ever lecture in Irish on chemistry, proving that, despite its critics, Irish was suitable for science.[40]

Branches organised trips to local beauty spots and to 'the Irish-speaking areas'. By 1906, the *Irish Independent*, under the heading 'The Gael in the Pale', reported that it may not have been necessary to go to the Gaeltacht shortly as an Irish speaking club was to set up in Dublin.[41] Irish-speaking cycling clubs were also established. St Brendan's branch held its third annual 'excursion crusade' on Sunday 10 June 1900. Beginning in Johnson's Court it went through Grafton Street, College Green, Westmoreland Street, Sackville (O'Connell) Street etc. and then to Bray with its members singing songs and only speaking Irish.[42] The missionary-type zeal extended to the members of the Michael Dwyer branch based in nearby York Street who made a point of speaking Irish on the city pavements.

A particular target of the league was the Post Office. The campaign to get it to accept letters and parcels addressed in Irish culminated in thousands of letters so addressed flooding the system, and on one day in March 1905 150 league supporters descended on the G.P.O. bearing parcels addressed in Irish.[43]

The wearing of so-called 'Irish dress' was promoted by some, but not without a degree of self-consciousness. In 1906 female members of the Ardchraobh founded Cumann na gClóca (sic) to encourage the wearing of what they called cloaks of Irish character and material, 'thus making the test of individual courage somewhat less severe than it might be if confined to a few.'[44] The women of the Rathmines branch had cut a dash three years previously at the great language demonstration, where 'the red Connemara cloaks of the cailíní were most conspicuous.'[45]

The purported dress of the Gael was receiving attention again in the 1911-12 period. An exhibition of Irish dress led to the founding of another association for reforming Irish dress. As Dublin's Irish week of 1912 approached, *An Claidheamh Soluis* reported that every year more and more kilts were being worn in Dublin and that 'we are beginning to cease to stare at one in the street.' Irish Irelanders also distinguished themselves by the sporting of specially designed Gaelic League caps and badges.[46]

Gaelicising the calendar

The Irish Ireland calendar in the capital was punctuated by a series of festivals and gatherings. The year began with the annual social event organised by the Ardchraobh. By 1910 this was described as 'a representative gathering or nearly so of the Gaelic League as the reception of delegates during Oireachtas week.[47] The Oireachtas was the annual cultural festival, discussed below.

When the league was established, St Patrick's Day was seen as an excuse for indulgence in alcohol unworthy of the dignity of a national holiday. The league with the support of the clergy decided to do something about this. In 1902 the league began to press for the day to be declared 'a national holiday in fact as well as in name'. In particular it pressed for the voluntary closing of public houses on the day. A National Holiday Committee was set up and in 1902 it was stated that a queue of publicans waited outside the league offices for specially printed window cards stating that they were observing the day by a closure. By 1902 the week around St Patrick's Day was a period of intense activity and designated 'Seachtain na Gaeilge'.

However ambitions for the national day ran much higher than just this. Sermons were given in Irish - from one in 1903 to six in 1908, including one in a Protestant church. Also St Kevin's Church of Ireland church on the south side of the city had an annual service in Irish, with, in 1907, P. Ó Connail (Conal Cearnach) presiding.[48] By 1912, Holy Communion in Irish was being held in St Patrick's Cathedral on St Patrick's Day with an afternoon service in Irish in St Ann's, Dawson Street.[49]

The greatest event associated with St Patrick's Day was the large language demonstration through the streets of the city, that of 1903 being probably the greatest and best-remembered, featuring for the first time a display of Irish industries. On Sunday of St Patrick's week that year, up to 40,000 people marched through the city streets, taking two hours to pass the O'Connell Monument, to a meeting in the Mansion House, presided over by the Lord Mayor.[50] For a number of years *An Claidheamh Soluis* published a map of the route of the demonstration, with the assembly point of the different sections. The day ended up with a rally held in various public spaces. In 1905 the demonstration finished up in Smithfield, where the Roman Catholic archbishop of Dublin, William Walsh, together with Hyde, graced the platform. An important feature of the demonstration was the collection of money by street collectors for the league in what became known as 'Ciste na Teanga'. One-third of the money collected was kept at local level and the rest augmented central funds. In 1907, the demonstration and collection in Dublin was, for unspecified 'local' reasons, moved from St Patrick's week to June, while they continued to be held in March elsewhere in the country.[51]

In 1896 it was decided to establish an annual festival at which prizes would be awarded 'for readings, recitations, songs and dramatic sketches in Irish.' The inspiration for this was the highly successful annual Eisteddfod in Wales. To this end a meeting was held in the Café Royal on 25 August 1896 and a committee formed to organise the festival for the coming year.[52] The first Oireachtas was held in the Round Room of the Rotunda on 17 May 1897 and would be held in Dublin annually until it moved to Galway in 1913. A highlight was the Oireachtas of 1903. The Thursday night of the festival was described by *An Claidheamh Soluis* as 'the greatest night in the history of the League.' When An Craoibhín (Hyde) appeared on the stage the air was said to be electric and that he was 'nearly unmanned by the reception'.[53] The camaraderie of all those striving for a common goal was celebrated:

> As a common centre for all those interested in the language movement, the festival was also a genuine success. The Gresham Hotel never contained a more varied assembly than that at the reception. People from every part of Ireland - from Aran to Dublin and from Cork to Donegal - as well as visitors from England, from Wales, and from the Highlands were present. They were well-to-do (we do not know of one rich Gaelic Leaguer) and poor, cleric and lay, learned and unlearned, young and old, Protestant and Catholic, but they all fraternized - the tie of a great hope and a great struggle binding them together.[54]

The Oireachtas received much official backing: William Walsh, Roman Catholic archbishop of Dublin was an early subscriber and in 1907 the viceroy, the Highland Scot, the Earl of Aberdeen, and Lady Aberdeen attended.[55]

Apart from the competitions in traditional singing and dancing, more advanced attempts were made to develop the music tradition: in 1902 an Oireachtas choir was established, and in 1909 an opera *Éan an Cheoil Bhinn* was written by Robert O'Dwyer and performed during the festival.[56] This was followed, in 1910, by a second opera, *Eithne*, with music by Ó Duibhir and libretto by Fr Tomás Ó Ceallaigh. It was performed on the stage of the Gaiety Theatre and played to 'enthusiastic if not large audiences.'[57]

This was not the first appearance of the Irish language on the stage. What is regarded as the first proper drama in Irish *Casadh an tSúgáin* by An Craoibhín was held in the Gaiety Theatre on 21 October 1901. This was followed the following year by *An Tobar Draíochta* by an tAthair Peadar in the Rotunda.

Exhibitions of the industries and art of the Irish-speaking areas became an annual feature at the festival. During the Oireachtas of 1900 the first representative meeting, or

Ardfheis, as it came to be known, of the league's then 120 branches was held. By 1907, the Ardfheis was being proclaimed as the 'parliament of Irish-Ireland', the year when it first conducted its business in Irish only. This was seen as 'a crushing answer to the pessimists about the language.'[58]

By 1899 the Leinster Feis, succeeded by Feis Átha Cliath, was under way. This was seen as an attempt, by way of competition, of raising the standard among the Dublin branch members of their skills in the spoken language and traditional arts. Some saw a feis at this time for 'Anglicised Leinster' as being too early. The feis was run on efficient lines by its enthusiatistic secretary, Éibhlín Nic Niocaill.[59] In 1910, what was described as a 'Gaelic League athletic carnival', including an Irish eight-mile marathon, was held in mid-summer. This was such a success that it was held annually and became known as 'Súgradh Gael'.[60]

Traditional practices were re-introduced to the city area. The lighting of bonfires on St John's Eve was revived by the league in 1903; bonfires blazed at Ticknock and other high points around the city, and ten years later a storytelling conference was held in the league's library in Rutland Square.[61]

The movement developed a minor cult of martyrs from its ranks - those who died young, often regarded as having given their lives by overwork for the cause. The earliest in 1901 was that of Willie Rooney, a highly influential writer and activist, followed by that of Fr O'Growney two years later. Two heavy blows followed in 1908 and 1909 respectively, the death of the writer, Mícheál Breatnach of TB, and of the young enthusiast, Éibhlín Nic Niocaill, by drowning. Nic Niocaill had taught at Craobh na gCúig Cúigí and had been secretary of Coiste Chathair Átha Cliath. Romantically associated with Patrick Pearse on slender evidence, she drowned off the Great Blasket on a summer visit there attempting to save the life of the son of the writer Tomás Ó Criomhthain.

Re-Gaelicising the landscape

In 1912, *An Claidheamh Soluis* reviewed P. W. Joyce's local history work, *The neighbourhood of Dublin*. The anonymous reviewer expressed the wish that the task that Joyce had done in recovering the very much anglicised history of the area would be done also for Gaelic Dublin.[62] This desire to re-Gaelicise the landscape was core to the league's activities. When the Rathmines branch held a band and choir recital in Kenilworth Square they renamed the park 'Cluain na nGael'. Their musical endeavours were intended to replace military recitals in the park and the branch sought the help of other branches to stamp out military fixtures of the same kind held in south Dublin. The Dún Laoghaire branch did not need much persuasion; in 1902 it had adopted unanimously the motion 'that military band parades and coon entertainments' were directly opposed to the spirit of the Gaelic League.[63] This rebranding also applied to people. The task of discovering the authentic Irish version of their surnames was facilitated by the publication of the book *Sloinnte Gaedheal is Gall* by Patrick Woulfe in 1907.[64]

A key strategy in the Gaelicisation of the city was the campaign for the erection of Irish language street names. In 1901, Dublin Corporation passed a resolution to the effect that where nameplates were being renewed they would be bilingual.[65] The very active and early Blackrock branch seems to have led the way for the provision of Irish language road name plates. As early as 1899 the branch asked the Blackrock township to place Irish nameplates above the English ones on Cross Road at the junctions of Merrion Avenue and Temple Road, this was reported as having been done and a later one was erected at Cross Avenue.[66] In May 1901, the Dalkey branch put up the name of the railway station there in Irish with the permission of the Dublin, Wicklow and Wexford Railway.[67] Not all approved of these new developments. *The Daily Express* complained that a sign pointing to Baile Átha Cliath, Dún Laoghaire and Carraigdubh (sic) was confusing.[68]

Increasing pressure was put on Dublin Corporation to take action on street names, and in August 1901, it was reported that at last 'on a corner house in that centre of fashion and West Britonism, Grafton Street, appears the inscription Sráid Énrí with the English name, Harry Street, underneath. These Irish name-plates will help to remind us that the capital of Ireland is not in what London theatrical managers call the provinces.'[69] Despite pledges from the Corporation that all nameplates replaced would be bilingual, by the end of 1904 the league was unhappy with progress made. It claimed that 'obscure places' were being given bilingual plates but that the main ones were staying in English only and so accused the paving committee, which was in charge of nameplates, of going back on its pledges.[70] By 1909, substantial progress had been made. In that year Donnchadh Ua Dubhghaill, a city councillor, in a letter in *An Claidheamh Soluis* listed the names of streets on which bilingual signs had been erected, and, more tellingly, the streets not yet done, and urged readers to use the Irish version.[71]

The City Council was praised for steps taken for the Gaelicisation of its internal structure. In 1899, it was reported that it was to have an Irish-language seal engraved - notwithstanding objections from certain Nationalist members. It was claimed that other bodies had already done this.[72] Later it directed that its various offices have their names in Irish and that the names of all members of the Corporation listed in its bound records be in Irish; gummed slips were to be provided to clerks who could not master the Gaelic script.[73] In 1906 a resolution was passed by the Corporation by 17 votes to four to have names in Irish on all rolling stock. An amendment to have them in both languages was rejected.[74]

Support for the language became a plank in the platform of candidates for the city council. In January 1903, Daithí Ua Cuain of Drumcondra placed a notice in *An Claidheamh Soluis* stating that the language revival was part of his platform. However by 1905 such support was sought on a more organised basis. The league lobbied candidates in elections for the Corporation asking them to fill in questionnaires as to where they stood on the language issue and their replies were published, and in 1908 candidates were asked if they were members of the league and if so to name the branch.[75]

City councillors were active in the campaign to have their names in Irish on their horse-drawn vehicles. Councillor Patrick O'Carroll of Blacklion House, Inchicore and Alderman Walter Cole were fined for doing so, and Alderman Cole had his apples and onions seized.[76] During the controversy over compulsory or 'essential' Irish in the National University in 1909 the Corporation was urged to pass a scholarship rate only in the case of Irish being compulsory for the university.[77]

An indication of how the language movement had impacted on Dublin Corporation is seen in the fact that out of the 11 people presented with the Freedom of the City between 1900 and 1920, three were awarded to those associated with the language revival movement: these were Douglas Hyde in 1906, Kuno Meyer, the Celtic scholar, and the writer, Peadar Ó Laoghaire in 1912.[78]

Despite the early agreement over nameplates in Blackrock, matters in general were not so happy with the suburban townships, seen as less favourable to the national outlook than the Corporation. The league saw ground for advance in two important facilities under the control of the townships, these were public libraries and technical schools. The Rathmines branch wrote to the local township board requesting that the league's publications be stocked in the local library, and in Dún Laoghaire. The case of a youth, Patrick Grant, who was ordered out of the public library for signing his name in Irish, was highlighted.[79] In Rathmines the township board was accused of rejecting Irish in its commercial school. A more serious allegation was made against the Pembroke council. In what the league termed 'the Pembroke scandal' a teacher was allegedly dismissed for being a Gaelic leaguer and a Nationalist.[80]

As already pointed out, a great dilemma for the league was that, while it had its origins in middle-class Dublin, the heartland of the spoken living language was in the rural far west; while it wished for the Gaelicisation of the city it would be a defeat if the

Gaeltacht died. It never really managed to resolve this dilemma. Hyde articulated this at the Ardfheis of 1902 when he stated all major movements in Ireland came from the people up, but that the Gaelic League was coming from the 'daoine barántúla' (people of worth) in Dublin; to succeed it must root itself in every parish in Ireland.[81] But as the capital of Ireland, Dublin was important for the movement. Its status as a deposed capital and a perceived provincial city of the United Kingdom rankled with the league. This view was well-expressed by Hyde at the great language demonstration of 1909, when, looking at the vast multitude gathered from the Parnell Monument (then under construction) in Sackville Street and stretching down to O'Connell Bridge, he depicted the street as 'a street that was as fine as could be found in any capital in Europe' and added 'may this beautiful city never be the capital of an English suburb.'

It was clearly seen, especially by the visionary founders of the movement, that a barrier to the progress of the language revival in the city was the language's association with rural poverty and backwardness. As Eoin MacNeill stated at a meeting of the Ardchraobh in 1899 'the question of the national language was the greatest national question at present. Yet the language movement was but a ripple on the stream of public life in Dublin. But Dublin should be shaken up. The crust of snobbery and conventionality should be broken.' He went on to say that could be done by the zeal and constant individual effort by leaguers.[82] This radical anti-snobbery, anti-convention note should have made it perhaps fertile ground for left-wingers, but when 'left wing' was used it usually referred to radical Nationalists.

The league and the workers

In the final year under consideration, 1913, Dublin was torn apart by class warfare. The revival movement was not unaffected by these great events, and did not hesitate to comment on them. Controversy over James Larkin and the language movement had surfaced in 1911, the year in which Larkin, with the assistance of Mícheál Ó Maoláin, filled out his census form in Irish.[83] Larkin attended the great language demonstration that year with a group of his followers and was allowed to speak to the assembly. Fr Myles Ronan, an historian and priest attached to the Pro-Cathedral, took grave exception to this. In a letter to the *Irish Independent*, he demanded to know who had invited 'Larkin's crowd' to the event and on whose authority had he been allowed to speak.

In the subsequent war of words it was claimed that Larkin had attacked the Oireachtas exhibition and members of the Gaelic League. The fact that Sinn Féin members with placards had been allowed to attend the meeting was also criticised.

Éamonn Ceannt supported Larkin, claiming that he was learning Irish. Indeed Larkin's paper, *The Irish Worker,* largely supported the language and regularly carried articles in Irish, news of league events and Irish cultural activities. However it did have reservations. It expressed fears of xenophobia and the denigration of other cultures and that it might make Irish youth too 'self-centred'. It pointed out that the enemy of an Irish revival was the crushing forces of capitalism, stating that 'you cannot learn starving men Gaelic' (sic).[84]

2. Coal delivery with police escort, *An Claidheamh Soluis,* 1 Nov. 1913.
DCLA

In one letter to *An Claidheamh Soluis* it was claimed that the coiste gnótha of the league had been taken over by 'socialists, anti-clericals, anti-teachers, extreme Sinn Féiners, and Provincialists, who for very different reasons, at the moment have joined together and secured control of the last Ardfheis.'[85] Concern over a Larkinite faction in the league reached to the very top. J. E. and G . W. Dunleavy have pointed out that the presence of such a group in the organisation was anathema to Douglas Hyde.[86]

The mainstream labour movement in the city co-operated with the league in promoting the language. In the same year as the controversy over Larkin and the language demonstration, a meeting of the Joint Dublin Trades Council and the coiste ceantair of the league met to look into the question of Irish in the city schools. It is also worth noting that the league had forged links with trade unionists through the formation of branches within individual unions and the participation of unions in the great language demonstration. For instance, the British-based Amalgamated Society of Railway Servants voted to take part in the demonstration of 1906.[87]

The Irish Worker remained generally supportive of the league and gave coverage to its activities. It did criticise it when it felt the need arose. In July 1911, the league's carnival committee obtained prizes for a sports event from Kilkenny Woodworkers, a company which had locked out its workers. Going on to condemn the purchase the paper asked 'if there is any body of men in Ireland who have been more favourably disposed towards the Gaelic League – who have stood by it throughout its career than the workers of Ireland we would like to know them.'[88]

An Claidheamh Soluis published a number of articles relating to the Great Lockout which engulfed Dublin over the summer of 1913. While a variety of opinions were expressed, the journal was conscious of not alienating support for the language. Consequently good and bad aspects of both the bosses' and the workers' sides were discussed. The influence of British unions on Irish workers was looked upon with suspicion, however, and the stance taken that unity among all sections of Irish society should be maintained as long as a foreign power was in control of the country, and that class disputes should be put aside until the common object of independence was achieved – whatever form that may have taken.

The paper came out in praise of the courage of Larkin. He had sent his son to St Enda's. Indeed Seán O'Casey had enlisted Larkin's help to print and distribute 5,000 leaflets publicising the school's pagent of 1913 put on to relieve serious financial problems. When Larkin was released from prison late in 1913 the paper published an article under the heading 'Cosa Dubha' (Blacklegs).

> Prison did not defeat Larkin. He came out a week ago healthier and braver than ever. Whatever opinion Gaels may have about the teaching of this man, it must be admitted that he gives courage and stamina to his followers. He said on the day that he came out of prison that he would start a general strike in Britain if any more 'black legs' were sent to Dublin. Every Gael hates the black legs from England. They are rabble and the dregs of the human race. They destroy the

working class and they destroy mannerliness (béasaíocht) everywhere they are given work.

Both sides, the workers and the men, get help from England. The men get help of money and the masters get the help of the foreign army from England. Both sides have a part in the strike. Neither side is free from blame.[89] [Author's translation]

móRSluá5 á5 hálla ná sáoiRse. —." Inóepenóenc
Cácar á5 pái lcíú roirh án loRcánác án lá á ócáiní5 sé ás pRíosún.

3. Crowd at Liberty Hall, to greet Larkin on his release from prison, *An Claidheamh Soluis*, 22 Nov. 1913. DCLA

The article goes on to hope that the workers will stand on their own two feet and not look to get help from England. During the height of the labour crisis *An Claidheamh Soluis* regularly published articles highlighting slum conditions in Dublin and the plight of the workers. In September 1913, *An Claidheamh Soluis* published a long piece in Irish on the cause of the workman. Pointing out that some Irish speakers believed that the workers had been led astray, it disagreed. It concluded:

Gaels should think deeply on all these questions. They will come to the conclusion that the cause of Irish and the cause of civilisation depends on the cause of the workers – the intellectual workers and the craft workers.[90] [Author's translation]

Internal dissention and decline

Publicising, as was its *raison d'etre*, the achievements of the league, the impression could have been given that the story, as covered in the pages of *An Claidheamh Soluis*, was one of success after success gained in a spirit of unanimity of purpose. This was far from the case, and the journal, especially under Pearse, did not hesitate to reveal some disquieting developments. A decline in the Gaelic League over the previous few years began to be noticed from 1905. In that year a number of the Dublin branches were deleted from the books because they had 'collapsed' or were incorporated with others, including Craobh na bPléimeannach, Craobh Naomh Bríde (Francis Street), Gobán (Taobh na Coille) and branches in Dundrum, Haddington Road and Rathgar.[91]

The matter was brought before the Ardfheis of 1907. Figures were produced to demonstrate that the organisation was not 'falling to pieces' as some expressed. It was claimed that in 1906-07, 553 branches were affiliated nationally compared to the 473 of 1905-06; it was accepted that there was a falling off in Britain over the same period from 54 branches to 44.[92] But this is still down on the 593 branches recorded in 1904.[93] Further decline was reported in 1908, with a falling off in Fingal reported.[94] Lessening enthusiasm is evident in the amount of money raised in the annual language collection in Dublin: this was £2,261 in 1905, £1,692 in 1906 and £1,643 in 1907.[95]

While the annual demonstration continued to be held, by 1908 activists like Éamonn Ceannt and Hyde were lamenting the fact that the vital contact with the people of the city had not lived up to its potential, and that the movement had become more closed and inward-looking. Ceannt, stating that 'most Dublin Leaguers will recollect that the Language Procession was the event which marked the coming of the League from out the Catacombs', when 'the populous was with us', but that now the league had not much appeal for outsiders.[96]

The decline in the number of branches was attributed by some critics within the organisation to a lack of direction. While it was claimed that the coiste ceantair in Dublin had given the branches a programme to follow and examiners sent out to inspect them, criticism still continued.[97] The need for so many unco-ordinated small branches in Dublin, many run by 'incompetent cliquish committees' was questioned by a Seán Ó Catháin. He was doubtful of the whole need for branches, pointing out that many branches did not mean progress. He argued that the branch organisation might have suited other organisations in Ireland from whom the league copied the system, but may not have suited its needs. He suggested that one branch may have been enough in Dublin.[98]

Sᵹoıl Éᴀnnᴀ,

ᴛeᴀċ ꝼeᴀᴅᴀ ċuılınn, ʀáᴛ ó máıne.

Oıᴀ Sᴀᴛᴀıʀn, Oıᴀ Ooṁnᴀıᵹ, ᴀᵹuʀ Oıᴀ Luᴀın,

5, 6, 7 ꝼeᴀᴅʀᴀ, 1910, ᴀn ᴀ 8 ᴀ ċloᵹ ᴛʀáᴛnónᴀ,

Léıʀeoċᴀıᴅ mıc léıᵹınn nᴀ sᵹoıle

"THE DESTRUCTION OF THE HOSTEL"

(páoʀᴀıc mᴀc cuılm ᴅo ʀᵹníoḃ)

ᴀᵹuʀ "íosᴀᵹán"

(páoʀᴀıc mᴀc pıᴀʀᴀıs ᴅo ʀᵹníoḃ).

ᴀn cláʀ.

"THE DESTRUCTION OF THE HOSTEL."

ᴀn ꝼuıʀeᴀnn ᴀnnʀo ʀíoʀ :

LOMNA DRUTH FERROGAIN FERGABAR	foster-brothers to Conaire, High King of Ireland.	Éᴀmonn Ḃuılꝼın (Eamonn Bulfin). Oeᴀʀṁuṁᴀ Ó Rıᴀın (Desmond Ryan). Muıʀıʀ Ó ꝼeᴀʀᴀċᴀıʀ (Maurice Fraher).
INGCEL, a British outlaw.		Sᴀṁᴀıʀle Mᴀc Ᵹᴀʀḃᴀıᵹ (Sorley MacGarvey).
MAINE HONEYMOUTH, son of Meadhbh of Connacht.		Oonnċᴀḃ Mᴀc ꝼınn (Denis Gwynn).
CONALL CERNACH CORMAC CONDLOINGEAS, son of Conchobar BRICRIU of the Evil Tongue	Heroes of the Red Branch.	Pʀoınnʀıᴀʀ Ó Conᵹᴀıle (Frank Connolly). Ooṁnᴀll Ó Concuḃᴀıʀ (Donal O'Connor). Éᴀmonn Ó Nuᴀlláın (Eamonn Nolan).
MAC CECHT, the King's Champion		Uınnʀeᴀnn Ó Ooċᴀʀᴛᴀıᵹ (Vincent O'Doherty).
NI-FRI-FLAITH		Rıʀᴛeᴀʀᴅ Ó Rᴀᴛᵹᴀılle (Richard O'Rahilly).
THE THREE RED PIPERS FROM THE ELF-MOUNDS		ꝼeᴀʀᴅoʀċᴀ Ó Ooċᴀʀᴛᴀıᵹ (Fredrick O'Doherty). Mᴀolṁuıʀe Mᴀᵹ Seᴀʀʀᴀıᵹ (Milo MacGarry). eoın Ó Oúnlᴀınᵹ (John Dowling).

4. Programme from a Sgoil Éanna production, 1910.
DCLA

Continued decline led to a deeper examination as to its causes. The activities of branches consisted of Irish classes, singing and dancing, indeed in some classes only. The more progressive had the courage to take up Irish history, although this was too academic for some. The monotony of class work, it was pointed out, had been fatal to many branches. The gap between classes and a conversational level had not been crossed, leading to frustration and a failure to persevere.[99] In 1910, it was regretted that the old spirit had evaporated. It had been replaced by an arid, soulless obsession with language teaching method and grammar, which had become a form of idolatry. Many friends of the league, it was claimed, held back from forming new branches because of the difficulty of keeping them alive.[100]

As branches closed and the language demonstration was cut back, Patrick Pearse began to run into trouble at St Enda's, with enrolment falling from 130 in 1909-10 to 60 in 1912-13. The girls' school, St Ita's, closed in 1912. In the same year, disappointment was expressed that the Oireachtas had 'not yet begun to exercise a far-reaching influence on Irish life', as was hoped it would do.[101]

Energy was sapped by bitter internal disputes and personality clashes in the league in Dublin. The rapid growth of the league and the coming together of a large number of fervent, intelligent and motivated writers and activists in the excitement of a newly-discovered cause was almost guaranteed to lead to conflicts over ideology, strategy and personal differences. An early dispute arose over the attempt to establish a Pan-Celtic Congress with its headquarters in Dublin. Many less Nationalistic and indeed Unionist Irish language enthusiasts supported this. However the league leadership opposed it fearing that it might dissipate their energies.[102] The fact that P. J. Keawell, the manager of *An Claidheamh Soluis*, was one of its leading opponents, may have contributed to the paper's strong anti-Pan-Celtic stance.

Squabbles over dialect were reported as early as 1901. The presence of large numbers of Munster men - especially from Cork and Kerry - with an awareness of the strong literary tradition associated with the language of that province led to a superior attitude on their part to their dialect and a disparagement of others, especially that of Connacht. In March 1901 S. J. Barrett, speaking at the central branch, pointed out that not enough Connacht men were active in the movement, and that nearly all the writers wrote Munster Irish, and that a Connacht branch should be formed in Dublin.[103]

Before the month was out a Connacht branch, known as the MacÉil Branch, was founded. At the same time it was reported that the Munster men had met in the Gresham Hotel with the aim of starting a Munster branch and would 'seek out Munster men in the city and make leaguers out of them.' The report in *An Claidheamh Soluis* hoped that this development would not lead to 'paróisteachas' (parochialism) in the league. Both these branches had a larger percentage of native speakers amongst their ranks and quickly became almost totally Irish-speaking.[104]

The Munster branch, known as Craobh an Chéitinnigh (Keating Branch), meeting over the years at various addresses in the Rutland Square area, would have a key role in the revival movement and the later revolutionary struggle. It quickly established itself as an élite within an élite, holding inter-branch debates, proposing new policy and winning the Oireachtas shield three years in a row. It had such prominent members as Fr Dineen, Shán Ó Cuív and Piaras Béaslaí. Cathal Brugha was president for many years. It was described in 1910, with Cathal Brugha as president, as 'now a great teaching institution and an active centre of vigorous national thought.'[105] The Céitinnigh faction were often at odds with many members of the coiste gnótha which had a sizable number of Connacht Irish speakers, including Patrick Pearse and Douglas Hyde.

Fr Dineen and the Céitinnigh opposed Pearse's application for the post of editor of *An Claidheamh Soluis* in 1903, with Dineen standing for the post himself. However the coiste gnótha was looking for a candidate who could stand up to the Munster clique and Pearse got the job.[106] The two factions had support in the journalistic world of Dublin. *The Freeman's Journal* and *The Leader* supported the Céitinnigh while W. J. Ryan of the new *Irish Independent* supported the coiste gnótha and Pearse.[107]

In 1907 and 1908, the squabbling grew more intense. Fr Dineen addressed the Céitinnigh and spoke of division in the ranks – 'class against class, caste against caste', as he termed it.[108] *An Claidheamh Soluis* went on the offensive in March 1908 in an editorial headed 'Lucht an Fheill' (The Treacherous Faction). It accused the Munster men for five years now of attempting to destroy the league, and implicated especially Dineen and Dr Dónal Ó Loinsigh, a strong member of the Munster faction from Ballyvourney, Co. Cork.[109]

While this in-fighting might be seen as confined to the leadership of the movement there was concern that the disputatious nature of league activity was a handicap to progress at branch level. *An Claidheamh Soluis* opined in January 1910: 'To perform is far more necessary than to criticise. The truth of this will be seen by our readers if they remember the number of towns and parishes in which all Gaelic League work has been made impossible by the severe criticism of thoughtless workers.'[110] The Céitinnigh faction were dubbed by a letter writer to *An Claidheamh Soluis*, Úna Ní Dhubhlaoich, 'the evil spirit of the Gaelic League, and the extreme Left Party' which was trying to control the organisation. Peadar Ó Maicín (Peadar Macken) replied that if this was true the converse was also true – an extreme right conservative wing afraid of innovation also existed.[111]

Matters came to a head on 7 July 1913. Douglas Hyde, speaking at a meeting of the coiste gnótha, threw down the gauntlet and sent out a message to all branches of the organisation for support against politics in the league. If his view did not prevail he would resign. Messages and motions of support for Hyde came in from all sides, including Coiste Chathair Bhaile Átha Cliath, and his detractors backed off.

Hyde survived for a further two years, but with the establishment of the Irish Volunteers as a result of Eoin MacNeill's 'The North Began' article in *An Claidheamh Soluis*, and Pearse's public dismissal of the league as the harbinger to the coming revolution, it must have been clear to many that a new phase had begun in which language revival would take the back seat to political, and indeed, military action.

Notes

1   Timothy G. MacMahon, '"All creeds and classes": just who joined the Gaelic League?' in *Éire-Ireland* xxxvii, 3-4 (2002), pp 118-68.

2   D. G. Boyce, *Nationalism in Ireland* (3rd ed., London, 1995); Tom Garvin, *Nationalist revolutionaries in Ireland 1858-1928* (Oxford, 1987); John Hutchinson, *The dynamics of cultural nationalism: the Gaelic revival and the creation of the Irish nation state* (London & Boston, 1987); Maurice Goldring, *Pleasant the scholar's life: Irish intellectuals and the construction of the nation state* (London, 1993).

3   *Freeman's Journal*, 7 June 1906.

4   Correspondence and associated documents re. The founding of the Gaelic league, mainly 1893 (NLI, MS 10,895).

5   MacMahon, "All creeds and classes", p. 122.

6   *An Claidheamh Soluis* (*ACS*), 8 Apr. 1899.

7   Ibid.

8   *ACS*, 24 Feb. 1900.

9   *ACS*, 5 Jan. 1901.

10   *ACS* , 17 Mar. 1900; 21 Apr. 1900.

11   Proinsias Ó Conluain, *Seán T: scéal a bheatha á insint ag Seán T. Ó Ceallaigh* (Baile Átha Cliath, 1963), p. 58.

12   MacMahon, "All creeds and classes", p. 139.

13   Martin B. Margulies, *The early life of Séan O'Casey* (Dublin, 1979), pp 36-7.

14   Seán O'Casey, *Drums under the windows* (London, 1945), p. 8.

15   *ACS*, 20 Oct. 1900.

16   *ACS*, 14 Oct. 1905.

17   *ACS*, 21 Mar. 1903.

18   *ACS*, 28 Nov. 1908.

19   *ACS*, 15 July 1899.

20   *ACS,* 29 Sept. 1900; Nov. 1900; 5 Jan. 1901.

21   *ACS*, 27 Apr. 1907.

22   *ACS*, 14 Apr. 1906.

23   *ACS*, 28 May 1907.

24   *ACS*, 18 May 1907

25   *ACS*, 18 May 1907.

26   Margulies, *Early life,* p. 44.

27   *ACS*, 27 July 1901; Oct. 1901.

28   *ACS*, 25 Jan. 1902.

29   *ACS*, 11 Apr. 1903.

30   *ACS,* 7 Oct. 1903.

31   *ACS*, 3 May 1903.

32   *ACS*, 14 Mar. 1903.

33   *ACS*, 15 Aug. 1908.

34   *ACS*, 29 Dec. 1900.

35   *ACS*, 1 Dec. 1901; 5 July 1902.

36   *ACS*, 1 Feb. 1902.

37   *ACS*, 26 Feb. 1910.

38   *ACS*, 14 Feb. 1903; 9 Nov. 1912.

39   *ACS*, 27 Oct. 1900; 16 Feb. 1900; Feb. 1902.

40   *ACS*, 17 Feb. 1900.

41   *Irish Independent*, 27 Oct. 1906.

42   *ACS*, 23 June 1900.

43   *ACS*, 11 Mar. 1905.

44   *ACS*, 31 Mar. 1906.

45   *ACS*, 14 Mar 1903.

46   *ACS*, 12 Aug. 1911; 29 June 1912.

47   *ACS*, 1 Jan. 1910.

48   Earnán de Blaghd, *Trasna na Bóinne* (Baile Átha Cliath, 1957), p. 129.

49   *ACS*, 16 Mar. 1912.

50   *ACS*, 7 Mar. 1903.

51   *ACS*, 27 Jan. 1907.

52   Donncha Ó Súilleabháin, *Scéal an Oireachtais* (Baile Átha Cliath, 1984), p. 11.

53   *ACS*, 24 May 1903.

54   *ACS*, 24 June 1899.

55   *ACS*, 10 Mar. 1900; 10 Aug. 1907.

56   *ACS*, 7 Aug. 1909.

57   *ACS*, 21 May 1910.

58   *ACS*, 20 July 1907; 17 Aug. 1907.

59   *ACS*, 31 July 1909.

60   *ACS*, 18 Feb. 1911; June 1912.

61   *ACS*, 4 July 1903.

62   *ACS*, 12 Oct. 1912.

63   *ACS*, 14 June 1902.

64   *ACS*, 19 Jan. 1907.

65   *ACS*, 9 Jan. 1901.

66   *ACS*, 1 July 1899.

67   *ACS*, 11 May 1901.

68   Ibid., 8 Nov. 1905.

69   *ACS*, 3 Aug. 1901.

70   *ACS*, 31 Dec. 1904.

71   *ACS*, 29 May 1909.

72   *ACS*, 29 July 1899.

73   *ACS*, 14 Sept. 1907.

74   *Freeman's Journal*, 10 July 1906.

75   *ACS*, 14 Jan. 1905; 11 Jan. 1908.

76   *Freeman's Journal*, 6 Sept. 1905.

77   *ACS*, 23 Oct. 1909.

78   *ACS*, 8 Aug. 1906; Apr. 1912.

79   *ACS*, 24 May 1902.

80   *ACS*, 27 Jan. 1906.

81   *ACS*, 13 July 1912.

82   *ACS*, 1 July 1899.

83   See 1911 census online (www.census.nationalarchives.ie/reels/nai000081064/).

84   Quoted originally by James Connolly, *Worker's Republic*, 1 Oct. 1898.

85   *ACS*, 27 Jan. 1907.

86   J. E. and G. W. Dunleavy, *Douglas Hyde: a maker of modern Ireland* (Berkeley, 1991), p. 315.

87   *Irish Independent*, 21 Feb. 1906.

88   *Irish Worker*, 8 July 1911.

89   *ACS*, 22 Nov. 1913.

90   *ACS*, 13 Sept. 1913.

91   *ACS*, 25 May 1905.

92   *ACS*, 24 Aug. 1907.

93   Tomás Ó hAilín, 'Irish revival movements' in Brian Ó Cuív (ed.) *A view of the Irish language* (Dublin, 1969), p. 97.

94   *ACS*, 1 Feb. 1908.

95   *ACS*, 22 Feb. 1908.

96   *ACS*, 8 Aug. 1908.

97   *ACS*, 18 Mar. 1905.

98   *ACS*, 1 Apr. 1905.

99   *ACS*, 20 Mar. 1909.

100 *ACS*, 29 Oct. 1910; 27 Sept. 1913.

101 *ACS*, 4 May 1912.

102 ACS, 9 Sept. 1899; Patrick Maume, 'D. P. Moran' in *Dictionary of Irish biography* (Cambridge, 2009).

103 *ACS*, 2 Mar. 1901.

104 *ACS*, 6 Apr. 1901.

105   *ACS*, 29 Oct 1910.

106   Séamas Ó Buachalla (ed.), *The letters of P. H. Pearse* (Gerrards Cross, 1980), p. 66-7.

107   Ibid., p. 91.

108   *ACS*, 6 July 1907.

109   *ACS*, 14 Mar 1908.

110   *ACS*, 8 Jan. 1910.

111   *ACS*, 11 May 1912; 18 May 1912.

Leanḃaíḋe sgoile i mbaile Áṫa Cliaṫ ag foġluim rinncí Danarḋa. Nar córa ḋóiḃ beiṫ ag   " freeman."
foġluim rinncí Gaeḋlaċa.

5. Dublin school children learn Irish dancing.
An Cliadheamh Soluis, 20 Dec. 1913.

14.

In pursuit of Patrick Donegan, Guinness boatman, 1895-1955: a case of family history

....

Patrick Coughlan and Francis Devine

Patrick Coughlan was employed in Guinness Brewery from March 1952 until his retirement in March 1993. He was a labourer initially in the brew house and then, by turns, in the container department, fermentation, and engineers' department. Coughlan was a committed company employee who took pride in his work and in the brewery.[1] He had reservations about the company's paternalism, however, and was always active in the Workers' Union of Ireland (WUI), remembering it 'coming into the Brewery' and, although seldom seeking union office or position, 'rarely missing a meeting'.[2] Coughlan did serve as WUI relief shop steward in the brew house in the 1960s and remains active in the Guinness Pensioners' Association.[3]

Coughlan's mother Elizabeth ('Bessie' or 'Babs') was a Donegan. Her mother, Bridget Donegan, lived in 53.1 Bow Lane and died of consumption [TB] on 21 October, 1910, aged 39, leaving eight children, aged between 15 and three years of age, motherless.[4] Her husband was Patrick Donegan, Coughlan's grandfather, who worked for Guinness and about whom there were family stories concerning his involvement in the 1913 Lockout and dismissal by Guinness, along with other boatmen. After some fruitless searches for details of Donegan's dismissal, Coughlan approached the Irish Labour History Society (ILHS) for suggestions as to how he might investigate this family story. How could one individual among the thousands dismissed, suspended or locked out in 1913 be traced? The Irish Transport and General Workers' Union (ITGWU) were not thought to have even organised in Guinness and, in any case, union records for the period were scarce. After consulting secondary sources, however, details of Donegan's case emerged and his story was gradually recovered from personnel files in the Guinness Archive and ITGWU material in the William O'Brien Papers in the National Library of Ireland.[5] It became an interesting case of family labour history.

Guinness: benevolent employer and organising target for Jim Larkin

Guinness prided itself on being a good employer. At its height, 3,500-4,000 workers were employed at St James's Gate. The workforce was regarded as the 'lifeblood of the Brewery'. The company 'recognised this and took measures to ensure the well-being of their workforce, earning in the process a reputation as a fair and benevolent employer, caring for the workers, as the saying goes, "from the cradle to the grave".[6] These progressive policies included provision of 'sickness allowances, pensions, gratuities, donations to those in need' and 'annual leave, beer allowances and medical healthcare' for workers and their families. Behind this, however, there was a stern and rigid paternalism and a strong suspicion of trade unionism among the general operatives and, especially, a deep distrust of the threatening potential of Larkinism after 1908. In return for their enlightened management and, as they saw it, generosity towards their men, the brewery demanded total loyalty from staff.

In correspondence cited below, the company suggest that they never raised any objection to their employees being organised and that they worked 'in close harmony' with trades unions. They had certainly long recognised and dealt with the Coopers' Society and other craft trade unions but strongly resisted organisation of their general operatives, by far the biggest section of the workforce.[7] 'Larkinism', however, proved another matter entirely for the apparently benign Guinness Board. In 1912, ITGWU General Secretary Larkin was, according to William O'Brien, 'anxious to spread the union' and 'proposed to organise the tramway men and Guinness's'.[8] O'Brien echoed the standard external view of the brewery and its management when he told Larkin:

> As to Guinness's, their conditions were so good that I doubted if it would be possible to organise them. Larkin held that there were two black spots in the trade union movement and that he would go ahead with it.[9]

Emmet Larkin thought that James Larkin was 'at the height of his power' and that he 'controlled almost all the unskilled labour in Dublin.' The two nuts left to crack were the Dublin United Tramway Company and Guinness. Efforts at gaining a toehold in Guinness were thwarted however.

> Guinness, which was directed by Lord Iveagh, the philanthropist, proved to be too much even for Larkin's organising genius.[10] The wages paid by Guinness were the best in Dublin, and Lord Iveagh treated his workers with a benevolent paternalism that was rare in his day. He provided houses at reasonable rates near the brewery, medical care, and all 'the eating and drinking' that was in a pint of the best Guinness 'XX'. Guinness proved to be impregnable because there was no discontent.[11]

Whatever discontent among the workforce there might have been was conditioned by the 'snakes and ladders' effect. Dublin's general employment market was over-supplied with cheap, readily-available labour. The cost of losing a 'steady' job in Guinness was high and, which employer would look kindly at a worker who had left, or worse, had been rejected by Guinness?[12]

1. Cartoon of Lord Iveagh, seated on a cask on a Guinness barge. The bargeman can be seen at the back of the vessel. *The Lepracaun*, 13 Sept. 1913.
DCLA

Guinness and industrial intelligence

In common with other employers, however, the infection that was Larkinism spread alarm at Guinness. In the second edition of *The Irish Worker*, June 1911, under a heading 'Sweating in the Brewery Trade', Larkin gave examples of poor wages and conditions in brewing. It was not Guinness he was referring to but, to the undoubted alarm of St James's Gate, the company did get a mention.

> Oh, you may say Guinness's men are not treated badly, well, I am not referring to Guinness's at present; perhaps if some of you worked there you would find there is a fly in the ointment – of that more anon.[13]

It was that 'more anon' that perhaps caused the deepest shiver. An immediate victory was signalled in brewers Watkins, Jameson, Pim and Co. who agreed to an advance in wages; a penny on the overtime rate; a systemising of overtime to avoid excessive hours; and a general improvement in hours and conditions. Larkin reminded his readers that he did not drink himself but for:

> men foolish enough to consume strong drink, it would be better that they should drink the liquor, stout or beer made by such firms as Watkins, Jameson, Pim & Co who not only employ Irishmen in every department, but who, I am informed, use practically all Irish-grown grain.[14]

Larkin still had Guinness in his sights. On 23 July 1911 in Beresford Place at a mass meeting to hear news of the international shipping strike, he directly challenged any brewery workers in attendance. Buoyed by ITGWU success in other breweries, Larkin claimed that Guinness would not object to trade union organisation.

> I wish to say a word about Guinness's men. Is it not time you took your place by your class and organised yourselves? Now, Guinness does not object to your organising, and it would be no harm if you promoted a trades union that would be helpful to every man. It should not be left to a few men out of Darcy's to organise. Guinness's men should be the pioneers. I hope they will come together and promote their organisation.[15]

The ITGWU were making rapid advances and a typical, 'one week's work accomplished' by the union in August 1911, included advances for Keenan's labourers; sandwich-men; Bewley and Draper's mineral men; Halligan's Millers draymen; Paul and Vincent's maltsters; Barrington's Soap Works; Gallagher's Master Carriers; Brooks Thomas's labourers; and Laird Line dockers.[16] For brewery labourers, most significant of all, however, was the announcement of advances in Watkins, Jameson, Pim, brewers and Darcy's Brewery where two shillings was won. Even in Guinness, the outer barriers of the company's defences seemed to be crumbling as the ITGWU announced 'new arrangements of work equal to three shillings a week for contractors' men.'[17]

At a meeting 'of immense proportions' in the Phoenix Park on Sunday, 20 August, to celebrate victorious joint action by the ITGWU and Amalgamated Society of Railway Servants, Larkin, as ever the final and most rousing speaker, concluded his praise of transport workers and the women of Inchicore by taking the opportunity to once again challenge brewery workers.

> Now I want to say a word to the Guinness men. How is it that you are not in a trade union? Can you give any reason why you are not? Only that you are a self-sufficient lot of men? Suppose we play the game with you for a couple of months, and we are well able to do it. Suppose the Transport Workers' Union and the railwaymen decide and say, 'We will handle no goods from Guinness until they join the Union'. Think of that, my friends. Remember that the firm is making three millions out of you. Don't be frightened of Guinness when all the railway magnates could not beat the railwaymen, Guinness could not beat you. I am going to give you an invitation. Why not have a 'Brewery Workers' Union'; I want to see Guinness's men co-operating with D'Arcy's men and Pim's.[18]

Guinness were sufficiently alarmed by these reports to engage in some industrial research. On 22 September 1911, the Confidential Enquiry Agency of Michael Sheehan, 'late Sergeant, Detective Department, Dublin Castle' sent a lengthy hand-written report to Charles G. Sutton, solicitor to the brewery. His brief had been to report on the ITGWU. Sheehan correctly claimed that the union 'was started in Dublin by Jim Larkin' but thought 'about four years ago', 1907, rather than 1909 as it was.[19] Sheehan thought the ITGWU had 'about 5,000' members with branches in Belfast, Cork, Waterford, Wexford, Drogheda, Dundalk and 'other seaport towns'. Membership was in fact probably three or four times that with a figure of 18,089 being returned to the Registrar of Friendly Societies for January 1912.[20] The union 'is not amalgamated with any English Society and is depending entirely on Irish support', a fact that Sheehan clearly saw as an Achilles' heel, limiting the union's membership and financial potential and signalling the probability that it would not survive a large-scale strike or lock-out by a stalwart employer. He noted that the ITGWU was in affiliation to the Dublin Trades Council but that some affiliates 'refused to recognise or affiliate' with it, further evidence of the union's supposedly flimsy base.

Sheehan then lists ITGWU objects and benefits – legal assistance, funeral allowance, 'a weekly allowance for members who are out of work thro' no fault of their own, or as a result of obeying the demands of the Union', and dispute pay of 10s. and 12s. 6d. per week – before concluding that the union 'is pure and simple a Socialist Society' primarily for the benefit of Larkin and his organisers. He then reassures his anxious clients:

> The funds of the Union never amounted to much, and are nearly exhausted at present, through the Wexford and Dublin Timber strikes. The allowance of the members are now getting cut down, and should the strike last much longer Larkin will be in for some rough handling.

Suggesting that Larkin 'dare not put in an appearance in Cork or Belfast', Sheehan goes on to comment on other ITGWU personalities. P. T. Daly, a compositor by trade, was noted for his previous membership of Dublin Corporation and being a 'Sinn Féiner in politics'. He 'travelled a good deal on some mysterious business', particularly to America 'on the call of some Irish socialists there.' An 'apparently poor man', Daly 'spends a lot of money travelling, so that he must get it from some peculiar quarter.' James Connolly's compositor background was also noted, together with his 'travelling abroad lecturing on Socialism.'[21] Walter Carpenter, 'an Englishman and a former speaker on Socialism in High Park [sic] and Trafalgar Square', 'a sweep by occupation', had been recently imprisoned for 'defaming the King'.[22] Finally, the secretary was a 'man named Tom Greene, who was a coal porter up to two years ago but since his appointment to the union he got elected as Poor Law Guardian to the North Dublin Union.'[23] These pen-pictures are reasonably accurate allowing for the clear bias and desire to see the worst. Larkin was described as a native of Rostrevor who moved to Lancashire at an early age, worked in coal-mines in Lancashire and South Wales before becoming a 'fireman on trading ships' and seeing a 'great deal of the world'.[24] Continuing the suggestion that the union was a milch-cow for its organisers, Sheehan reported that Larkin:

> is said to have a salary of £3 a week out of the Society but the true fact is that no one knows how much he draws for he and those mentioned can do what they like with the funds of the Society.

To gain the affections of the 'poor, foolish labouring classes', Larkin 'pretends to be a relation of the Larkin of Manchester [Martyrs] fame' so that they believe 'he is a dangerous individual. He is neither one or the other, and the only danger I can see about him is getting poor senseless labourers to leave their employment, and having the handling of their money.'[25]

Sheehan concluded by reassuring his client that 'there is great discontent' among the membership; that if the current strike lasted much longer Larkin's union 'will be wiped out'; and that a Women's Branch has been started together with a 'Labour Paper' with 'very little circulation outside Dublin'. The latter were references to what became the Irish Women Workers' Union and *The Irish Worker*.[26]

Sheehan wrote to Sutton again on 6 October 1911, enclosing an ITGWU rule book, and insisting from a source 'who knows the inner working of the Union that 8*d.* out of every shilling goes towards the expenses of Jim Larkin and his Organisers.'[27] The Timber Trade strike was supposedly causing such anger against Larkin that, with the fall in strike pay, some members 'are swearing vengeance against Larkin for having brought them out and others have gone so far as to say that they will throw him into the Liffey.' Sheehan assured his client that 'there is no doubt but Larkin is nearly beaten to the ropes.' Presumably impressed by Sheehan's reports, but again operating through their solicitors, Sutton, Guinness received a further report on 31 July 1913, a month before the onset of the Great Lockout. Sheehan had trawled the offices of the Registrar of Friendly Societies and reported, a little confusingly, on the ITGWU Burial and Tontine Society, as well as the union proper. He reproduced the union's returns showing ITGWU income for the year 1912 and its expenses. He suggested that 'if all the members' were paying their subscriptions it would amount to £18,000 rather than £4,000, the implication being that some sort of misappropriation of funds had taken place but making no allowance for recalcitrant members, the retention of a portion of income by the branches themselves, or for the fact that the accounts were audited and acceptable to the registrar.[28] It is significant, however, that Guinness were keeping an eagle eye on the potential threat posed by the ITGWU and were anxious to have some measure of the potential membership and financial strength of a possible opponent. The ITGWU's gathering strength and Larkin's public identification of Guinness as an organising target undoubtedly prompted company concerns.

Dismissal of the Guinness boatmen, 1913

The ITGWU finally made headway in Guinness in January 1913. *The Irish Worker* carried a notice for 'all Guinness's employees except tradesmen' to attend a meeting at 74 Thomas Street, a venue convenient for the brewery, on 26 January at 1 p.m. Speakers would include Councillor William Partridge and ITGWU organiser P. T. Daly.[29] The notice concluded with the rally cry: 'It is important that every man in Guinness's employ should attend. Be slaves no longer!'[30] Another meeting was recorded on Sunday, 1 June 1913.[31] It is not clear how many attended as the paper makes no further reference to Guinness and the union generally became preoccupied in shipping and dock-working disputes and mounting recruitment campaigns among rural workers in Co. Dublin.[32] The ITGWU had, however, organised some 500 members in Guinness – out of a total workforce of 2,400 – and McCarthy and Donegan were among the general labourers and the boatmen who would, on a daily basis, as they sailed up and down the river, be in contact with ITGWU dockers, porters, carters, canal-men and malt-men. Indeed, an ITGWU badge/card might have been proving increasingly necessary to gain access to or be accepted by organised employments. Clearly not recognised by Guinness, the ITGWU nevertheless continued to gather strength. One of the comments in the correspondence cited below to the effect that the union 'had, in any case, intended to ask for increased wages and improved conditions for boatmen' suggests that recruitment among the outdoor staff, the river and street workers in Guinness had advanced.

2. Guinness barges, Patrick Donegan worked as a Guinness bargeman on this type of barge.
A visit to St James's Gate Brewery (London, 1896).
DCLA

Larkin wrote to the 'Manager, Shipping Department' in Guinness on behalf of the dismissed boatmen on 7 October 1913. Edward McCarthy, captain of the motor boat *Tolka*, had been ordered to collect empties from Tedcastle's Wharf. Larkin explained that 'there being a lock-out there he was under the impression that he might be the means of effecting your traffic' and, 'I understand he refused to convey such empties and he was immediately suspended.'[33] McCarthy's fellow-boatmen handed in a week's notice but this was 'withdrawn' when a statement was made that 'if McCarthy apologised to Mr Thring, Head of the Department, he would be reinstated.' Larkin goes on that 'without consulting the Union', McCarthy did apologise but 'instead of being reinstated, he was summarily dismissed.' The five crew, including Donegan, handed in notice but 'were paid off at once.' Larkin lists the men and their service to the brewery: John Noonan, eight years; James Kirwan, nine years; Michael Butler, nine years; Thomas Doyle, eight years; and Patrick Donegan, 20 years. Larkin pointed out that these men were 'all good, competent workmen against whom there has been no complaints.' In McCarthy's case, the letter observes that he 'himself has given thirteen years of his life in the service of Guinness.'

Having stated the facts as he knew them, Larkin then made the case that the union 'think the dismissal of these men is a most unjust action on your part' and, linking the affair to the wider labour conflagration in the capital, 'feel that this is on a par with the action of the other employers ... trying to destroy Trades Unionism.' The central issue of trade union recognition, at the heart of the Lockout itself, was felt to be at stake as the brewery's action was 'denying' the men '(a) the right to belong to a Trades Union' and '(b) to associate with their fellows for the betterment of their class.' Larkin followed this with the observation that 'since your Company depends upon the good-will of the working-class who are the principal consumers of your product we think we are entitled to ask you to reinstate these six men in their formal grades', adding that the ITGWU had, in any case, intended to ask for increased wages and improved conditions for boatmen. Larkin argued that wages were lower than English equivalents and yet the cost of living was higher in Dublin and that the company was generating 'enormous profits'. Larkin concludes with a vague threat that failing reply,

> steps will be taken both at home here in Ireland and in Great Britain and other places where your commodity is put on sale so that sufficient pressure will be brought to bear upon you that you will realise that the workers in the twentieth century have not only a right to combine in Trades Unions, but also have a right to demand that their grievances shall be treated in a business like way.

Given all that was happening, Guinness did not see such threats as idle, although, as James Connolly's letter below indicates, the ITGWU had threatened an embargo on Guinness products. H. W. Renny-Tailyour, managing director, Guinness, replied to Larkin on 14 October 1913, pointing out, in a pure crystallisation of 'Free Labour' philosophy, that it is 'not our usual practice to discuss questions regarding our employees with anybody except the men themselves, who are well aware that the Board are open at all times to discuss and consider any question that they may wish to raise.'[34] Despite the limited organisation within Guinness, the letter suggested that the board 'have never objected to our employees being members of any Trades Union, and are pleased to feel that we have at all times worked in close harmony with Trades Unions both in Dublin and elsewhere.' The company 'never objected to our men associating together for their betterment both of themselves, of their wives and of their children.' The niceties dispensed with, McCarthy's direct refusal of an order – for 'his ordinary daily duties' – was cited as incontrovertible reason for his dismissal for 'insubordination' and that the other men gave seven to ten days' notice 'although they had previously been warned that such notice would prevent them ever being re-employed.' They were paid a week's wages in lieu and Renny-Tailyour concluded by proudly stating that Guinness 'rely with the utmost confidence on the loyalty of our employees, and that so far as our treatment of our men is concerned, we at all times submit without hesitation to the criticism of public opinion.' Company hands and consciences were now quite clearly thoroughly washed.

On Friday 12 December 1913, Connolly, acting as General Secretary, ITGWU, rang Guinness and requested to speak with one of the directors. Ernest Guinness took the call.[35] He reported that Connolly had asked the company to reconsider the 'slight trouble existing between us' over the dismissal of six boatmen in the previous October who had refused to handle 'tainted goods' at Tedcastle's Wharf.[36] Two of the men, boat skipper Edward McCarthy and deck hand Patrick Donegan, who had come out in sympathy with him, had nearly 40 years' service in the company and 16 children between them. Connolly had said to Guinness that he was 'very wishful of having a Christmas gift of peace to people, and … he was very anxious that the port should now open.'

Ernest Guinness, maybe infected by the approaching season, appeared to have been a sympathetic listener as he followed up the telephone conversation with a letter containing tentative proposals for a general settlement of the 'unfortunate dispute in Dublin'. Yeates notes that Connolly, writing with the authority of the ITGWU General Executive Committee, said the union was lifting the embargo on Guinness's products as the result of the dismissal of a few of your men. Without at all making it a condition of our action, we desire to suggest to you that if your firm could see their way to the reinstatement of the six men in question, the act would help greatly to straighten out the tangle on the quays, and thus clear the way for the final greater settlement now being sought by all parties concerned.[37]

Connolly's appeal to the heart was referred by Ernest Guinness to his father Lord Iveagh, telling him that the situation was 'very hard on the men'. Iveagh, predictably, took the view that the punishment must stand as example to others. Colonel H. Renny-Tailyour replied to Connolly thanking him for his 'courteous tone' and noting that Connolly's letter had clearly been based on a 'misapprehension', but merely reiterated the company's position that they had no objection to employers being members of 'any Trades Union' but reserving the right to dismiss them for 'insubordination'.[38] This reply was somewhat disingenuous as Guinness were accessing labour through the strike-breaking organisation, the Shipping Federation, and, given its resources, had become persuaded to purchase its own, directly-controlled specialist barges, thus leaving itself less vulnerable in future disputes.[39] Before the first purpose-built ships arrived, the *Barkley* was purchased and was in service when Connolly received his reply.[40] On the matter of McCarthy, Donegan and their comrades, the company was not for turning.

3. Guinness Malt Store, Robert Street
A visit to St James's Gate Brewery, Dublin (London, 1896).
DCLA

The threat to boycott or 'black' Guinness products was never really implemented, perhaps because of the demands on ITGWU resources and attention elsewhere around the city. In addition, although Larkin was 'a teetotaller himself and a vehement denunciator of the evils of drink' he knew the tactic would not work for the 'most popular beverage in the country' was Guinness. The token blacking was a symbolic gesture as Guinness employees collected all brewery supplies in James's Street.[41] Equally, Guinness steered clear of total involvement in the conflict by resisting overtures from William Martin Murphy and the Dublin Employers' Federation (DEF).[42] The brewery board met a DEF delegation on 16 September 1913 but politely declined Murphy's invitation to add 'the moral support of the great company of Guinness'. Instead, they offered a donation of £100 to the DEF contingency fund, doubling the previous highest individual donation from Murphy himself.[43] Ernest Guinness, writing to his father, Lord Iveagh, cautioned against any provocative course with the ITGWU:

> It would be not do for us to accuse any of our men [of] being foolish as to belong to Larkin, but that if we have any trouble … the men who gave the trouble should

be got rid of at once and never taken back again, as that I believe will do more than anything to prevent more of our men joining Larkin.[44]

To avoid difficulties in the strike-bound Dublin port, Guinness sent cargo by the Great Southern and Western Railway to Cork, from whence it was shipped to London.[45] Guinness estimated ITGWU membership as between 200 and 450 and sought to neutralise the union's growing presence. Ernest thought they 'owe it to the other employers ... to make a firm stand now.' What he proposed was 'nothing like so drastic' as was being carried out elsewhere and, tellingly for McCarthy and Donegan, thought the policy likely to cause little

> trouble at all, but even if all our boatmen left us I believe I could replace them all in a couple of weeks. If I prove to be wrong, and all our Draymen [and] Motor drivers do go out in sympathy. I should feel that we are much better able to fight it out now, cost what it may, than later on when Larkin has mastered his plans, and we are possibly under Home Rule.[46]

Thus, from the beginning, McCarthy and Donegan's case was hopeless and merely the example the brewery had, if not sought, then readily taken as a pre-emptive strike against the potential terrors of Larkinism.

In fact, the ITGWU appear to have maintained some organisation in Guinness until June 1920 when John Hill, 'late employee of Messrs Guinness' was dismissed for union activities, acted as secretary, brewery section 'without remuneration'. This suggests continuing problems regarding union activity within the brewery but ironically came at a point when the ITGWU was at its zenith with 120,000 members.[47]

Brigid McCarthy's plea

In January 1914, Brigid McCarthy, wife of dismissed skipper Edward McCarthy, wrote to Guinness managing director Renny-Tailyour, clearly very distressed by lack of money and her husband's inability to obtain work. She wrote that McCarthy had:

> all his things ready to go away to sea, which is breaking my heart. Would you be so kind as to try and get him back, or would you try and get some money for me as I am very badly off with eight small children. I was talking to him today and he said if he was taken back he would give up all unions ... I would not mind if he was put in some other part of the Brewery as he does not like the boats. Would you be so kind and let me know what you can do for me before he goes away.

4. Patrick Donegan with his greyhound 'Fluther', c. 1950.
Courtesy Patrick Coughlan.

Kindness was not Renny-Tailyour's strong suit apparently as Brigid McCarthy's persistent correspondence until August bore no dividend.[48] Patrick Donegan, whose motherless family of eight were similarly distressed, threw himself on the charity of Dublin Lord Mayor Lorcan Sherlock. A collection was taken up 'to secure a horse and dray by which to earn a livelihood for himself and family.'[49] Patrick Coughlan recalls that his grandfather was 'no businessman'. The horse that was purchased for him 'was nearly blind' and as Donegan went through the streets as a 'bellman', many customers took part sacks of coal promising to 'pay him on Friday' but, of course, 'Friday never came'. Donegan's business failed and he went to work in Inchicore Works in the smithy shop. Here he had a small accident to his foot, was discharged and received a tiny pension. The ITGWU pursued an unsuccessful compensation case for Donegan against the Great Southern and Western Railway under the Workmen's Compensation Act that concluded in court in November 1923.[50] Always loyal to the ITGWU, Frank Robbins, theatre branch secretary, got Donegan employment as a 'queue man' outside the Tivoli Theatre in Francis Street where his six feet height proved formidable in controlling and managing the crowds.

Patrick Donegan's employment record and continuing ITGWU efforts on his behalf

Patrick Coughlan, having read something of Donegan's dismissal, now pursued his grandfather's records in the Guinness Archive.[51] Donegan was employee 6983 having been employed on the B list in the forwarding department of the brewery on 2 May 1895. This document indicates that he was born on 14 September 1872 in Ballymore-Eustace, Co. Kildare.[52] His application to the brewery was supported by Rev. Herbert Kennedy, rector, Hollywood, Ballymore-Eustace, by letter of 17 February 1894.

> I beg to recommend bearer, Patrick Donegan, for employment in the Brewery – I have known his father for a considerable length of time and have a high opinion of him – Patrick Donegan bears good recommendations from worthy parishioners of mine who have known him from childhood, Mrs Kennedy of Armfield and Mr West of [indecipherable] near whose places he lives – I believe you would find him thoroughly honest, sober, quiet, and trustworthy; and I hope you will be able to give him employment.[53]

On 7 May 1896, on the recommendation of Robert Herd, and with his conduct 'satisfactory' and his efficiency 'good', Donegan was promoted to the A list.[54] Donegan's dismissal on 27 September 1913 from the forwarding department was approved by the board on 30 September. His wages were 29 shillings a week. Guinness regarded Donegan as having 'resigned' for the reasons 'in sympathy with the dismissal of E. McCarthy and on principle.' His 'character', 'efficiency' and 'attendance' were all noted as 'good'.[55]

After Donegan's coal business failed, the ITGWU made further representations on his behalf. John Bohan, TC, branch secretary, ITGWU Dublin No. 3 branch, based at 74 Thomas Street, wrote on behalf of Donegan,[56] McCarthy and three other men involved in the original incident, T. Coyle, J. Kerwan and M. Butler on 2 March 1922. Bohan acknowledged that the men were dismissed because of their 'sympathetic action, in which they refused to perform certain duties whilst employed as Boatmen.' Bohan referred to their service, 'from 7 to 18 years', and to the fact that the company had regarded them as 'first-class workmen, until this unfortunate affair took place.' Bohan then sought their reinstatement or that 'some compensation would be allowed in each case according to service.' Bohan's opportunity was apparently presented by recent beneficence shown by the company to others.

> Having regard to the fact that a number of men have been reinstated recently who were dismissed from your employment during the troubled period of 1916, we trust that your Board will extend to the above men the same treatment and consideration.[57]

Quite separately, and apparently unknown to Bohan, ITGWU general treasurer William O'Brien, had already written a similar plea on 27 February 1922. O'Brien's letter followed a similar logic but only appealed on behalf of Donegan and W. McCarthy [sic] -

> in view of the fact that your firm has recently decided to re-employ those dismissed in consequence of the political situation which existed for some time past, I have been directed to ask if your Board would be good enough to extend that privilege to the two men referred to.[58]

O'Brien's letter identified the boat as the *Anna Liffey*. T. B. Case replied to O'Brien on 3 March saying that after giving 'full consideration by our Board', 'we regret that we cannot see our way to accede to the request of your Union, as we are not prepared to take these men back into our service.'[59] Bohan received a similar reply.[60] An internal board memo from the registry department, dated 28 February 1922, signed by the managing director, J. H. A. Guinness, indicated that Donegan had made three previous applications to be re-employed and that the board had determined on 9 September 1914 that he 'cannot ever be re-employed by us.' Further detail is supplied on Edward McCarthy. He had been first employed on 14 November 1901 as a labourer in forwarding and finally as a skipper 'on one of our boats'. He was dismissed for 'insubordination' on 19 September 1913 as he 'refused to go to Tedcastle Berth to collect empties when directed to do so.' As with Donegan, his previous character, efficiency and attendance were 'good'.[61] The ITGWU bargaining position was relatively poor as they were only beginning to organise in the brewery. Donegan was clearly held in regard, however, to have both his branch secretary and O'Brien lobby on his behalf. The cachet of being a '1913 martyr' clearly held currency.

Donegan's plight in his old age provoked Frank Robbins, secretary, ITGWU Dublin District Council and Donegan's branch secretary in No. 7 branch, theatre and cinema, to write, hopefully, to Guinness on 17 January 1949. By now Guinness general staffs were organised in the Workers' Union of Ireland (WUI).[62] Robbins nevertheless repeated the history of the event, acknowledged previous unsuccessful pleas but concluded that:

> Mr Donegan is almost 70 years of age and his circumstances at the moment are not very good. We are placing this case before you for your sympathetic consideration in view of his previous service.[63]

M. Morrissey, registry department wrote a memo to the managing director, re Donegan 'Reg No 6983, ex Brewery Employee, Application For Assistance' on 21 January 1949, rehashing details from previous files but with the hand-written comment 'report the Board cannot see their way to help.'[64] Donegan was 76 years and four months old. This not entirely unexpected, cold news was conveyed to Robbins in a terse letter of 24 January 1949 from Morrissey. It ended the appeals. The brewery's paternalism had un-breachable limits.

Patrick Donegan died in 1955. He had remained a committed trade unionist all his life and an active ITGWU member. The union had done its best on his behalf, maintaining his case from 1913 until 1949 to no avail. Donegan, despite staying loyal to the ITGWU, maintained a solid admiration for James Larkin, which he conveyed to his family. Donegan remained a Larkinite all his life. Indeed, he had gone to Dún Laoghaire in April 1923 to greet the great man on his arrival back from over eight years' exile in America and is recorded in a photograph of the occasion. Given Donegan's admiration for Larkin, it seems odd that he apparently remained loyal to the ITGWU rather than transfer to the WUI after 1924 with the majority of ITGWU members in Dublin. In fact, the likelihood is that he did join the WUI and was, as a consequence, part of the fractious and ultimately disastrous strike in Inchicore Railway Works in August, 1924. The strike, forced against the wishes of WUI branch secretary – former Irish Citizen Army man and Communist Party of Ireland member, Seán McLoughlin – resulted in mass dismissals. The greatest, and for Donegan, probably most disillusioning, shock was the breaching of WUI picket lines at Kingsbridge Station by a lorry from the Dublin Rapid Transit Company, 'known by every worker in Dublin to be the property of the Larkin family.' The company was owned by Larkin's sister Delia's husband Patrick Colgan and operated out of the house Larkin lived in. According to Jack Carney, writing to Seán O'Casey in 1948, 'from that day to the hour of his death, Jim never spoke to Delia.' McLoughlin emigrated to Britain not long after the strike, his 'belief in Larkin – until then unquestioning – shattered.'[65] Donegan may have been equally disillusioned and, once re-employed, rejoined the ITGWU. Donegan was fortunate to get his job back. He told his grandson, Patrick Coughlan, that as the foreman came along the line of hopefuls, hand-picking the lucky few, Donegan used his impressive height and physique, strengthened by his toil in the smithy, to suggest to the foreman that, 'if he didn't pick me, he might not be able to eat solids for a few weeks.' The foreman saw sense and Donegan was favoured.[66]

Donegan still continued to regard himself as a follower of Big Jim. It was in this spirit that he took his original actions in 1913, actions for which he and his family paid a high price in economic terms. Donegan's grandson, Patrick Coughlan, and the wider family have rightly drawn great pride from the heroic commitment of Patrick Donegan, Edward McCarthy and their crew-mates in 1913. The successful pursuit of Donegan's case is reward for their desire to recover the family's labour history.

Acknowledgement

This article arose out of meetings between Patrick Coughlan and Francis Devine, the last being on 10 November 2005, and Coughlan's search of the Guinness Archive where Clare Hackett and Éibhlín Roche proved of immense encouragement and assistance. Original scanning was done by Eileen Meier, SIPTU College. We are grateful to the assistance of Ken Finlay, *Dublin Historical Record*, and Ed Penrose, ILHS.

Notes

1   For a history of Guinness see P. Lynch and J. Vaizey, *Guinness's brewery in the Irish economy, 1759-1876* (Cambridge, 1960); Andy Bielenberg, 'The Irish brewing industry and the rise of Guinness, 1790-1914' in Richard G. Wilson and Terence R. Gourvish (eds), *The dynamics of the modern brewing industry since 1800* (London, 1998); Oliver MacDonough and S. R. Dennison, *Guinness, 1886-1939: from incorporation to the Second World War* (Cork, 1998).

2   For the WUI 'coming into the brewery' see Martin Duffy, *The trade union pint: the unlikely union of Guinness and the Larkins* (Dublin, 2012), pp 9-16.

3   For further discussion of the WUI into Guinness see Francis Devine, *Understanding social justice: Paddy Cardiff and the discipline of trade unionism* (Dublin. 2002), pp 7-11. For general views of working in Guinness see Mary Muldowney, 'A world of its own': recollections of women workers in Guinness's brewery in the 1940s', *Saothar 23* (1998), pp 103-18; Al Byrne, *Guinness time: my days in the world's most famous brewery* (Dublin, 1990). For a pictorial view see *St James's Gate Brewery: history and guide* (Dublin, 1931); and Finbarr Flood's farewell collection, *The Guinness Dublin Brewery, St James's Gate*, (Dublin, 1994). Clare Hackett, 'The Guinness Archive employment records, 'from the cradle to the grave', *Irish Archives, Journal of the Irish Society for Archives*, vol. 9, ns (Winter 2003-2004), pp 67-71.

4   Death certificate in possession of Patrick Coughlan. The children were Anne, 15, a domestic servant; Bessie, 13; Bernard, 12; Mary, 10; Martin, 9; Patrick, 7; Bridget, 5; and Margaret, 3. (www.census. nationalarchives.ie/pages/1911/Dublin/Usher_s_Quay/Bow_Lane_West/71826/).

5   Pádraig Yeates, *Lockout: Dublin 1913* (Dublin, 2002) describes the Donegan-McCarthy case in detail.

6   Hackett, 'The Guinness Archive employment records', p. 68.

7   The Regular Dublin Operative Coopers' Society claimed to have been founded in 1666 and on its stationary the even earlier date of 1501, the year a charter was granted to the Coopers' Guild, the

Guild of St Patrick. The union was affiliated to the Irish Trade Union Congress, 1894-1910, and later the Congress of Irish Unions and, until its final dissolution in 1983, the Irish Congress of Trade Unions. Membership was 230 in 1892; 300, 1900; 340, 1910; 252, 1945; 193, 1960; and 109, 1970. Its demise was purely a function of technology and the loss of the old wooden cooperage craft. The Guinness Storehouse contains many artefacts of the trade and some emblems of the society. See Sarah Ward-Perkins, *Select guide to trade union records in Dublin* (Dublin, 1996), pp 229-30.

8   William O'Brien, 23 January 1881-30 October 1968, was a tailor and active in the Amalgamated Society of Tailors and Tailoresses, serving on the executive of Dublin Trades Council, 1909-19, including secretary, Lockout Committee, 1913-14. Associated with Connolly in the Irish Socialist Republican Party after 1896, O'Brien was secretary, Dublin Labour Party, 1911-15 and T.D. for Dublin South, 1922-23; and Tipperary, 1927, 1937 and 1938. In 1918, O'Brien was elected ITGWU general treasurer, 1919-24, and, after Larkin's expulsion, served as general secretary, 1924-46. O'Brien was president, ITUC, 1913, 1918, 1925 and 1941. O'Brien's bitterness to Larkin ultimately culminated in splits in the Labour Party in 1944 with the creation of the short-lived National Labour Party, and the ITUC, with the formation of the Congress of Irish Unions, 1944-59. See Charles Callan and Barry Desmond, 'William O'Brien (1881-1968)', *Irish labour lives* (Dublin, 2010), pp 204-9; Francis Devine, *Organising history: a centenary of SIPTU, 1909-2009* (Dublin, 2009), p. 760; Arthur Mitchell, 'O'Brien, William (1881-1968), labour leader and trade union official', *Dictionary of Irish biography* (Cambridge, 2009); Thomas J. Morrissey. *William O'Brien, 1881-1968: Socialist, republican, Dáil deputy, editor and trade union leader* (Dublin, 2007).

9   William O'Brien, *Forth the banners go Forth the banners go: reminiscences of William O'Brien as told to Edward MacLysaght* (Dublin, 1969), p. 60.

10   The first earl of Iveagh, Edward Cecil Guinness, 1847-1927, was the son of Sir Benjamin Guinness, had managed the brewery with his brother Arthur since 1870, acquiring Arthur's shares in 1876. He oversaw the flotation of Guinness as a public company in 1886 and remained chairman until 1890, although he continued to effectively be the brewery's ultimate decision-maker. To mark his retirement, he provided £250,000 to erect working-class housing in Dublin and London, and created the Iveagh Trust. He was raised to the peerage in 1891, Diarmuid Ferriter, 'Guinness, Edward Cecil (1847-1927), 1st earl of Iveagh, businessman and philanthropist', *Dictionary of Irish biography*.

11   Emmet Larkin, *James Larkin, Irish labour leader, 1876-1947* (London, 1965), p. 118. If there was 'discontent' it had little means of expression but perhaps the rising general discontent in Dublin from 1910 on was catching an echo in the brewery.

12   For a brief discussion of the early organisation of Guinness staffs see Francis Devine, 'Foreword' in Duffy, *The trade union pint*, pp 9-16.

13   *Irish Worker*, 24 May 1911.

14   *Irish Worker*, 10 June 1911. For insights into the history of Dublin brewing see (www.breweryhistory.com/journal/index.html) (2011); and *Dublin historic industry database*, (www.gsi.ie/) (2012).

15   *Irish Worker*, 29 July 1911.

16   *Irish Worker*, 26 Aug. 1911.

17   *Irish Worker*, 24 May 1911; 31 May 1911.

18   *Irish Worker*, 26 Aug. 1911.

19   Michael Sheehan to Charles G. Sutton, 22 September 1911 (GA, GDB/C004.06/0062). The ITGWU was formed on 28 December 1908 and registered from 4 January 1909.

20   (NAI, Registrar of Friendly Societies, Trade Union File 275T). The figure is cited in C. Desmond Greaves, *The Irish Transport and General Workers' Union: the formative years, 1909-1923* (Dublin, 1982), p. 70.

21   P. T. Daly, 1870-1943, was a printer and active in the Dublin Typographical Society and Dublin Trades Council. He was a member of the IRB becoming a member of the supreme council until expelled in 1910 having admitted to mishandling funds. By now he had left Sinn Féin and was active in socialist politics. He had held a Corporation seat, 1903-09. He was elected secretary, ITUC, 1910-18 and became secretary Dublin Trades Council. Daly acting as honorary secretary, ITGWU during Larkin's imprisonment in 1910 and was chosen by Larkin to succeed him while he travelled to America in 1914 until persuaded by Tom Foran and William O'Brien to appoint Connolly instead and put Daly in charge of the ITGWU National Health Insurance Approved Society. By 1918, Foran and O'Brien had ousted Daly from most key positions and Daly was identified with the Larkinite minority who agitated until Larkin's

return, the apparently inevitable split and the formation of the Workers' Union of Ireland in 1924. Daly remained secretary, Dublin Trades Council, even after the ITGWU-led breakaway Workers' Council reunited with the DTC in 1929. Daly died on the steps of the DTC premises on 20 November 1943, see Séamus Cody, 'The remarkable Patrick Daly', *Obair 2* (January 1985), pp 10-11. James Connolly, 1868-1916, was appointed Ulster organiser, ITGWU, 1910 and acting general secretary during Larkin's absences in 1913 and after his departure for America in 1914, see C. Desmond Greaves, *The life and times of James Connolly* (London, 1961); and Donal Nevin, *James Connolly: a full life* (Dublin, 2005).

22 Walter Carpenter was an activist in the Socialist Party of Ireland and appears to have become involved in the ITGWU about 1911 before becoming general secretary, International Tailors', Machiners' and Pressers' Union in 1913. The union had been formed among Jewish immigrant workers in 1908. It changed its title to the Irish Garment Workers' Industrial Union in 1922. Under Carpenter, the union fought against sweat-shop employers and reflected a truly international membership and concern. In 1915, the Tailors and Pressers, incorporated into their rulebook lines written by Young Ireland leader Joseph Brennan, for the distribution of which Walter Carpenter had served three months in prison in 1911, 'The right Divine of Labour, To be first of earthly things: That the Thinker and the Worker Are Manhood's only Kings.' Carpenter was to the van of all such activity until ill-health forced his retirement in 1925. He died shortly afterwards, a mere 55 years old. When the union wound up, its remaining funds were drawn to erect a headstone to Walter Carpenter in October 1948. In their final return to the Registrar of Friendly Societies, Carpenter is described as 'Secretary of Union 1915 to 1925. Died 25 February 1926, Prominent in national and labour circles 1913, 1916, 1922. Figure of historical interest.' See, Joe Mooney, 'Walter Carpenter – from sweep to revolutionary – a forgotten figure from 1913 Lockout' (http://1913committee.ie/blog/?p=542).

23 Thomas Greene, a Dublin carter, was first secretary, National Union of Dock Labourers, Dublin, and first secretary, ITGWU No. 1 Branch. 'Shaken by the allegations of socialism', Greene resigned as secretary in October 1911 and was succeeded by John O'Neill. Greene's 'refuge' appeared to be the Workers' Union. He was 'soon mixing in the shady company of P. J. McIntyre, E. W. Stewart and John Saturnus Kelly, nefarious characters who spent time railing against Larkin and the ITGWU and publishing various yellow press papers. In February 1914, no doubt hoping to pick up crumbs from the collapsing Lockout table, Greene announced the formation of the Irish Dockers' & Workers' Union, see Devine, *Organising history*, pp 23, 28, 46, 50, 73; Greaves, *ITGWU*, pp 23-4, 45, 53, 53, 57, 70, 79, 115.

24 Larkin was in fact born in Liverpool in 1874, see Donal Nevin, *James Larkin: lion of the fold* (Dublin, 1998). His grandson James Larkin maintains that Larkin was born in Tamnaharry, Burren in 1876, see *In the footsteps of Big Jim: a family history* (Dublin, 1996).

25 The Manchester Martyrs – William Allen, Michael Larkin and Michael O'Brien – were members of the Irish Republican Brotherhood (IRB) executed for their part in the killing of policeman Charles Brett in the attack on a horse-drawn prison van to release two IRB leaders Timothy Deasy and Thomas J. Kelly who were being transported to Belle Vue Gaol. A crowd of around 10,000 witnessed the public hanging of the martyrs outside Salford Gaol on 23 November 1867. See Paul Rose, *The Manchester Martyrs: the story of a Fenian tragedy* (London, 1970).

26 The IWWU was founded in April 1911 as a subsidiary organisation within the ITGWU. Jim Larkin was president and his sister Delia general secretary. By 1912 the union had moved to a more independent status. Connolly, acting general secretary, ITGWU, and Helena Molony struggled to keep the union alive and by 1918 it claimed 5,300 members. Louie Bennett became general secretary in 1919, a position she held until 1955. Never rising to more than 7,000 members, the IWWU finally merged with the Federated Workers' Union of Ireland on 1 September 1984. See Mary Jones, *These obstreperous lassies: a history of the Irish Women Workers' Union* (Dublin, 1988). *The Irish Worker* has been described as 'Larkin's oratory congealed in print', see Greaves, *ITGWU*, p. 64. It had a mass circulation in 1912-14 and was 'unchallenged as the informed and rousing voice of working-class grievance, expectation and hope. To read it even today is to experience excitement and a joyous self-confidence and to access the most significant expression yet of Irish working-class culture on a sustained basis. The paper was doing much to strengthen the spine of a class whose backs would have to endure so much in 1913', Francis Devine, 'Larkin and the ITGWU, 1909-1912' in Nevin, *Larkin: lion of the fold,* p. 35. See also John Newsinger, 'A lamp to light your feet: James Larkin, the *Irish Worker* and the Dublin working class', *European History Quarterly*, vol. 20 (1990), pp 63-69.

27 Michael Sheehan to Charles G. Sutton, 6 October 1911 (GA, GDB/C004.06/0062).

28 Michael Sheehan to Sutton & Co, 31 July 1913 (GA, GDB/C004.06/0062).

29 Partridge was born in Sligo in 1874 but reared in Ballaghaderreen, the son of a railway engine driver. Partridge served an engineering apprenticeship in Sligo and Broadstone and became active in Dublin No. 2 Branch, Amalgamated Society of Engineers, Dublin Trades Council and Conradh na Gaeilge. A City Councillor in Kilmainham, 1904-06 and 1913-17, he became an ITGWU organiser and central figure during the 1913 Lockout. An Irish Citizen Army member, he served in the Royal College of Surgeons in 1916 under Michael Mallin and Constance Markievicz and was subsequently imprisoned in Dartmoor and Lewes. Suffering from Bright's Disease, he was released in April 1917 and died in Ballaghaderreen on 26 July. See Hugh Geraghty, *William Patrick Partridge and his times (1874-1917)* (Dublin, 2003) and Lawrence William White, 'Partridge, William Patrick ('Bill') (1874-1916), trade unionist and revolutionary nationalist', *Dictionary of Irish biography*.

30 *Irish Worker*, 25 Jan. 1913.

31 *Irish Worker*, 31 May 1913.

32 Eugene Coyle, 'Larkinism and the 1913 County Dublin farm labourers' dispute', *Dublin Historical Record*, lviii, no. 2 (Autumn 2005), pp 176-90.

33 (NLI, William O'Brien Papers, MS 13,921); James Larkin to manager, shipping department, Guinness's Brewery, 7 October, 1915 (GA, GDB/C004.06/0062). There is some confusion over the name of the barge as later it is referred to as *Anna Liffey*.

34 Ibid.

35 Arthur Ernest Guinness, 1876-1949, was the younger brother of the 2nd earl of Iveagh, Sir Rupert Guinness, 1874-1967. Ernest was assistant managing director, 1902-1912, and vice chairman, 1913-1947, Bill Yenne, *Guinness: the 250 quest for the perfect pint* (Hoboken, New Jersey, 2007), p. 284.

36 (GA, Board memoranda, 2144-431 and ITGWU correspondence, Box 6). See also (NLI, William O'Brien Papers, MS 13,921).

37 Yeates, *Lockout*, pp 479-81.

38 (GA, Board memoranda, 2144-431 and ITGWU correspondence, Box 6). See also (NLI, William O'Brien Papers, MS 13,921).

39 L. H. Powell, *The Shipping Federation: a history of the first sixty years, 1890-1960* (London, 1950).

40 Tim Magennis, 'Where are the barges now?', *Iris na Mara*, pp 7-8, 28; Peter Walsh, 'Six pairs of oars and an anchor', *Guinness Extra: The Brewery Community Bulletin*, vol. 11 (June 1993), pp 14-15. The *Barkley* was purchased in 1913, a 569 ton coaster, built in the Ailsa Shipyard, Troon, Ayrshire, Scotland in 1898 and purchased second hand from John Kelly & Sons, Belfast. She was requisitioned by the Admiralty in 1916 and carried stone to Guernsey, timber and cement to Britain, and pig iron from Glasgow to Dunkirk. She was `released back to Guinness in 1917 at 7 p.m. on 12 October, 1917, seven miles from the Kish Lightship she was struck by a German U-boat and sunk. Five crewmen perished and nine were saved. Yeates suggests 'tankers' but at that time the barges carried wooden hogsheads until the mid-1960s when steel tanks, equivalent to five hogsheads, replaced the timber barrels. The first purpose built tankers came in the mid-1980s.

41 Yeates, *Lockout,* p. 233.

42 The Dublin Employers' Federation (DEF) was founded by William Martin Murphy on 30 June 1911. Its intention was to 'prevent strikes' and oppose 'intimidation and violence' so that men 'desirous of retaining or returning to their employment, are prevented from doing so.' Championing the 'free labour' cause, DEF objects were 'mutual protection and indemnity of all employers of labour' and 'to promote freedom of contract between employers and employees.' Devine, *Organising history*, p. 44.

43 Ibid, pp 233-4, citing secretary's Annual report for 1913 (GA, Board memoranda 2144-431; ITGWU correspondence, 1913). See also MacDonagh and Denneson, *op. cit.,* pp 144-46.

44 Yeates, *Lockout*, p. 234.

45 *Irish Worker*, 22 Nov. 1913.

46 Ibid, citing (GA, Board memoranda 2144-431).

47 *Workers' Republic*, 31 July 1920. ITGWU membership was 102,823 in September and 120,000 by December, see ITGWU, *Annual report for 1920.*

48   Mrs B. McCarthy to 'Mr Taylor', 4 January, 1914 (GA, ITGWU correspondence, Box 6); Yeates, *Lockout,* p. 548.

49   (GA, Board memoranda, 2144-431). The subscription list is contained in the (DDA, Walsh Papers, laity file); Yeates, *Lockout,* p. 548.

50   In response to the ITGWU's first letter from O'Connor, Solicitors, on 6 February, 1923, the company made 'an offer of light work' to which the 'applicant had no objection' providing that 'he is paid his old rate of wages and an agreement entered into to preserve his rights; or in the alternative, he would accept a lump sum' (NLI, ITGWU Special List A8, Ms 27,054 (7)). Matters went to and fro until in November, 1923, Donegan attended court 'when no Order made, applicant to return to work, liberty to re-enter.' There is no record of re-entry and, according to Coughlan, the 'small pension' perhaps resulted from a settlement at local level.

51   Hackett, 'The Guinness Archive employment records'.

52   Personnel File, Patrick Donegan (GA, GDB/C004.06/0062). Donegan was actually born in Coolgreany, Gorey, Co. Wexford, birth certificate in the possession of Patrick Coughlan.

53   Reference written by Rev. Herbert Kennedy, 17 February 1894 (GA, GDB/C004.06/0062).

54   Personnel File, Patrick Donegan (GA, GDB/C004.06.0062).

55   ibid.

56   John Bohan was ITGWU No. 3 Branch (High Street) secretary and a member of Dublin Corporation, 1912-1915. A constant thorn in the ITGWU executive's side, he was secretary WUI No. 1 Branch in 1924 but quickly fell out with Larkin and was sacked in 1930. His subsequent life remains a mystery. See Devine, *Organising history,* p. 972.

57   John Bohan, ITGWU Dublin No. 3 Branch to chairman, Guinness, 2 March, 1922 (GA, GDB/C004.06.0062). Notice that the name Coyle does not appear on the original *Tolka* crew list.

58   William O'Brien to Guinness, 27 February 1922 (GA, GDB/C004.06.0062).

59   T. B. Case to O'Brien, 3 March 1922 (GA, GDB/C004.06.0062).

60   T. B. Case to Bohan, 3 March 1922 (GA, GDB/C004.06.0062).

61   Report by managing director, H. J. A. Guinness to registry department, 28 February, 1922 (GA, GDB/C004.06.0062). Interestingly, an Edward McCarthy, 28 Arran Quay, turns up as an ITGWU delegate to the Congress of Irish Unions, Waterford, 1947, see CIU, *Third annual report*, p. 37. Surely it cannot have been the same Edward McCarthy?

62   For details of the WUI organisation see Duffy, *The trade union pint*.

63   Frank Robbins, branch secretary, Dublin No. 7 Branch, ITGWU to Guinness, 17 January, 1949 (GA, GDB/C004.06.0062).

64   M. Morrissey, Memo to managing director, 21 January, 1949 (GA, GDB/C004.06.0062).

65   Seán McLoughlin, 'How Inchicore was lost' (NLI, William O'Brien Papers, MS 15,670); Carney to O'Casey, 27 July, 1948 (O'Casey Papers), cited in Niamh Puirséil, 'Seán O'Casey Papers', *Saothar 31* (2006), pp 129-31; *Voice of Labour*, 24 Jan. 1925; Devine, *Organising history,* pp 211-12; Charlie McGuire, *Seán McLoughlin, Ireland's forgotten revolutionary* (London, 2010), pp 119-22.

66   Related to Francis Devine by Patrick Coughlan (16 January 2013).

5. Food ship arrives in Dublin, *An Claidheamh Soluis*, 13 Dec. 1913.
DCLA

15.

George Russell and James Stephens: class and cultural discourse, Dublin 1913

....

Leeann Lane

The poverty of Dublin slum dwellers depicted in James Stephens' *The charwoman's daughter*, serialised in the *Irish Review* in 1911-12,[1] found its way into the cultural discourse of the period, most notably in the context of the 1913 Lockout. In October 1913 George William Russell (Æ) penned a letter to the employers of Dublin denouncing their refusal to allow unionisation and their treatment of their employees. This letter, 'To the Masters of Dublin', was published in *The Irish Times* on 7 October 1913; it was reproduced in *The Irish Worker* four days later, on 11 October. This essay will examine the manner in which many of the Anglo-Irish leaders of the cultural revival engaged in a battle and a war of words with the new Catholic elite in waiting, the most iconic figure being William Martin Murphy; the issues around which this cultural war was waged crystallised in 1913 with the Lockout and the Hugh Lane Gallery controversy. Cultural discourse across Dublin in 1913 was sharply class focused. Crucially, in this cultural battle, the voice of the working classes was mediated, represented by the Anglo-Irish cultural revivalists in the context of their own class needs and issues. In putting forward this argument, the essay will use George William Russell's intervention in 1913 on behalf of the locked out men as a case study. The dichotomy in living standards and material wealth which Russell identifies in his letter was also reflected in one of the key novels of the period, James Stephens' *The charwoman's daughter*. Stephens' novel is particularly interesting by virtue of the fact that, unlike Russell, he was of the working classes. Both Russell and Stephens were part of the same literary circle in Dublin in 1913; Russell, indeed, is credited with discovering Stephens and introducing him to key cultural practitioners in the city. Both, however, engaged with the plight of Dublin in the period from different class perspectives and needs.

For many who lived in Dublin in 1913 the cultural war between Anglo-Ireland and the emerging new Catholic elite within the middle classes had little resonance or impact. Activities such as a trip to the theatre or the newly arrived cinema were enjoyed as a night of entertainment with no apparent political or class connotation. And yet, cinema and theatre were sharply divided by class in terms of access, offerings and even the behaviour expected of audiences. In 1913 culture and leisure activities reflected the class and wealth divisions that marked Dublin. The Georgian houses of Merrion

Square, the growing middle-class suburbs, the fine shops in Grafton Street all reflected affluence and at times the architectural beauty of Ireland's capital city. At the opposite side of the spectrum, in the tenements of Dublin, people lived in grinding poverty and squalor. This sharp discrepancy between absolute poverty and gradations of affluence was delineated a year previous to the Lockout in James Stephens' novel, *The charwoman's daughter*. Unlike James Plunkett's *Strumpet city* published in 1969, *The charwoman's daughter* offers a key into poverty and deprivation from a contemporary perspective. *The charwoman's daughter* sharply portrays the manner in which invisible barriers in terms of access to amenities and opportunities existed between the classes in Dublin despite their often close proximity on the streets and parks of the city centre. The central character, Mary Makebelieve, entertains herself while her mother works, by sitting in St Stephen's Green and by walking through O'Connell Street and Grafton Street perusing the shop windows. The descriptions underscore the exclusion of the poor and the manner in which the characters in the novel gaze longingly at the material goods they desire but can lay no claim to.

> She always went along the right-hand side of the street going home, and looked in every shop window that she passed; and then, when she had eaten her lunch, she came out again and walked along the left-hand side of the road, looking at the shops on that side; and so she knew daily everything that was new in the city, and was able to tell her mother at night time that the black dress with Spanish lace was taken out of Manning's window … or that the diamond ring in Johnson's marked One Hundred Pounds was gone from the case …[2]

This juxtaposition of poverty and wealth in Dublin had been previously depicted in fiction most notably in George Moore's 1886 Big House novel, *A drama in muslin*. Moore depicted the manner in which the roads to Dublin Castle on the night of the Vice-regal Ball were lined with:

> vagrants … waifs … troops of labourers battered and bruised with toil … Never were poverty and wealth brought into plainer proximity. In the broad glare of the carriage lights the … every stain of misery were revealed to the silken exquisites who, a little frightened, strove to hide themselves within the scented shadows of their broughams …[3]

In 1913 Dublin Castle was still the focus of government social life,[4] so the fictional scenes depicted by Moore could conceivably be those of this later time period. However, *The charwoman's daughter* was the first fictional depiction of poverty from the perspective of the Dublin tenement rather than from that of the Big House. James Stephens himself had spent some of his childhood in the north side slums of the capital and was therefore writing from experience. Born either in 1880 or 1882, Stephens was the son of a van driver. In 1886 he was sent to the Meath Protestant Industrial School for street begging and in later life told stories of hunger and vagrancy.[5] In the 1911 census he was recorded living with his wife, two children and a servant girl at 54.4 Mount Street, Lower, Dublin; he listed his occupation as that of clerk. The dwelling in Mount Street occupied by the family comprised two rooms in a 12 room house; six families in total lived in the house.[6] Such poor housing conditions indicates that although Stephens had in 1907 been 'discovered' by Russell and introduced into Dublin literary circles,[7] this did not translate into economic advancement.

THE DUBLIN STRIKE.

BY "Æ" (GEORGE W. RUSSELL).

"Irish Worker" Press, Liberty Hall, Dublin, Ireland.

1. *The Dublin strike*, includes three items by Æ: 1. A plea for the workers. 2. An open letter to the employers. 3. An appeal to Dublin citizens. Published at the Irish Worker Press, Liberty Hall, 1913.
DCLA

Underscoring the dichotomy in material possessions and expectations amongst the classes in the period portrayed in Stephens' novel, Russell quite possibly penned his letter to the 'Masters of Dublin' in his head as he travelled from his house in affluent, middle-class Ranelagh to the office of *The Irish Homestead*, the organ of the Irish Agricultural Organisation Society (IAOS) established in 1894. In the spacious Georgian office in 84 Merrion Square, Russell, as editor of the paper from 1905, constructed an idealised image of small-holder life in rural Ireland. Now in 1913 the poet, painter and journalist had intervened on the side of the urban worker. Indeed, commentators were quick to point out that a poet had intruded in an apparently economic matter. In one letter of response to Russell's contribution to the debate he was described as a 'good poet who had sought to convert ... into a bad economist.'[8] That same year, and also in the context of the Lockout, Russell's friend and fellow cultural revivalist, W. B. Yeats published, once again in *The Irish Times*, 'Romance in Ireland', later renamed 'September 1913', a poem decrying the materialistic values of the Catholic middle classes. Yeats depicted the Catholic middle classes in thrall to a church underpinned by the very materialistic, grasping and vulgar values adhered to by their flock. The middle classes depicted in the poem compile inventories; prayers are added up in the same way as money in a description that portrays the lack of real spirituality and humanity in religious sentiment:

> What need you being, come to sense,
> But fumble in a greasy till
> And add the halfpence to the pence, until
> You have dried the marrow from the bone?
> For men were born to pray and save:
> Romantic Ireland's dead and gone,
> It's with O'Leary in the grave.[9]

Literary Dublin and the doyens of the cultural revival such as Russell and Yeats, were not just desirous to attack the Catholic business elites of Dublin in the context of the Lockout but linked to this was the Hugh Lane Gallery controversy of 1913. William Martin Murphy was not just decried as a cruel employer; he was also denounced as a man without aesthetic or cultural taste. That the city of Dublin would not find the money to build an art gallery to house Hugh Lane's bequest was testament to this.

Russell's intervention on behalf the locked out workers in 1913 should be seen in the context of his wider writings and opinions in *The Irish Homestead*. It is this wider context that allows the argument that Russell's plea on behalf of the workers was more layered and complex than a humanitarian reaction to injustice, starvation and sordid tenement life. In the pages of *The Irish Homestead*, Russell constructed a certain view of poverty and created an idealised peasant.[10] Russell's 'created' peasants were small holders, primitive and backward in the material needs of the life but filled with an innate dignity and willing to be lead into the joys of an idealised rural way of life which bore little resemblance to the realities of commercial farming in Ireland.

Russell's descriptions of the rural life that the small farmer ought to strive for were, in many cases, literary constructs designed to act as a counter to what he saw as the materialism of Catholic bourgeois Ireland. In the letter to *The Irish Times* in 1913 Russell refers repeatedly to his work as part of the IAOS and draws analogies between the plight of the tenant farmer and the urban worker. There is no doubt that Russell was genuinely appalled at the treatment of the men, women and their families during the strike. In no uncertain terms he laid bare the levels of poverty in the Dublin slums denouncing the lack of civic responsibility:

> You have allowed the poor to be herded together so that one thinks of certain places in Dublin as of a pestilence. There are 20,000 rooms, in each of which are entire families, and sometimes more, where no function of the body can be concealed, and delicacy and modesty are creatures that are stilted ere they are born. The obvious duty of you in regard to these things you might have left undone, and it be imputed to ignorance or forgetfulness; but your collective and conscious action as a class in the present labour dispute has revealed you to the world in so malign an aspect that the mirror must be held up to you, so that you may see yourself as every humane person sees you.[11]

THE CHARWOMAN'S DAUGHTER

BY

JAMES STEPHENS

MACMILLAN AND CO., LIMITED
ST. MARTIN'S STREET, LONDON
1912

2. *The charwoman's daughter*, first edition, London, 1912.
DCLA

Indeed, in 1913, 79 elected members of Dublin City Council owned 89 tenements and second class houses.[12] The census returns of 1911 show that 26,000 families lived in inner city tenements of which 20,000 lived in single rooms like Mary Makebelieve and her mother in *The charwoman's daughter*; Dublin in that year had the worst housing conditions of all cities in the United Kingdom.[13] Mary Makebelieve lives with her mother, a widow, in one top story room in a big house; this is a room without even a table. They eat breakfast with the bread, condensed milk and tea cups balanced precariously on the bed. Cockroaches emerge at night from cracks in the wall. Mary lies awake listening to the gnawing of rats' teeth in the skirting; there

4

you back them up to-day they will be able to fight their own battles to-morrow, and perhaps to give you an example. I beseech you not to forsake these men.

II. AN OPEN LETTER TO THE EMPLOYERS.

By " Æ."

SIRS,—I address this warning to you, the aristocracy of industry in this city, because, like all aristocracies, you tend to grow blind in long authority, and to be unaware that you and your class and its every action are being considered and judged day by day by those who have power to shake or overturn the whole social order, and whose restlessness in poverty to-day is making our industrial civilisation stir like a quaking bog. You do not seem to realise that your assumption that you are answerable to yourselves alone for your actions in the industries you control is one that becomes less and less tolerable in a world so crowded with necessitous life. Some of you have helped Irish farmers to upset a landed aristocracy in this island, an aristocracy richer and more powerful in its sphere than you are in yours, with its roots deep in history. They, too, as a class, though not all of them, were scornful or neglectful of the workers in the industry by which they profited; and to many who knew them in their pride of place and thought them all-powerful they are already becoming a memory, the good disappearing together with the bad. If they had done their duty by those from whose labour came their wealth, they might have continued unquestioned in power and prestige for centuries to come. The relation of landlord and tenant is not an ideal one, but any relations in a social order will endure if there is infused into them some of that spirit of human sympathy which qualifies life for immortality. Despotisms endure while they are benevolent, and aristocracies while "noblesse oblige" is not a phrase to be referred to with a cynical smile. Even an oligarchy might be permanent if the spirit of human kindness, which harmonises all things otherwise incompatible, is present.

You do not seem to read history so as to learn its lessons. That you are an uncultivated class was obvious from recent utterances of some of you upon art. That you are incompetent men in the sphere in which you arrogate imperial powers is certain, because for many years, long before the present uprising of labour, your enterprises have been dwindling in the regard of investors, and this while you have carried them on in the cheapest labour market in these islands, with a labour reserve always hungry and ready to accept any pittance. You are bad citizens, for we rarely, if ever, hear of the wealthy among you endowing your city with the munificent gifts which it is the pride of merchant princes in other cities to offer, and Irishmen not of your city, who offer to supply the wants left by your lack of generosity, are met with derision and abuse. Those who have economic power have civic power also, yet you have not used the power that was yours to right what was wrong in the evil administration of this city. You have allowed the poor to be herded together so that one thinks of certain places in Dublin as of a pestilence. There are twenty thousand rooms, in each of which live entire families, and sometimes more, where no functions of the body can be concealed, and delicacy and modesty are creatures that are stifled ere they are born. The obvious duty of you in regard to these things you might have left undone, and it be imputed to ignorance or forgetfulness; but your collective and conscious action as a class in the present labour dispute has revealed you to the world in so malign an aspect that the mirror must be held up to you, so that you may see yourself as every humane person sees you.

The conception of yourselves as altogether virtuous and wronged is I assure you, not at all the one which onlookers hold of you. No doubt,

3. An open letter to the employers, published in *The Dublin strike*, 1913.
DCLA

were three rat holes in the room. Mary does not look out the grimy window often because she would have to wash the falling soot from herself and water had to be carried up 'hundreds and hundreds of stairs'; Mary consequently 'disliked having to use too much water'. Her mother 'seldom washed at all'. Eight people occupied the next room in the house; Mr Cafferty, a labouring man, his wife and six children.[14] Stephens portrays the subsistence lifestyle of the tenement dwellers where any unexpected event causes untold hardship and deprivation. When Mary's mother is ill they are forced to pawn their paltry items of furniture and shabby clothes.[15] The novel treats of the constricting employment possibilities in Dublin in the period and the manner in which this impacts on the poorest families. Despite his willingness to work Mr Cafferty cannot find anyone to employ him. In this time period unskilled labourers were forced to rely on 'work that was often casual, broken and seasonal. There were estimated to be 24,000 men, one quarter of adult males of the city dependent on such labour and many went for weeks without any work at all.'[16] The latter is the situation Mr Cafferty found himself in, leading to hardship for his family; his wife 'now had less money than she had been used to, but she still had the same rent to pay, the same number of children to feed, and the same personal dignity to support as in better days ...'[17] Stephens writes in a manner that underscores the poverty trap in which the tenement dweller lives:

> while many wild creatures are able to make thrifty provision against the bad time which they know as certainly and periodically as the good times. Bees and squirrels ... fill their barns with plentiful overplus of the summer fields, birds can migrate and find sunshine and sustenance elsewhere; and others again can store during their good season a life energy by means whereof they may sleep healthily through their hard times. These organizations can be adjusted to their environment because the changes of the latter are known and can be predicted from any point. But the human worker has no such regularity. His food period does not ebb and recur with the seasons. There is no periodicity in the changes, and, therefore, no possibility for defective or protective action.[18]

In this context of an excess of labour over employment, Russell notes and condemns the Dublin employers for conducting their industries 'in the cheapest labour market in these islands, with a labour reserve always hungry and ready to accept any pittance.'[19] This reserve labour force was central to the manner in which Dublin employers such as Murphy could drive down wages in the period and stymie attempts at unionisation. Yet, despite denouncing the conditions of the Dublin worker in his 1913 letter, Russell's writings in many respects idealised poverty in the context of his hatred of the materialism and, as he saw it, vulgarity of the new Catholic middle classes and his intervention during the Lockout should be interpreted in this wider context. Russell, while genuinely horrified at conditions in the Dublin slums, used the occasion of the Lockout to once again denounce the rising Catholic middle classes as he had done and continued to do in *The Irish Homestead*. The opinions Russell enunciated and the attitudes he expressed in his role of editor of *The Irish Homestead* have to be viewed in the context of social, economic and political change in Ireland at the time. By the closing decades of the 19th century a new rural elite in place of the Anglo-Irish landlord class had emerged in Irish society. This new elite, comprising large farmers, shopkeepers, merchants and professional men, was the product of 'the post-Famine social, economic and political transformation of Ireland.'[20] Despite Russell's theosophical concern to promote the brotherhood of man, he was primarily concerned to better the life of the small farmer and an examination of his editorials and weekly notes in *The Irish Homestead* show him to be opposed to the larger farmer who he viewed negatively as a member of the rising middle class in early 20th-century Ireland. Throughout the pages of *The Irish Homestead* the large farmer was described negatively and pejoratively. He, together with the gombeenman,[21] was presented as the source of ill in the Irish countryside, such descriptions were an indication of Russell's discomfort with, and dislike of, the new configuration of social, economic and political power in late 19th-, early 20th-century Irish society. Throughout his writings Russell stressed the uncultured aspects of the Irish middle class, often contrasting their, as he argued, lack of cultural achievement with the glory of the Anglo-Irish contribution to Irish literature and the arts in general. In particular, this new middle class was Catholic and thus Russell's sense of the uncreated nature of Irish Catholicism coalesced with his hatred of middle-class materialism and lack of culture. These issues that he discussed in the context of his view of agricultural co-operation came to the fore in an urban context in 1913. And crucially, in his letter of 1913 he repeatedly castigated the employers of Dublin for failing to act as did 'merchant princes in other cities' and 'endow your city with munificent gifts.' Russell made direct reference in the letter to the gallery controversy:

> That you are an uncultivated class was obvious from recent utterances of some of you upon art … Irishmen not of your city who offer to supply the wants left by your lack of generosity are met with derision and abuse.[22]

This reference to the Hugh Lane bequest and its stipulations in the context of the effects of the Lockout is noteworthy. Russell's letter expressed more than concern at the deprivations experienced; the 1913 Lockout provided a vehicle to express cultural concerns and class issues from his own wider Anglo-Irish perspective. The new Catholic elites were a class, he wrote in *The Irish Homestead* in 1913, who preferred the 'decorations in a gaudy public house to a poem in stone by Lutyens', the British architect who was to have designed the new art gallery. It should be noted when considering Russell's appreciation of the art of Edwin Lutyens and his support for his proposed commission, that the council of the Royal Institute of Architects of Ireland adopted a wholly different view on the basis of jobs and opportunities within Ireland. During the debate on the proposed gallery the following resolution was sent to the Lord Mayor, Lorcan Sherlock, the Hon. Secretary of the site committee and to the press:

> That the Council deprecates the apparent intention of the promoters of the new Municipal Art Gallery building to withhold from Irish architects the opportunity of submitting designs. The Council further regrets that it is proposed to associate an Irish architect with Mr Luytens. Similar action has prevented Irish architects from exhibiting their skill in design on more than one occasion in recent years. The Council would suggest that an open competition for the design be inaugurated, and that Mr Lutyens be asked to act as Assessor. [23]

In contrast to the lack of cultural leadership demonstrated by the wealthy Catholic business men of 1913 Dublin, the large cultural dimension to the Irish trade union movement, notably the theatrical productions of Liberty Hall and the literary components of *The Irish Worker* would have appealed to Russell.[24] Over 80% of the 1912 Christmas Number produced by *The Irish Worker* was devoted to fiction, poetry and drama. Standish O'Grady, long revered by Russell as the man who had re-introduced the values of the Irish heroic past to Irish literature, wrote the first piece in the Christmas Number entitled 'Heroes and the heroic: an address to Young Ireland'; O'Grady, indeed, contributed 20 pieces to *The Irish Worker* over the period of its run from 1911-14.[25]

The co-operative values preached by Russell in *The Irish Homestead* were an attempt to grapple with social change. Far from a utilitarian self-aid paper for farmers concerned with pig farming and livestock rearing, the subtext of *The Irish Homestead* was an idealistic attempt to halt the effects of mass democracy in Irish society and to retain a leadership role for the Anglo-Irish. Russell believed that it was possible to diminish the impact of the vulgar Catholic bourgeois class in Irish society. He hoped to create an affiliation between the Anglo-Irish and the smaller farmers in Irish society, the latter released by agricultural co-operation from debt bondage to the Irish gombeenman, representative for Russell of the rise of the new materialistic middle class in Irish society;[26] The 'Masters' of Dublin were the analogous class in a 1913 urban setting.

Through rural reconstruction and agricultural co-operation Russell desired to create a new role for the Anglo-Irish who had been relegated to the fringes of Irish society by the end of the 19th century. Recreated as an aristocracy of intellect and character, the Anglo-Irish would establish themselves as the leaders of a rural Ireland, newly reconstructed through agricultural co-operation. In 1908 Horace Plunkett published *Noblesse oblige*, *an Irish rendering*, an appeal to the landlords of Ireland to use their superior education and character to work for the future social and economic betterment of Irish society, thereby ensuring themselves a place in the new Ireland. In his editorial published in *The Irish Homestead* on 1 February 1908, Russell ringingly endorsed the sentiments expressed in the pamphlet, sentiments he himself expressed and enlarged on repeatedly in his co-operative writings. In the past, Russell argued, Irish farmers followed those who helped them in the land struggle. In the future support, he declared, would be granted by the farmers to those who served them in solving the problems of the small proprietor.[27] Russell's call to the Irish landlord class to work to better the future of Irish society drew on his beliefs in the merits of a hierarchical past which was underpinned by notions of reciprocal duties and rights between classes and where social relations were mediated through patronage and the concept of a moral economy. Co-operation ensured a leadership role for the Anglo-Irish in the new Ireland. As early as 1899 Russell wrote that co-operation brought to the assistance of the simplest and poorest the intelligence and wealth of the rich and better educated, and yet without weakening the poorest members' 'feeling of self-respect.'[28] In his October 1913 letter Russell made explicit reference to his belief in the concept of *noblesse oblige*.

> Despotisms endure while they are benevolent, and aristocracies while noblesse oblige is not a phrase to be referred to with a cynical smile. Even an oligarchy might be permanent if the spirit of human kindness, which harmonises all things otherwise incompatible, is present.[29]

Although Russell accepted the right of the workers to unionise, the reference to the idea of *noblesse oblige* needs to be highlighted. The IAOS was founded on a contradiction; created to meet a purported need for a 'self-supporting, spontaneous and democratic federation of co-operative farmers' by Horace Plunkett, whose watchword was *noblesse oblige*.[30] Analogously, to refer to the latter concept in the context of urban trade unionism in 1913 marked a fundamental contradiction in Russell's analysis and understanding. His sense of aiding the small farmer through agricultural co-operation was, therefore, strongly paternalistic in viewpoint and an anathema to the trade union concept he appeared to endorse in 1913.

Russell saw the Anglo-Irish as the guardians of culture in Ireland; if they were permitted to leave the country following the completion of land purchase measures Ireland's intellectual future was, he argued, in jeopardy. Without culture, he declared, a country becomes 'barbarous and the standard of life, morals and civilization sinks lower and lower.'[31] Again in 1908 he put forward the same message, exhorting the Anglo-Irish to fulfill their role as culture givers, thereby preserving 'the influence and place of their class in Ireland.' A country he declared, 'without a cultivated upper class would make a poor show.'[32] And that poor show was, he made clear in his October letter, to the fore in 1913 in the failure of Dublin's industrial elites to make provision for the Hugh Lane bequest. Indeed, Russell's focus on the achievements of the Anglo-Irish also was expressed in other articles in *The Irish Worker*, a curious sentiment in a trade union paper. Standish O'Grady's first page article in the paper in the 1912 Christmas Number echoes many of Russell's ideas. The article engages with the idea of labour and work in a very idealistic way that does not reflect on the brutal realities of the poverty of the urban. While the article denounces 'those who live without labour on the labour of others', it glorifies the rural worker and does not engage at all with urban poverty. The 'Heroic ideal of our century', O'Grady wrote, necessitates 'life in the open air and the light; therefore in the country.' Moreover, while the urban worker is not mentioned as one of O'Grady's heroic types, the Anglo-Irish Ascendancy, as in Russell's 1913 letter, are described as having 'the right to be included in our heroical types.'[33]

During the cultural revival years Russell constructed a literary ideal of a spiritualised Ireland receptive to heroic thought. While he certainly viewed this vision of a spiritualised Ireland as a means of keeping at bay, what he saw as a movement to bring English commercial ideals to Ireland,[34] he also juxtaposed the idealism of men like the Young Irelander, Thomas Davis, with the squalidness of the Catholic bourgeois Ireland then in the process of creation. This was very much Yeats's message also in 'September 1913' with his reference to the romance and political passion of the Fenian, John O'Leary, in opposition to the grasping Catholic middle classes. This class antagonism can be seen again in 'The fisherman' published in *The wild swans at Coole* in 1919. In this latter poem Yeats imagined a new audience, a wise, dignified, west of Ireland fisherman in defiance of the reality:

> The witty man and his joke
> Aimed at the commonest ear,
> The clever man who cries
> The catch-cries of the clown,
> The beating down of the wise
> And great Art beaten down. [35]

Crucially, Russell was not interested in the politics of Davis, Robert Emmet or Wolfe Tone. What he extracted instead for use in his literary creation of an ideal heroic, spiritualised Ireland was the idealism they exhibited, one of the necessary characteristics, he believed, for the development of a noble humanity in the Ireland of the future. Although Russell's desire to make the Irish more spiritual was vague in meaning, it must be viewed as his counter or response to the increasing growth of material and middle-class values in late 19th-, early 20th-century Irish society. For Russell the things of the spirit were art, music, literature, and a closeness to nature. Above all to be spiritual meant being opposed to materialism and, by connection, to middle-class values. When Russell talked of nobility of spirit or of noble human beings, again, to a large degree, imperceptible descriptions, he was referring to those for whom things of the spirit were more important than material concerns. In some respects *The Irish Worker* betrayed a similar sentiment. The short story by W. P. Ryan in the 1912 Christmas Number described a festival in Liberty Hall in terms which prioritise the 'dreamer' and the 'visionary'; 'creative dreams' and the 'mental world' are stated to produce the 'real, the undying workers' Ireland'.[36] Yet for starving workers in Dublin in the period the 'sense of spiritual electricity' can have meant little. Interestingly, this is very close to Russell's discussion of 'the uses of the soul from a co-operative point of view.' In this article Russell stated that men had to be encouraged 'out of the ignoble way of regarding co-operation solely as a means of taking in more cash ... It enables him to build the City Beautiful in his mind ...'[37]

Russell's refusal to allow the small farmers and, by connection in 1913, the poor of Dublin, any materialistic impulses was certainly not the depiction of the desires of the tenement dwellers; their very different aspirations are encoded in Stephens' *The charwoman's daughter*. This difference in portrayal underscores the manner in which the poor, both rural and those of urban Dublin in 1913, are for Russell used to make wider cultural and class arguments. By contrast to Russell's poor who transcend mere material concerns, Mary and her mother in *The charwoman's daughter* are all the time conscious of their lack of material goods; their daydreaming of future happiness is itemised in the language of acquisition. Mary's mother cries because she is not rich. Her imaginings and daydreams revolve around money and goods 'she would play at imagining that someone had died and left her a great fortune, or that her brother Patrick had come back from America with vast wealth and then she would tell Mary Makebelieve of the things she intended to buy and do the very next day.' Mary's mother refurnishes the room again and again in her mind, putting down a 'Turkey carpet', purchasing a mahogany chest of drawers, a rosewood piano and a shining brass fender. She imagines a vast new wardrobe with dresses for different social occasions, travelling dresses, dresses for driving in a carriage. She imagines Mary's future husband laying stress on his wealth and goods.

> She also discussed, down to the smallest detail, the elaborate trousseau she would provide for her daughter, the extravagant presents the bridegroom would make to his bride and her maids, and those, yet more costly, which the bridegroom's family would send to the newly-married pair.

At night her dreams are 'fierce'; she was 'demanding from a sleep world the things she lacked in the wide-awake one.'[38] When she takes on a new job as charwoman she returns and 'enumerates all the rooms in the house' and itemises all the goods in the house, the 'different ornaments', the 'little framed photographs', the 'carved looking glass'.[39] Indeed, Mary's mother never held a position for long because she is both conscious of and angry at the disparity in wealth and consequently status:

> Mrs Makebelieve's clients were always new. She could not remain for any length of time in people's employment without being troubled by the fact that these folk had houses of their own and were actually employing her in a menial capacity.[40]

Mary herself finds her happiness slightly clouded on a trip to the Phoenix Park; her sense of lack is on a material level, in this case her shabby clothes contrast unfavourably with those of others on the street. She defines herself against those that have material affluence and possessions and finds she lacks.

> Now and then a darker spot flitted through her mind, not at all obscuring, but toning the brightness of her thoughts to a realizable serenity. She wished her skirts were long enough to be held up languidly like the lady walking in front: the hand holding up the skirt had a golden curb-chain on the wrist which drooped down to the neatly-gloved hand, and between each link of the chain was set a blue turquoise, and upon this jewel the sun danced splendidly. Mary Makebelieve wished she had a slender red coral wristlet; it also would have hung down to her palm and been lovely in the sunlight, and it would, she thought, have been far nicer than the bangle. [41]

The charwoman's daughter depicts a vibrant Dublin, mostly closed to the Makebelieves except in an observational capacity. The novel delineates the various affluent shopping streets of the capital and the opportunities for theatre going. In 1892 Douglas Hyde in 'The necessity for de-Anglicising Ireland', a lecture given to the Irish National Literary Society, called for action to arrest the decay of the Irish language; he criticised the Irish for the manner in which despite desires for political independence, they were culturally enslaved to England.

A year later in 1893 Hyde and Eoin MacNeill founded the Gaelic League. Yet in the early 20th century the commercial theatres and music halls of Ireland were still heavily influenced by British popular cultural productions.[42] The Abbey Theatre founded in 1904 as the successor to the Irish National Literary Theatre of 1897, stood as a counter to this with its focus on plays based on Irish subjects. In the early 20th century the theatre still had the potential to be a participatory activity for the audience although Yeats as director of the Abbey Theatre was concerned to introduce changes. He discontinued the practice of allowing the sale of half-price tickets after 9.15 p.m., a tradition in the Queen's Theatre, and he darkened the theatre during the performance.

These reforms, Irish theatre historian Christopher Morash argues, 'were [to] bring to an end the centuries-old pleasures of theatre going, which involved talking to other people, smoking, commenting on the play, applauding or hissing the characters, eating oranges, calling out witty responses to the action on stage, an getting up for a drink when the action hit a dull spot.'[43] For the majority of Dubliners with the arrival of film to Ireland in the late 19th century, cinema could be added to a trip to the theatre as a night of entertainment. Of course for the very poor in 1913 such entertainments were not affordable as they struggled to buy the basic necessities of life. Ironically in this context, the Queen's Theatre showed twice a night during the week of 23 June 1913, less than two months before the Lockout, *From mill to mansion: or, the story of a great strike*. The publicity bills declared: 'All we ask is a fair day's wage for a fair day's work, but the masters grudge us even that.'[44] Entry to this play would not have been accessible for the poorest of Dublin's tenement dwellers, those who could not find work in the stagnant, oversupplied labour market. For Mary Makebelieve and her mother the knowledge and enjoyment of the theatre was at one remove:

> In the night time her mother and herself went round to each of the theatres in turn and watched the people going in, and looked at the big posters. When they went home afterwards they had supper, and used to try to make out the plots of the various plays from the pictures they had seen, so that generally they had lots to talk about before they went to bed.[45]

Mary, having become friendly with a policeman on her walks around Dublin, is dismayed to see him enter the theatre with another woman. Mary had gone to the Gaiety Theatre:

> to watch from outside 'a certain actor ... whom all the women of Dublin made pilgrimages, even from distant place to look at; and by going at once they might be in time to see him arriving in a motor-car at the stage door, when they could have a good look at him getting out of the car and going into the theatre.

Mary had been taken to a restaurant twice by this policeman and had hoped that he might take her to the theatre,[46] a cultural space she could, by virtue of her economic status, only aspire to viewing from the position of observer or outsider. In many ways then, from Russell's intervention in the Lockout to the depiction of labour unrest and lack of unemployment in the theatre, those representations of the poor in cultural discourse and representation were not direct; their voices and experiences were mediated through the lens of middle-class values and needs. Richard Hoggart's discussion of the representation of the English working classes by middle-class Marxist historians in the first half of the 20th century is apt in this context:

He pities the betrayed and debased worker, whose faults he sees as almost entirely the result of the grinding system which controls him. He admires the remnants of the noble savage and has a nostalgia for those 'best of all' kinds of art, rural folk-art or genuinely popular urban art ... He pities and admires the Jude-the-Obscure aspect of working people. Usually he succeeds in part-pitying and part-patronizing working-class people beyond any semblance of reality.[47]

Indeed, one response to Russell's letter highlighted the manner in which those who represent the poor are often not of the poor or have transcended their social origins: 'Is Mr. Larkin without his "three square meals a day". Does he contemplate "sleeping under canvas in Croydon Park", as some workers have been advised to do? I think not.'[48] While Russell offers an example of a commentator on poverty from outside the working classes, Stephens was of the poor, albeit in an increasingly different class.

In many respects *The charwoman's daughter*, while it depicts poverty, simultaneously denies how absolute it was for so many living in Dublin in 1913. Augustine Martin has described the novel in terms of a fairy tale, noting that in its principal elements 'it retells the Cinderella story'.[49] This fairy tale element to the novel is highlighted by the surname Makebelieve. In this context of genre, the novel takes refuge in an escapism that formed a large part of the cinema experience in the period. The first moving picture was shown in Ireland in April 1896 at Dan Lowrey's Star of Erin Theatre of Varieties, while the first permanent cinema was the Volta, opened in 1909 by James Joyce.[50] By 1916 there were 149 cinemas and picture halls listed in Ireland.[51] Kevin Rockett argues that while there were certain venues in which film was shown that attracted a middle-class audience, notably the Antient Concert Rooms and the Rotunda, the majority of Dublin cinema going audience was 'working class, or, at least, clerical grades and other aspiring lower middle-class men and women.'[52] The cinema represented an escape from the drudgery of life, the interiors tended to emphasis luxury with plush carpets and seating. Many cinemas, Rockett writes:

> offered a sumptuous environment – central heating, plush carpets, sensuous décor and seating – which contrasted with the cold, poorly-lit, wooden floored, or at best linoleum covered floors, of working-class homes ... [53]

The renovation of the Theatre Royal in late 1913 showed a similar desire to create an escapist cultural space:

> Much work has been spent on the re-decoration of the vestibule, which, with its marble steps, always makes such a favourable impression. The paneling of the alcove is new, and is in conventional Arabesque style, in keeping the aspect

of the vestibule itself … A new style will be found to have been adopted in the numerous hangings which go to add to the luxurious air of the theatre.

Notably, the report of the re-opening of the theatre following such renovations stated that the 'whole of the work has been carried out by trade union labour.'[54]

An examination of the newspapers for 1913 indicates a broad range of films offered from those based on classic novels or plays to the more popular orientated detective and cowboy films. *The Irish Worker* advertised cinema on a regular basis. The Christmas Number in 1912 urged 'Workers' to 'Support the Only Picture House in Dublin Owned by an Irishman', the 'Irish Cinema' on Capel Street.[55] On 19 May 1913 *The Freeman's Journal* reported shows in the Princess Cinema in Rathmines daily from 3 to 10.30 p.m. with a complete change of programme on Mondays, Thursdays and Sundays. Of course, those of the working classes who had employment would not have been in a position to attend an afternoon screenings. All films in this cinema, as in all cinemas at this time, were accompanied by a full string orchestra. The management, committed to giving patrons the best and latest films were, the newspaper reported, sending their film manager to Europe to secure 'the latest and best productions.'[56] Later that month the paper reported that the 'great Vitagraph Masterpiece', an adaption of Charles Dickens' *The tale of two cities* was attracting large crowds.[57] Indeed, in September 1913 theatre and cinema coalesced according to a writer in *The Freeman's Journal* reporting on the George Edwardes Gaiety play, *The girl on the film*, playing that month in London. The 'novel feature of this latest "Edwardes" production' according to the report was that this was the first time cinema had been used as the central angle around 'which a plot has been woven'.[58] Throughout 1913 reporters tended to compare cinema to the stage, in instances noting where the former triumphed over the latter. On 18 September a reporter from *The Freeman's Journal* attended a private exhibition of *Hamlet* by the French film company Gaumont which began producing films in 1897. This film version of the play was acted by the Theatre Royal, Drury Lane company with J. Forbes Roberston in the leading role. The reporter noted that the film of two hours in duration represented the full play and commented on the potential issue of the lack of words, particularly in the context of the leading actor having acted the part on stage.

> Two hours long 'Hamlet' without words might seem to some people like the play without Hamlet, but any such notion is soon dispelled by the extraordinary beauty of the pictures and the success with which the work of one of the most scholarly and impressive living actors of 'Hamlet' has been reproduced.

The reporter continued by discussing the advantages the cinematic production had over that of the original stage play, noting that the appearance of the ghost is 'managed without any undue call on the senses and the play scene is also carefully managed.'

Again, Dublin audiences, who could view the film from 29 September, were treated to an orchestra that rendered 'appropriate music throughout'.[59]

The nascent cinema industry in Ireland gave rise to a discussion in December 1913 as to the suitability of certain films for children and the possibility of a special programme being introduced in the holiday period. The reportage underscores the newness of the medium and the potential.[60] Indeed, a number of advertisements appeared in the Dublin papers in 1913 by men desirous of investing in the cinema business.[61] Discussing the manner in which the youth of Dublin enjoyed with whoops of delight any representation of the cowboy on screen, the report on 17 December 1913 claimed that some of the best educators in Dublin lauded the influence of the cinema on the basis that 'boys gain from them a surprising acquaintance with strange manners, customs and scenes, and that there is a broadening of the mind like that which travel gives.'[62] In 1913 steps were taken by the Recorder of Dublin Corporation to introduce a comprehensive set of conditions for the granting of cinema licenses, up to this only safety related conditions were in place.[63] The *Irish Independent* reported in April that Gaumont was to install in Lord Edward Street equipment 'for the home production of films representing Irish scenes and occurrences.'[64] At the end of June the Rotunda Picture House was showing, amongst other films, *Dublin Dan*, a comic film about a Dublin detective, produced in 1912 by the American Solax Film Company. That same week the programme of the Rotunda included 'Wolfe Tone Memorial' shot the previous Sunday at the annual Bodenstown pilgrimage. This latter again shows the fluid nature of cinema showings in Dublin, mixing the local with the international.[65]

The language of the new medium of cinema even entered into the discourse about the Lockout. Russell condemned the lack of humanity amongst the employers. 'Cry aloud', he declared, 'to heaven for new souls. The souls you have got cast upon the screens of publicity appear like the horrid and writhing creatures enlarged from the insect world, and revealed to us by the cinematographer.'[66] However, with this description of the employers of Dublin as alien creatures, the creation of the new cinematography, the reality of the brutality of the Lockout is rendered otherworldly and in that way represented as a world apart from the world of normal experience.[67] This elision of brutality underscores the manner in which Russell's intervention during the 1913 Lockout has to be seen in the wider context of his discourse on the position of the Anglo-Irish in the early 20th century. His genuine concern at the position of the workers notwithstanding, the plight of Dublin's urban poor were for Russell part of his wider anxieties in the context of the rise of a new Catholic middle-class elite. Social reality is denied in the conclusion to *The charwoman's daughter*, which is more surprising given Stephens' class origins. The poverty of the Makebelieves is not eliminated through social revolution.[68] There is no strike by workers (such as Mr Cafferty) as would occur in 1913; there is, indeed, not one reference to trade unionism in the novel. Instead, Mary's mother receives a letter;

she is the sole beneficiary of her brother Patrick who made a fortune in New York. Just as Mrs Makebelieve had itemised on so many occasions in the novel all the material goods she desired, the letter offers an inventory of all she has acquired, stocks, shares, tenement buildings, 'pictures, prints, plate, line glass'.[69] Unlike Seán O'Casey's 1924 play on tenement life, *Juno and the paycock*, where the apparent inheritance comes to nothing, Mary is able to achieve her material ambitions; 'Hats were mentioned, and dresses, and the new house somewhere.' As the first fictional depiction of tenement life, *The charwoman's daughter* ultimately therefore denied social realism. As Curry and Devine note, this other worldly aspect to the novel in which unexpected good fortune prevails to rescue characters from poverty can be seen in some of the short stories published in *The Irish Worker*.[70] The reality was the brutality of poverty and the class and labour struggles between the 'Masters of Dublin', to use Russell's phrase, and the men and women of the tenements, which resulted in the Lockout of 1913. This reality was not represented in its full brutality in contemporary cultural discourse; it would take Plunkett's historical novel, *Strumpet city* to move towards such realistic representation.

Notes

1   The novel was published in book form in 1912.

2   James Stephens, *The charwoman's daughter* (Dublin, 1972), p. 15. This edition has an introduction by Augustine Martin.

3   George Moore, *A drama in muslin* (Gerrards Cross, 1981), p. 171.

4   Catriona Crowe (ed.), *Dublin 1911* (Dublin, 2011), p. 95.

5   Patrick Maume, 'Stephens, James', in James McGuire and James Quinn (eds), *Dictionary of Irish biography* (Cambridge, 2009). (http://dib.cambridge.org/viewReadPage.do?articleId=a8278).

6   Census 1911 (http://www.census.nationalarchives.ie/pages/1911/Dublin/South_Dock/Mount_Street__Lower/84621/)

7   Maume, 'Stephens, James'.

8   'Criticism of 'A.E.'s Letter', *Irish Times*, 8 Apr. 1913.

9   W. B. Yeats, 'September 1913' in A. Norman Jeffares (ed.), *Yeats's poems* (Dublin, 1989), p. 210.

10   For a fuller discussion see Leeann Lane, '"It is in the Cottages and Farmer's Houses that the Nation is Born": Æ's *Irish Homestead* and the cultural revival', *Irish University Review* 33: 1 (Spring-Summer, 2003); Leeann Lane, '"There are compensations in the congested districts for their poverty": Æ and the idealized peasant of the agricultural co-operative movement', in Betsey Taylor FitzSimon and James H. Murphy (eds), *The Irish revival reappraised* (Dublin, 2004).

11   *Irish Times*, 7 Oct. 1913.

12   Kevin Rockett, *Irish film censorship: a cultural journey from silent cinema to internet pornography* (Dublin, 2004), p. 37.

13   Crowe (ed.), *Dublin 1911*, p. 85.

14   Stephens, *The charwoman's daughter*, p. 9; pp 12-13.

15   Ibid., pp 59-60.

16   Crowe (ed.), *Dublin 1911*, pp 121-2.

17   Stephens, *The charwoman's daughter*, p. 91.

18   Stephens, *The charwoman's daughter*, pp 89-90.

19   *Irish Times*, 7 Oct. 1913.

20   Donald E. Jordan, *Land and popular politics in Ireland: County Mayo from the plantation to the land war* (Cambridge, 1994), p. 7.

21   The gombeenman, often a local shopkeeper, loaned money or advanced goods at high rates of interest.

22   *Irish Times*, 7 Oct. 1913.

23   'Dublin Municipal Art Gallery', *Irish Times*, 9 Apr. 1913.

24   The anti-alcohol message in *The Irish Worker* would also have appealed strongly to Russell who repeatedly wrote on the perils of drink and the malign influence of the public house on Irish life.

25   James Curry and Francis Devine (eds), 'Introduction', 'Merry May your Xmas Be & 1913 Free from Care': *The Irish Worker* 1912 *Christmas Number* (Dublin, 2012), p. 7.

26   See Lane, '"It is in the Cottages and Farmers' Houses that the Nation is Born"'.

27   'The future of the Irish aristocracy', *Irish Homestead*, 1 Feb. 1908. See also, 'The resignation of Lord Monteagle', *Irish Homestead*, 28 Oct. 1905 where Russell praised Monteagle's performance as president of the IAOS and lauded him as one who brought to his other public and philanthropic work 'the motto of his class, "Noblesse Oblige"'.

28   'Among the societies', *Irish Homestead*, 7 Jan. 1899.

29   *Irish Times*, 7 Oct. 1913.

30   Cyril Ehrlich, 'Sir Horace Plunkett and agricultural reform,' in J. M. Goldstrum and L. A. Clarkston (eds), *Irish population, economy and society: essays in honour of the late K. H. Connell* (Oxford, 1981), pp 273-4.

31   'Villagers' libraries', *Irish Homestead*, 31 Mar. 1906.

32   'Or is it the first chance?', *Irish Homestead*, 7 Mar. 1908.

33   Standish O'Grady, 'Heroes and the heroic: an address to Young Ireland', *Irish Worker*, Christmas 1912, p. 2.

34   George Russell to W. B. Yeats [October 1896] (NLI, P. 8388).

35   W. B. Yeats, 'The fisherman', in Jeffares, *Yeats's poems*, p. 251.

36   Liam P. O Riain, 'On a tram car in Wonderland', *Irish Worker*, Christmas 1912, p. 6.

37   'A lay sermon to co-operators', *Irish Homestead*, 2 Jan. 1909.

38   Stephens, *The charwoman's daughter*, pp 11, 13, 16, 21.

39   Ibid., pp 41-2.

40   Ibid., p. 28.

41   Ibid., p. 34.

42   Rockett, *Irish film censorship*, p. 23.

43   Christopher Morash, *A history of Irish theatre 1601-2000* (Cambridge, 2002), p. 131.

44   Morash, *A history of Irish theatre*, p. 153.

45   Stephens, *The charwoman's daughter*, p. 15.

46   Ibid., pp 52, 54.

47   Richard Hoggart, *The uses of literacy. aspects of working-class life* (London, 2009), p. 6. First published 1957

48   'Criticism of 'A.E.'s Letter', *Irish Times*, 8 Oct. 1913. Croydon Park in Fairview, Dublin, was the drilling grounds of the Irish Citizen Army. At the end of 1913 the Larkin family were evicted and were forced to squat in the Park. My thanks to Francis Devine for this information.

49   Martin, Introduction to The charwoman's daughter, p. 5.

50   Rockett, *Irish film censorship*, pp 2, 29.

51   Diarmaid Ferriter, *The transformation of Ireland 1900-2000* (London, 2004), p. 103.

52   Rockett, *Irish film censorship*, p. 23.

53   Ibid., p.27.

54   'Theatre Royal', *Irish Times*, 18 Dec. 1913.

55   *Irish Worker*, Christmas Number 1912, p. 13.

56   *Freeman's Journal*, 19 May 1913.

57   Ibid., 27 May 1913.

58   Ibid., 17 Sept. 1913.

59   Ibid., 19 Sept. 1913.

60   Ibid., Dec. 1913.

61   See, for example, *Freeman's Journal*, 26 Aug. 1913.

62   *Freeman's Journal*, Dec. 1913.

63   Rockett, *Irish film censorship*, p. 37.

64   *Irish Independent*, 28 Apr. 1913.

65   *Freeman's Journal*, 24 June 1913.

66   *Irish Times*, 7 Oct. 1913.

67   Murphy was similarly reviled in *The Irish Worker* which used imagery that portrayed him as an alien, malign creature and consequently less than human. He was described, for example, as an 'industrial octopus' and a 'blood-sucking vampire'. Curry and Devine (eds), 'Introduction', p. 5.

68   Martin, Introduction to *The charwoman's daughter*, p. 5.

69   Stephens, *The charwoman's daughter*, p. 123.

70   Curry and Devine (eds), 'Introduction', p. 8.

16.
From *Disturbed Dublin* to *Strumpet city*: the 1913 'history wars', 1914–1980

....

John Cunningham

When the Lockout ended with the drift back to work in the early months of 1914, the industrial struggle gave way to disputes over its interpretation. Continuing over several decades, these disputes were prompted mainly by concern about the reputations of the major historical actors, but also by the wish to assert the importance of the episode itself. Such are the concerns of 'public history' everywhere. The term 'history wars' has been applied to the heated and politicised debates about the interpretation of the past in other countries – notably Australia[1] – and although discussion of the Lockout has not occupied the public sphere to the same extent as these other history wars, such bitterness surrounded the way it was remembered that the concept becomes useful. This chapter will focus on the public (as opposed to the academic) history of the Lockout up to about 1980.

Disturbed Dublin

The epic character of the Lockout was recognised by contemporaries, and the efforts to influence its historical interpretation commenced immediately. In the spring of 1914, Arnold Wright began work on a book that would be published in October of the same year as *Disturbed Dublin*. Wright was an English journalist, who had 'a singularly varied career' in England, India and Australia, according to an obituarist. A parliamentary correspondent and a writer of travel books, his reputation derived mainly from *Twentieth century impressions of Ceylon*, written following his short visit to that outpost of empire in 1906.[2] In his ambition to 'furnish a complete picture of Dublin industrial life' within a few months, Wright recalls P. G. Wodehouse's satirical creation, Lady Malvern, who, having written *India and the Indians* on the basis of four weeks on the sub-continent, was confident she could complete research for a companion volume on America in an even shorter time.[3]

In the preface to *Disturbed Dublin*, Wright announced his intention of providing 'a succinct and impartial account of the Larkinite movement', before proceeding in the same sentence to describe that movement as 'a peculiarly pernicious form of Syndicalism.'

DISTURBED DUBLIN

THE STORY OF THE GREAT STRIKE
OF 1913–14

WITH A DESCRIPTION OF
THE INDUSTRIES OF THE IRISH CAPITAL

BY

ARNOLD WRIGHT

LONGMANS, GREEN, AND CO.
39 PATERNOSTER ROW, LONDON
FOURTH AVENUE & 30TH STREET, NEW YORK
BOMBAY, CALCUTTA, AND MADRAS
1914

1. First edition of *Disturbed Dublin*, published in London in 1914.
DCLA

His claim to impartiality was further compromised in the table of contents, with chapter titles including 'An orgy of anarchy,' 'The methods of the yahoo,' and 'The ignoble art of intimidation.' It was believed (though not explicitly acknowledged) that Wright was paid £500 by the Dublin employers, and he certainly told the story of the Lockout from their point of view. But would even William Martin Murphy himself have supposed that he resembled a 'typical family solicitor of the old school ... who blends the milk of human kindness with an unswerving rectitude of conduct'?[4] The choice of Wright and the placing of the work with a prestigious London publisher indicate a concern to repair reputational damage in Britain arising from the report of the Askwith inquiry and from adverse press coverage and political commentary during the dispute. If the intention had been to form Irish opinion, a native hack writer would have been more effective. But much of the actual leg-work was carried out by such a writer in any case, as is indicated by Wright's 'special acknowledgements' to Terence O'Hanlon, for his 'much-appreciated assistance in collecting and collating the great mass of published material relating to the strike.' O'Hanlon was well-placed to assist Wright – and he needed the money. Still in his twenties, he was a staff journalist with Independent Newspapers until ill-health obliged him to relinquish his position in 1912. Thereafter, he was a freelance writer, mostly for Independent titles. Coincidentally, O'Hanlon was a native of Camlough, in South Armagh, just a few miles from the place where Larkin's father was raised, and which Larkin claimed as his own birthplace.[5] Wright revealed, almost inadvertently, that another version of his story was in preparation, when he reported on an effort to interview Larkin: 'I found him at first unwilling to discuss the question, in view of the fact that Mr Connolly, his chief lieutenant, was bringing out a book on the subject of the strike.'[6]

Disturbed Dublin attracted relatively little attention. It was not noticed by *The Freeman's Journal*, *The Irish Times*, *The Times*, or, it would seem by many of the Irish local newspapers,[7] but it was very warmly reviewed in the *Irish Independent*. Echoing the book's preface, the anonymous critic commended the 'impartial history of last year's great labour upheaval that ended in the glorious defeat of an insidious attempt to establish a vicious form of Continental Syndicalism,' before acknowledging the 'industrial Wellington who was pitted against the Larkinite Napoleon on that occasion ... Mr Wm M. Murphy.' No less a figure than the 'industrial Wellington' himself wrote to his own paper a few days later, amplifying a point made in discussions of the book about his refusal of a knighthood.[8]

Academic reviews were mixed but all agreed that Wright displayed a strong pro-employer bias. Even for the well-disposed reviewer in the *Journal of Political Economy*, Wright should not have so carelessly worn his heart on his sleeve: 'In his overenthusiasm for the cause of the employers … Mr Wright has indulged in a great amount of eulogy, which is to say the least unnecessary.'[9] The most devastating of the academic reviews, in the *Economic Journal*, was by Charles Bastable, professor of Political Economy at Trinity College.[10] Identifying serious errors, he criticised Wright's presentation of certain episodes, his 'thoroughly prejudiced treatment' and his economic illiteracy. 'The best prospect for industrial peace,' wrote Bastable, 'was to be found rather in the growth of effective labour institutions than by exalting the power and authority of the employing class.'[11] *Disturbed Dublin* then was propagandist in design, but in its transparent one-sidedness, it was ineffective propaganda.

Connolly's book on the Lockout never appeared, but he lectured on it, and it was a central concern of his *Reconquest of Ireland*, published in 1915.[12] Probably his most substantial post-hoc engagement with the topic was his long review of Wright on the front page of *The Irish Worker*. Like Bastable, Connolly highlighted errors of fact, of interpretation and of naked bias: 'The achievement of the employers is written as if the book was dealing with struggle of a puny David against a mighty Goliath, the employers being David and Jim Larkin being the giant Goliath.' For Connolly, it was the work of a 'hack writer ... which found its inspiration in the councils of the employers.'[13] Significantly, he took the opportunity to define the parameters of the story as it might have been told by 'a Labour writer', by 'one of those literary men ... who stood so grandly by the workers in that titanic struggle' or by any 'man or woman with honesty in their hearts.' The key elements of the story for Connolly were as follows:

- the employers' determination to wipe out the ITGWU and their lack of scruple as to method;
- the support for the employers from the press of 'every shade of religions and politics';
- the state's commitment to the employers and the violence unleashed on Dublin's working class;
- the violation of domestic privacy and 'the most sacred feelings of womanhood' by drunken police;
- the deliberate use of starvation as a weapon;
- the end of deference among the previously brow-beaten labourers;
- the solidarity shown by the families of the locked-out workers;
- the support for the workers from the 'men and women of genius';
- the failure of British labour leaders to fully 'realise of the grandeur of the opportunity';
- the inaccuracy of the view that the result was the 'rout of Larkinism'; rather, it was 'a drawn battle'.

These key elements of the story of the Lockout would become its most familiar features, and it is noteworthy that it was the concise narrative shaped for an ephemeral workers' paper that prevailed in what may be regarded as the first of the 1913 history wars, rather than the version that appeared between authoritative-looking hard covers. There were other elements of the story that would assume significance as a result of Connolly's rebellion and martyrdom at Easter 1916 – notably the founding of the Irish Citizen Army (ICA). And with hindsight, as we shall see, the Lockout would come to be represented by many as a kind of dress-rehearsal for the Easter Rising.

Lockout: early anniversaries

In the earliest biography of Connolly, a 24-page pamphlet by the Gaelic revivalist Seán Mac Giollarnáth in 1917, almost three pages were devoted to the Lockout, in the course of which an interesting comparison was made: 'The Dublin masters acted towards the new Labour movement as the landlords had acted towards the Land League.'[14] The story of the Lockout occupied about 10% of W. P. Ryan's history of *The Irish labour movement* published in 1919, and it was naturally central to Seán O'Casey's short history of *The Irish Citizen Army* which appeared in the same year.[15] O'Casey, whose reputation as a dramatist would be secured during the following decade, was for some months in 1914 the secretary of the ICA. In the earliest 'official' history of Irish labour, published in the *Reports and memoranda* prepared by the Irish Labour Party and Trade Union Congress (ILP&TUC) to introduce itself to the Socialist international gathering in Berne, Switzerland, in February 1919, the 'great Dublin struggle' of 1913-14 loomed large. In this document, Connolly's 'drawn battle' interpretation was significantly stretched: 'The material damage was heavy, but morally Labour had won a startling victory.'[16]

If the Lockout had already entered 'history', circumstances in August 1923 were not conducive to anything like a commemoration of its tenth anniversary. The civil war, consequent to the Anglo-Irish Treaty, had only ended in April, and battle had already been joined in the labour 'civil war' which followed the return to Dublin of James Larkin on the very day that the republican ceasefire was announced. Fresh out of prison and more than eight years out of Ireland, he seemed determined to take up the reins of ITGWU leadership that he had reluctantly left in Connolly's hands in 1914. Those who steered the union in his absence, building a professional apparatus and a membership which surpassed 100,000 at one point, were not willing to relinquish control, so a conflict ensued which was both personal and ideological. It was a conflict which extended from the picket line to the higher courts and from committee room debate to a physical battle for control of the union headquarters.[17]

THE STORY OF THE IRISH CITIZEN ARMY

By P. O CATHASAIGH

The first account that has been given of the formation of the Irish Citizen Army during the Dublin strike of 1913-14, and the part played by it in the subsequent history of Ireland. The author, who was himself a leading figure in the movement, writes with vigour and conviction upon the role of labour in Ireland, and expressing a very definite opinion as to the relations of the workers to the National movement. The book contains original character sketches of Larkin, Connolly, Captain White, and Madame Markiewicz, and some facts bearing on the relations between the Citizen Army and the Volunteers now emerge for the first time.

MAUNSEL & CO., LTD.

ONE SHILLING NET

2. Seán O'Casey, writing as P. O Cathasaigh, published a history of the Irish Citizen Army in 1919.
DCLA

There was occasional reference to the Lockout in the course of the battle for the soul and the control of the ITGWU, mostly on the part of the Larkinites.[18] Addressing a meeting in Liberty Hall in November 1923, Larkin stated that 'the spirit which animated Dublin from 1907 to 1913 was now lacking,' that 'most of the organised workers in Dublin did not care a damn about anyone but themselves.' An 'attempt was being made to drive [those animated by the spirit of 1913] out of the union,' and they should resist, ensuring that they paid their dues and remained 'in good standing so that when the time came they could take the power in their own hands.'[19]

Larkin and his followers would lose the significant battles, and they formed a breakaway union, the Workers Union of Ireland (WUI). A personal feud between the ITGWU's William O'Brien and Larkin ensued, which continued to be prosecuted by the former even beyond Larkin's death in 1947. That the history of the Lockout became one of the fields of contention almost immediately is confirmed by the following quotation from an ITGWU publication in 1924:

> The year 1913 is memorable for the great struggle of the Dublin workers against the combined attack of the Dublin employers. Unfortunately, it is memorable at the same time for the boiling over of the egoism of James Larkin ... It required all the strength and steadiness of James Connolly ... and others to prevent disaster and debacle. Before and after the struggle ended the Dublin members were reduced to sore straits indeed ... Verily the Dublin men and women were starving. In the middle of it all, Larkin could fiddle with hot-house gardening in Croydon Park and order from Liverpool – not from Ireland – 'seed, plants, etc.', up to a value of £20. A veritable marvel of constructive leadership![20]

The references to his egoism and to his English hot-house plants did not exactly flatter Larkin, but they at least testified to his presence during the Lockout – a fact that the ITGWU would not always acknowledge. If it seems inconceivable that a history of the Lockout could be written without mentioning Big Jim, William O'Brien did just that in 1934, the 21st anniversary, when he published *Nineteen thirteen – its significance* without a single reference to Larkin. James Connolly, by contrast, was invoked more than a few times.[21] O'Brien, who had been secretary of the Lockout committee, had no doubt about the importance of the struggle:

> What is truthfully called the Labour War of 1913 was the biggest and most extensive struggle in the whole history of the Irish labour movement. Indeed in some respects it was one of the greatest events in the history of Labour in these islands, and undoubtedly the year 1913 made a red-letter mark in the annals of the entire Trade Union movement.[22]

O'Brien continued:

> The fight had aroused a splendid fighting spirit in the Labour forces and within a comparatively short time the fruits of struggle were gathered ... James Connolly soon took charge and rallied the remnants of the Union around him, compelling employer after employer not only to recognise the Union again but under the new circumstances brought about by the War, to concede wages and conditions they had stubbornly resisted before. With the Irish Citizen Army which had been organised as a workers' Protective Force during the struggle of 1913-14, he forced the Insurrection of Easter Week 1916. Within three years of the close of the dispute the Irish Transport and General Workers Union had spread all over Ireland as a result of the events of Easter Week, the execution of Connolly, and the situation caused by the European War.[23]

3. Liberty Hall, leased by the ITGWU in 1912, and later purchased.
Fifty years of Liberty Hall: the Golden Jubilee of the Irish Transport and General Workers' Union, 1909-1959 (Dublin, 1959).

Deftly, he establishes Connolly's role in transforming the 'drawn battle' of 1913-14 into a 'startling victory' while simultaneously diminishing Larkin. O'Brien's pamphlet, drawn from the text of an article in a union periodical, had several incarnations, notably in 1959 when it was reprinted without substantive change in the commemorative *Fifty years of Liberty Hall*. Although retired for more than a decade, O'Brien remained a key interpreter of the history of the ITGWU. Other articles in that jubilee publication do mention Larkin, albeit grudgingly.[24] It was similar with regard to a public announcement in the *Irish Press,* where units of the ITGWU sent greetings to their National Executive on the occasion of the same jubilee. In the text and photographs accompanying the messages, James Connolly was given pride of place, and Larkin was mentioned only in passing, and then somewhat disrespectfully in that his first name was omitted which was not the case for Connolly and the other union leaders mentioned. Insofar as the union was promoting its heritage, it was 1916 that was embraced rather than 1913. This was apparent too in 1958, when information was released to the press relating to interesting artefacts that were uncovered during the demolition of Liberty Hall. First was an 'old Singer sewing machine which, it is thought, was used in the manufacture of ammunition belts and bandoliers before the 1916 Rising.' Next, a 'bread-slicing machine was recovered [which] was used during the 1916 Rising and was believed to have been used also during the "lock-out" of 1913.' Given that there was a soup-kitchen in Liberty Hall during 1913, the antique bread slicer was almost certainly acquired then, yet it was a possible connection with 1916 that was emphasised.

Even in 1963, on the 50th anniversary of the Lockout, the ITGWU impulse was to focus on 1916, thereby denying Larkin any attention. Publicity issued for a commemoration in Cork began:

> A photostat copy of Pádraig Pearse's handwritten draft of his oration at the grave of O'Donovan Rossa will be among the historic exhibits on view in Cork next month, when the Cork branches of the ITGWU commemorate the golden jubilee of 'The Big Lockout' in Dublin in 1913. Also on display will be a leaflet issued from the then beleaguered GPO ...[25]

Other 'documents of this historic era' would also be displayed, but their nature was not specified.[26] Cork ITGWU had clearly embraced the idea that 1913's significance was as a curtain raiser for 1916.

Commenting on the 1959 jubilee publication, Seán O'Casey wrote that it 'mentions Jim but once or twice ... These fellows' hatred seems to be pathological or is it just the hatred of the little maneens for the Big Fellow.' According to Donal Nevin, the 'maneens' were William O'Brien and Cathal O'Shannon.[27] A substantial review of the same volume in *The Irish Times* by James Plunkett (introduced fully below) was generally favourable, but there was a sting in the tail:

> An exception to the general tone of fairness is the section on 1913, which so plays down the dynamic role taken by Larkin that here is indeed Hamlet without the Prince. The uninformed will read it without suspecting that the employers

dubbed the movement 'Larkinism' and that the little children marked the arrival of the food ships by singing to the air of Alexander's Ragtime Band: 'Come on along, come on along / And join James Larkin's union / You'll get a loaf of bread / And a pound of tea / And a belt of a baton from the DMP.[28]

The Lockout in historical discourse

If the meaning of the Lockout was a concern of people connected with the trade union movement, what was its status in historical discourse generally? Until the 1960s, as Fergus D'Arcy has established, the large circulation general histories which appeared had little to say about 1913. D'Arcy cites as an exception the eighth volume of Monsignor D'Alton's *History of Ireland*, published in 1928, which devoted half a page to the Lockout, but treated it 'as an isolated episode intruding into the general narrative of events.'[29] A similar point might be made about the several editions of Dorothy McArdle's *The Irish Republic*, first published in 1937.[30] P. S. O'Hegarty's influential *History of Ireland* (1951) was even more cursory. An ex-IRB man 'unable to accept the economic or class-conscious interpretation of history', O'Hegarty mentioned the Lockout only obliquely during a brief discussion of what he described as the 'playacting bellicosity' of the Citizen Army.[31]

Of the histories of the revolutionary period published in those years, probably the most widely read were the 'fighting stories' of several of the more active counties during the revolutionary period, which were published by *The Kerryman* in the late 1940s. Therefore, the account of the Lockout most familiar to Irish people generally prior to the 1960s may well have been Séamus O'Brien's 13 pages in the Dublin volume in the series.[32] The author evidently had unpleasant encounters with Larkinites while an organiser with the ITGWU,[33] but he did not allow this to prejudice his representation of Larkin:

> Larkin had himself sprung from the docks and knew all about the hardship and slavery of the work. He had little regard for formulae and rules. When he saw a condition of affairs to be remedied, he set about the job ... The English headquarters of the union resented this assumption of authority on the part of Larkin ... Larkin refused to accept defeat. He felt he had a purpose in life – and he set about the formation of an Irish union without any hindrances or any control from outside the country.[34]

The Lockout of course featured in many publications, academic and political, which, due to limited circulation did not significantly shape public perceptions. There were two popular historians, however – R. M. Fox and T. A. Jackson, both Englishmen – who wrote Irish history from a labour or socialist perspective and who had an impact. Fox

(1891-1969), a journalist and cultural critic who married the Irish children's author Patricia Lynch, and was active on the left of the British movement before the First World War, treated the Lockout in his short biographies of Connolly (1943), Larkin (1957), and Louie Bennett (1958), as well as in his study of the Irish Citizen Army (1943) and his work *Green banners: the story of the Irish struggle* (1938).[35] Jackson (1879-1955), also prominent in the British left before 1914, was a founder of the British Communist Party. He had a long-standing interest in Ireland, but his book *Ireland her own* (1946) devoted only two of its more than 400 pages to an assessment of Larkin and the Lockout. Moreover, in this significant if brief presentation of the socialist republican interpretation of the events of 1913-14, the following was the aspect of the Lockout's legacy that was most emphasised: that it 'gave rise to the Citizen Army' and that it fostered 'close relations between the young neo-Fenian intellectuals and the labour movement.'[36] Except in giving due credit to Larkin, Jackson's differed little from the William O'Brien interpretation.

4. Éamonn O'Doherty's statue of James Connolly facing Liberty Hall, commissioned by the Irish Congress of Trade Unions and erected in 1996.

(Photo: Andrew Sneyd) DCLA

A number of significant dramatists also engaged with the Lockout, the first being Andrew Patrick Wilson whose play based on the dispute was on the Abbey Theatre stage in November 1914, just weeks after the publication of *Disturbed Dublin*. It was entitled *The slough*, and its author was the Abbey's general manager, having previously been a prolific contributor to *The Irish Worker*.[37] Another play based on the dispute and on Larkin's role, *The labour leader* by Daniel Corkery, was presented in the Abbey in 1919.[38] The playwright with the closest connection with the events of 1913-14 was Seán O'Casey, whose work in the words of one authority was characterised by 'a sense of answerability to disadvantaged communities, a desire to valorise their counter-hegemonic character, and a wish to undo their historiographic invisibility.'[39] O'Casey was an Irish Citizen Army member and its first historian – and a life-long Larkinite. Characters in two of his plays, *A star turns red* (1940) and *Red roses for me* (1942) were based on Larkin although the former was not produced in Ireland until 1978. While none of the major plays of O'Casey's Dublin trilogy, *The shadow of a gunman* (1923), *Juno and the paycock* (1924) and *The plough and the stars* (1926) are set during that particular conflict, their audiences are constantly reminded of the Lockout by the attitudes struck by the cast of Dublin working class characters. James Plunkett's, *The risen people*, which was performed in the Abbey in 1958, will be discussed below.

Lockout commemorations

Significant commemorations of the Lockout were held on the 50th anniversary in 1963, the most ambitious of which were under the auspices of the Dublin Council of Trade Unions in September, and co-ordinated by its president Paddy Donegan and by Michael Mullen T.D. of the ITGWU.[40] Mullen told the council in March that the cost would be £10,000 – a fabulous sum in 1963 – also advising that 'employers would take part' and that the Royal Dublin Society (RDS) would be the venue.[41] There were two elements in the commemoration: a theatrical pageant, described as 'a masque', and 'the biggest exhibition of its kind ever mounted by a trade union organisation' on these islands.[42] The exhibition told 'the graphic story of the lock-out and the days which followed in documents and rare photographs', but this was only a small element of the whole. As the following (excerpted from the official publicity) indicates, a recasting of the Lockout story was at the core of the endeavour, and the re-casting was ideological. In previous interpretations, the Lockout was a heroic example of militant defiance; now it was the first step on the journey to 'a promised land,' a land that had finally been reached:

> This exhibition shows the fulfilled vision of Irish Labour … The great struggle began fifty years ago when a seemingly unsurmountable difference and bitterness divided labour and management. This week at the RDS you can see people at work under conditions that have been brought about largely by Trade Union

principles, organisation and incentive, resulting in the harmonious dove-tailing of employer and employee for the greater good of the individual and the country as a whole.[43]

That there was something of the spirit of the Lemass era about it all was made explicit in a reference to the Second Economic Plan in a leading article on the anniversary in the *Irish Press*.[44] And Eamon de Valera, president of Ireland, performing the official opening, was very much in line with this in commending 'understanding, goodwill and proper co-operation between the several partners in industry.' If the president referred specifically to the Lockout, which he would have well recalled, the reference was not reported, although he did acknowledge the social contribution of trade unions: 'An fhorbairt agus an forás atá le feiceáil bhí páirt ar leith iontu ag na hoibrithe agus na ceardchumainn.'[45]

But the reality of class tensions would disrupt the corporatist *aisling*. First, RDS officials objected to the staging of the masque on their premises – perhaps recalling the adverse impact of the tram strike on their 1913 Horse Show! – on the basis that they had given permission only for 'a pageant or a concert and that the original terms of the letting precluded political or controversial matter.' The masque consequently had to be moved to the Olympia.[46] There was further controversy when striking deep-sea dockers insisted on the exclusion of the stand of Irish Shipping Ltd. on the grounds that it was a member of the Irish Master Stevedores Association, a party to their dispute.[47]

Like the expelled Irish Shipping, the participating employers were semi-state organisations or else educational bodies such as the Dublin Vocational Education Committee. And it was very much an industrial exhibition, featuring Bord Fáilte's promotional 'Everyman's industry' and an Electricity Supply Board (ESB) stand, 'The kitchen through the ages', alongside a display of modern electrical appliances.[48] The services of the ESB were also in evidence in the huge centrepiece of the exhibition, 'symbolic of the rise and progress of Irish trade unionism' which overlooked all the stands:

> The huge phoenix head is in gold and the fire and ruins are indicated by a series of large zig-zag scarlet streaks. This huge set-piece is illuminated by 900 electric light bulbs, portion of which, inset behind the red streaks, flick on and off giving the impression of a continuously glowing fire.[49]

Visitors were lured to the RDS by an opportunity to acquire free tickets to the theatrical show, but the winners were presented with a very different and rather traditional telling of the Lockout story in the Olympia. This did not mean that the Dublin Trades Council was at war with itself over the interpretation of 1913, but rather it reflected trade union circumstance – where both militant and conciliationist aspects had their vital place. To satisfy the former tendency, Seán O'Casey was invited to provide a script for the pageant but he declined, pleading his 83 years. An eminent substitute was available, however.

Let freedom ring: a masque of 1913-1916 was written by Donagh MacDonagh, who, as well as being a playwright, poet and broadcaster, was a district justice and son of the martyr of 1916. According to the critic Desmond Rushe, his show drew 'liberally on the words and speeches of many authors' and was 'directed with originality and cleverness' by Vincent and Jack Dowling.[50] It featured familiar songs, performed to the accompaniment of a 'section of the ITGWU band', but also MacDonagh's own 'Dublin 1913.' This song, oft-recorded in the following decades, was one element of the jubilee that left a lasting mark, its image of Larkin 'like a mighty wave' etched in the imagination of generations, and its narrative structure copper-fastening the connection between 1913 and 1916 in popular memory:

> It was in August the boss man told us, no union man for him could work. We stood by Larkin and told the boss man, we'd fight or die, but we would not shirk. Eight months we fought and months we starved; we stood by Larkin through thick & thin; But foodless homes and the crying of children, they broke our hearts, we could not win.
>
> When Larkin left us we seemed defeated, the night was black for the working man, But on came Connolly, with hope and counsel; his motto was that we'd rise again. In 1916 in Dublin city, the English soldiers they burnt our town, They shelled the buildings, and shot our leaders; the harp was buried beneath the crown ...[51]

Coinciding with the Trades Council events, Radio Éireann presented a special Thomas Davis Lecture on the Lockout featuring Professor T. Desmond Williams. The station also broadcast Proinsias Mac Aonghusa's two-part documentary which included interviews with Nora Connolly O'Brien, Barney Conway and Desmond Ryan. For their part, the daily newspapers commissioned articles to mark the anniversary. *The Irish Times* had contributions from Cathal O'Shannon and James Plunkett, while the *Irish Press* reprinted William O'Brien's hoary 'Nineteen thirteen – its significance', that item's fifth incarnation since 1934.[52] As he had been on a previous occasion by James Plunkett, O'Brien was taken to task by a letter-writer to the paper for failing to mention the ITGWU founder: 'One assumes that Mr O'Brien had heard of the part that Larkin – and Larkinism – played in lifting the Irish worker off his knees.'[53]

One who would take full account of Larkin was Donal Nevin, research officer of the Irish Congress of Trades Unions, activist in the clerical branch of the WUI, and confidant of Jim Larkin Jr.[54] Nevin edited an important publication for the WUI, entitled *1913: Jim Larkin and the Dublin lock-out* which although it did not appear until mid-1964 was intended to mark the Lockout in a 'permanent form' and ensure that 'the present and future generations of trade unionists might learn and understand something of the heroic struggles of those who built our Irish trade union movement.'[55] It was a modest-looking publication – 124 pages plus plates in plain-covered paperback – aimed at a 'general reader' and consisting of 55 documents written by participants and contemporaries, as well as tremendously vivid selection of photographs. As things turned out, the expectations of the publisher were more than fulfilled and this extremely useful compendium must be ranked as among the most influential on the Lockout. With the evidence of the many contemporary documents placed before the public, Larkin could never again be written out of the Lockout story.

James Plunkett

The individual who has done most to shape popular perceptions of the Lockout has been James Plunkett Kelly (1920-2003). As well as putting the working class of Dublin at the centre of the story and redeeming Larkin, he ensured that in popular perception the Lockout narrative came to be centred on the Lockout itself, and that it would no longer be regarded as principally a curtain-raiser for something else. Indeed, he seems to have deliberately disentangled 1913 from 1916.[56] This mild-mannered man was an unlikely history warrior but his sense of mission in respect of the Lockout story is indicated by the fact that he publicly tangled on at least two occasions with the by-then-venerable William O'Brien over the latter's distorted representation of events.[57]

Educated at the Synge Street Christian Brothers School in Dublin, Plunkett Kelly was a chauffeur's son who grew up to be an accomplished classical musician and an inter-county Gaelic footballer. Following his father's early death, he went to work as a clerk with the Dublin Gas Company, where he became active in the WUI. In 1946, he was recruited as a full-time official by his union, so he worked alongside James Larkin during the last year of the latter's life. All the while, he was writing. By his own account, his earliest published work was satirical verse in Dublin labour periodicals, *The Worker* and *Torch* when he was 17 or 18. By the time he was 20, the literary magazine, *The Bell*, had accepted his first story, which was entitled 'Working class.'[58] A collection of his short stories was published in 1954, under the shortened version of his name, James Plunkett, by which point several of his radio plays had been broadcast by Radio Éireann. The roles of writer and trade union official came into conflict when Plunkett was one of a delegation of Irish writers who visited the USSR and, on the grounds that he was a Communist sympathiser, an effort was made to have him dismissed from his trade union post. The effort was unsuccessful, but he resigned in 1955 to take a position as a producer with Radio Éireann.[59]

Already, in 1954, Radio Éireann had broadcast his play on the Lockout, *Big Jim*, which, to quote from the pre-publicity, was a 'realistic portrayal of a Dublin family who were just a few of the twenty-six thousand involved ... and with the untold suffering which [Larkin's] first allies, the workers, faced with good-humoured heroism.'[60]

This radio play was the earliest template for *Strumpet city*, and it would be expanded upon and developed over the following 25 years. If there was a superficial similarity between Plunkett's and William O'Brien's renderings of the Lockout, it was in the virtual absence of Larkin from both, but their purposes were very different. In Plunkett's work, in the words of one literary scholar, 'the myth of Larkin is skilfully developed by his spectral presence.'[61] Following a second broadcast, the text of the play was published in 1956, and reviewed in the *Irish Press* by Thomas Kinsella. While the young poet expressed some reservations, he was generally enthusiastic:

> The handling of the principal figures, major personalities in the play though minor in the politics of the time, is what makes 'Big Jim' one of the best plays which Radio Éireann has given us in recent years. They are, in a sense, stock characters, reminiscent in many ways of Seán O'Casey's *dramatis personae* ... but in a series of clever following-movements back and forward in time he has succeeded in the difficult task of presenting what might be called the heroism of boredom, of doing nothing for eight months but starve.[62]

There was already speculation about a rewrite and a transfer to the Abbey, and when this took place in September 1958, the play was titled *The risen people*. An inevitable comparison with O'Casey in *The Irish Times* review was softened as follows: 'The comparison is no denigration. Mr Plunkett's play is a foster-child that the author of *Juno* could be proud to own.' A particular point of comparison noted by the critic was the device of having 'Larkin himself appearing mostly in the way Pearse appears in *The plough and the stars* ... for the most part a background character, yet his messianic presence inhabits the whole drama.'[63] *The risen people* was revived in the Gate in 1959, when it was presented by the Jim Larkin Theatre Group, when one of the principal players was Frank Cluskey, future leader of the Labour Party, but then a young WUI official who had cut his thespian teeth with the WUI Dramatic Society.[64] Tomás MacAnna directed an Abbey revival of the play in August 1963 to coincide with the 50th anniversary of the Lockout.[65]

Plunkett signed a contract in 1958 with London publisher, Hutchinson, to write a novel based on his *Big Jim/The risen people* story, receiving a substantial advance. Progress was slow, not least because of his busy working life as a TV producer from the establishment of the Irish television service at the end of 1961, and it was 1969 before the doorstopper of 200,000 words finally appeared. At the launch in the Bailey in Duke Street, Minister for Education Brian Lenihan Snr., paid tribute to the literary merit of the work, but said that it was 'also a notable and valuable social document ... which attempted to picture the entire social scene in Dublin.' The effort to marry social history and fiction prompted mixed reviews outside of Ireland. For some critics, it was hopelessly old-fashioned narrative fiction, while others drew very favourable comparisons with the work of Dickens.[66]

For the literate public in Ireland, the first contact with *Strumpet city* was in the reviews and commentary in the national papers, and these therefore deserve some attention. That they were written by some of Ireland's leading literary figures of the day adds to their interest. Hutchinson (and James Plunkett himself) were effective publicists, and anticipation was created through occasional references in newspapers in the months before publication. Reviews appeared, in an evidently coordinated fashion, in the three national dailies on the Saturday before publication, prompting further discussion.

What of the reviews, then? In the *Irish Independent,* the poet and leading literary critic John Jordan was generally quite complimentary about Plunkett's endeavours, but he did express one reservation:

> I am less happy with the author's presentation of the young or youngish active Larkinists, though they are all sharply differentiated. The trouble is that they are all, as members of the human communion, too good, too loyal, too brave, too generous, 'goodies' in fact. No political, social, or religious movement is without its cowards or its bullies, or its traitors. One cannot credit that Big Jim led a band of angels.[67]

In *The Irish Times,* novelist Terence De Vere White damned it with faint praise:

> This is a good book by a good man: and if that sounds stuffy, I can't help it ... Compared with the Behan picture of Dublin, it may seem somewhat subfusc, as if everyone is seen through a slight mist. And Mr Plunkett's characters never attain the dramatic proportions of O'Casey's workers. This is not merely because he has avoided the conjunction of four letter words with holy names. He has an ingrained respect for humanity, and a feminine tenderness ... No doubt, his purpose was to show his working-class characters as kindly and humane if sometimes weak. There is nothing of the satirist, no bitterness in this writer's composition. As a result, one leaves the book down with something of the same sensation as one ended *Dr Zhivago*, with a renewed faith in the essential decency of people.[68]

Of all of the papers, the *Irish Press* pulled out all of the stops to greet *Strumpet city*, something for which David Marcus, the paper's literary editor was responsible. Marcus, a champion of the short story genre with which Plunkett was most associated, carried out a two-part interview with the author; excerpts from the novel were published on two days; there was extensive coverage of the launch; and the playwright Denis Johnson was engaged to write the review. The choice of Johnson was singularly appropriate, for he was the first to apply the term 'strumpet city' to Dublin. In his play *The old lady says no*, premiered in the Abbey in 1929, the following lines are uttered by the Robert Emmet character 'Strumpet City in the sunset, suckling the brats of Scot, of Englishry, of Huguenot.'[69] For Johnson, it was 'refreshing to be able to welcome a major novel that concerns itself not with the geography, decor, and linguistic side of our liberation, but with poverty, economic slavery and the most horrible slums in western Europe' and he was effusive in his praise. At the same time, he was crankily anxious to deny the story any contemporary relevance towards the end of what has been characterised as 'the decade of upheaval'[70] in Irish industrial relations:

> The struggle of Larkin's strikers were real enough, but they seem strangely dated in these days of Labour Courts and Conciliation Boards – arbiters whose views on fair treatment can more readily be defied by unions than by employers. Strikes are bigger and better now that we have the blessing of nationalised services, where the public rather than some profit-seeking boss can be made to foot the bill, and to suffer in the meantime by walking to work or sitting in the dark.[71]

If the critics were half-hearted, the general reception was enthusiastic. The author earned an early bonus in the form of TV and film options, and his book was an instantaneous hit. As it happened, 1969 was the first year that such best-seller lists were compiled in Ireland, and *Strumpet city* was far and away the best-selling book in that year, when its rivals included Christy Brown's *My left foot*, and Tim Pat Coogan's very topical history of the IRA.[72] As early as the month of July, *The Farmers Journal* was reporting that it was 'on sale in every huckster shop around the country.'[73] There was further success when it was issued in paperback, with substantial sales in the United States and Britain, and translation into other languages, including Russian.

In the period after the initial publication, *Strumpet city* continued to attract attention. Publicity surrounding Plunkett's follow-up novel of 1977, *Farewell companions*, brought its predecessor back into the best-sellers' list. Long before the proliferation of book clubs, a Dublin Literary Society was discussing the novel in the Brazen Head pub, and somebody was naming their prize dog, 'Strumpet city.' The novel's title was drawn into public discourse in all sorts of ways as indicated by a number of examples: Fr Peter McVerry, referring to the difficulties that elderly people faced in heating their homes said that 'Strumpet city is the present day reality.' A letter to *The Irish Times* from a spokesperson for the Dublin City Business Association made reference 'to the streets of their Strumpet City.'[74] And if such a public association seems surprising from a business source, it must be considered even more surprising from the Cavan branch of the Irish Farmers' Association. In January 1977, a Mr Donohue told his comrades at a meeting in the Farnham Hotel that he had recently been reading a book called *Strumpet city*, which described a 'struggle by James Larkin and his labour associates.' Most of them 'ended up in jail, but the labour movement prevailed and became what it is today.' 'The IFA should take note of this,' he advised.[75] The novel was adapted for radio in 1978 – while a question regarding its authorship featured in the Garda entrance exam – and a revival of 'The risen people' by the pioneering Project Arts Company was promoted as 'the stage version of *Strumpet city*.'[76]

The seven-part RTÉ television series, broadcast in the spring of 1980 was the high point of James Plunkett's dissemination of the story of the Lockout. It was a high point also in the history of Irish television, being the central element of an RTÉ strategy to achieve international credibility as a producer of high quality television drama. Indeed Peter Ustinov and Peter O'Toole, actors of international repute, were cast with this objective in mind. The prospect of selling the series abroad justified the unprecedented level of expenditure required to attain the production values necessary to attract customers.[77] In this regard, the early responses of Irish critics was encouraging: one wrote that it was a 'very credible lively mass audience television serial that is going to appeal to an audience that enjoyed *The Forsyte saga*; another that it was 'RTÉ's epic answer to *Roots*.'[78] Ultimately, the series would be screened in 52 countries, even if RTÉ's ambitions for the series in America were disappointed, because commissioning editors believed that 'the accents would have been incomprehensible' to their viewers.[79]

It took director Tony Barry two years to bring the story on to the screen, the adaptation being carried out by Hugh Leonard, a well-known dramatist and newspaper columnist who was also a screenwriter for the BBC. It was acknowledged that Leonard's script was faithful to the novel, but if it was, he was as careful (in his *Sunday Independent* column) as Denis Johnson had been earlier to show that his immersion in labour matters had not increased his sympathy for the protagonists in the strikes of his own day.[80]

Almost 60% of RTÉ's audience did not have access to any other television channel so viewing figures were high. There was an almost uniformly positive reaction to the series, one indication being the resolution adopted by Kells Urban Council congratulating RTÉ for throwing 'a direct light on the struggle of the working class.' The initial enthusiasm in this instance was that of Councillor Tommy Grimes of the Labour Party.[81] The *Irish Press* sought out the sons of Larkin and Connolly to report on their reactions. For Denis Larkin, who was pictured on the front page watching the programme with a miniature version of Óisín Kelly's statue of his father beside the television, it was 'an accurate portrayal of life in those days.' For Roddy Connolly, the opening episode was 'a splendid recall of Dublin in those days, with good character acting.' The young Dermot Keogh, who watched 'with the jaundiced eye of the historian' for the *Irish Press*, was drawn 'inexorably into the drama' by the 'excellence of the acting and the fluency of the storyline.'[82] The only fly in the ointment was the widely-circulated criticism of the depiction of the Dublin Metropolitan Police by the police historian and curator of the Garda Museum, Gregory Allen. He accused the RTÉ Authority and all others concerned of gross irresponsibility in their 'incitement to hatred of the police.' To those who thought that the unfavourable representation of a long-abolished force did not matter much, he issued a warning:

> But the police in every age standing against the outcry of radical forces for absolute freedoms in society are at mercy of articulate minorities, including some writers, who succeed at least in perpetuating the old bogeyman image of the police, especially in the minds of impressionable young people in a sensitive period in our history.[83]

Given the representations of Catholic clergymen in both novel and series, some criticism might have been anticipated on those grounds, but the indications are that it was scant. The novel did feature in the Redemptorist magazine, *Reality*, in an article which was reported in several newspapers. In the article, Fr Anthony McHugh posed the question about *Strumpet city*: 'Has the author been as true to clerical Dublin as he has been to working class Dublin?' It was a fairly nuanced discussion that followed, however, which cited the papal encyclical *Rerum novarum*, acknowledging that the Catholic clergy of early 20th-century Dublin 'were so anxious to reject the condemned form of socialism that they ended up by unwittingly also the forms that were good.'[84]

That in reality, as in *Reality*, the historicity of *Strumpet city* came to be generally accepted was the greatest tribute to the power of its storyline.

Conclusion

The historical importance of the Lockout is indicated by the trouble taken to shape its interpretation to their own purpose by everyone from Arnold Wright for the Dublin employers, to James Larkin, William O'Brien, and even the Dublin Trades Council. But the distinction of having had the greatest popular impact remains with James Plunkett, who used four distinct vehicles for his fictional version: the radio play of 1954, the stage play of 1958, the novel of 1969 and the television series of 1980. The status acquired by the Plunkett narrative was indicated in the selection of *The risen people* by the Irish Congress of Trade Unions as the centrepiece of its centenary celebration in 1994.[85]

5. Óisín Kelly's Larkin monument in O'Connell Street, unveiled in 1979.
(Photo: Andrew Sneyd) DCLA

Plunkett did not have the last word, however, for in the interval between the appearance of *Strumpet city* the novel in 1969 and the TV series in 1980, historians had begun to show an unprecedented curiosity about both the Lockout and Larkin. This was an Irish manifestation of an increasing interest internationally in social and labour history.[86] As far as the dissemination among the broader public of knowledge about the period was concerned, the most important publications of the period were F. S. L. Lyons's *Ireland since the famine* (1971) widely used as a history textbook both at second and third level, and the Curriculum Development Unit's *Divided city: portrait of Dublin, 1913* (1978).[87] Other official and semi-official expressions of recognition of the Lockout legacy during the 1970s included the issuing of Larkin postage stamps in 1976, and the commissioning from sculptor Óisín Kelly of the Larkin monument, unveiled in Dublin's O'Connell Street by Patrick Hillery, president of Ireland, in 1979. Notably, that monument, which references the Lockout in overlooking the scene of 1913's Bloody Sunday, proved problematic for the film-makers when trying to recreate the same scene for *Strumpet city.*

At the same time, the Lockout was becoming became part of a long 'history war' in Ireland, the so-called revisionist controversy, when, in response to the crisis in Northern Ireland, writers inside and outside academia challenged Nationalist historical orthodoxies, especially those relating to the 1912-23 period which were perceived to legitimise 'armed struggle.' As far as labour history was concerned, this frequently meant emphasising Larkin and the struggle associated with him at the expense of what came to be regarded as the more problematic legacy of James Connolly.[88] Eoghan Harris, a prominent figure in the fiercely revisionist Official Sinn Féin / Workers' Party milieu, recently disclosed how such a revisionist impulse informed his drama 'The ballad of James Larkin' commissioned for the WUI commemoration of the 61st anniversary of the Lockout in 1974.[89]

Have we seen the last of the 1913 history wars? Probably not. The research and the public debate which has been prompted by the centenary will generate fresh interpretations, and current trade union circumstance makes it likely that there will be sharp debate in labour circles at least about the lessons of the Lockout.[90] And there are indications that the debate may be rather wider than that in recent comments from columnist Kevin Myers (in relation to what he described as 'that risible travesty, James Plunkett's *Strumpet city*') and by former Fine Gael Taoiseach John Bruton who, in urging restraint in relation to commemorating the Irish revolution, suggested among his alternative emphases that the achievements of the Irish trade union movement during the Lockout and subsequently 'must not be eclipsed by other commemorations as they were for many years.'[91]

Notes

1   Katie Holmes and Stuart Ward (eds), *Exhuming passions: the pressure of the past in Ireland and Australia* (Dublin, 2011), passim; Stuart Macintyre and Anna Clark, *The history wars* (Carlton, 2003), passim.

2   *The Times,* 17 Feb. 1941.

3   P. G. Wodehouse, 'Jeeves and the unbidden guest,' in *My man Jeeves* (London, 1919), pp 18-36.

4   Arnold Wright, *Disturbed Dublin: the story of the great strike* (London, 1914), pp v-x, 78.

5   Philip Rooney, 'Terence O'Hanlon: an appreciation', *Seanchas Ardmhacha: Journal of the Armagh Diocesan Historical Society*, vol. 1, no. 2 (1955), pp 192-215. O'Hanlon wrote *The highwayman in Irish history* (Dublin, 1932).

6   Wright, *Disturbed Dublin,* p. 259.

7   As part of research for this essay, the author has reviewed Irish local newspapers available in digital format by end December 2012.

8   *Irish Independent,* 4, 6, 7 Nov. 1914.

9   'Disturbed Dublin by Arnold Wright,' *Journal of Political Economy*, vol. 23, no. 8 (October 1915), pp 855-6.

10   J. G. Smith, 'Obituary: C. F. Bastable,' *The Economic Journal*, vol. 55, no. 217 (April 1945), pp 127-37.

11   C. F. Bastable, *The Economic Journal*, vol. 25, no. 97 (March, 1915), pp 64-6.

12   James Connolly, *The reconquest of Ireland* (Dublin and Belfast, 1972 ed.), pp 27-31, 67-74; *Irish Worker,* 29 May 1915.

13   *Irish Worker,* 28 Nov. 1914.

14   Published under the name G. B. O'Connor, *James Connolly: a study of his work and worth* (Dublin 1917). Mac Giollarnáth had earlier published, also pseudonymously, a pamphlet biography of Padraic Pearse, his predecessor as editor of *An Claidheamh Soluis.*

15   W. P. Ryan, *The Irish labour movement: from the 'twenties to our own day* (Dublin 1919), pp 214-37; P. O'Cathasaigh (Seán O'Casey) *The story of the Irish Citizen Army: The first account that has been given of the formation of the Irish Citizen Army during the Dublin strike of 1913-14, and the part played by it in the subsequent history of Ireland* (London, 1919), passim.

16   Irish Labour Party and Trade Union Congress, *Reports and memoranda prepared for the International Labour and Socialist Conference, in Switzerland, 1919* (Dublin, 1919), pp 4-22.

17   Francis Devine, *Organising history: a centenary of SIPTU* (Dublin, 2009), pp 132-40, 148-65; Emmet O'Connor, *A labour history of Ireland, 1824-2000* (Dublin, 2011), pp 130-3; D. R. O'Connor Lysaght, 'The rake's progress of a syndicalist: the political career of William O'Brien, Irish labour leader', *Saothar: Journal of Irish Labour History,* 9 (1983), pp 48-62; Thomas J. Morrissey, SJ, *William O'Brien, 1881-1968: Socialist, republican, Dáil Deputy, editor and trade union leader* (Dublin, 2007), pp 214-38.

18   *Irish Times,* 8 Mar. 1924.

19   *Irish Times,* 5 Nov. 1923.

20   National Executive Council, ITGWU, *The attempt to smash the Irish Transport & General Workers Union* (Dublin, 1924), p. xiv.

21   William O'Brien, *Nineteen-thirteen: its significance* (Dublin, 1934), passim. The text was first published in *An Díon*, the periodical of the Post Office Workers' Union.

22   Ibid.

23   Ibid.

24   *Fifty years of Liberty Hall: the Golden Jubilee of the Irish Transport and General Workers' Union, 1909-1959* (Dublin, 1959), pp 34-9 and *passim*; Emmet O'Connor, *James Larkin* (Cork , 2002), p. 115.

25   *Irish Press,* 13 Sept. 1963.

26   Ibid.

27   Donal Nevin, 'Seán O'Casey on Jim Larkin', in Donal *Nevin, Larkin: lion of the fold* (Dublin, 1998), pp 412, 529, fn. 2. O'Shannon (1893-1969) was an ITGWU veteran, an official of two trade union congresses, and a long-time workers' representative in the Labour Court. He was the compiling editor of *Fifty years of Liberty Hall.*

28   *Irish Times,* 20 Feb. 1960.

29   F. A. D'Arcy, 'Larkin and the historians' in Nevin, *Lion of the fold,* pp 371-8.

30   Dorothy Macardle, *The Irish Republic; a documented chronicle of the Anglo-Irish conflict and the partitioning of Ireland, with a detailed account of the period 1916-1923* (London, pbk ed., 1968), pp 88-9.

31   Cited in D'Arcy, 'Larkin and the historians', p. 373.

32   S. O'Brien, 'The great Dublin strike and Lockout, 1913', in *Dublin's fighting story, 1916-21: told by the men who made it* (Tralee, 1949), pp 12-24. There were ITGWU organisers named Seamus O'Brien and Seumas O'Brien in the 1920s (Francis Devine, personal communication). One of them married James

Connolly's daughter, Nora, but it has not been possible to definitively establish that it was he who was the author of the article.

33   Devine, *Organising history*, pp 166, 197.

34   S. O'Brien, 'The great Dublin strike', p. 13.

35   P. Beresford Ellis, '[R. M. Fox]: An influential historian of Irish labour', Irish Labour History Society website (http://www.irishlabourhistorysociety.com/pdf/R%20M%20Fox.pdf), (12 Jan. 2013).

36   T. A. Jackson (with C. Desmond Greaves), *Ireland her own: an outline history of the Irish struggle* (London, 1976), pp 376-8; D'Arcy, 'Larkin and the historians', p. 373.

37   James Curry, 'Andrew Patrick Wilson and *The Irish Worker*, 1912-13', in D. Convery (ed.), *Locked out: a century of Irish working-class life,* forthcoming (2013) from Irish Academic Press.

38   Donal Nevin, 'Larkin in literature and art', in *Nevin, Larkin: lion of the fold,* pp 406-11.

39   M. Pierse, 'The shadow of Seán: O'Casey, commitment and writing Dublin's working class', *Saothar,* 35 (2010), pp 69-85.

40   Michael Mullen was a Labour T.D. between 1961 and 1969. He served as general secretary of the ITGWU from 1969 until his death in 1982. Paddy Donegan was general secretary, National Engineering Union, at the time of the jubilee, but he was appointed an ITGWU National Industrial Group secretary the following year.

41   *Irish Times*, 13 Mar. 1963; see also 22 Jan. 1963.

42   *Irish Press,* 17 Sept. 1963.

43   *Sunday Independent,* 15 Sept. 1963.

44   *Irish Press,* 19 Sept. 1963.

45   *Irish Press,* 18 Sept. 1963. Workers and unions played a special part in the development and growth that can be seen (today).

46   *Irish Times,* 12 Aug. 1963.

47   *Irish Times,* 18 Sept. 1963.

48   *Irish Press,* 17 Sept. 1963.

49   Ibid.

50   *Irish Independent,* 17 Sept. 1963.

51   The song, which borrowed its tune from the popular standard 'Preab san ól', was also recorded under the title, 'Ballad of James Larkin.' For the full text, see John McDonnell (ed.), *Songs of struggle and protest* (Cork, 1986), pp 86-7. For the classic version from 1969 by Christy Moore (http://www.youtube.com/watch?v=-GXTWp54gAc) (12 Jan. 2013).

52   *Irish Times,* 26 Aug., 17 Sept. 1963; *Irish Press,* 17 Sept. 1963. O'Brien's 'Nineteen-thirteen' was published in *An Díon* in December 1934, the ITGWU pamphlet in the same year, another ITGWU pamphlet in 1943 (O'Connor, *A labour history,* p. 164) and ITGWU, *Fifty years of Liberty Hall.*

53   *Irish Press,* 21 Sept. 1963. O'Brien did discuss his relationship with Larkin in his memoir narrated to Edward MacLysaght published shortly after his death, *Forth the banners go* (Dublin, 1969).

54   See Francis Devine, obituary of Donal Nevin (1923-2012) (http://www.irishlabourhistorysociety.com/pdf/Donal%20Nevin%20RIP.pdf) (12 Jan. 2013).

55   'Introduction', Workers Union of Ireland, *1913: Jim Larkin and the Dublin lock-out* (Dublin, 1964), p. 5. While Nevin's name did not appear on the title page, his editorship was acknowledged in the 'Introduction'.

56   D. R. O'Connor Lysaght, 'Would it have been like this? James Plunkett and *Strumpet City*' in *History Ireland*, vol. 12, no. 4 (Winter 2004), p. 9.

57   *Irish Times,* 24, 30 Mar. 1956; 24 Feb. 1960.

58   Another of his stories, 'The mother,' however, appeared in *The Bell*, before 'Working class.' Biographical details compiled from the following: James Plunkett, *The gems she wore: a book of Irish places* (London, 1972), passim; 'James Plunkett: a supreme storyteller whose life remained true to trade unionism' (obituary), *Irish Times*, 31 May 2003; David Marcus, 'A portrait of Dublin,' first of a two-part interview with Plunkett, *Irish Press,* 24 Apr. 1969.

59   Ibid. Under another *aimn cleite*, Séamus Ó Ceallaigh, Plunkett Kelly shared his thoughts on developments in Irish trade unionism: 'Triocha blain de cheardchumannachas', *Comhar*, iml. 13, uimh. 7 (Jul. 1954), pp 9-11.

60   *Tuam Herald,* 23 Oct. 1954.

61   Lawrence Wilde, 'Making myth: the image of "Big Jim" Larkin in *Strumpet City',* in *Journal of European Studies*, vol. 41, no. 1 (2010), pp 63-75.

62   Thomas Kinsella, 'A play about Big Jim', *Irish Press,* 12 May 1956.

63   *Irish Times*, 24 Sept. 1958.

64   Ibid., 16 Dec. 1959.

65   See discussion in *Irish Times,* 11 Oct. 1994.

66   *Irish Times,* 29 Apr., 25 Aug. 1969, *The Times,* 3 May 1969.

67   *Irish Independent,* 26 Apr. 1969.

68   *Irish Times,* 26 Apr. 1969.

69   P. F. B., 'Obituary: Denis Johnson, 1901-84', *Dublin Historical Record*, 38, no. 1 (December 1984), p. 36.

70   Charles McCarthy, *Decade of upheaval: Irish trade unions in the nineteen sixties* (Dublin, 1973).

71   *Irish Press,* 26 Apr. 1969.

72   Rónán McDonald, '"Anything about Ireland?": reading in Ireland, 1969-2000,' in Clare Hutton (ed.), *The Oxford history of the Irish book*, vol. 5 (Oxford, 2011), p. 203.

73   *Farmers Journal,* 12 July 1969

74   *Irish Press,* 19 Feb. 1977; *Irish Times,* 26 Apr. 1978.

75   *Anglo-Celt,* 28 Jan. 1977.

76   *Irish Press,* 29 Sept. 1978; *Sunday Independent*, 23 Nov. 1980; *Farmers Journal,* 30 Apr. 1977.

77   Martin McLoone, 'Strumpet City: The Irish working class on Irish television' in Martin McLoone and John MacMahon, *Television and Irish society: 21 years of Irish television* (Dublin, 1984), pp 53-88.

78   *Irish Times,* 17 Mar. 1980; *Sunday Independent,* 17 June 1979.

79   Helena Sheehan, *Irish television drama: a society and its stories* (Dublin, 1987).

80   Ibid. *Sunday Independent,* 12 Feb. 1978.

81   *Meath Chronicle,* 29 Mar. 1980.

82   *Irish Press,* 17 Mar. 1980.

83   *Irish Independent,* 30 Apr. 1980. See also, for example, *Irish Press,* 31 Mar. 1980.

84   Coverage of *Reality* article: *Sunday Independent*, 24 Aug. 1969; *Nenagh Guardian,* 6 Sept. 1969.

85   *Irish Times,* 11 Oct. 1994.

86   Indications in Ireland of this phenomenon included the establishment of the Irish Economic and Social History Society in 1970, and the Irish Labour History Society in 1973.

87   D'Arcy, 'Larkin and the historians', pp 374-8.

88   D'Arcy, 'Larkin and the historians', pp 374-8; Gearóid Ó Tuathaigh, 'Irish historical "Revisionism": state of the art or ideological project?' in Ciaran Brady (ed.), *Interpreting Irish history: the debate on historical revisionism* (Dublin, 1994), pp 306-26; D. G. Boyce, '1916: interpreting the Rising', in D. G. Boyce and Alan O'Day, *The making of modern Irish history: revisionism and the revisionist controversy* (London, 1996), pp 163-87.

89   Eoghan Harris, 'Jim Larkin would have lashed the Labour Party', *Irish Independent*, 16 Sept. 2012. Harris evidently discounted evidence tending to contradict his assertion that Larkin was 'the least nationalist of Irish socialists' For such evidence, see Adrian Grant, *Irish socialist republicanism, 1909-36* (Dublin, 2012), pp 30-47; Emmet O'Connor, 'Red Jim was green man', *Irish Democrat,* 3 Oct. 2002, (http://www.irishdemocrat.co.uk/features/larkin/) (12 Jan. 2013).

90   M. Clancy and J. Cunningham, 'Editorial: Labour and the decade of centenaries', *Saothar* 37 (2012), pp 3-4.

91   *Irish Independent,* 11 Jan. 2013; John Bruton, 'All sacrifices of 100 years ago must be honoured', *Irish Times,* 11 Nov. 2011.

Index

Note: page references in italics denote illustrations

P

Sutton, Charles G., 315, 317
Swan, R.L., 84
Sweden, 29, 48, 49
Swifte, E.G., 8, 206
Swords, Co. Dublin, 246
sympathy strikes, 42, 45, 63, 169, 177, 204, 227
    Connolly and, 42, 181
syndicalism, 5, 17, 28, 30, 35, 38,
        45, 48, 49, 51, 182, 225
    industrial militancy and, 36–42
    Larkinism as, 19, 353, 355
    policies, 38–9
Synge Street Christian Brothers School, 367

T

Taft Vale judgment, 216
Tale of two cities (Dickens), 348
Tapestry Project, 2
Tara Street Baths, 110, 111, 119, 140
Tate Gallery, 267
TB (tuberculosis), 60, 61, 84, 97,
        151, 157, 270, 295, 311
    deaths from, 157
    medical courses, 89–90
    sanatoria, 60, 90, 97
Tchaykovski, Dr Barbara, 121
Tedcastle's Wharf, 318, 320, 325
Temple Street, 150
tenements, 4, 10, 57, 79, 84, 129, 145–50, 208,
        270, 276, 334. see also housing conditions
    character of tenement dwellers, 158–61
    Church Street collapse (1913), 10, 65–7,
        66, 71, 129–30, 142, 145, 276–7
    Corporation members, owned by, 73, 74, 337
    and death rates, 58, 150–1
    and disease, 60, 97, 150–5
    housing inquiry (1913), 67–79. see
        also housing inquiry
    literary depictions of life in, 333, 334–5. see
        also Charwoman's daughter (Stephens)
    numbers and population, 4, 73, 75,
        130, 146, 148, 153, 154, 337
    occupations and wages, 156–7
    overcrowding, 4, 57, 58, 61, 146, 149, 276
    poverty. see poverty
    sanitary and water facilities, 57,
        72–3, 76, 147, 153, 155

tax rebates for landlords, 73–4
    visual record of life in, *130, 132,* 145–61, *146,*
        147, 148, 150, 151, 153, 154, 155, 157, 160
Terenure, 167, 289, 291
Textile Operatives Society, 41
theatre, 345–6, 348, 364, 368
Theatre Royal, 347–8
Thomas, J.H., 45
Thomas Street, 149, 317, 324
Thompson, N., 102
Thompson, Sir W.J., 102
Thom's Directory, 92
Thring, Mr, 318
Thunder's Court, 156
Tickell's Court, 148, *148*
Tillett, Ben, 36, 39, 45, 46, 47, 252
timber merchants, 43, 170
Times, 21, 33, 35, 68, 116, 180, 355
Tivoli Theatre, 324
Tobar Draíochta, An, 294
Toiler, 7
Tolka (Guinness boat), 318
Tone, Theobald Wolfe, 200, 201, 202, 203, 343
Tonypandy lockout and riots (1910), 30, 33
Torch (periodical), 367
Total Abstinence and Workmen's Club, 264
Tower Bar, *159*
Townsend, George, 254
Townsend Street, 145, 155
Trade Disputes Act, 1906, 171
trade union movement, British, 5, 27, 30–1, 37, 48
    and Dublin Lockout, 2, 3, 10–13, 28–9,
        42–7, 224–6, 232, 356. see also food
        aid; Trades Union Congress (TUC)
    and Irish trade unions, 27, 28–9
    and Larkin, 3, 10, 13, 45, 46, 225
    New Unionism, 28, 30
    radicals' criticisms of, 37, 38
    strike wave. see 'Great Unrest' (1910-1914)
trade union movement, Irish, 4–5, 7, 10, 12,
        20, 216, 312. see also Irish Trade Union
        Congress (ITUC); Irish Transport and
        General Workers' Union (ITGWU)
    British movement, relations with, 27, 28–9
    cultural dimension, 341
    membership, 5, 47
trade union organisation, 30, 37, 48
    new approaches, 28, 39–42

Y

Yates, Rose Lamartine, 119
Yeates, Pádraig, *Lockout,* 1, 13, 16, 17, 20, 46,
62, 123, 138, 226, 228, 229, 239, 320
  on child beggars, 135
  criticism of, 35–6
  epilogue, 18
  'Save the Kiddies' scheme, 140, 141
Yeats, Jack B., 263
Yeats, William Butler, 167, 263, 265,
277, 291, 336, 345–6
  'The fisherman,' 343
  'September 1913,' 174–5, 336, 343
York Street, 264, 292
York Street Spinning Company (Belfast), 61
York Street Workingmen's Club (Dublin), 287
Young Ireland, 343
Ypres (Belgium), 18